Slide Libraries

A Guide for Academic Institutions, Museums, and Special Collections

Second Edition

Betty Jo Irvine
Fine Arts Slide Librarian
Indiana University

With the assistance of P. Eileen Fry
Slide Librarian
Indiana University

Libraries Unlimited, Inc.- Littleton, Colorado
1979

LIBRARIES UNLIMITED, INC.
P.O. Box 263
Littleton, Colorado 80160

Library of Congress Cataloging in Publication Data

Irvine, Betty Jo.
    Slide libraries.

    Bibliography: p. 241
    Includes index.
    1. Libraries--Special collections--Slides (Photogra-
phy) I. Fry, Eileen, joint author. II. Title.
Z692.S65I7   1979   025.17'73   79-17354
ISBN 0-87287-202-5

This book is bound with James River (Scott) Graphitek®–C Type II nonwoven
material. Graphitek–C meets and exceeds National Association of State Textbook
Administrators' Type II nonwoven material specifications Class A through E.

Dedicated to

ELEANOR COLLINS

Curator
Slide and Photograph Collection
University of Michigan
1946-1973

ACKNOWLEDGMENTS

Grateful thanks are extended to all the slide librarians, curators, and media professionals who assisted in the original and recent data compilations for this book. The combined efforts of these individuals and the following colleagues helped to make this publication possible: Catherine R. Clawson, C-E Refractories, Pennsylvania; Eleanor Collins (formerly at the University of Michigan); William J. Dane, Newark Public Library; Nicholas DeMarco, Vassar College; Edith M. Dunn, Georgia Institute of Technology; Dawn Donaldson, State University of New York at Buffalo; Mary Ann Dutt (formerly at the Philadelphia Museum of Art); Bonita L. Everts, Walker Art Center; Toni Graeber, University of California at Los Angeles; Gail Grisé, Indiana University; Nadine Hamilton (formerly at the University of Illinois at Chicago Circle); Jennifer Hehman, Ohio State University; Kaz Higuchi (formerly at Princeton University); Virginia Hotchkin (formerly at the State University of New York at Binghamton); Sue Janson (formerly at Cornell University); Paul Lazar, Indiana University; Concetta Leone, University of Pennsylvania; Kathryn McKenney, Wintherthur Museum; Stephen Marjolies, Brooklyn College; Richard Martin (formerly at Columbia University); Mary Meihack, University of Minnesota; Margaret P. Nolan, The Metropolitan Museum of Art; Elizabeth M. Lewis (formerly at the U.S. Military Academy, West Point); Marie R. Light, University of Michigan; Mod Mekkawi, Howard University; Olivera Mihailovic, University of Chicago; Marlene Palmer, National Collection of Fine Arts, Smithsonian Institution; Sara Jane Pearman, The Cleveland Museum of Art; Anne von Rebhan, National Gallery of Art, Washington, D.C.; Julia Sabine (formerly at the Newark Public Library); Sister Louise Lovely, Marycrest College; Elsie H. Straight, Ringling School of Art; Christine L. Sundt, University of Wisconsin; Luraine Tansey, San Jose City College; Mildred E. Thorson, University of Washington, Seattle; Rosemary M. Williams, Ball State University; Victoria Wilson (formerly at Indiana University); Virginia Yarbro (formerly at The Art Institute of Chicago); and Susan Watters, The World Bank, Washington, D.C. I am particularly appreciative of the photographic and special materials provided by the following individuals: Rosann Auchstetter, The Art Institute of Chicago; John Caldwell, Philadelphia College of Art; Helen Chillman, Yale University; Cynthia Clark, Princeton University (formerly at Harvard University); Melanie Ann Crawford, The Evergreen State College; Nancy DeLaurier, University of Missouri— Kansas City; Eleanor Fink, National Collection of Fine Arts, Smithsonian Institution; Jane Goldberg, University of Illinois—Urbana; Thomas H. Ohlgren, Purdue University; Helene E. Roberts, Harvard University; Ramona Roters, Syracuse University; Wendell Simons, Christine Bunting, and Kathleen Hardin, University of California, Santa Cruz; Charlotte Tannenbaum, University of Houston; and Carol Terry, Stanford University.

I would not have undertaken work on a second edition of *Slide Libraries* without the assistance of my colleague, P. Eileen Fry, Fine Arts Slide Librarian at Indiana University. We carefully reviewed the first edition line by line and agreed on all omissions, inclusions, and revisions of the original text and illustrations. In addition to being a constant source of information about current activities in slide librarianship, she was responsible for revising and preparing new text for

Chapters 5, 8, and 9. Her contribution to the second edition has been substantial, and I am indebted to her for continuing support throughout this project.

The vast resources of the Indiana University Libraries were heavily utilized for all bibliographic research. I especially want to thank my library associates for sharing their specialized expertise with me: Lois Lehman, Education Library; Margie Hickman and Julie Nilson, Cataloging Department; Margaret Carter, Eva Kiewitt, and Mary Popp, Graduate Library School Library; and the staffs of the Main Library Reference Department and the Interlibrary Loan Office. Rosanna Blakely, Cataloging Department, and Carolyn Snyder, Public Services, allowed me to use materials that expedited the preparation of cataloging examples. Reg Heron, Fine Arts Department, and Phil Spaulding, A-V Center, were most helpful in supplying current and relevant information about photographic techniques and innovations, and about media equipment.

The following individuals contributed to the final preparation of manuscript materials: Barbara Brennan (second edition, Diagrams 13, 15, 17, and 18), and Christopher Richards (all other diagrams); Jill Caldwell (original bibliography and directory preparation); David Lee Carl (processing and developing of all photographs), and David Schalliol (second edition processing of Photographs 7 and 11); and Dave Greischar and Jan Herron (typing of bibliographies and directories).

In order to fulfill the demands of time and energy required for the second edition, our immediate staffs in the Fine Arts and Slide Libraries conscientiously and faithfully overcame our frequent absences—especially mine—and kept operations there running smoothly and effectively: Sam Grupper; Phil Heagy; Jan Herron; Sue Ramage; and Teresa Rohrabaugh. These co-workers also submitted cheerfully and willingly to numerous telephone requests for information needed by me as I worked at home on the manuscript revisions. My husband and daughter suffered gladly as I spent many hours at the library, in my home office, and, generally, in a state of mind far removed from the obligations of a family.

The first edition was prepared through funding provided by Advanced Studies of Indiana University, which supported my original research trip to East Coast slide libraries, and by the Council on Library Resources (Washington, D.C.), which contributed support during the leave period when the original manuscript drafts were prepared. For the second edition, I was granted a half-time leave of absence from the Indiana University Libraries, which was expeditiously approved by Wilmer Baatz, Assistant Director for Administration. Without the generous assistance of these institutions, the first and second editions of *Slide Libraries* could not have been written.

A topic as specialized as slides requires that a publisher be innovative and courageous. Without the encouragement and sustained support of Christine L. Wynar, Editor, and Libraries Unlimited, Inc., *Slide Libraries* would not have been published.

PREFACE TO THE SECOND EDITION

Since 1973, the extraordinary increase in professional activity and in the number of publications by slide librarians, curators, and media professionals has been the most salient and encouraging aspect of preparing the second edition of *Slide Libraries*. Moreover, the combined efforts of both print and nonprint media specialists in the cataloging field have contributed to the development of standardized practices, which were only being suggested in the 1960s. Another area that prompted extensive treatment in the second edition was automation applications for slide collections. Sophisticated indexing techniques utilizing both manual and machine systems have been given expanded coverage. Although neither the first edition nor this one was intended as a guide to the use of slides in instruction or for student study, several photographs and floor plans have been added that provide examples of how the slide library can better serve user needs. "Using Slides for Instruction," in the Selected Bibliography, was also updated. Additional examples of cataloging and classification applications have been included to offer expanded guidelines on this topic both for slide librarians and for students studying the organization of nonprint media. A new section has been devoted to a subject that was only mentioned in the first edition—environmental controls and preservation measures for slides. Although the need for such measures has always been important for slide collections, recent experimental research and active interest in this topic make its inclusion in this edition particularly relevant.

The considerable increase in publishing has created what may appear to some to be a burdensome number of bibliographic citations in the text. However, the value of the second edition is certainly enhanced by these references, which deserve the attention of those who plan to use *Slide Libraries* to its greatest advantage— both for immediate reference and for research purposes. The bibliographies at the end of each chapter have been limited as much as possible to the most important citations. The Selected Bibliography at the back of the book has a considerable number of additional references. The reader is advised to use both chapter and Selected Bibliography entries when desiring complete references on a given topic. To insure against any serious omissions, all available bibliographic indexes, reference sources, and unindexed journal runs were examined, beginning with 1971 imprints.

The first preface is still relevant to the objectives of the second edition and provides useful information about the original data compilations for *Slide Libraries*. Hopefully, the expanded treatment of numerous topics, the careful review and revision of the entire text, and the addition of new concepts such as graphic card catalogs should make this edition a useful complement to the general literature on nonprint media.

PREFACE TO THE FIRST EDITION

The materials explosion of the 1960s has demanded formal recognition of the complex nature of visual resource libraries and of the need to establish valid criteria for their effective utilization and development. The purpose of this guide is to state these criteria for slide libraries so that they will be available to individuals in the art, audiovisual, library and instructional media fields. The chapters that follow outline standard administrative practices, classification systems, production methods, physical facilities, and supplies and equipment, indicating basic guidelines for the efficient organization and administration of these visual resource collections. In the past it took months or even years to learn to cope with the complexities of an audiovisual resource collection; it is hoped that this work will facilitate that learning process for those in academic institutions and museums.

In recognition of the lack of published information on slide libraries, a comprehensive study and survey was instituted, covering the history of the problem. the present status of slide collections, practical matters (such as equipment and photographic processing) and more formal library considerations (such as the use of classification systems, source or accession files and authority files). The base of departure for this research was art slide libraries in colleges, universities, and museums in the United States. An eight-page questionnaire was sent to the librarians and curators of these collections, and a selected number were interviewed personally.

From 1968 to 1970, 150 questionnaires were mailed to slide librarians in colleges, universities, and museums in the United States. A total of 120 (80%) responded either by writing directly or by returning the questionnaires; as a result, 101 questionnaires were tabulated for the study. Letters are included in the total number of responses but not as part of questionnaire tabulations. (See the directory of slide libraries for a list of contributing collections.)

Although initially an attempt was made to limit the size of the collections covered, the base of 25,000 was dropped because not all sources consulted (*The American Art Directory*, *The American Library Directory*, and *The Directory of Special Libraries and Information Centers*) gave the exact sizes of slide collections; moreover, in view of the tremendous growth rates of many collections, it seemed unfair to omit them under such an arbitrary standard. Thus, the frequent lack of such data, coupled with the desire to include as many academic collections as possible, negated the use of a size-limitation factor for the inclusion or exclusion of slide collections in the initial study; the size of slide libraries studied ranges from 1,000 to over 200,000 slides.

Because the emphasis in the original study was on academic collections, only a select number of museums were included. It was not considered necessary to obtain information on every slide collection in the United States in order to develop an overview of organizational and administrative procedures. The bibliographical research for this manual, however, has included all potential subject reservoirs on this topic: audiovisual, art, education, library, and science literature. Historically, art education and art history curriculums have had the greatest demand for this particular visual medium, which originated in the seventeenth century; consequently, these areas have been the primary research sources. The visual documentation of art works through the use of slides for educational purposes has been a natural function of the medium. Only recently have other disciplines discovered the advantages and flexibility of this rather "old" visual tool.

In addition to the use of questionnaires as a data base, 28 collections were directly observed and studied; in such cases each slide librarian was interviewed so that information could be collected on the day-to-day operation, organization, and general administration of each facility. Extensive photographic coverage was also undertaken of all collections directly observed. Except as noted, the photographs included here were taken by the author. Another 550 questionnaires were mailed to manufacturers and distributors of slides, equipment, and general supplies used in slide libraries. The results of this final mailing are included in the various chapters on equipment and supplies and in the directories.

Because slide libraries in the United States had never been studied in depth, the questionnaire and direct observation methods were considered critical to the formulation of guidelines for the operation of such collections. Additional research through audiovisual education, and library literature has provided the necessary supplementary information; literature from approximately the last 15 years in the audiovisual, education, and library fields was studied. Bibliographical indexes from 1876 to the present were searched specifically for the treatment of slides or lantern slides in art, education, and library literature. One of the most beneficial results of this undertaking is the extensive and comprehensive bibliographic compilations; these serve as guides to supplemental reading on related topics and, in other instances, indicate the availability of more detailed information. This work is designed not to duplicate the research and publications of others but to generate new concepts and to complement previously established ones.

One aim of this manual is to show, whenever possible, the correlation of slide library procedures with established library practices on an organizational and administrative level. Further, the guidelines and principles set forth should be useful regardless of the subject orientation of the slide library. Those working in a previously established slide library should find the guide as helpful as those interested in building a collection.

The name "library" has lost its etymologic meaning and means not a collection of books, but the central agency for disseminating information, innocent recreation, or best of all, inspiration among people. Whenever this can be done better, more quickly or cheaply by a picture than a book, the picture is entitled to a place on the shelves and in the catalog.

. . . A generation ago the lantern slide was little known except in magic lantern entertainments, and it required some courage for the first schools to make it a part of the educational apparatus. Today there is hardly a college or university subject which is not receiving great aid from the lantern. No one thinks of it as a course in art or discusses it from an ethical standpoint. It is needed by the engineer, physician, botanist, astronomer, statistician, in fact in every conceivable field, but of course, it is specially adapted to popular study of fine arts because they are so dependent on visual examples, and the lantern is the cheap and ready substitute for costly galleries.

Melvil Dewey
1906

"Library Pictures," *Public Libraries* 11:10 (1906).

TABLE OF CONTENTS

DIRECTORY OF SLIDE SOURCES (cont'd)

LIST OF FIGURES

LIST OF DIAGRAMS

LIST OF PHOTOGRAPHS

1–BACKGROUND FOR SLIDE LIBRARIANSHIP

HISTORICAL INTRODUCTION

The earliest noted slide collections in the United States date from the 1880s to 1900 and were initiated in the following institutions: American Museum of Natural History of New York City; Bryn Mawr College; Buffalo Society of Natural Sciences; Art Institute of Chicago; Cornell University; Dartmouth College; Massachusetts Institute of Technology; the Metropolitan Museum of Art; Mount Holyoke College; Princeton University; the University of Illinois; the University of Michigan; the University of Rochester; Wellesley College; and Williams College. These collections represented a vast range of subjects from architectural history to travel or geography. Other areas were archaeology, art, cultural history, design, education, general and local history, nature, and science.

It was not until 1884 that George Eastman patented the roll film system; consequently, collections begun prior to this time depended solely upon the lantern slide, which is a 3¼x4-inch glass slide with glass used as the medium upon which the image is printed. Originally, lantern slides that date from the seventeenth century were hand-painted, and many were works of art in their own right. Prominent collections of these early lantern slides can be examined at the Library of Congress and the George Eastman House in Rochester, New York.

The American Museum of Natural History of New York City was one of the early promoters of museum instruction to the public, and by 1900, it was providing lantern slides, filmstrips, and other teaching materials to the schools (Saettler, 1968, p. 87). By 1923, the Chicago Bureau of Visual Instruction had built a slide library totalling 85,000 slides (ibid., p. 155).

In the 1930s, color dye processes were perfected by Leopold D. Mannes and Leopold Godowsky, Jr., in collaboration with the Kodak Research Laboratory. The result of this work was the introduction of the Kodachrome three-color film process. Until the perfection of this particular technique, 35mm or 2x2-inch slides were not widely accepted. Although the period of growth of slide libraries begins in 1880, the most significant number of collections were established between 1930 and 1960. This increase was very likely due both to the added benefit of color slides and to the fact that they were, and still are, less expensive to produce than standard lantern slides. Consequently, it was financially feasible for colleges, museums, schools, public libraries, and universities to have begun their collections at that time. These birth trends might also be indicative of the steady rise of art history studies as more than a mere humanities adjunct to the liberal arts education in the United States.

The wide range of subjects in early slide collections was not unusual in light of the immediate acceptance and consequent exploitation of the full teaching potential of this medium. Moreover, the study of fine arts itself is multidisciplinary and includes research in history, literature, philosophy, religion, and the sciences. By the 1960s, there were over 5,000 art, historical, and science museums in the United States and Canada, and thousands of colleges and universities included the arts in their humanities programs. Slides are readily adapted to lecture programs of all types, and with the advent of the Kodachrome 35mm three-color film process, they have been well within the financial and physical constrants of institutions desiring to build a slide library. Teachers, librarians, and students could easily take slides while vacationing or on research trips, thereby developing art, travel, or geography collections. In addition, most science, historical, and art museums have available slides of their collections, and these could also be obtained by beginning slide libraries.

Today, the utilization of slides is a fundamental and integral part of every visual arts curriculum in colleges, art schools, and universities. The majority of art museums have slide collections that are heavily used by the curatorial staff for group lectures and by nearby academic institutions that may have inadequate collections. For example, the Art Institute of Chicago and the Metropolitan Museum of Art have slide loan procedures (fees are charged on either an institutional or individual basis) for institutions within their areas. In addition, the general public borrows slides from museums and, in some cases, from academic institutions for both community programs and for private use.

Few public libraries have slide collections available for loan purposes. In 1974, Mrs. Mary G. Sell, Art Division, Carnegie Library of Pittsburgh, surveyed nineteen public libraries, requesting information about slide collections (Page, 1976). Ten libraries responded, providing data about staffing, circulation procedures and statistics, budgets for collection development, and so forth. The following institutions were documented by this study (slide collection size in parentheses): Carnegie Library of Pittsburgh (92,247); Chicago Public Library (8,000); Cleveland Public Library (5,800); Enoch Pratt Free Library of Maryland (32,197); Minneapolis Public Library (35,920); Newark Public Library (15,000); Philadelphia Public Library (1,780); St. Louis Public Library (15,600); St. Paul Public Library (11,000); and the Tulsa Public Library (100 sets and individual slides) (ibid., p. 86). In this same report, Page describes the planning and budgeting procedures for the Rochester Public Library's establishment of a slide collection, providing useful information for any public librarian who might be concerned about handling slides (ibid.). Another public library having slides is the Public Library of Cincinnati and Hamilton County (25,000). Based upon Page's observations, slides can provide a beneficial service to public library patrons, but expectations for service must be matched by a commitment to separate staff and budget allocations specifically designated for slides.

Administration of early visual resource libraries was given minimal attention. More often than not, such collections as slides, photographs, architectural drawings, and maps were begun in a non-library situation by people who gathered materials in a haphazard manner. Slide collections in most United States colleges and universitites were initiated by the art faculty to illustrate lectures. These collections were often small, consisting of several boxes of slides relating to only a few specialized subject areas. Because of the size of these collections and the limited demands and size of the faculty, it was generally assumed that these incipient slide libraries required minimal supervision and attention to basic library principles such as cataloging and classification. Generally, part-time students in a department aided the faculty in the performance of clerical tasks. When the collection expanded to burdensom proportions, a full-time person, usually with a visual arts background but rarely with library training, was hired. Occasionally, the collection was actually established within the library so that professional supervision was automatically instigated. Approximately 20% of the academic and museum collections surveyed in 1968 indicated that their collections were initially supervised by a professional—

an individual with a graduate or undergraduate equivalent degree in library science or in art history. The majority of the professionally degreed supervisors had a background in library science rather than in art. Museums were more likely to have begun their slide collections under the supervision of the library because it provided a natural location for the organization and development of a collection for the entire museum staff's use. In some instances on the academic level, when the art library was physically a part of an art department, this collection was also placed under the librarian's jurisdiction. It is interesting to note that of the 101 collections returning a completed questionnaire, 19 responded that their collections began under professional guidance. The slide libraries of the following 19 institutions began in this manner:

Massachusetts Institute of		National Gallery of Art	1941
Technology	c. 1900	Indiana State University	1950
Princeton University	c. 1900	Miami University, Ohio	1952
University of Rochester	c. 1900	University of California,	
Art Institute of Chicago	c. 1904	Los Angeles	1953
Rhode Island School of Design	1915	University of California, Davis	1955
Cleveland Museum of Art	1916	University of California,	
Grinnell College	c. 1920	Riverside	1956
Indianapolis Museum of Art		University of California,	
(formerly Herron Museum of Art)	c. 1920	Santa Cruz	1966
City Art Museum of St. Louis	c. 1925	Elmhurst College	1967
Cincinnati Art Museum	1937	School of Visual Arts, New York	1967

Table 1 (p. 28) illustrates the relationships among art schools, colleges, museums, and universities regarding the age, initial and present staffing, and the size of the slide collection. Individual institutions are not identified because the status of an individual collection may differ from one year to the next, particularly in size and professional staffing. Instead, the information provided is intended as a general indication of how collection size affects the size of its staff. Another factor that greatly affects staff size is the expansion rate of the slide library. Individual institutions tend to use different methods for recording their growth rate; consequently, such information could not also be included for comparison purposes. Moreover, a given collection may undergo rapid growth within a given year that does not reflect its normal expansion pattern. A summary of Table 1 indicates that 50% of the collections have a full-time professional staff (with graduate library and/or art history degrees), 85% have a part-time staff ranging from one to twenty employees, and 50% maintain collections of over 50,000 slides. When an academic or museum collection exceeds 50,000 slides, professional staffing patterns are usually established. Collections having 100,000 slides or more are usually staffed with from one to four full-time professionals.

Today, with the emphasis on instructional media centers, it is generally considered more desirable to administer and maintain all audiovisual collections in one location to avoid duplication of equipment, facilities, and staff rather than to disperse them throughout an institution. With the general resistance of the librarian in the past to accept the role of nonbook materials as basic and necessary to a library, it was natural that these collections originated within the proximity of the user rather than the professional administrator such as a librarian. Although this guide is primarily concerned with slides, they cannot be divorced from their

(Text continues on page 31)

Relationships Among Institutional Type, Age, Initial and Present Staffing, and Collection Size

TABLE 1. Collections Established from 1880 to 1930

Institution	Date Est.	Staff When Est.	STAFF (1970) Professional Degree	No.	F	Clerical Degree	No.	PT No.	Size
U	1880	F	-	-	-	BA	1	5	150,000
U	1880s	F	L	1	-	-	-	3	55,000
C	1890	F	-	-	-	BA	1	3	80,000
C	1892	F	-	-	-	BA	2	3	48,000
U	1900	PR/L	H	1	-	BA	2	3	90,000
U	1900	F	H	1	-	BA	3	-	160,000
C	1900	F	-	-	-	-	-	2	20,500
U	1900s	F	-	-	-	BA	1	1	40,000
M	1904	PR/L	H	2	-	NC	2	5	82,000
			L	2					
M	1905	PT/CL	H	1	-	BA	2	2	70,000
C	1905-8	F	H	1	-	-	-	10	100,000
M	1907	PT/CL	H	4	-	BA	1	9	270,000
C	1910	F	-	-	-	NC	1	2	47,000
U	1910	F	-	-	-	BA	1	2	90,000
U	1911	F	H	1	-	BA	2	4	135,000
			L	1					
U	1911	F	-	-	-	BA	1	3	100,000
U	1914	F	H	1	-	BA	2	7	93,000
			L	1					
C	1915	CL	BA	1	-	-	-	9	60,000
AS	1915	PR/L	-	-	-	BA	2	-	46,000
M	1916	PR/L	H	1	-	BA	4	9	140,000
			L	1					
C	1917	F	-	-	-	BA	1	4	130,000
M	1920	PR/L	L	1	-	-	-	-	22,000
C	1920	F + PR/L	-	-	-	-	-	2	22,500
U	1920	F	H	1	-	-	-	10	100,000
U	1920s	F	-	-	2	-	-	10	22,000
U	1920s	PT/CL	H	1	-	NC	1	4	90,000
C	1920s	F	-	-	-	BA	1	4	92,000
U	1923	F	L	1	-	-	-	2	137,000
U	1924	CL	L	2	-	BA	3	6	170,000
U	1925	F	-	-	-	BA	2	4	119,000
						NC	1		
M	1925	PR/L	-	-	-	-	-	1/L	11,000
U	1926	F	-	-	-	NC	1	1	15,500
U	1927	CL	L	1	-	BA	1	4	170,000
U	1927	F	-	-	-	-	-	3	20,000
								1/L	
M	1930	UNK	L	2	-	NC	1	1	36,500
U	1930	PT/CL	H	1	-	-	-	UNK	200,000
U	1930s	F	-	-	-	BA	1	1	90,000

TABLE 2. Collections Established from 1931 to 1950

Institution	Date Est.	Staff When Est.	Professional Degree	No.	F	Clerical Degree	No.	PT No.	Size
C	1931	UNK	-	-	-	NC	1	2	37,000
C	1933	PT/CL	-	-	-	BA	1	none	14,000
U	1934	F	-	-	-	BA	1	15-20	300,000
U	1935	F	H	1	-	-	-	9	100,000
U	1935	F	L	1	-	L	1	10	190,000
U	1935	F	-	-	-	BA	3	1	66,000
U	1935	F	L	1	-	-	1	3	50,000
U	1935	F	H	1	-	-	-	17	94,000
M	1937	PR/L	L	1	-	BA	1	-	20,000
C	1938	F	-	-	1	BA	1	3	95,000
U	1938	F	H	1	-	-	-	4	130,000
U	1938	F	-	-	-	BA	1	-	20,000
U	1938	F	H	1	-	BA	2	15	85,000
M	1939	CL	H	2	-	BA	2	6	89,000
U	1940	F	H	1	-	BA	1	5	34,000
						NC	1		
AS	1940	F	-	-	1	-	-	3	25,000
M	1941	PR/BA	BA	1	-	-	-	1	53,000
C	1943	F	0	1	-	-	-	4	33,000
U	1946	F	-	-	1	-	-	3	35,000
U	1947	F	-	-	-	BA	1	3	100,000
U	1947	F	H	1	-	-	1	21	106,000
U	1948	F	-	-	-	BA	1	11	35,000
U	1948	F	-	-	-	BFA	1	4	65,000
U	1948	F	-	-	-	NC	4	1	60,000
AS	1949	PR/H	-	-	-	-	-	1/L	10,000
U	1950	CL	H	1	-	-	-	3	33,000
AS	1950	UNK	-	-	-	-	-	3	15,000
U	1950	PR/O	PR/O	1	-	-	1	-	2,000
U	1950s	PR/L	L	1	-	BA	2	-	25,000
U	1950s	PT/CL	H	2	-	-	-	12	75,000

TABLE 3. Collections Established from 1951 to 1967

Institution	Date Est.	Staff When Est.	Professional Degree	No.	F	Clerical Degree	No.	PT No.	Size
U	1951	F	H	1	-	-	-	7	70,000
U	1952	CL	L	1	-	-	-	3	55,000
U	1952	PR/L	H	2	-	-	-	2	24,000
U	1953	F	-	1	-	-	-	5	45,000
U	1953	F	H	1	-	-	-	9	60,000
U	1953	CL	H	1	-	BA	1	5	164,000
U	1953-5	F	-	-	-	-	-	2	46,000
U	1954	F	-	-	-	MFA	2	5	34,000
U	1955	F	-	-	-	-	1	12	33,000

(Table continues on page 30)

TABLE 3. (Cont'd)

Institution	Date Est.	Staff When Est.	STAFF (1970) Professional Degree	No.	F	Clerical Degree	No.	PT No.	Size
U	1956	PR/H	-	-	-	BA	1	5	50,000
M	1956	PR/O	-	-	-	BA	1	-	40,000
M	1957	PT/CL	H	1	-	-	-	-	11,000
			L	1					
U	1958	F	L	1	-	-	-	4	50,000
U	1959	F	L	1	-	-	-	3	10,000
U	1959	F	-	-	-	BA	1	3	37,000
AS	1959	F	H	1	-	-	2	2	95,000
U	1959	F	H	1	-	-	-	3	30,300
AS	1959	CL	-	-	-	BA	1	-	40,000
C	1959	F	L	1	-	-	UNK	UNK	16,000
U	1959	PT/CL	H	1	-	BA	1	2	12,000
AS	1960	F	-	-	1	BFA	1	.	2,500
AS	1960	UNK	L	1	-	-	-	1	20,000
U	1961	PT/CL	L	1	-	-	1	3	50,000
M	1961	CL	-	-	-	MFA	1	5	5,500
AS	1963	F	-	-	-	-	2	1	48,000
U	1964	F	-	-	-	-	-	1	15,500
C	1964	UNK	L	1	-	-	2	2	20,000
			H	1					
U	1965	F	-	-	1	BA	1	5	52,000
U	1966	PR/L	L+H	1	-	BA	1	3	58,000
U	1966	F	H	1	-	-	-	5	76,000
AS	1967	PT/CL	-	-	-	-	-	1	1,000
AS	1967	F	-	-	-	BFA	1	-	6,000
C	1967	PR/L	L	1	-	-	-	2	6,000
U	1967	F	H	1	-	-	-	5	15,000

* * *

Key to Abbreviations Used in Table

AS	art school	L	librarian/graduate library degree
C	college	MFA	master of fine arts degree
M	museum	NC	no college degree
U	university	O	other professional degree, e.g.,
BA	bachelor's degree		master's degree in education
BFA	bachelor of fine arts degree	PT	part-time
CL	clerical	PR	professional
F	faculty	UNK	unknown
H	graduate degree in art history		

relationship to filmstrips, phonorecords, and other media, which can be used in conjunction with slides and which all should be housed and administered in the manner most advantageous to the user, whether a museum curator, a university professor, or a student.

LITERATURE SURVEY

Slide libraries, like other audiovisual resource collections, have suffered from general neglect in the literature until very recently. The earliest study in visual education was a survey by F. Dean McClusky entitled "The Administration of Visual Education: A National Survey," which is an unpublished report made to the National Education Association in 1924 (Saettler, 1968, p. 154). City school systems were analyzed in McClusky's report, one of the conclusions of which was that in 1923, slides were the most widely used visual media (ibid., p. 155). Although slides were widely used by 1923, and even though Melvil Dewey had applauded their use in a 1906 article in *Public Libraries* (1906, p. 10), the literature in general did not offer an abundance of information on these early collections. Two of the earliest articles of note were by E. L. Lucas (1930) of the Fogg Art Museum Library, Harvard University, and L. E. Kohn (1932) of the Art Institute of Chicago. Both discussed the classification of their respective collections. Miss Kohn especially emphasized the treatment of slides in a similar manner as books by making a title page for slides as part of the cataloging process (1932).

As a logical consequence of the development of the three-color film process in the 1930s and the widespread emergence of slide libraries, papers concentrating on production methods for slides sporadically began to appear in the literature. In 1943, the merits of the color 35mm slide and the black and white lantern slide were argued by two art historians in the *College Art Journal* (Beam, 1943; Carpenter, 1943). Although almost 30 years old, these articles are relevant today because many slide librarians and curators still face problems of using lantern slides, dispensing with them, buying them, or occasionally producing them (on roll film). The film discussed in the two papers mentioned above was Kodachrome.

Margaret Rufsvold pointed out in 1949 that "the literature of the audiovisual field is especially rich in its treatment of the classroom uses of media. However, little attention has been given to the reference uses of these materials in the library by individuals or groups. Also neglected is the whole field of cataloguing, organizing, and distributing audio-visual materials according to standard library practices" (Rufsvold, 1949, p. III). The slide was no exception to this pattern. The next two decades, however, would help to fill this vacuum.

By the 1950s, the color 35mm slide was established as an important and necessary part of a slide library. Several articles discussed the relative ease of building a 35mm slide library, placing special emphasis on the economy factor of these slides (Bibler, 1955; Bridaham, 1951; Ellis, 1959; Walker, 1953). Other areas of concern at this time were the classification, filing, and general retrieval problems associated with slide collections (Perusse, 1954; Tselos, 1959; Walker, 1957). Several general audiovisual cataloging manuals of note that included the treatment of slides appeared at this time, especially those by Virginia Clarke (1953) and Eunice Keen (1955). The finest general overview of the problems encountered in handling slide and photograph collections was written by Phyllis

Reinhardt, who was the Art Librarian at Yale University at that time (1959). She discussed the general characteristics of these collections, the importance of developing a quality collection, cataloging and classification methods used at Yale, and staff training. Hers was one of the first papers to stress the critical need for a properly trained professional to supervise these collections.

The major emphasis in the 1960s was on classification and cataloging problems. Slide libraries came of age as they entered the computer era. During this period, an art, history, and science slide and picture classification system was devised by Wendell Simons and Luraine Tansey at the University of California at Santa Cruz. A preliminary edition of their work was issued in 1969; the final edition was published in 1970 (Simons and Tansey, 1970).

While the Santa Cruz system was being developed on the West Coast, individuals on the East Coast were also making contributions to research in this field. Elizabeth Lewis (1969) of the United States Military Academy Library at West Point and Boris Kuvshinoff (1967) of Johns Hopkins University discussed two methods of establishing a visual aid card catalog that could be used manually and by machine indexing. In addition, Robert M. Diamond (1969) of the College of Fredonia, State University of New York, developed a retrieval system for 35mm slides used in the arts and humanities. Audiovisual cataloging and organization manuals that include slides also enjoyed the publication boom (Colvin, 1963; Gambee, 1967; Harris, 1968; Hicks and Tillin, 1967; Hopkinson, 1963; Strout, 1966; Westhuis, 1967).

The 1970s will be recognized as a time of prolific accomplishment and publication activity for nonprint media; and as nonprint media prospered, so did slides. Beginning with the 1970 edition of the Santa Cruz classification system, the period from 1970 to 1978 has benefitted from an accumulated literature that eclipsed what had been published since the beginning of the century. These recent contributions were made primarily by American, British, and Canadian slide librarians, media specialists, and other professionals committed to documenting their work with slides and slide collections.

A benchmark book of the 1970s, *Bibliographic Control of Nonprint Media* (1972), resulted from an institute sponsored by a grant from the U.S. Office of Education and was conducted in a series of sessions from 1969 to 1970. Robert M. Diamond (Director, Instructional Resources Center, State University College, Fredonia, New York) and Wendell Simons contributed papers that include information about Diamond's descriptor system and the Santa Cruz classification schedule, and about general problems related to the storage and retrieval of slide collections (ibid., 1972, pp. 346-73). Published in 1974, *Slide Libraries* (Irvine) was the first monograph devoted to the general study of slide collections. In this same year, Dr. Juan Freudenthal (School of Library Science, Simmons College) prepared an excellent state-of-the-art report entitled "The Slide as a Communication Tool," covering subjects as diverse as copyright and visual materials. The following year, *Library Trends* dedicated a single volume to "Music and Fine Arts in the General Library," which included three articles on slides: "Organization and Management of Art Slide Collections," by Betty Jo Irvine, Fine Arts Librarian, Indiana University; "Classification of Research Photographs and Slides," by Luraine Tansey, Art Historian and Slide Consultant, San Jose City College; and "Slides for Individual Use in the College Library," by Wolfgang Freitag, Librarian, Fine Arts Library, Harvard University (1975, pp. 401-426, 495-99). (For additional references on instructional uses of slides, see section XIV, "Using Slides for Instruction," in the Selected Bibliography.) In an effort to provide much-needed guidance about the organization and utilization of nonprint media in academic libraries, Pearce Grove, Library Director, Eastern New Mexico University, edited a series of papers that were published as part of the "ACRL [Association of College and Research Libraries] Publications in Librarianship" (*Nonprint Media in Academic Libraries*, 1975). For this volume, Freitag and Irvine jointly prepared a chapter on "Slides" that summarized historical data on slide collections, acquisition and selection tools, and production techniques relevant to academic collections (1975, pp. 102-121).

By mid-decade, another monograph on slides had been published: *The Management of 35mm Medical Slides*, by Alfred Strohlein, Staff Advisor, Media Resources Branch, National Medical Audiovisual Center, Atlanta, Georgia (1975). Although primarily directed to the medical or science slide librarian, Strohlein's handbook contains a great deal of information valuable to anyone working with slides, e.g., sections on computer and data processing applications for slides, circulation procedures, and a table listing the cost-storage ratio of various slide cabinets. Continuing a tradition established in 1972, Nancy DeLaurier (Curator, Slides and Photographs, Department of Art and Art History, University of Missouri—Kansas City) prepared a third edition of the *Slide Buyer's Guide* in 1976. This guide has become a standard source of information for commercial and museum sources of slides and is commonly cited in the literature. Although numerous non-art sources are listed by DeLaurier, her primary focus has been art and art-related slide producers and/or distributors. A useful complement to the *Guide* is the *Index to Educational Slides* prepared by the National Information Center for Educational Media (NICEM) (1977). Both the *Guide* and NICEM indexes are updated regularly. Working in association with the Art Libraries Society of the United Kingdom, Philip Pacey (Art Librarian, Preston Polytechnic) prepared the *Art Library Manual*, which includes 26 chapters on topics ranging from general art bibliographies to microforms (1977). The chapter devoted to "Slides and Filmstrips" was written by Pacey (ibid., pp. 272-84). In 1978, members of the Art Libraries Society/ North America (ARLIS/NA) compiled a *Directory of Art Libraries and Visual Resource Collections in North America*, which represents the most comprehensive inventory available of art slide, photography, and other media resources.

In addition to the general publications cited, the 1970s reflected the increasing concern among slide curators, librarians, and media specialists with cataloging and classification. Slides, along with other nonprint media, benefitted from expanded treatment in the AECT, second Anglo-American, and Canadian cataloging rules (Tillin and Quinly, 1976; 1978; Weihs, 1973). Articles were written about the cataloging, classifying, and indexing of art and art-related slides (Bogar, 1975; Sedgley and Merrett, 1974; Zahava, 1978) and about medical or science slide collections (Clawson and Rankowski, 1978; Raymond and Algermissen, 1976; Visser, 1977). A significant increase in the number of publications about computer or data processing applications for slide retrieval also occurred during this period (Lewis, 1976; LoPresti, 1973; *Illuminated Manuscripts . . . ,* 1977 and 1978; Ohlgren, 1978 and 1979; Rahn, 1975). At Columbia University, a dissertation was prepared on the comparative use of visual indexing in microfiche, Super 8, and videotape and on conventional access via card catalogs and permuted computer print-outs for slide retrieval (Lewis, 1974). Through locally prepared manuals, slide librarians and media specialists described sophisticated systems outlining the application of automation techniques in their institutions: African Studies Program Slide Archives, Indiana University; Architecture and Planning Library, Howard University; and the National Collection of Fine Arts Slide and Photograph Archive (Ohrn, 1975; *SLIDEX*, 1978; NCFA . . . , 1978).

During the 1970s, there was a marked increase in activity by professional organizations and their members. Formal programs, business meetings, and workshops on slides are now regular features at the annual conferences of the Art Libraries Society/North America (ARLIS/NA), the College Art Association (CAA), and the Mid-America College Art Association (MACAA). Regular columns on visual resources appear in each issue of the *ARLIS/NA Newsletter*, 1973- . Slide and photograph curators prepare their own newsletter under the sponsorship of MACAA: the Mid-America College Art Association Slides and Photographs *Newsletter*, 1974- . Canadian curators now have their counterpart to the MACAA *Newsletter*, entitled *Positive*, 1976- . In 1977, both the ARLIS/NA and the CAA endorsed a statement on the professional status of slide curators, and this was published in the *CAA Newsletter* ("Professional status . . . ," 1977). The following year, MACAA slide and photograph librarians began publishing a series of visual resources guides, of which the *Guide to Equipment for Slide Maintenance and Viewing* (1978), edited by Gillian Scott (University of California, Santa Barbara) is a noteworthy example (1978). (For additional references, see the bibliographies at the end of each chapter and the Selected Bibliography.)

INTRODUCTION TO MANAGEMENT, ORGANIZATION, AND STAFFING

Many of the problems encountered in managing, organizing, and staffing slide libraries are endemic to audiovisual collections. Initially such materials may have been ignored, but the general profundity of nonprint media and their acceptance by instructional systems have created a demand for making them accessible in a manner suited to the medium. Such modes of accessibility have not always been strictly aligned with traditional handling of print materials by libraries. The fragility of lantern or glass slides, the small size of 35mm slides, the difficulty of circulating and housing single slides, and the absence of viable systems for organizing slides based upon subject content have forced many educators and librarians either to avoid slides or to treat them in a rather perfunctory manner. At the same time, however, their flexibility as a teaching tool, their relatively low cost, and their ease of production have sustained them as a popular instructional medium. A field that has maintained consistent and heavy use of slides is the fine arts; consequently, it is not surprising that the majority of slide libraries flourish in academic art departments and museums.

Although many other audiovisual materials have been integrated into library collections (filmstrips, phono recordings, and tapes in the last ten years), slides, while predating many of these media, are not commonly held and maintained by academic libraries. To compensate for the unavailability of slides, users began developing their own collections in academic departments or schools, usually acquiring part-time clerical or student assistance as the collection expanded. This pattern of clerical staffing continues to present a major bottleneck in the establishment of professional management of slide libraries, because it has tended to obscure the distinctions between professional, clerical, and technical duties and responsibilities. By contrast, slide libraries in art museums usually come under the management of the museum librarian or a professional slide librarian.

Although a single full-time clerical employee may be in charge of a slide library, additional part-time staff are usually required to meet user demands on a daily, weekly, or monthly basis. Characteristic of slide libraries is rapid expansion, which allows the collection to double or triple within a period of five years or less. Commonly, such expansion is accompanied by the hiring of more part-time staff rather than by a general review and analysis of changed staffing needs required by the size of the collection and by the increase in users that usually parallels collection growth. As this pattern continues, both the slide library staff and its parent faculty (or museum curatorial staff) begin to recognize that the collection has become increasingly complex in its coverage of a single field, that the original cursory approach to cataloging and classification is no longer adequate, and that more sophisticated records and techniques are needed to maintain control of the collection. Training in the principles of administration, organization, and retrieval and storage of instructional resources is required. Unfortunately, holdings of many collections exceed 50,000 slides before an attempt is made to resolve problems created by inadequate cataloging and classification systems, by the absence of standard library techniques and tools, and by insufficient staffing. Continued management by an individual with minimal qualifications (a bachelor's degree in a subject field without professional graduate training) and by part-time rather than full-time support staff rarely provides opportunities to overcome the problems cited. Occasionally, dedicated individuals on a clerical level will rise to the demands of both the collection and the users and develop a surprisingly sophisticated system for organizing and maintaining the library. Sound management patterns, however, should be based on more than serendipity.

Today, professional staffs manage most collections of more than 50,000 slides. Graduate degrees in library science and/or a subject field such as art history represent the backgrounds of professional slide librarians. Current trends indicate that, more and more, developing and established slide collections require the expertise provided by advanced degrees both in library science and in a subject field. Although subject training is needed for cataloging collections focusing on a single area, such preparation does not coincidentally prepare an individual to manage a slide library. Training for slide librarianship requires a background in administration, cataloging and classification principles, handling audiovisual collections, information science, reference, and selection. Computer applications and data processing techniques are being incorporated into the operations of many slide libraries, thereby requiring a greater degree of information processing sophistication by individuals managing these collections. All such training is commonly available in library schools. Many library schools, however, lack extensive programs on nonprint materials.

In order to compensate for the absence of courses on the handling of nonprint materials, prospective slide librarians must seek courses in departments of education, which emphasize the acquisition and selection of audiovisual media. The high degree of professional specialization also requires resident training in a major slide library (100,000 slides or more) under professional management. One of the major problems confronting individuals seeking training for slide librarianship is the lack of formalized programs specifically designed for special libraries, coupled with the meager nonprint media course offerings by library schools. Fortunately, many schools are beginning to alter their curriculums to meet the needs of librarians who intend to work with audiovisual collections. As more and more individuals demand curricular inclusion of courses and training in handling audiovisual materials, such programs will become an integral part of preparation for librarianship. Workshops conducted by slide and photograph curators or by library science faculty are a propitious indicator of the trend toward specialized training programs for nonprint media specialists. Such programs have been held at Columbia University, Simmons College, Syracuse University, the University of Missouri—Kansas City, and the University of Texas—Austin. Chapter 2 provides additional information on specialized training and outlines the parameters for professional, clerical, and technical staff classifications for slide libraries.

Indicative of their beginnings in academic art departments, slide libraries are typically organized according to a classification based upon broad media classes, art history periods, country or geographical areas, and artist entries for painting and sculpture. For architecture, after the main class divisions, buildings are usually organized by type under site or location entries. Initially, such a system sounds deceptively simple. What is generally missing, however, are authority files, which can prevent the misfiling of an artist under several variations of his name, under different nationalities, or within more than one historical period. Historians commonly argue about the beginning of one period, the end of another, and which art forms can be classed in one rather than another era. As long as a collection is small, broad general categories suffice, but as soon as there are more than one hundred slides on a given artist, building, or art form, the problems begin. Defining subject categories, dating works for chronological divisions under artist, and determining media types, particularly for contemporary artists, pose complicated questions for anyone not trained to understand theories of classifying and cataloging information. As one grapples with the major media, the decorative arts provide yet another range of possibilities for classification and cataloging. Different organization patterns may be required for the decorative arts because they do not conform to the standard creator/title identifiers associated with architecture, painting, sculpture, and the graphic arts.

Slide sets, as is the case with filmstrips, usually adapt to the standard systems of classification (Dewey Decimal and Library of Congress classifications) and basic subject heading lists. For in-depth collections of slides on a single topic, however, a corresponding classification and cataloging approach is needed to directly deal with the visual content of each image. In an attempt to determine systems that would adapt to the classification and cataloging of art forms, academic institutions and museums—although occasionally sharing systems—usually try to break new ground by developing their own classification schedules. As a consequence of such diverse and dispersed efforts, many institutions lack a unified and coherent classification and cataloging system. Although most do have systems that have a similar structure—media, period, artist, or site arrangement—the implementation of that structure varies in sophistication from one collection to another. Chapters 3 and 4 focus on the similarities of classification and cataloging approaches and on those library techniques and tools that, if consistently utilized, offer valid alternatives for the organization of slide libraries.

Problems in the acquisition and selection of slides reflect the absence of published selection tools and guides. Operating in an institutional vacuum has not been a conducive environment for informed collection building. At the same time, however, the general absence of published information about slide libraries would not have generated an optimistic view toward inquiry. Fortunately, this condition is changing. Publication activity and increased communication among slide librarians through the Art Libraries Society/North America (ARLIS/NA), the College Art Association (CAA) and the Mid-America College Art Association (MACAA) are helping to provide both the developing and newly established slide collections with sources that identify and evaluate slide distributors and producers. These sources are described in Chapter 5 and listed in the bibliography under the heading, "Acquisition and Selection—Slides."

Another aspect of acquisition is the local production of slides in academic departments, campus audiovisual centers, and museum photography divisions. Although there is a plethora of publications on producing slides, much of this literature seems to have been overlooked by individuals in slide collections having responsibility for local production. All too frequently, inadequate facilities have been set up, with the individual managing the collection also expected to shoot and develop slides. This diversity of roles is indicative of the previously cited lack of distinction between the character of the various functions performed in slide libraries. Many campuses have local production centers, which should be more consistently utilized for slide production. What is again plaguing slide collections is their isolation within academic departments, which has prevented broad-based solutions that are economical and effective. Reliance upon centralized production services may not even be considered a viable alternative to departmental slide production or processing, although it has been successfully implemented by a number of collections, e.g., Harvard University, Pennsylvania State University, University of Illinois—Urbana, and Yale University. The bibliography on acquisition and production of slides brings together many of the publications that will provide slide librarians a basis for making informed production and selection decisions. In addition, the text of Chapter 5 indicates the range of possibilities available for acquiring slides.

Another area that appears relatively simple at first glance is that of the selection of slide storage. This topic has received little attention in the literature and as a consequence, decisions on housing slides frequently do not take into full account the expansion schedule and organizational and use patterns that individual collections will have. Again, rather than planning the development of slide libraries on short- and long-term projections, many untrained individuals managing slide libraries make hasty decisions based upon what appear to be immediate expansion problems. The type of storage selected for slides has many ramifications for the use of the collection and can affect the implementation of organizational techniques such as interfiled shelflists and coordinated circulation systems. Unless unlimited funds are available for trying out a number of different storage facilities, the selection of slide cabinets should be based upon a critical examination of the development of a given collection and its future requirements. At the same time, however, several modes of housing may prove more practical than absolute adherence to the constraints of one type of facility. For example, a single library may have sets of slides stored in projector trays ready for classroom use, single slides filed individually in drawers, and a special collection on a given topic on visual display rack cabinets for immediate visual access.

Blame for not making informed decisions on slide storage, however, cannot be readily placed on individuals managing slide libraries. Listings of furniture for slide collections have been relatively non-existent. Except for occasional ads in photography magazines, an individual seeking information about slide cabinets was forced to conduct time-consuming correspondence surveys with other institutions to determine the various types of slide housing facilities. What may work well for one collection may not adapt readily to the needs of another. Chapter 6 and the "Directory of Distributors and Manufacturers of Equipment and Slide Supplies" provide a framework for the acquisition and selection of filing and storage cabinets for slides.

As slide collections expand, staffs enlarge, and users increase, corners of faculty or administrative offices or closet-sized spaces in museums and academic departments prove totally inadequate for a functioning collection. Requisites for designing slide library facilities in terms of standardized space needs based upon functions performed have been generally neglected in the literature. To date, other than the first edition of *Slide Libraries*, only two other publications have focused on this topic: Margaret Nolan's "The Metropolitan Museum of Art—Slide Library" and the MACAA guide on slide library management (1972, pp. 101-103; *Guide* . . . , 1978, pp. 5-27). Rooms, corners, closets—any space that could accommodate a desk, viewers, and cabinets—defined the physical environment of the slide library. Of course, the term "library" was rarely associated with the early modest quarters occupied by many collections. Like the acquisition, organization, staffing, and storage patterns of these incipient libraries, the physical area represented as minimal an allocation as possible. Of course, such areas may have proved quite adequate during the development of the collection but like many of the other problems facing slide librarians, the physical facility for the collection in many instances remained too small, with resulting inadequate arrangements to meet the demands that users place both on the staff and the slides. Guidelines for planning and designing slide library facilities are discussed in some detail in Chapter 7. The emphasis in this section is on the functions of slide libraries and the effect of user patterns on selection of furniture and equipment. A suggested building program and sample floor plans provide specific examples of slide library facilities.

Chapters 8 and 9 deal with the infinite variety of special equipment and supplies needed for slide libraries. Because of the numerous publications on projectors and projection systems, Chapter 8 is intended to complement the available literature and to offer a coherent picture of alternatives and selection considerations. Fortunately, projectors are frequently maintained by campus services or by photography departments in museums so that slide librarians are not always responsible for such equipment. At the same time, they should be aware of equipment types and of how projectors influence the general quality of projected slides. The purchase of inadequate projection systems is incompatible with the effective use and acquisition of high quality slides.

Various types of viewers, light tables, and magnifiers are necessary for slide preview in the slide library. Slide mounts, file guides, portable screens, and carrying cases are also among the variety of supplies and equipment utilized. Such equipment and supplies are within the acquisition jurisdiction of the slide librarian, who needs to be aware of the market options in all areas that affect slide library management.

The designing, equipping, managing, organizing, and staffing of any library are not simple tasks, but problems encountered in traditional libraries are compounded in audiovisual collections. Certainly, these problems are not insurmountable. First a general recognition and examination of operable procedures currently practiced is necessary. Second, an explanation of how such operations and procedures can be standardized making use of standard library techniques and tools should be provided. Third, through the subsequent realization of the complexities involved and expertise necessary to manage a slide library, professional, clerical and technical staffing patterns should be developed. Fourth, slide librarians should use and support the publication of articles and books that offer guidelines for informed decision making, which is critical to the effective management of these collections. And finally, slide librarians and curators must continue to seek alliance with strong professional organizations, which provide a forum for presenting issues and recommendations affecting the management, organization, and staffing of slide libraries.

REFERENCES

Anglo-American Cataloguing Rules. 1978. Second Edition. Prepared by The American Library Association, The British Library, The Canadian Committee on Cataloguing, The Library Association, and The Library of Congress. Edited by Michael Gorman and Paul Winkler. Chicago: American Librarian Association and Canadian Library Association.

Beam, P. C. 1943. "Color Slide Controversy." *College Art Journal* 2 (January): 35-38.

Bibler, Richard. 1955. "Make an Art Slide Library." *Design* LVI (January):105, 128.

Bibliographic Control of Nonprint. 1972. Edited by Pearce S. Grove and Evelyn G. Clement. Chicago: American Library Association.

Bogar, Candace S. 1975. "Classification for an Architecture and Art Slide Collection." *Special Libraries* 66 (December):570-74.

Bridaham, L. B., and C. B. Mitchell. 1951. "Successful Duplication of Color Slides; Results of Research at the Chicago Art Institute." *College Art Journal* 10 (Spring):261-63.

Carpenter, J. M. 1943. "Limitations of Color Slides." *College Art Journal* 2 (January):38-40.

Clarke, Virginia. 1953. *Non-Book Library Materials. A Handbook of Procedures for a Uniform and Simplified System of Handling Audio-visual Aids, Vertical File, and Other Non-book Materials in the School Library.* Denton, Texas: Laboratory School Library, North Texas State College and North Texas State College Print Shop.

Clawson, Catherine R., and Charles A. Rankowski. 1978. "Classification and Cataloging of Slides Using Color Photocopying." *Special Libraries* 69 (August):281-85.

Colvin, Laura C. 1963. *Cataloging Sampler: A Comparative and Interpretive Guide.* Hamden, Connecticut: Shoe String Press.

Dewey, Melvil. 1906. "Library Pictures." *Public Libraries* 11:10.

Diamond, Robert M. 1969. *The Development of a Retrieval System for 35mm Slides Utilized in Art and Humanities Instruction.* Washington, D.C.: Bureau of Research, Office of Education, U.S. Department of Health, Education, and Welfare (Final Report, Project No. 8-B-080).

Diamond, Robert M. 1972. "A Retrieval System for 35mm Slides Utilized in Art and Humanities Instruction." In *Bibliographic Control of Nonprint Media*, edited by Pearce S. Grove and Evelyn G. Clement, pp. 346-59. Chicago: American Library Association.

Directory of Art Libraries and Visual Resource Collections in North America. 1978. Compiled by the Art Libraries Society of North America (ARLIS/NA). Santa Barbara, California: American Bibliographical Center-Clio Press.

Ellis, Shirley. 1959. "Thousand Words about the Slide." *A.L.A. Bulletin* 53 (June):529-32.

Freitag, Wolfgang. 1975. "Slides for Individual Use in the College Library." *Library Trends* 23 (January):495-99.

Freitag, Wolfgang, and Betty Jo Irvine. 1975. "Slides." In *Nonprint Media in Academic Libraries*, edited by Pearce Grove, pp. 102-121. Chicago: American Library Association.

Freudenthal, Juan R. 1974. "The Slide as a Communication Tool: A State-of-the-Art Survey." *School Media Quarterly* 2 (Winter):109-115.

Gambee, Budd L. 1967. *Non-Book Materials as Library Resources.* Chapel Hill, North Carolina: The Student Stores, University of North Carolina. (Bibliographies for Chapters 1, 2, 4 and 5 were revised, June 1970.)

Guide for Management of Visual Resources Collections. 1978. Edited by Nancy S. Schuller. New Mexico: Mid-America College Art Association and the University of New Mexico at Albuquerque.

Guide to Equipment for Slide Maintenance and Viewing. 1978. Edited by Gillian Scott. Albuquerque, New Mexico: Mid-America College Art Association and the University of New Mexico.

Harris, Evelyn J. 1968. *Instructional Materials Cataloguing Guide.* Tucson, Arizona: The University of Arizona, College of Education. Bureau of Educational Research and Service.

Hicks, Warren B., and Alma M. Tillin. 1967. *The Organization of Nonbook Materials in School Libraries.* Sacramento, California: California State Department of Education.

Hopkinson, Shirley L. 1963. *The Descriptive Cataloging of Library Materials.* San Jose, California: San Jose State College, Claremont House.

Illuminated Manuscripts: An Index to Selected Bodleian Library Color Reproductions. 1977. Compiled and edited by Thomas H. Ohlgren. New York: Garland Publishing, Inc.

Illuminated Manuscripts and Books in the Bodleian Library: A Supplemental Index. 1978. Compiled and edited by Thomas H. Ohlgren. New York: Garland Publishing.

Index to Educational Slides. 1977. 3rd edition. Los Angeles: National Information Center for Educational Media (NICEM).

Irvine, Betty Jo. 1975. "Organization and Management of Art Slide Collections." *Library Trends* 23 (January):401-416.

Irvine, Betty Jo. 1974. *Slide Libraries: A Guide for Academic Institutions and Museums.* Littleton, Colorado: Libraries Unlimited.

Keen, Eunice. 1955. *Manual for Use in the Cataloging and Classification of Audio-Visual Materials for a High School Library*. Lakeland, Florida: Lakeland High School.

Kohn, L. E. 1932. "A Photograph and Lantern Slide Catalog in the Making." *Library Journal* 57:941-45.

Kuvshinoff, B. W. 1967. "A Graphic Graphics Card Catalog and Computer Index." *American Documentation* 18 (January):3-9.

Lewis, Elizabeth M. 1969. "A Graphic Catalog Card Index." *American Documentation* 20 (July):238-46.

Lewis, Elizabeth M. 1974. "A Cost Study of Library Color Microimage Storage and Retrieval: Visual Indexing in Microfiche, Super-8 and Videotape." Ed.D. dissertation. New York: Columbia University.

Lewis, Elizabeth M. 1976. "Visual Indexing of Graphic Material." *Special Libraries* 67 (November):518-27.

LoPresti, Maryellen. 1973. "An Automated Slide Classification System at Georgia Tech." *Special Libraries* 64 (November):509-513.

Lucas, E. Louise. 1930. "The Classification and Care of Pictures and Slides." *A.L.A. Bulletin* 24:382-85.

NCFA Slide and Photograph Archive. Division of Office of Slides and Photography, National Collection of Fine Arts. 1978. Washington, D.C.: Smithsonian Institution.

Nolan, Margaret P. 1972. "The Metropolitan Museum of Art—Slide Library." In *Planning the Special Library*, edited by Ellis Mount, pp. 101-103. New York: Special Libraries Association.

Nonprint Media in Academic Libraries. 1975. Edited by Pearce Grove. Chicago: American Library Association.

Ohlgren, Thomas H. 1978. "The Bodleian Project: Computer Cataloguing and Indexing of Illuminated Medieval Manuscripts." *Transactions of the First International Conference on Automatic Processing of Art History Data and Documents*, pp. 290-318. Pisa, Italy: Scuola Normale Superiore.

Ohlgren, Thomas H. 1979. "Computer Indexing of Illuminated Manuscripts for Use in Medieval Studies." *Computers and the Humanities*. In press.

Ohrn, Steven G. 1975. "Cataloguing in Context: The African Studies Program Slide Archives." Bloomington, Indiana: African Studies Program, Indiana University.

Pacey, Philip. 1977. "Slides and Filmstrips." In *Art Library Manual*, edited by Philip Pacey, pp. 272-84. New York: Bowker.

Page, Julie A. 1976. "Slides in the Public Library." *ARLIS/NA Newsletter* 4 (April):84-86.

Perusse, L. F. 1954. "Classifying and Cataloguing Lantern Slides." *Journal of Cataloguing and Classification* X (April):77-83.

"Professional Status for Slide Curators." 1977. *CAA Newsletter* 2 (December):9.

Rahn, Hans C. 1975. *Rahn'sche Fabdiapositivsammlung: eine ikonographische Klassifizierung von Meisterwerken der Malerei von 1430-1810 (Rahn's Coloured Slide Collection: An Iconographical Classification of Masterpaintings from 1430-1810)*. Bern: H. Lang.

Raymond, Sue L., and Virginia L. Algermissen. 1976. "Retrieval System for Biomedical Slides Using MeSH," *Medical Library Association Bulletin* 64 (April):233-35.

Reinhardt, Phyllis A. 1959. "Photograph and Slide Collections in Art Libraries."
    Special Libraries 50 (March):97-102.
Rufsvold, Margaret I. 1949. *Audio-Visual School Library Service, A Handbook for
    Librarians*. Chicago: American Library Association. 116pp.
Saettler, Paul. 1968. *A History of Instructional Technology*. New York:
    McGraw-Hill.
Sedgley, Anne, and Bronwen Merrett. 1974. "Cataloguing Slide Collections:
    Art and Architecture Slides at RMIT [Royal Melbourne Institute of Tech-
    nology]. *Australian Library Journal* 23 (May):146-52.
Simons, Wendell. 1972. "Development of a Universal Classification System for
    Two-by-Two-Inch Slide Collections." In *Bibliographic Control of Nonprint
    Media*, edited by Pearce S. Grove and Evelyn G. Clement, pp. 360-73.
    Chicago: American Library Association.
Simons, Wendell W., and Luraine C. Tansey. 1970. *A Slide Classification System
    for the Organization and Automatic Indexing of Interdisciplinary Collec-
    tions of Slides and Pictures*. Santa Cruz, California: University of California.
Slide Buyer's Guide. 1976. Edited by Nancy DeLaurier. 3rd edition. New York:
    College Art Association of America.
"SLIDEX: A System for Indexing, Filing, and Retrieving Slides and Other Visual
    Aids." 1978. Prepared by Mod Mekkawi, Laura H. Palmer, and Woodrow W.
    Lons, Jr. Washington, D.C.: Howard University.
Strohlein, Alfred. 1975. *The Management of 35mm Medical Slides*. New York:
    United Business Publications.
Strout, Ruth French. 1966. *Organization of Library Materials II*. Madison, Wis-
    consin: University Extension Division, University of Wisconsin.
Tansey, Luraine C. 1975. "Classification of Research Photographs and Slides."
    Library Trends 23 (January):417-26.
Tillin, Alma M., and William J. Quinly. 1976. *Standards for Cataloging Nonprint
    Materials; An Interpretation and Practical Application*. 4th edition. Washing-
    ton, D.C.: Association for Educational Communications and Technology.
Tselos, Dmitri. 1959. "A Simple Slide Classification System." *College Art Journal*
    18 (Summer):344-49.
Visser, Ora. 1977. "Stellenbosch University Medical Library Slide Classification,
    Storage, Retrieval, and Issue System." *Medical Library Association Bulletin*
    65 (July):377-79.
Walker, Lester C., Jr. 1953. "Low Cost Slide Production for Teaching Aids."
    College Art Journal XIII (Fall):39-41.
Walker, Lester C., Jr. 1957. "Slide Filing and Control." *College Art Journal* XVI
    (Summer):325-29.
Weihs, Jean Riddle, Shirley Lewis, and Janet MacDonald. In consultation with the
    CLA/ALA/AECT/EMAC/CAML Advisory Committee on the Cataloguing
    of Nonbook Materials. 1973. *Non-Book Materials: The Organization of
    Integrated Collections*. 1st edition. Ottawa, Canada: The Canadian Library
    Association.

Westhuis, Judith Loveys, and Julia M. DeYoung. 1967. *Cataloging Manual for Nonbook Materials in Learning Centers and School Libraries*. Rev. edition. Ann Arbor, Michigan: Michigan Association of School Librarians, The Bureau of School Services, The University of Michigan.

Zahava, Irene. 1978. "Use of Extensive Subject Headings for an Art Slide Collection." *ARLIS/NA Newsletter* 6 (November):97-100.

2–ADMINISTRATION AND STAFFING

INTRODUCTION

The administration and staffing of a slide library vary, depending upon whether the collection is under the jurisdiction of an instructional materials center on the academic level, a departmental or library system of a college or university, or an art school or museum. Because the instructional materials center concept has not been fully implemented as an efficient *modus operandi* for media organization, it is still necessary to discuss the administration and staffing of a slide library within varying institutional contexts. What are the functions of the chief administrator and the staff? Before administration and staffing can be discussed, this question must be answered.

According to Robert De Kieffer (Director of the Bureau of Audiovisual Instruction at the University of Colorado), there are "five primary functions and four secondary functions in any educational program:

Primary functions:	Secondary functions:
1. Informing	1. Reporting
2. Educating and training	2. Recommending
3. Supplying	3. Cooperating
4. Producing	4. Evaluating"
5. Assisting	

(1965, p. 100).

Informing is the process of making teachers and other users aware of "the types of audiovisual materials, equipment, facilities, and services available to them." The second function involves *educating* teachers and users in the use of media. *Supplying* and *producing* audiovisual materials and *assisting* users or teachers in how to use media are the remaining primary functions outlined by De Kieffer. The secondary functions include *reporting* on present and long-term needs, *cooperating* with the various areas within a system so that coordination of objectives is possible, and *evaluating* methods of operation and the overall effectiveness of a program (ibid., 1965, pp. 101-103).

If a slide library is part of an instructional materials or media center within a larger organization such as a college, the general director of the center will be assuming the functions defined by De Kieffer and will be delegating the authority to accomplish those functions when appropriate. If slides are located within a department or branch of a library, academic complex, or museum, the individual in charge of that branch or department may be responsible for these functions and for their delegation to subordinate staff members. Of course, there is always the possibility of a collection's growing and expanding without any directional guidance so that its functions often reflect its haphazard expansion pattern. In the majority of academic slide libraries in the United States, the collections began in such a manner. Slides were necessary to support the teaching of art, thereby forcing the faculty to develop their own private or departmental collections, which they initially organized or turned over to clerical or student supervision. As a consequence, if any of the functions defined by De Kieffer were performed, it was more by chance than by design. Accidental collection building of this type may have sufficed at the turn of the century, but today it is both economically inefficient and administratively unwise. Museum collections have usually developed under the aegis of the museum library, but this has not necessarily been the case in art schools, even though they frequently have their own library facility.

Because of the materials explosion and rapid development of technological competence over the past two decades, a collection of slides can double or triple within a year or less. This rapid expansion potential contributed to the immediate need to establish patterns of administration and staffing that both provide short- and long-term solutions to the fulfillment of a collection's primary and secondary functions. For the academic campus system that is working to develop or to maintain an instructional media program, the literature offers both questions and solutions through publications including *Administering Instructional Media Programs* (Erickson, 1968), *Criteria for Planning the College and University Learning Resources Center* (Merrill, 1977), *Developing Multi-Media Libraries* (Hicks and Tillin, 1970), *Library Uses of the New Media of Communication* (Stone, 1967), *Media Milestones in Teacher Training* (De Kieffer, 1970), "Organizing and Collecting Non-Print Materials in Academic Libraries" (LeClercq, 1975), and others. Such works have contributed to this chapter's objective to define the professional and support staffs of slide libraries and to offer recommendations on administration and staffing.

COLLEGES AND UNIVERSITIES

The majority of slide libraries in the United States were faculty initiated and supervised in academic institutions. As the collections expanded, they became too cumbersome for the faculty to administer on a part-time basis. Full-time staff, usually on the clerical level, was hired to supervise the collection; occasionally, a professional staff member took over the collection. In rare instances, the collection was begun under the direction of a librarian. Although art collections were the primary focus for the study, they do not vary from the general supervision patterns of slides in other academic disciplines. For example, a survey taken at Indiana University revealed the separate development of ten slide collections in addition to the one in the Fine Arts Department. All of these were initiated without professional library supervision and are under part-time faculty or clerical guidance. The demand for slides as a teaching tool speaks for the need to consolidate as much as possible in order to make materials widely available in the most efficient and economic manner. Consolidation through instructional materials or learning resource centers perhaps will be the most advantageous solution to the problem. Particularly in academic communities, large slide collections have developed that are searching for answers to the administrative and staffing problems engendered by their haphazard birth. As C. Walter Stone points out:

> It would seem that the most significant work being done with new media on the college or university campus takes place outside libraries and that, when all types of libraries have been surveyed, only those school programs which have followed an instructional materials center philosophy are demonstrating any significant gains. (1967, p. 179).

As early as 1960, the Standards for Junior College Libraries stressed the importance of audiovisual materials as part of the junior college library concept (Christensen, 1965). In the same paper on the Standards, the author points out, however, that the concept of incorporating audiovisual materials into the college library program goes back to 1946, "when a postwar planning committee of college and university librarians recommended the library as the 'logical agency to handle these teaching aids' " (ibid., p. 121). The Standards also include the administration of audiovisual services under the auspices of the library (ibid., p. 128). In an article appearing in the *Junior College Journal* in 1970, the author notes that the 1960 Standards are being revised and that the *Standards for School Media Programs* will certainly be considered as useful for standardization of "terminology, staffing, organization, and services" for library-college media centers (Fusaro, 1970, p. 42).

Administration and staffing guidelines were set forth for public schools in the *Standards for School Media Programs*, prepared jointly by the American Association of School Librarians, ALA, and the National Education Association (1969). In 1975, these standards were replaced by *Media Programs: District and School*, authored by the AASL and the Association for Educational Communications and Technology (formerly with the NEA). Chapter 4 of the new standards describes the "Personnel" of media programs, who are defined as the media professionals (which include "media specialists," "head of the school media program," and others), and the support staff (which include "media technicians" and "media aides") (ibid., 1975, pp. 21-35). Additional guidelines defining the functions and role of media professionals are offered by the School Library Manpower Project (SLMP) in *Occupational Definitions for School Library Media Personnel* (1971) and *Jobs in Instructional Media* (JIMS), prepared by the Association for Educational tional Communications and Technology of the NEA (1970). With the groundwork laid by the various standards, JIMS, SLMP, and other activities and publications within the media profession, Margaret E. Chisholm (Vice President of University Relations and Development, University of Washington, Seattle) and Donald P. Ely (Trustee, Dewitt Community Library, New York) wrote *Media Personnel in Education: A Competency Approach* (1976). Chapter 3, "The Emerging Role of the Media Professional," specifically builds on the JIMS and SLMP studies, offers additional guidelines for and examples of the functions performed by media professionals and support staff, and describes the concept of competency for the professional (ibid., pp. 27-50). Educational training guidelines for media staff are also indicated (ibid., pp. 31-40). This work is a useful reference tool for the media professional working within *any* type of institutional or organizational context.

If a college or university is developing a media program or center, the proper administration of the slide collection belongs to this program and should include appropriate professional and support staff. *Media Programs* and *Media Personnel in Education* amply describe the types of positions and the functions and responsibilities that these staff members fulfill. With slight modification, most of the principles outlined can be applied to the university or college media center concept. In addition, the basic terminology patterns used in these publications should be utilized when applicable.

Large university libraries are rarely involved in the administration of a slide library or, for that matter, in the administration of any type of media facility. The following statement represents the conclusions of Fred F. Harcleroad (President of California State College at Hayward) in his article "Learning Resources Approach to College and University Library Development":

> Although the large libraries may have to be separate because of their large book collections and enormous problems of storage and retrieval, ideally there should be some relationship between the other learning resources on the campus and the basic part of the learning resource of any campus, the book and magazine collections. At the present time, however, the most promising organizational developments for using learning resources are taking place outside the library in large research universities, and in a new division of educational services or learning resources which includes the library in smaller, instructionally-oriented colleges and community colleges. (1967, p. 239).

Published ten years later, *Criteria for Planning the College and University Learning Resources Center* generally reflects the same absence of coordination between print and nonprint collections as noted by Harcleroad in 1967 (Merrill and Drob, 1977, pp. 38-40).

The traditional splintering of educational resources in academic institutions has parallels in the diversified administration of slide libraries in colleges and universities. In those institutions where the slide collection is within the administrative jurisdiction of an academic department, the head of the collection might be a faculty member, a curator who may or may not have professional status, or a clerk. If the head of the collection is part of an academic library system, the position might be that of a librarian, a para-professional, or a clerk. The academic qualifications required for a given position often provide an indication of whether that position is professional, i.e., having administrative, faculty, and/or librarian's status, or is a clerical or a support staff position. As found in the author's 1970 study, about 50% of academic slide libraries included professional staff members with graduate library and/or art degrees administering the collections and receiving commensurate library or administrative rank as part of their positions (Irvine, 1974, p. 18). In 1974, the Professional Status Committee (a sub-committee of the College Art Association Visual Resources Committee) attempted to update data on slide library staffing and to provide a comprehensive picture of the qualifications and functions of slide library administrators (DeLaurier, 1975a, 1975b, 1975c). The 1974 report included an analysis of both full- and part-time administrative staffing patterns in 164 academic institutions and 17 museums (DeLaurier, 1975b, p. 2). In a pattern similar to that of the author's earlier study, the 1974 staffing data indicate that in about half of the 182 collections documented, the chief administrator had academic, faculty, or librarian status (ibid., p. 2; 1975c, p. 2). Although the use of title designation varies, academic, faculty, and librarian ranks are generally assumed to be descriptive of professional positions. There is a trend toward full-time professional slide library administration complemented by full-time support staff; however, both the 1970 and 1974 studies indicate that the varied administrative jurisdictions of slide collections contribute to the confusion regarding what constitutes professional leadership. Another effort to provide supportive information on slide library staffing is offered in the *Guide for Management of Visual Resources Collections*, a booklet prepared by the Visual Resources Committee of the Mid-America College Art Association (1978, pp. 39-54). This booklet provides numerous descriptive lists of the tasks and responsibilities of administrative, professional, clerical, and technical staff in a slide library, and it includes sample job descriptions for each of these levels as well.

A major controversy existing in academic and museum slide libraries is the question of staffing qualifications based on library versus subject versus media training. Should the slide librarian have a graduate degree in a subject area rather than in library science if the collection is composed of slides on a single topic? One of the reasons that this question is frequently asked is that traditional library school programs do not yield much helpful information to individuals desiring to administer media collections of any type. As one prominent professional who heads a slide and photograph library pointed out, "library school grads usually want to work in a general reference library rather than a slide and photo collection and there is usually not any direct relationship to the program of library science schools and media handling." Many slide librarians or curators lament that "no one will treat it like a library." This is indicative of the casual birth and awkward adolescence that most collections have experienced when professional administration was not present from the collection's inception. Generally, if the collection was started on a professional level by a professional staff, the collection and the staff enjoy a commensurate level of respect.

Another aspect of the nebulous professional and non-professional role of the slide librarian is the profusion of titles given to this individual and to what is being supervised: audiovisual curator; curator of the slide collection; curator of visual resources; director of the section of slides and photographs; slide curator; slide librarian; and slide room supervisor. The collection of slides itself varies in title from slide room to visual resource collection. Frequently, slides and photographs are included in the title of the collection and its administrator. In those cases in which a media title is applied, the individuals are rarely under the supervision of a campus media center or program. Although the term curator is most commonly associated with museum staffs, this title is more common to the academic slide library administrator than to the museum slide librarian.

How can these titles be adjusted to the national patterns defined by *Media Programs* and *Media Personnel in Education* (1975; 1976)? Based upon the terminologies utilized in these works, and their relevance to the "library-college media center," it is possible to use similar titles when applicable (Fusaro, 1970). The professional staff of the slide library should be considered "media professionals," and the supportive staff, "technicians" and "aides." The combined title "slide library media specialist" is redundant, while "slide librarian" signifies the logical coordination of library plus media expertise necessary to administer a slide collection. If the slide collection is within an academic media center, a media specialist would be the primary supervisor unless slides composed such a major portion of the collection that a specialist in slides only is necessary; therefore, the following administrative hierarchy would prevail: head of the media center, media specialist, slide librarian. Supportive staff for a single slide library could be termed slide library aides and slide library technicians, while these individuals functioning in a media center that housed a variety of media including slides would maintain their titles—media technicians and media aides.

ART SCHOOLS AND MUSEUMS

In art schools and museums, the logical location for the administration of the slide collection is within the library. If the institution is unable to hire a full-time slide librarian, the collection should be under the supervision of the professional library staff. Even if the collection is small—less than 50,000 slides—it should be established within the framework of professional administration. Occasional faculty or curatorial supervision is inadequate and places responsibilities and duties on those frequently not qualified and without ample time to administer a visual resource collection. It is the responsibility of the librarian in a museum or art school to be informed about and prepared to administer all learning resources within that institution. If the library and library staff are sufficiently large in relationship to the size of the institution, one or more media professionals should be made responsible for the slide and photograph collection. It is quite common to have slides and photographs considered as a single collection and administered by the same staff members. As much coordination as possible should be encouraged between the slide and photograph collections. Many of the problems relating to cataloging and classification, authority, source and subject files, and so forth, are common to both media. The same status and benefits of the professional library staffs in art schools and museums should be provided for the professional slide library staff. Qualifications, training, and general management functions of slide librarians are the same for academic institutions and for museums.

QUALIFICATIONS FOR PROFESSIONAL STAFF

Slide collections are highly sophisticated instructional resource libraries that need to be managed and organized for maximum retrieval and utilization. Media professionals who manage slide libraries require a diversity of educational and empirical expertise. They need training in the principles of library and information science, in the management of nonprint media, in the operational requirements of highly specialized slide libraries, and, as appropriate, in the subject concentration of given collections. Emphasis on only one of these areas of competency is not adequate for effective and efficient slide library management.

The majority of library schools provide curricula on data processing and computer applications to information management—an area becoming increasingly important to slide libraries. In addition, general courses on administration and personnel management, cataloging and classification, and reference and selection techniques and tools have relevance particularly as collections, budgets, staff, and user demands increase. Although general courses in nonprint media are offered by the majority of library schools, the descriptions of these courses do not emphasize media in academic contexts or indicate study of individual media such as slides (Fry, 1975, p. 2). Especially significant to slide librarians are the programs being developed to train library subject specialists, e.g., programs in law, medical, music, and documents librarianship. Such programs indicate an awareness by library school faculty of the need to provide specialized professional curricula in addition to the general library science education. A 1975 study of accredited library school curricula cited one program, "Visual Arts Librarianship" offered by Queens College and the Metropolitan Museum of Art Slide and Photograph Library, that includes courses in "Art Slide Librarianship," "Picture Resources in Libraries," and "Multimedia Documentation in the Visual Arts" (ibid., p. 3). This combination of subject area, nonprint media, and library science instruction represents a highly desirable structure for education for slide librarianship. However, for the majority of individuals preparing to become slide librarians, other educational options should be investigated. For those attending library schools deficient in courses on nonprint media, additional coursework should be taken through the audiovisual or educational technology program within schools or departments of education. Such coursework should be within a graduate program in educational technology that is designed for the preparation of media professionals in schools and colleges. The graduate degree in library science and/or educational technology is commonly considered the professional degree for the media professional (Chisholm and Ely, p. 39).

Until professional training in slide librarianship is commonly available, resident training in a major academic or museum slide library (100,000 slides or more) operated by a full-time professional staff should be arranged through the library school as part of the specialized preparation required for slide librarians. In addition to the benefits to be gained through programs such as that at Queens College, workshops sponsored by library schools and/or academic institutions provide an in-depth examination of slide librarianship, often in the context of a specific collection. In 1975, a three-day institute on slide librarianship was sponsored by the School of Library Service, Columbia University, the Metropolitan Museum of Art Slide and Photograph Library, and the Art Libraries Society/North America (Lemke, 1975a, 1975b). Simmons College has also held a workshop on slides ("Continuing Education," 1973). The Curator, Slides and Photographs, Nancy DeLaurier, at the University of Missouri–Kansas City, has given a course and conducted a summer workshop on slide librarianship annually since 1976 (Holcomb, 1976). Such workshops, when intensive, might provide an alternative to resident training when such training is not readily available.

For slide collections concentrated in a single subject area, such as the fine arts, either a bachelor's degree or an additional master's degree in the appropriate subject field is desirable. Such slide libraries will be common to art museums or to university art departments and will also tend to have collection sizes of 50,000 slides or more.

The following is a summary of the training recommended for a media professional who specializes in academic or museum slide librarianship:

> master's degree in library science with emphasis on audiovisual materials and
>   information science;
> resident training in a major academic or museum slide library;
> bachelor's degree in relevant subject area or an additional master's degree in a subject
>   are (if applicable).

For large single subject collections requiring several full-time catalogers, the emphasis may be placed on in-depth knowledge of a single field; consequently, a master's degree in a subject area complemented by coursework in library science may be preferable in some instances.

STAFF FUNCTIONS AND STATUS

As noted above, the professional staff should have a coordinated training program providing subject expertise, if necessary, and library school and media coursework. The professional staff is responsible for the primary and secondary functions outlined by De Kieffer and those in *Media Programs* and *Media Personnel in Education*. The supportive staff performs clerical routines such as typing slide labels and guidecards, plus technical tasks such as producing slides. The professional staff includes the following positions: head of the slide library; cataloger(s); and reference librarian(s). Each should be identified as a "slide librarian," with the appropriate position title added to this basic title, e.g., slide librarian, reference. The following titles should be given to the supportive staff: binders; filers; photography technicians; projectionists; and typists. Based upon the tasks performed, each is identified as either a slide library aide or technician.

The professional staff of the slide library should have the following responsibilities and duties:

Professional Staff

cataloging and classification of slides which includes:
    development of catalog headings
    development of authority file
    development of shelflist and auxiliary catalogs to the collection
    revision of cataloging and classification system and/or revision of a section or entire
        collection

educating, training and informing the users of the services and equipment available from
    the slide library

providing reference service to the users of the collection

determining and planning the activities of the clerical and technical staff

directing the production of slides by the slide library

selecting and evaluating commercial and museum sources of slides

evaluating the methods of operation

selecting equipment for the slide library

reporting on and planning for the long- and short-term needs of the slide library and
    recommending changes and policy decisions on the operation of the slide library

developing channels of cooperation and communication within a department, college,
    museum, or university

The professional staff should have faculty status and salary equivalent to that for the professional library, media, and/or administrative staff of the college, museum, or university. The standards for the professional staff and benefits should be no less than those specified by the Association of College and Research Libraries

(ALA), the American Association of Community and Junior Colleges, and the Association for Educational Communications and Technology:

> Every professional staff member has faculty status, together with all faculty benefits and obligations.
>
> Faculty status for professional staff includes such prerogatives as tenure rights, sick leave benefits, sabbatical leaves, vacation benefits, comparable hours of duty, retirement and annuity benefits, and inclusion on the same salary scale which is in effect for faculty members engaged in classroom teaching. Where academic ranks are recognized, ranks are assigned to the professional staff independent of internal assignments within the center based on the same criteria as for other faculty. (American Library Association . . . , 1973, p. 57).

In order to support the professional status of slide librarians, the following "Statement of Professional Status for Curators/Directors of Visual Resources Collections for the Fine Arts" was endorsed by both the Art Libraries Society/North America and the College Art Association boards of directors in 1977:

> A qualified professional is mandatory for the efficient operation and development of a fine arts visual resources collection.
>
> The professional status of qualified visual resources personnel should be recognized. This status should require academic qualifications or their full equivalent and carry a professional title; this status should be accorded a rank equivalent to that of other parofessionals in the institution, with commensurate salary and benefits.
>
> Participation in the activities of national and regional organizations and attendance at related conferences, are essential for the visual resources professional and, therefore, should be facilitated by the institution in every feasible manner. ("Professional Status . . . ," 1977, p. 9.).

This statement should be utilized with the staffing guidelines outlined as appropriate.

The supportive staff of the slide library should have the following responsibilities and duties:

Slide Library Technicians

> making of all materials for the slide library, e.g., color and black and white slides (this individual may be a professional photographer who is on contract to perform this function or a student or part- or full-time employee skilled in slide production; or campus audiovisual services or museum photography departments may perform this function)
>
> maintaining and making available equipment for showing slides (this may be performed by a) an audiovisual department of a college or university, or b) by the staff of the slide library with or without the assistance of the campus audiovisual center, and c) in museums, by the photography department)
>
> training slide projectionists, binders, and filers (this function may be performed by the slide library technicians or by slide library aides)

Slide Library Aides

performing circulation routines and record keeping

typing slide labels, correspondence, purchase orders and other slide library records

binding, filing and projecting slides

If the slide library supportive staff is small, there may be an overlap between tasks performed by technicians and aides, although aides should only be expected to assist in such duties normally expected of technicians on a minimal level. If the slide library does not handle its own production and maintenance of equipment, a full-time technician may not be necessary. For every full-time professional, there should be a minimum of one full-time slide library aide. The necessary number of staff members will, of course, depend upon the size of the collection and production and expansion rates.

At least 50% of academic collections are still under the sole administrative supervision of a clerical staff member, although many of these individuals have undergraduate degrees in fine arts. An individual with such training, however, cannot be expected to make short- and long-term administrative decisions and to plan effectively for future collection development. If the individual hired on a clerical level is able to perform such responsibilities, then the collection, department, and college or university have momentarily enjoyed a propitious staff selection. To expect every worker hired and paid on a clerical scale to perform on a professional level is an unreasonable and invalid expectation. A position should not be based upon the qualifications of a temporary staff member but upon an accurate and appropriate job description that defines a position, thereby placing it on a professional, clerical, or technical level but *not* on all three simultaneously.

SUMMARY

Whether a slide library exists in an art school, college, museum, or university, it should be placed within the logical jurisdiction of other learning resources within that institution. In schools and museums having unified media programs for both print and nonprint materials, slides should be circulated, housed, and organized under the general administration of the program's staff. In centralized academic library systems, the slide collection should be administered within a general library setting. For decentralized or branch library systems, the slide collection should function as a branch library under the immediate jurisdiction of a corresponding subject library, i.e., an art slide collection within a fine arts branch library. Although the preceding options are recommended for the administrative placement of a slide collection within academic institutions or museums, organizational patterns that work well for one institution may not be readily adapted to another; consequently, variations from the administrative structure mentioned are possible. For example, a slide library might function on a co-equal basis with other libraries in a given system. In any case, each media professional should be titled a slide librarian, with salary, status, and benefits commensurate to those provided other professional staff, and should be provided the necessary supportive staff to expedite the effective and efficient operation of the library.

REFERENCES

American Association of School Librarians and the Department of Audiovisual Instruction of the National Education Association. 1969. *Standards for School Media Programs*. Chicago and Washington, D.C.: American Library Association and the National Education Association.

American Association of School Librarians, ALA and Association for Educational Communications and Technology. 1975. *Media Programs: District and School*. Chicago: American Library Association.

American Library Association (Association of College and Research Libraries), American Association of Community and Junior Colleges, Association for Educational Communications and Technology. (ALA-AACJC-AECT). 1973. "Guidelines for Two-Year College Learning Resources Programs," *Audiovisual Instruction* 18 (January):50-61.

Association for Educational Communications and Technology. 1970. *Jobs in Instructional Media*. Washington, D.C.: Association for Educational Communications and Technology.

Chisholm, Margaret E., and Donald P. Ely. 1976. *Media Personnel in Education: A Competency Approach*. Englewood Cliffs, New Jersey: Prentice-Hall.

Christensen, R. M. 1965. "Junior College Library as an A-V Center." *College and Research Libraries* 26 (March):121-28.

"Continuing Education." 1973. *ARLIS/NA Newsletter* 1 (October):30.

De Kieffer, Robert E., and Melissa H. De Kieffer. 1970. *Media Milestones in Teacher Training*. Washington, D.C.: Educational Media Council.

De Kieffer, Robert E. 1965. *Audiovisual Instruction*. New York: The Center for Applied Research in Education, Inc.

DeLaurier, Nancy. 1975a. "Professional Status Survey of Slide Curators: A Report." *ARLIS/NA Newsletter* 3 (October):108.

DeLaurier, Nancy. 1975b. "Report on the Professional Status Survey of Slide Curators." Mimeographed. Kansas City, Missouri: Department of Art and Art History, University of Missouri.

DeLaurier, Nancy. 1975c. "Slide Curators Professional Status Survey: Additional Statistical Report." Mimeographed. Kansas City, Missouri: Department of Art and Art History, University of Missouri.

Erickson, Carlton W. H. 1968. *Administering Instructional Media Programs*. New York: The Macmillan Company.

Fry, P. Eileen. 1975. "Nonprint Media Training in Graduate Library Science Curriculums." Mimeographed. Bloomington, Indiana: Indiana University. 4pp.

Fusaro, J. F. 1970. "Toward Library-College Media Centers; Proposal for the Nation's Community Colleges." *Junior College Journal* 40 (April): 40-44.

Guide for Management of Visual Resources Collections. 1978. Edited by Nancy S. Schuller. Albuquerque, New Mexico: Mid-America College Art Association and the University of New Mexico at Albuquerque.

Harcleroad, Fred F. 1967. "Learning Resources Approach to College and University Library Development." *Library Trends* 16 (October):228-40.

Hicks, Warren B., and Alma M. Tillin. 1970. *Developing Multi-media Libraries*. New York: Bowker.

Holcomb, Alice T. 1976. "Basic Training for Slide Curators." *ARLIS/NA News-letter* 4 (Summer):119.
Irvine, Betty Jo. 1974. *Slide Libraries: A Guide for Academic Institutions and Museums*. Littleton, Colorado: Libraries Unlimited.
LeClercq, Anne. 1975. "Organizing and Collecting Non-Print Materials in Academic Libraries," *North Carolina Libraries* 33 (Spring):21-28.
Lemke, Antje B., and Meg Estabrook. 1975a. "A Selective Bibliography of Recent Publications for the Slide Librarian." Mimeographed. New York: Syracuse University School of Information Studies.
Lemke, Antje B. 1975b. "Slide Librarianship' A Contemporary Survey," *ARLIS/ NA Newsletter* 3 (Summer):85.
Merrill, Irving R., and Harold A. Drob. 1977. *Criteria for Planning the College and University Learning Resources Center*. Washington, D.C.: Association for Educational Communications and Technology.
"Professional Status for Slide Curators." 1977. *CAA Newsletter* 2 (December):9.
School Library Manpower Project. American Association of School Librarians. 1971. *Occupational Definitions for School Library Media Personnel*. Chicago: American Library Association.
Stone, C. Walter (ed.). 1967. "Library Uses of the New Media of Communication." *Library Trends* 16 (October):179-80.

3—CLASSIFICATION AND CATALOGING

INTRODUCTION

The necessity for an acceptable system by which to organize knowledge for book libraries to provide coherent and utilitarian accessibility is no longer argued. But what has happened to the so-called "nonbook materials"? The reasons for organizing slides or any other type of media are the same as those for books, and to submit that one is more or less ephemeral than the other (thereby deserving more or less organizational attention) is to deny the usefulness and need for more than one medium of communication.

A noted authority in the field of classification, W. C. Berwick Sayers, has written several manuals explaining how and why classification it utilized. The following statements have been selected from one of his manuals to provide some cursory background to the principles that he so wisely and yet succinctly provides the reader:

> When the librarian uses the word "classification" he means the work of sorting and arranging the material—books, manuscripts, documents, maps, prints—with which he has to deal. His primary business is to select books and other printed and graphic records for the use of others; and he is successful if he is able to marshal this material so effectively that it can be placed before his readers in the least possible time. In short, to save the time of readers in their pursuit of knowledge, information or even amusement, is his ultimate work as a librarian. (Sayers, 1958, p. 2).

> Nothing can be more confusing than a disorderly, unrelated mass of books, unless it is a mass of pamphlets, cuttings, prints, photographs and the other ana of civilized life. Anyone who has tried to find something in the lumber room of a library which has been merely a place where things are collected in the hope that some day someone will arrange them, understands the waste of effort and the futility involved in disorder. It is to bring system out of the confusion of things that classification has been devised. (ibid.).

Sayers further states that:

> In order to make a classification scheme a practical instrument for the arranging of books, the nature of books themselves must be recognized. Books are not subjects, but may be statements of subjects. (ibid., p. 13).

This observation is particularly relevant to a discussion of the classification of visual resource materials, because the immediate, yet simple difference between much book and nonbook material is set forth. Pictures or slides are, in most instances, the "subjects" themselves and communicate instantly to the individual whether that person is able to read or not. Intellectual interpretation of that visual communication may differ among individuals, as with textual material, but the initial differences in the information transfer process vary because the actual information medium is not the same. For example, a written or verbal picture of a bucolic scene including various forms of rural architecture and domesticated animals can evoke a wide range of intellectual conceptions, while the actual picture provides some semblance of a concrete reality not so easily conjectured. To say that the "subjects" themselves can be classified in exactly the same manner as the verbal renderings is highly debatable. The point is not, however, to say that one is less valuable than the other—book versus visual image—but to say that "the nature of books" as opposed to visual images "themselves must be recognized."

In light of the preceding discussion, the reader is asked to keep the differences between books and visual images in mind while reading the following passages from Sayers:

> Likeness governs classification and the likeness we choose we call the characteristic of classification. (ibid., p. 8).

> A natural classification is one that exhibits the inherent properties of the things classified: an artificial classification depends upon some arbitrarily chosen characteristic or accident of the things classified and has no direct relation to their inherent properties. (ibid., p. 34).

> Practically the whole history of the classification of knowledge is a gradual working forward from the artificial schemes of arrangement to more and more natural ones. In describing the difference between natural and artificial classification, the scientist tells us that artificial classification is classification by *analogy*, that is to say, things are classified by their external likeness and apparent purpose; while natural classification depends upon *homology*, the likeness that resides in the structure and function of the things classified. (ibid., p. 35).

In a recent publication on the classification of slides and pictures, Simons and Tansey defend their development of a distinct classification of visual media by emphasizing and explaining the basic differences between the printed concept and the visual one. They particularly emphasize the need for a separate classification for collections of individual slides and pictures, because visual material that already has a pre-determined sequence such as filmstrips or motion pictures can readily be adapted to standard book schemes (Simons and Tansey, 1970, pp. 2-3). The basic problem is to recognize the essential differences in the natures of slides or pictures and books. One of the most useful and yet confounding aspects of a unitary image collection is the fact that each individual unit can be classified, cataloged, stored, and retrieved individually; they then can be re-assembled according to a specific teaching function without regard to the previous organization of the file. A filmstrip, or motion picture, however, cannot be adapted to this type of re-definition of utilization patterns without destroying the original function and continuity of the sequenced material.

There are three basic methods of organizing a slide collection: accession number order, classified order, and subject order. The arrangement of slides in sets can be used in any of these three systems. In *accession number* order, the slides are filed numerically according to the sequence of acquisition, with the internal subdivisions based upon the numerical sequence of the slides; e.g., every twenty or thirty slides might have a subdivision guide card with the accession number sequence indicated. Useful with this type of filing system are contact prints of the slide image on catalog or subject cards; these provide the user with an immediate visual record of the slide without first checking the slide files. *Classified order* depends upon a formal classification system such as the Dewey Decimal, Library of Congress, a

modification of these systems, or a specially devised scheme with a correlated notation. In order to provide for efficient use of the collection, however, auxiliary
catalogs or indexes should be used. *Subject order* is based upon the alphabetical
organization of subject classes and divisions. Using this arrangement, a collection
is considered self-indexing and may not require supplemental catalogs or indexes.
Even with this system of organization, there are a restricted number of access
points to an individual slide. If the user is not familiar with the terminology upon
which the subject classes and divisions are developed, then there may be difficulty
in locating specific types of information.

The following terms represent the major elements of a classification. These
will be used throughout this chapter to indicate the hierarchical levels of each
system:

> Main classes.
> > Divisions.
> > > Sub-divisions.
> > > > Sections.
> > > > > Sub-sections,
> > > > > > etc. (Sayers, 1958, p. 12).

MEDIA STUDIES, HANDBOOKS, AND MANUALS

If there is a consensus on the cataloging and classification of audiovisual materials, it is on the proliferation of approaches and the lack of standardization. As
William J. Quinly (Director, Educational Media Center, Florida State University)
has pointed out: "One of the major bottlenecks in getting educational media from
the producer to the patron has always been the cataloging and catalog production
process. . . . Furthermore, the majority of audio-visual specialists have fallen into
the practice of cataloging their own material, duplicating the almost identical efforts
of the other cataloguers" (1967, p. 276). In the same publication, Jay E. Daily
(Professor, Graduate School of Library and Information Sciences, the University
of Pittsburgh) stated that "there are no books which tell a librarian precisely how
best to process non-book materials nor which provide a better rule of thumb than
the general one of treating each collection of nonbook materials as a separate and
special entity" (1967, p. 287). This latter comment was made in a paper analyzing
the relevance of the 1967 edition of the *Anglo-American Cataloging Rules* to non-
book materials. Even though the acceptance of audiovisual materials by most
education institutions is considered a *sine qua non* of their teaching functions,
"educational specialists lament the deplorable lack of organization of 'media' for
utilization in the learning process," according to Pearce Grove (Library Director
at Eastern New Mexico University) (1969, p. 299).

Louis Shores (Dean Emeritus of the Library School, Florida State University)
succinctly summarized the scope of materials organization when he wrote that,
"For the first time in the history of education, instructional materials are so many
and so varied that individual differences in students can be matched with individual
differences in media" (1968, p. 11). A pioneer in media education, Dr. Shores has
been a primary force in the movement toward the total integration of all library
materials. To him, "what audio-visual really means is an extension of the means
of communication between learner and environment; consequently, the librarian

must make himself as knowledgeable in these other formats of the generic book as he now is with those which are lumped together under the heading of print" (ibid., p. 15).

How are the preceding comments relevant to the individual who administers a slide collection? To ignore the problems of the organization and retrieval of audiovisual media on a broad level is to operate in a vacuum regarding the optimal possibilities of media utilization and standardization potentials. As Dr. C. Walter Stone (Director of the Center for Library and Educational Media Studies and Director of the University of Pittsburgh Libraries) points out:

> ... in the future our concern is going to be with information, not with its possession, processing, and distribution. In many parts of the United States the definition of a librarian, audiovisual specialists, or media specialist tends to be an individual whose concern is to buy packages of material. But in the future we are not going to care about the form in which information is packaged; we shall seek the information itself. (1969, p. 5).

The operation and administration of any media collection, whether it is specialized or generalized in terms of subjects or by types of materials covered, should be approached in the context of contemporary research and models for development. If the slide librarian or curator faces daily tasks by submitting to whatever organization vagaries are imposed, then that individual compounds the complexity of tasks, duplicating and wasting effort, expense, and time. What is mandatory is that the primary forces—directors of instructional media centers, museums, and chairmen of academic departments—effecting the organization of slide libraries recognize the value of standardizing procedures for handling all materials, no matter what their "form" may be. The remainder of this chapter examines organizational alternatives that are available to a slide collection at the present time and recommends guidelines on the use of these alternatives.

What progress has been made in the past thirty years in the literature on the cataloging and classification of audiovisual materials? This section provides a general survey of existing publications with an emphasis on the organization of slides.

In 1948, a survey of the cataloging, arrangement, and storage of motion pictures, filmstrips, and 2x2-inch slides was undertaken by a student as part of her thesis requirements at Florida State University, with Louis Shores acting as one of the consulting professors for this project (Daughtry, 1948). Questionnaires were mailed to 88 audiovisual centers throughout the United States, with 61 responding. The following conclusions resulted from her study:

> Eighty-four percent of the surveyed audio-visual centers include 2" x 2" slides in their collection. The methods of cataloging 2" x 2" slides used by the surveyed a-v centers are similar to those used for motion pictures and filmstrips. The two methods most frequently used for indexing 2" x 2" slides are (a) subject and title and (b) subject only. Fifty-one percent of the surveyed audio-visual centers index 2" x 2" slides by subject and title; thirty-three percent index by subject only. Ten percent index by title only. (ibid., p. 45).

> In contrast to the relative uniformity of cataloguing and classification, there is no system of shelf order or rack arrangement used by more than approximately one-third of the surveyed audio-visual centers. The two most frequently used methods of shelf

order or rack arrangement of 2" x 2" slides are (a) alphabetically by subject and (b) Dewey Decimal classification. Thirty-five percent of the audio-visual centers surveyed arrange 2" x 2" slides alphabetically by subject and thirty-one percent arrange them by Dewey Decimal classification. (ibid., p. 40).

The third most frequently used shelf arrangement was by accession number (ibid., p. 50).

The following year, Margaret Rufsvold of Indiana University published one of the standard works in the audiovisual field, *Audio-Visual School Library Service: A Handbook for Librarians* (1949). She attempted to fill the vacuum existing in the "whole field of cataloging, organizing, and distributing audio-visual materials according to standard library practices" (ibid., p. iii). She recommended the use of title main entries and added entries when important for audiovisual materials, and that units or sets of materials should be entered under the title of the set (ibid., p. 58). For slides, she offered the following guidelines:

> To process slides assign one classification or one identification number to all slides in a unit or series and form the call number by placing SL or SM before this number. . . . Catalog by unit using title or subject of the entire series as the main entry; . . . Make added cards for subjects only . . . and file all cards in the public card catalog. (ibid., p. 61).

Summarily, she recommended the same type of cataloging as is used for print or book materials and discussed the use of Dewey Decimal or "identification" (accession) numbers as possibilities for classification (ibid., p. 55). Her final statement in the section on "Classification" still proves critical to media accessibility: "In the final analysis it becomes apparent that only through the card catalog can all materials on a subject be brought to the attention of the library patron" (ibid., p. 56).

In 1952, 1953, and 1955, respectively, Dixie Thompson (1952), Virginia Clarke (1953), and Eunice Keen (1955), published their manuals on handling audiovisual materials in the school library. In order to allow for the lack of background in the Dewey Decimal classification by library personnel, Thompson advised the use of accession numbers for shelving material and a symbol system for classification, so that a media symbol combined with the accession number formed the call number (1952, p. 2). Slides would be cataloged by set or unit, using a title or subject main entry with added entries made for subjects only (ibid., p. 23). Clarke recommended the inclusion of all materials—book and nonbook—in one subject catalog, their arrangement by media code and accession numbers, the main entry under title, and the use of *Sears List of Subject Headings for Small Libraries* (1953). Keen stated that the call number should be a symbol for lantern or 2x2-inch slides over the Dewey number, the main entry, a subject entry (if the slides did not have a distinctive title), title, imprint, collation, and notes should be on the catalog card in that order (1955, p. 10).

In a *Primer of Non-Book Materials in Libraries* (1958), Mason stated that "slides can be arranged in alphabetical subject, classified, or accession order. While the first two methods appear to be ideal the accession number method with its fixed location does avoid constant moving of the slides and thus lessens the risk of breakage" (1958, p. 46). The problem of breakage so commonly associated with lantern or 3¼x4-inch slides was still used to pre-determine the organization of slides in many libraries at this time.

By the end of the decade, the Descriptive Cataloging Division of the Library of Congress published a preliminary edition of the *Rules for Descriptive Cataloging in the Library of Congress: Pictures, Designs, and Other Two-Dimensional Representations*; this was superseded by the 1967 edition of the *Anglo-American Cataloging Rules* (1967). Both works make the same general entry recommendations that maintain as much consistency as is feasible with those rules designed for book materials with main entries under artist (or studio), architect (or architectural firm), and anonymous works under title.

During the 1960s, the universality of the organizational problems inherent in media collections was generally recognized by most individuals handling these materials; consequently, a proliferation of solutions was offered. The following manuals have been selected to demonstrate both the diversity and similarity of suggested standards during this ten-year period.

In *Instructional Materials* (1960), Louis Shores indicated the cataloging entry sequence for slides as "(1) Title, format. (2) Imprint. (3) Number, size" (ibid., p. 25). He did not make any definite suggestions for their classification except by the following: "In the Materials Center books are universally arranged by DC. Periodicals usually are arranged by title. Some centers also arrange disk recordings, filmstrips, and films by DC . . . but as a rule film collections are not arranged by DC numbers" (ibid., p. 18). He did, however, recognize the trend at that time to interfile the catalog cards for all library materials (ibid., p. 21).

The Descriptive Cataloging of Library Materials, published in 1963 (Hopkinson, 1963), followed basically the *Rules for Descriptive Cataloging* for the Library of Congress. The author recommended that title main entries be used either for individual or sets of slides and the use of a media code preceding the call number (ibid., pp. 40-41). In a guide intended for use in a library science course at the University Extension of the University of Wisconsin, Department of Library Science, the author stressed the use of title main entries for slides, filmstrips and motion pictures except when a set of slides were by the same artist. In this latter instance, the slides would be entered under the artist or the compiler. When a compiler was absent and more than one artist was included, then the title main entry was used. If a title was not supplied, then one was created for the main entry.

In 1967, Warren B. Hicks (Director of Library Services, Chabot College, Hayward, California) and Alma M. Tillin (Technical Services Librarian, Library Center, Berkeley Unified School District, California) wrote *The Organization of Nonbook Materials in School Libraries* (1967). In the introduction, they state that "the decisions on cataloging precedure are based on the fundamental principle that the organization of printed and audio-visual materials by subject reinforces the learning and extension of experiences and skills already acquired by pupils and teachers" (ibid., p. 1). They also indicated that a California State Department of Education survey revealed that the accession number and Dewey Decimal systems were the two systems used in school libraries for audio-visual materials (ibid., p. 7). Briefly, they outlined the advantages and disadvantages of these two methods. For the most part, they support the use of the Dewey Decimal over the accession number system because it directly relates to the classification of books, thereby preventing the total separation of book and media materials, and maintains the same subject approach through the classification system to all materials (ibid., pp. 7-8). They also indicate the shelving advantages of different media by using the DDC, but they point out the slower cataloging rate involved in the assignment of call numbers. Title main entries are recommended for all materials, in addition to a media code plus a number (accession, DDC, or LC) and a Cutter number for the call number (ibid., p. 15). Their thorough approach to the various types of classification systems and methods of cataloging that can be used for nonbook materials make this publication one of the most useful published during this period. The trend throughout the publications on this topic has been toward a total materials center concept whereby all types of materials are available through the same retrieval device—the card catalog.

The *Instructional Materials Cataloging Guide* (1968) was written by Evelyn Harris, the Instructional Materials Librarian at the University of Arizona. She recommended the use of *Sears* for subject headings but did not really offer advice regarding the classification of materials except for the following: "choice of classification scheme is largely dependent on physical facilities available for housing materials in some kind of consistent order. The Dewey Decimal classification for all forms of materials is often unworkable because of space problems and other difficulties" (ibid., p. iv). She did, however, recommend the use of a classified listing in a separate card catalog of all materials (ibid., p. 25). Consequently, whenever an item was accessioned, it would also have to be assigned the DDC number in order to be placed in this catalog—this catalog was in addition to a regular shelflist for books (ibid.). If Dewey numbers are assigned, it would seem advisable to use them both as classification and as shelving tools. Intershelving of different forms of media, which does present storage problems as Harris indicated, is not mandatory. For general slides, title main entries are suggested, and for art slides, "artist and title analytics should be made for individual works represented, as listed in a contents note, unless separate entry is made for each individual slide" (ibid., p. 16). She recommended the *AAC Rules* as main entry authority.

As indicated earlier in the Daughtry survey, access by subject and title, and by subject only were the two most common indexing methods for slides in 1948. In fact, the strict subject arrangement has probably been the most frequently used method by most collections because of the directness of the retrieval approach. In 1968, *The Picture Collection Subject Headings* for the Newark Public Library was published. Although this same method could be used for slides, other subject approaches tend to dominate. For example, the slide collection at the Newark Public Library is classified by Dewey with Cutter numbers (ibid., p. vi), thus providing a subject approach that also groups works of one artist together, although separating one form of artistic medium from another by the same artist. The geographical arrangement under medium (architecture, graphic arts, engraving, painting, and sculpture) with further subdivision by artist is characteristic of both the DDC and LC systems.

Although Sayers's third edition of *A Manual of Classification* (1955) was completely revised and partly rewritten by Arthur Maltby in 1967, Maltby did not deem it necessary to alter Sayers's comments on the organization of lantern slides (Sayers, 1967). Sayers noted the importance of classifying slides and any other type of picture and indicated the feasibility of using the UDC (Universal Decimal Classification) (1955, pp. 306-307; 1967, pp. 327-28). He also stressed the use of subject cataloging. At the same time, however, he recognized the inconvenience of keeping individual slides in strict classified order when they would be continually removed from this set order to be used for lectures. He reluctantly reinforced their logical organization in "lecture sets," because this conformed best to their use patterns (1955, p. 307; 1967, p. 328). (Maltby's fifth edition of Sayers [1975] is primarily devoted to print media and does not include information on handling slides.) Filing slides by set versus filing slides individually will be discussed in detail in Chapter 4.

By 1966, the Department of Audiovisual Instruction (now called the Association for Educational Communications and Technology, AECT) of the National Education Association organized a task force to develop "(1) standards for cataloging education media and (2) coding standards for computerized cataloging and scheduling" (National Education Association, 1968, p. iii). A revised and third edition of the *Standards for Cataloging Nonprint Materials* were also published (Association for Educational Communications and Technology, 1971; 1972). The *Standards* outline a ten-entry sequence ranging from title main entries to the use of tracings (subject added entries or others when relevant). In addition, a classification number using the LC or DDC numbers to allow for subject organization of materials was recommended (ibid., p. 8). Whether slides were cataloged individually or in sets, the main entry was under title (ibid., p.1). Tracings provided an artist or a subject approach to a slide.

In 1969, Virginia Clarke published a revised edition of her handbook for nonbook materials. This later edition includes thirteen pages on the handling of art slides (ibid., pp. 63-75). She also included a bibliography of books suggesting lists of headings that may provide some authority for establishing subject lists. In addition to the standard practice of main entry under title, she suggested added entries to satisfy the need for information on the medium, nationality, period, and visual content or subject of the slides. A list of headings for the art history periods and a list taken from *Sears*, 9th edition, are also included (ibid., p. 74).

Akers's *Simple Library Cataloging*, 5th ed., has one chapter devoted solely to "Audio-visual Materials" (1969, pp. 199-222). The author indicated that she does not think it worthwhile to use a classification system for audiovisual materials because of the lack of integrated storage or shelving; she instead suggested the common use of accession numbers plus media codes (ibid., p. 200). For slides, as for other materials, she recommends title main entries (ibid., p. 219) and stresses the use of a catalog for access to the materials.

In Wetmore's general guide to the organization of library materials, she recommended the use of accession order filing and title main entries (1969, p. 128). *Special Libraries*, by Silva, also noted the widespread use of accession order or alphabetical subject filing and title main entries (1970, p. 52).

In *Developing Multi-Media Libraries* (1970), Hicks and Tillin again joined forces to provide a great deal of practical information on the development of media collections within a library. They discuss the widespread use of an accession number or subject classification (DDC or LC) for media materials and title main entries, with art materials under artist (ibid., pp. 62, 73).

Following in the tradition of Virginia Clarke's coverage of slides in her 1969 handbook, the authors of *AV Cataloging and Processing Simplified* devoted ten pages to the accessioning, processing, and cataloging of slides (Johnson, et al., 1971, pp. 177-86). This manual recommended the use of DDC, *Sears List of Subject Headings*, and title main entries when possible.

By the middle of the 1970s, a number of key publications began to form the focal point for discussions regarding the organizational treatment of nonprint materials: 1) *Anglo-American Cataloging Rules, Chapter 12 Revised: Audiovisual Media and Special Instructional Materials*, published by the American Library Association (1975); 2) *Non-book Materials Cataloguing Rules*, prepared by the Media Cataloguing Rules Committee of The Library Association, 2nd edition (1974); 3) *Nonbook Materials: The Organization of Integrated Collections*, published by the Canadian Library Association (Weihs, 1973); and 4) *Standards for Cataloging Nonprint Materials*, 4th edition, published by AECT (Tillin and Quinly, 1976). Unlike earlier diverse efforts among individuals seeking to offer guidelines for cataloging nonprint materials, these publications represent an attempt to provide consistent patterns for handling nonprint media, and they reflect American, British, and Canadian cataloging expertise. Each of these works acknowledges and reflects the groundwork laid by the others. In general, these guides include recommendations to follow the the *Anglo-American Cataloging Rules* (*AAC Rules*) for cataloging audiovisuals, particularly the revised edition of Chapter 6 (1974), and the new Chapter 12 (1975). Title main entries are recommended when it is not possible to establish an author or creator. Examples of the application of the rules in Chapters 6 and 12 for the cataloging of nonbook materials are provided in the fifth edition of Bohdan Wynar's *Introduction to Cataloging and Classification* (1976). Both *Nonbook Materials* and the AECT *Standards* include information on the applicability of various classification systems—e.g., LC, DDC—and subject headings lists—e.g., *Sears*, LC, and MeSH for health sciences collections (Weihs, 1973, pp. 3-4; Tillin and Quinly, 1976, pp. 24-25). *A Nonbook Cataloging Sampler* (Loertscher, 1975) includes numerous examples illustrating the use of the Canadian *Nonbook Materials* cataloging guide. The use of a media code as part of a call number is no longer advocated; instead, the medium designation is indicated immediately following the title in brackets in the *AAC Rules* and the AECT *Standards* and in parentheses in the Canadian *Nonbook Materials*. For purposes of identifying nonprint media when shelved separately from books, the AECT *Standards* does note the usefulness of a code above the classification number to serve as a location device (1976, p. 28). The *Non-Book Materials Cataloguing Rules* was prepared as a British code for cataloging and as a "draft standard for the revision of the Anglo-American Cataloguing Rules" (1974, pp. 4-5). For additional information about the historical context and interrelationships among these cataloging guides, and for general background on this topic, refer to the excellent paper written by Suzanne Massonneau, "Developments in the Organization of Audiovisual Materials," in *Library Trends* (1977). Two papers published in *Library Resources and Technical Services* are particularly useful for discussions of the events that have led to the revision of the *AAC Rules* regarding nonprint media and to the contributing roles played by the Canadian and AECT publications (Hagler, 1975; Tucker, 1975).

Due to its publication date of 1973, the Canadian *Nonbook Materials'* recommendations on main entry and descriptive cataloging reflect the influence of the 1967 edition of the *AAC Rules*. In the section on slides, title main entries for general material and artist main entries for single slides are recommended (Weihs, 1973, p. 69). In general, the same rules apply to stereoscope and to microscope slides (ibid., pp. 56-57, 68). The fourth edition of the AECT *Standards* includes stereoscope, microscope, and audioslides within the framework of the medium designator "slide" (1976, p. 183). Indicative of its more recent publication date, the AECT

Standards utilizes the rule revisions made since the 1967 edition of the *AAC Rules*; specifically it cites the use of the revised edition of Chapter 6 (1974). For slides, title main entries are preferred except when a "creator" or artist can be identified (AECT, 1976, pp. 183-84).

The use of artist main entries for slides marks a significant departure from the third edition of the AECT *Standards*, which strictly recommended the use of title main entries for all media. Nine pages are devoted to slides in the fourth edition ((ibid., pp. 183-91), as compared with the three pages of the third edition (AECT, 1972, pp. 68-70). Reflective of the expanded coverage of all media in the 1976 edition, the section on slides includes descriptive text on determining the eight areas that represent the arrangement of the catalog data: 1) main entry; 2) title/medium designator/statement of creator responsibility; 3) edition; 4) imprint; 5) collation (physical description); 6) series; 7) notes; and 8) other identifying and organizational data (1976, pp. 183-87). Particularly useful are the statements on collation (5), which include the centimeter equivalents for the most common slide sizes: 1x3-inch=3x8cm; 2x2-inch=5x5cm; and 3¼x4-inch=8x10cm (ibid., p. 185).

In concert with the trend of the 1970s to integrate cataloging systems for print and nonprint media, the framework of a General International Standard Bibliographic Description (ISBD(G)) was published by the International Federation of Library Associations and Institutions (IFLA) in 1977. The AAC, AECT, British, and Canadian cataloging rules for nonprint media had recognized the need for such a description, which could be used both for print and nonprint materials and utilize the foundations laid by the ISBD(M) for monographs, which was published by IFLA in 1971. In the Canadian *Nonbook Materials* and in the AECT *Standards*, explanations were provided as to how the ISBD(M) could be applied to nonprint media (Weihs, 1973, p. 99; AECT, 1976, p. 32). The revised Chapter 12 of the *AAC Rules* also relied on the ISBD(M) for terminology, punctuation, and general arrangement of elements of description (1975, p. vii). The significance of the ISBD(G) is best summarized in the IFLA document:

> The primary purpose of the International Standard Bibliographic Descriptions (ISBDs) is to aid international communication of bibliographic information by (i) making records from different sources interchangeable, so that records produced in one country can be accepted easily in library catalogues or other bibliographic lists in any other country; (ii) assisting in the interpretation of records across language barriers, so that records produced for users of one language can be interpreted by users of other languages; and (iii) assisting in the conversion of bibliographic records to machine readable form (1977, p. 1).

The ISBD(G) does not replace cataloging rules but complements them by providing a framework for the ordering of cataloging elements and for prescribing punctuation, which allows either human or machine interpretation of the elements of the bibliographic description. While the actual elements of description might vary from one set of rules to another, these elements could still be identified either by eye or by machine if they are consistently ordered and punctuated. The following areas order and define the framework of cataloging elements for the ISBD(G):

1. Title and statement of responsibility
2. Edition
3. Material (or type of publication)
4. Publication, distribution, etc.
5. Physical description
6. Series
7. Note
8. Standard number (or alternative) and terms of availability (ibid., p. 2-3).

If international bibliographic control of all media is ever to be accomplished, consistent application of the ISBD(G) or of a possible derivative description is mandatory. Such control also depends upon the use of machine readable data bases, which would be required to store the immense number of records yielded by cataloging all published forms of print and nonprint materials.

The foundations for a computerized data base for nonprint media were laid by the Library of Congress in 1970 when its MARC (Machine Readable Cataloging) Development Office issued *Films: A MARC Format*. In 1972, the annual catalog, *Films and Other Materials for Projection*, issued by the Catalog Publication Division of LC, was enlarged "to include sets of transparencies and slides, with data supplied by producing and distributing agencies" (Massonneau, 1977, p. 677). *Films and Other Materials for Projection* "has been photocomposed from machine-readable cataloging records" since 1973 (Library of Congress, Catalog Publication Division, 1976, p. iii). A national network for on-line book cataloging, the Ohio College Library Center (OCLC), prepared guidelines for initiating on-line nonprint media cataloging in 1976, when draft copies of *Films Format: A Description of Fixed Field, Variable Fields, Indicators and Subfield Codes* were made available (Massonneau, 1977, p. 677). Members of the network can input nonprint cataloging data on-line and can receive computer-produced card copy from OCLC.

At the end of 1978, the second edition of the *AAC Rules* prepared by the American Library Association, the British Library, the Canadian Committee on Cataloguing, the Library Association (Great Britain) and the Library of Congress, was published. The primary contributing sources for the development of *AACR 2* regulations for nonprint media cataloging were the British *Non-book Materials Cataloguing Rules*, the Canadian *Nonbook Materials*, the AECT *Standards*, and the revised *AAC Rules* Chapter 12. In addition, *AACR 2* follows the exact framework outlined by the ISBD(G). Cataloging information previously encompassed by the revised *AAC Rules* Chapter 12 has been divided among Chapters 7 ("Motion Pictures and Videorecordings"), 8 ("Graphic Materials"), and 10 ("Three-Dimensional Artifacts and Realia"). The descriptive treatment of slides is included in Chapter 8. These three chapters are in Part I of *AACR 2*, which covers bibliographic descriptions for all media. Part II deals with "Choice of Access Points" or headings, uniform titles, and cross references. The Joint Editor of *AACR 2*, Michael Gorman, notes that "the rules in part 1 of *AACR 2* deal with print and nonprint materials on an equal basis. Descriptions for nonprint materials are not formulated as if a particular item were a deformed book but in terms of the particular material within the context of a neutral and comprehensive framework—the ISBD(G)" (1978, p. 214). Another significant aspect of *AACR 2* described by Gorman is the use of levels of detail in the description, which allows for three levels or degrees of detail for catalog entries (ibid., p. 215; *AACR 2*, p. 15). This option is particularly useful for nonprint media, because it makes it possible to enter these materials in the general library catalog or to submit cataloging copy to data bases such as OCLC in the same framework used for books but without the detailed description commonly associated with most print media. In addition, the three levels of detail also have value for those libraries that prefer a shortened catalog entry for all materials in their collection. The use of varying levels of descriptive cataloging is not new, and Gorman wisely points out that this idea has been revived for *AACR 2* because "networks and other cooperatives concerned with the exchange of bibliographic information can ask their members to adhere to standards without thereby being forced to ask for an impossibly high standard (i.e., all the descriptive information that a code can furnish) or being forced to devise a 'minimum standard' of their own" (ibid.). Historically, local standards have been the rule rather than the exception for nonprint cataloging. The equitable treatment of print and nonprint media in the *AACR 2* and the use of ISBD(G) should encourage more libraries to provide the cataloging records for all their library collections integrated within a central library catalog.

In order to illustrate both the similarities and differences inherent in the rules described, two slides have been cataloged using *AACR 2*, the AECT *Standards*, and the Canadian *Nonbook Materials*. Added entries are noted at the bottom of each card in accordance with the recommendations of each set of rules (subject entries are not given). The first set of cards was prepared for an art slide having a single author or creator primarily responsible for the work (Figures 1 to 3). The second set exemplifies use of a title access point as the primary entry (Figures 4 to 6, see pages 69 to 70).

Figure 1–Art Slide Catalog Card, AACR 2 (3x5-inches)

```
Class   O'Keeffe, Georgia.
No.         Black iris. [slide] / Georgia O'Keeffe. -- New
        York : Sandak, [1975?]
            1 slide : col. -- (Women artists : 18th to
        20th century ; set no. 752, PC344)

            Original painted in 1926.
            Original in The Metropolitan Museum of Art,
        New York.
            Original measures: 36 x 30 in.

            I. Title.  II. Series.
```

Figure 2—Art Slide Catalog Card, AECT Standards (3x5-inches)

```
Class   O'Keeffe, Georgia
No.        Black iris. [Slide]  Stamford, CT: Sandak,
        [1975?]
           1 slide (glass): col; 2 x 2 in.; plastic
        mount.  (Women artists: 18th to 20th century;
        752: PC344)
           Reproduction of her painting in oil, 1926.
           Original in The Metropolitan Museum of Art,
        New York.

        t/ser
```

Figure 3—Art Slide Catalog Card, Nonbook Materials (3x5-inches)

```
Class   O'Keeffe, Georgia.
No.        Black iris  (Slide)  Sandak [1975?]
           1 slide.  col.  2 x 2 in.  (Women artists:
        18th to 20th century, 752: PC344)

           Originally painted in 1926.
           The Metropolitan Museum of Art.




           I. Title.  II. Series.
```

**Figure 4–Nature Slide Catalog Card with Title Main Entry,
AACR 2 (3x5-inches)**

```
Class   American falls: Niagara Falls [slide] / --
No.         Rochester, N.Y. : Ward's Natural Science
        Establishment, [1970?]
            1 slide : col. -- (Ward's comprehensive
        geology color slide set. Streams and rivers :
        regional--New York and Ontario ; 173 W 1714)

        SUMMARY: View from Goat Island, Niagara Falls,
        New York.

        I. Ward's Natural Science Establishment.
        II. Series.
```

**Figure 5–Nature Slide Catalog Card with Title Main Entry,
AECT Standards (3x5-inches)**

```
Class   American falls: Niagara Falls.  [Slide]
No.         Rochester, NY:  Ward's Natural Science
            Establishment, [1970?]
            1 slide (glass): col; 2 x 2 in.; glass mount.
        (Ward's comprehensive geology color slide set.
        Streams and rivers: regional--New York and
        Ontario; 173 W 1714)
            View from Goat Island, Niagara Falls, NY


        ser
```

**Figure 6—Nature Slide Catalog Card with Title Main Entry,
Nonbook Materials (3x5-inches)**

```
Class    American falls: Niagara Falls  (Slide)
No.          Ward's Natural Science Establishment [197-?]
             1 slide.  col.  2 x 2 in.  (Ward's
         comprehensive geology color slide set.  Streams
         and rivers:  Regional--New York and Ontario,
         173 W 1714)
             View from Goat Island, Niagara Falls, New York.


         I.  Series.
```

Historically, the years from 1973 to 1978 have provided a series of benchmark publications, which should change the trend for cataloging nonprint media from one of diversity and multiplicity to unity and integration of direction. If nonprint materials are to enter the bibliographic mainstream, however, publications providing national and international standards for cataloging rules must be used. A 1977 study of the use of cataloging codes in school media centers indicated that "14 codes, manuals, or cataloging tools other than the three major codes" were being used by about half of the 45 state school library systems responding to this survey (Rogers, 1979, p. 46). The three codes cited were the *AAC Rules* (1967) and revised chapters, the AECT *Standards*, and the Canadian rules. As Margaret Chisholm stated in 1975: "To have a system which provides optimum effectiveness, one must take into consideration the need for standardization of terminology and of cataloging codes. This is essential in the establishment of national and international data banks," and "for exchange of information between . . . the myriad of . . . networks and communications systems which are rapidly developing" (*Reader in Media*, 1975, p. 350). Ultimately, "effectiveness" will be measured against the ability to satisfy user demands. The users of nonprint media have been plagued by access as diverse as the media themselves. In the future, the user should benefit from the unified approach to cataloging nonprint and print materials offered by *AACR 2*, which represents the consensus of library and media professionals. Until that consensus becomes widely accepted and implemented, access to nonprint materials will continue to be a multi-level topic.

SYSTEMS DESIGNED FOR SLIDES

Cataloging and classifying slides can be approached both from the perspective of the general user and from that of the subject specialist. The general user may be a teacher or student in a community college, school media center, or university who seeks interdisciplinary access to and use of visual materials. The cataloging and classification systems cited thus far can be used to meet the needs of most general users. The subject specialist has not commonly adopted national or international systems for organizing and gaining access to slides. National cataloging and classification patterns, if not already in use, could be adapted to subject area slide collections. For large collections having 100,000 or more slides, such adaptation would be prohibitively expensive unless costs could be shared in ways similar to those for print media. The fact that informal efforts toward sharing cataloging and classification information have existed among slide librarians and curators for many years is demonstrated by the similarities in handling slides among many collections. Cataloging and classification systems for art slides have not been systematically documented, yet these collections comprise the largest slide libraries in the United States. This section is devoted to an analysis of a selected number of relatively unpublicized systems for slides.

The existence of subject catalogs or indexes to the slide files, which are necessary when using a DDC, LC, or accession number arrangement, is uncommon in most academic institutions and museums. Art slide libraries prefer a self-indexing file arrangement, which is the same as the classification system and functions as an alphabetical subject index to the collection. The subject access is, of course, limited by the number of main classes, divisions, subdivisions, sections, subsections, and so forth. Basic to this different approach to the organization or classification of slides is the concept of the specialist versus the general user. In the majority of academic institutions, art slide libraries were begun by faculty who have a specialized subject background in the arts. Because of their subject training, they have usually preferred a slide collection organized within the historical framework of artistic periods or styles, while individuals outside the art field have preferred a subject access to art materials to compensate for their lack of knowledge of individual artists or architects. For example, the art historian preparing a lecture on seventeenth century landscape painting knows immediately which artists worked in this area. On the other hand, the general user desiring slides on this topic would find it quite difficult to extract those slides from an art historically classified collection without knowing beforehand the nationality and names of the artists in the seventeenth century who painted landscapes as their major occupation.

In order to clarify what is meant by an art history classification scheme, outlines of the systems used and/or devised at the following institutions will be examined: Columbia University Department of Art History and Archaeology; Corning Community College; Cornell University College of Architecture, Art, and Planning; Harvard University, Fogg Art Museum Library, and the University of Michigan Department of the History of Art; the Metropolitan Museum of Art; the National Collection of Fine Arts, Smithsonian Institution; the National Gallery of Art, Washington, D.C., and the Art Institute of Chicago; University of Minnesota Department of Art History; Yale University Art Library, and the University of California, Santa Cruz University Library. These collections range in size from the largest academic collection at Columbia University having approximately 430,000 slides to fewer than 40,000 slides at Corning Community College; they are representative of the major art history collections in the United States. Whether collections have more than, or less than 50,000 slides, their classification systems tend to be quite similar, although the smaller the collection, the frequently less refined, detailed, and extensive are the classification divisions, subdivisions, sections, subsections, and so forth. Unfortunately, most collections do not have formal classification systems that have been completely and accurately recorded in staff handbooks for classifying and cataloging information. Consequently, the only method by which complete comprehension of the total classification and organizational system can be obtained is by direct observation and study of the slide files themselves.

Columbia University

Although a complete guide to the classification system at Columbia University used in the Department of Art History and Archaeology is not available, a brief outline of their scheme is posted for the user. The following represents their user's guide to the collection:

I		Initial letters designate media [Main Classes]
	A	Architecture (Architecture is subdivided by country with sites arranged alphabetically under country and designated by a code number.)
	S	Sculpture
	P	Painting
	MINOR ARTS	
	B	Stone objects (generally prehistoric)
	C	Ceramics (including vase painting)
	D	Design, Perception, & Organic Form and Perspective
	F	Furniture
	G	Gems, Seals, Cameos, Jewelry
	H	Glass
	J	Ivories
	K	Metal Work
	L	Stained Glass
	M	Manuscripts (Typography is a subdivision of design.)
	N	Numismatics: Coins, etc.
	T	Maps
	V	Views
	W	Textiles
	X	Topography
	Y	Gardens & Garden Design
	Z	Social Customs (e.g., dance, ritual, literary texts)
II		Numbers following the initial letter designates periods and countries [Divisions]
	1	Prehistoric
	2	Egypt
	3	Mesopotamia and Assyria
	4	Western Oriental (Asia Minor, Syria, Persia, etc.)
	5	Pre-Hellenic (Minoan, Mycenean, Cycladic, etc.)
	6	Greece
	7	Etruscan
	8	Rome
	9	Ancient European
	10	Early Christian and Byzantine
	11	Coptic
	14	Pre-Romanesque (Merovingian, Carolingian)

16	Romanesque
17	Gothic
21-29	Renaissance (to 1700):

21	England
22	France
23	Germany, Austria, Switzerland
24	Italy
25	Low Countries
26	Spain and Portugal-
27	Central and North Europe, Russia
28	Latin America
29	North America

31-39	Eighteenth-Nineteenth Century (By country in same order as Renaissance.)
41-49	Twentieth Century (By country in same order as Renaissance.)

III   Special Categories

AP:	Architectural Techniques, Construction, Diagrams, etc.; precedes Architecture. Architectural Treatises are cataloged under Architecture by country; they appear in the slide drawers before the monuments proper.
ARC:	Archaeology. Greek, large slides only
E:	Examination, technical analysis, forgeries, etc.
EP:	Painting; ES: Sculpture. EP precedes Painting, ES precedes Sculpture.
NE:	Ancient Near East (designates small slides only)
O:	Oriental (designates small slides only)
OM:	Islamic (designates small slides only)
PM:	Mosaics (designates small slides only). In large slides, Mosaics are cataloged under painting, but appear in the slide drawers after other forms of painting.

If an architectural monument were being classified, it would be treated according to the following schedule:

    Medium (main class)
        Country (division)
            Period (subdivision)
                Site (section)
                    Type of building (subsection)

Another alternative to classifying architecture by site is to class it by architect, although site locations are usually easier to handle unless the collection is used solely by an architectural historian. The architectural sites and names of the buildings are designated by a Cutter number.

Painting and sculpture would be classed by medium, period, or country; by artist; and then by iconography or subject content:

    Medium
        Period or country
            Artist
                Subject

The manuscripts collection of slides is quite extensive at Columbia and is classified according to the following system:

Medium
    Period
        Site (city and name of owning library)
            Shelf number
            Folio number

A sample slide label illustrates how this system of cataloging and classification is applied:

Figure 7—Slide Label, Columbia University

```
1.    ┌──────────────────────────────────┐
      │      RODA BIBLE.   M53-P218       │
2.    │  DANIEL.                 LAT.6    │
3.    │                          f.66     │
4.    │  11th century.                    │
      └──────────────────────────────────┘

5.    ┌──────────────────────────────────┐
6.    │  Paris,BN,Lat.6,f.66             │
      │  Neuss,Katalan Bibel 33.         │
      │                                   │
      └──────────────────────────────────┘
```

Line 1:   manuscript title; M for manuscripts; 53 for Romanesque; P218 for Cutter number for Paris
Line 2:   initial or title of illustration; LAT.6 for shelf number
Line 3:   f.66 for folio number
Line 4:   date or approximate date
Line 5:   city and name of owning library with shelf and folio numbers
Line 6:   source of slide

For painting, sculpture or works having a known artist, the main entry would be under artist, for architecture under the site or name of the location of the building, and for manuscripts under the title of the manuscript.

Corning Community College

Corning Community College bases its system for art slides on the ones used in the *American Library Color Slide Catalogue of World Art, Teachers Manual for the Study of Art History and Related Courses* (1964), the Metropolitan Museum of Art, and at Yale University. In addition, they use the *Outline of the Library of Congress Classification* (Library of Congress Processing Department, 1970). Both art history and general history slides are filed according to the same period divisions, so that all material is historically related in the files no matter what the subject matter may be. For non-historical slides, Corning uses the relevant LC class and divisions. The Enoch Pratt Free Library of Baltimore, Films Department, and the Evergreen State College Library also utilize LC classification for slides. (See Chapter 4 for additional information on Evergreen.) In the Art and Music Department of the Newark Public Library, DDC is used to classify slides.

In their guide to the cataloging system, Corning provides the following broad outline:

All Historically-Oriented slides:
    I.   WESTERN (This term is understood but not used on labels or cards.)

A	Architecture	
B	Sculpture	
C	Painting	
D	Minor Arts	
E/F	History	
M	Music	
P	Language & Literature	According to *Outline of Library of Congress Classification*
U	Military History	
Z	Bibliography	

    II.   PRIMITIVE
    III.   ORIENTAL
    IV.   ISLAMIC
    V.   LATIN AMERICAN & PRE-COLUMBIAN

(Roman Numerals not used allow for later possible additions)

    X.   NON-HISTORICALLY ORIENTED SLIDES
        E
        to   (according to *Outline of Library of Congress Classification*)
        Z

After the preceding main classes, Corning uses basic time or period divisions for art, history, music, language and literature, military history, and bibliography:

1. 500,000-1500 B.C.
2. 1500 B.C.-approx. 500 A.D.
3. 500 A.D.-approx. 1400 A.D.
4. 1400 A.D.-1600 A.D.
5. 1600 A.D.-1800 A.D.
6. 1800-1900 A.D.
7. 1900-... or undated

After these basic divisions for western civilization, subdivisions are used for the periods from medieval through the twentieth century, i.e., from 3 through 7 as decimal numbers (e.g., 3.1 is Frankish or Merovingian within the medieval time division). Lower case letters are used for country designations.

Figure 8—Slide Label, Corning Community College

1.	Architecture.Med.Fr.Rom.
2.	Moissac, Abbey.
3.	1115-30 A.D.

4.	South Portal.
5.	IA3b.6 Loc.: Moissac,
6.	Moissac France.
7.	1

Line 1:   medium; general time period; country; subdivision period, Rom. for Romanesque

(Slide label description continues on page 76)

Line 2:   site, name of building or type of building
Line 3:   date
Line 4:   section of building illustrated
Line 5:   call number; I for Western civilization, A for architecture, 3 for 500 A.D.-
            approx. 1400 A.D., b for French, and .6 for Romanesque; location of site
Line 6:   second line of call number which gives site location; country
Line 7:   accession number, 1 is for the first slide in this category

Main entries are similar to those used at Columbia University. A card file similar to a standard library card catalog is also maintained for this collection.

Cornell University

In a format similar to that of other institutions, the College of Architecture, Art and City Planning of Cornell University provides a general guide to the classification of the slide collection. It is primarily devised for architectural history although it does allow for fine arts slides, which are classified by the following categories:

Media
    Country and/or period
        Geography (or country)
            Artist

Pre-20th century architecture and city planning slides are classified and cataloged by the following categories:

Medium (architecture, pre-20th century)
    Country or geographical location
        City (alphabetically within a country)
            Building type
                Name of building (alphabetically within type)

Modern architecture, i.e., 20th century, is classified by the following categories:

Medium (20th century)
    Architect (alphabetically)
        Building type
            Date
                Name of building (alphabetically within type)

The major classes that are primarily of a media type are the following:

A   MAPS (world and large geographic areas)
B   ARCHITECTURE
C   SCULPTURE
D   Drawing
E   PAINTING
F   Mosaics
G   Manuscripts
H   Book Arts

I	Prints
J	Photography
K	Landscape
L	Military (military camps, military organization, etc.)
M	Numismatics (coins, medals, seals)
MA	Modern Architecture (20th century)
N	Portraits
O	THEORY
P	Ornament
Q	Ceramics
R	Glass and Enamels
S	Jewelry, Jewels, Metalwork
T	Wrought Metal, Arms, Armour
U	Furniture
V	Tapestry, Textiles, Wallpaper, Embroidery
W	Culture and Civilization
X	Tools and Inventions
Y	Transportation
Z	Government

The classes comprising the most significant sections of the collection are in all capital letters. As is immediately apparent, this system and Columbia's are quite similar. For additional information on the categorization of architectural types, consult the *American Institute of Architects Filing System for Architectural Plates and Articles* (1956).

Information on cataloging and classifying architecture slides has been published for the following institutions: Georgia Institute of Technology Architecture Library (LoPresti, 1973), Liverpool School of Architecture (Havard-Williams and Watson, 1960), University of Melbourne School of Architecture (Swan, 1960), University of Michigan Art and Architecture Library (Bogar, 1975), and the University of Minnesota Architecture Library (Perusse, 1954). These collections represent a variety of approaches to handling architecture slides. The Liverpool School of Architecture arranges its slides in accession number order, while providing access via extensive author and subject catalogs. The University of Melbourne uses the system described by Perusse for the University of Minnesota Architecture Library, which is based on the following classified order: 1) period or art historical chronology, 2) geographical area, and 3) building types. Until Bogar developed a new system for the University of Michigan, LC had been used to classify the Art and Architecture Library's slide collection. Her article in *Special Libraries* fully describes and outlines and provides slide label examples for this system, which classifies architecture slides "alphabetically by country or continent, then alphabetically by city or geographic area, then by building type within each city or geographic area" (1975, pp. 571-73). The Georgia Tech Architecture Library uses the Santa Cruz classification, which is discussed later in this chapter.

Harvard University and the University of Michigan

The classification system utilized at the University of Michigan is based upon that of Harvard University's lantern slide and photograph classification schedule, with the latter being derived from the Metropolitan Museum of Art's scheme.

Because these two systems are almost identical, they will be outlined together, with differences indicated in brackets. This system is used by Michigan and Harvard both for their 2x2-inch and lantern slide collections. Harvard also uses this same classification for cataloging their photograph collection of about 390,000 items.

In this system, the arts are divided into nine main classes:

000	Maps [Harvard only]
100	Architecture
200	Sculpture
300	Painting and drawing
400	Work in mineral stuffs
500	Work in metals
600	Work in wood
700	Work in ivory, leather, etc.
800	Textiles, embroideries, lace, etc.
900	Prints

A combination of numerical, decimal, and alphabetical tables are provided for chronological divisions, geographical or country subdivisions, and subject content or architectural type sections. To include all of these tables in their entirety would be to include the entire classification system, which is not the intent of this chapter. Instead, the following summary of the subject content divisions is given:

a. Architecture
   1   General views, bridges, public squares, etc.
   2   Religious buildings
   3   Palaces, villas, etc.
   4   Manor houses, etc.
   5   Educational buildings
   6   Museums
   7   Public amusements
   8   Governmental and municipal buildings, etc.
   9   Other buildings not easily classifiable

b. Sculpture
   1-3   Religious subjects
   4   Mythological subjects
   5-6   Portraits
   7   Ecclesiastical sculpture
   8   Monuments and tombs

c. Painting
   1-3   Religious subjects
   4   Mythological subjects
   5-7   Portraits
   8   Landscapes and marines
   9   Animals
   90   Genre [Harvard only]

d. Minor Arts (separate sections by specific type of material or craft are used for each of the classes from 400 to 900; class 400, Work in mineral stuffs, illustrates a sampling of this section)

Work in Mineral Stuffs

1	Stone and marble (not sculpture)
2	Gems and precious stones (crystal, jade, etc.)
3	Mosaics and Cosmati
4	
5	Enamels, Cloisonne
6	Glass, stained and painted
7	Glass
8	Pottery (includes faience, lustre, majolica, etc.)
81	Stucco
82	Terracotta
83	Tiles
9	Porcelain

Basically, this system can be summarized as follows:

Medium
  Period (Ancient–all art till the beginning of the Christian era; Modern–art from the beginning of the Christian era)
    Country, geography or culture
      City (architecture)
        Artist or school and century (painting, drawing, sculpture, prints)
          School and century (minor arts)
            Architectural type (architecture)
              Subject content (painting, drawing, sculpture, prints)
              Specific type of material or craft (minor arts)

The major difference between the Harvard and Michigan uses of this system is their treatment of manuscripts that fall under class 700, Work in ivory, leather, etc. Harvard classifies their lantern slide manuscripts by collection (city, museum, manuscript number or shelf number, and folio number) in a format similar to Columbia's. Michigan classifies them by century, chronology, or country and then by manuscript type, e.g., gospel, evangelary, missal, and so forth. Michigan retains the use of the 700 class number, while Harvard uses a Cutter number for the city but letters or initials for the name of the library or owning body.

Figure 9 illustrates the cataloging and classification of a manuscript slide by the University of Michigan.

Figure 9–Slide Label, University of Michigan

1.	776 Mss., Span., 11th C.
2.	4.11 Roda Bible:
3.	19BR 66 Daniel
4.	11th cen.

5.	MS.Lat. 6, fol. 66
6.	Paris, Bibliothèque
7.	Nationale

(Slide label description on page 80)

Line 1:   700 for Work in Ivory, Leather, etc.; 076 for Spain; medium; country;
            period
Line 2:   4. for illuminated manuscript; 11 for century; manuscript title
Line 3:   19 for Old and New Testament Subjects Together; B for Bible; R for Roda;
            66 for folio number; title of illustration
Line 4:   date or approximate date
Line 5:   MS.Lat. 6 for manuscript shelf number; fol. 66 for folio number
Line 6:   city and name of owning library (Source data is typed on an interfiled
            shelflist card.)
Line 7:   continuation of Line 6

In order to clarify how the Harvard/Michigan system is applied, the following examples of slide labels are analyzed. Figure 10 illustrates a label prepared by Michigan and Figure 11, one by Harvard. Source data is given only on an interfiled shelflist card at Michigan, while Harvard includes abbreviated source information on the slide label and complete source data on a shelflist card. Harvard maintains both an interfield shelflist and a separate card catalog having main and added entries for slides and photographs. Figure 12 (see page 81) is a sample shelflist card for the Harvard label illustrated.

Figure 10–Slide Label, University of Michigan

1.	Gogh, Vincent Van	375
2.	Self-portrait at an easel	G553
3.	1888.	5G(n)
4.	Amsterdam,Stedelijk Mus.	

Line 1:   Gogh for artist main entry; 300 for painting and drawing; 075 for modern
            France
Line 2:   title of painting; G553 for Cutter number for Gogh
Line 3:   date; 5 for portraits of men; G for portrait of Gogh, i.e., self-portrait;
            (n) distinguishes different representations of the same subject by the
            same artist
Line 4:   location

Figure 11–Lantern Slide Label, Harvard University

1.		177
2.	Stonehouse (Devon), Royal	St 72
3.	Victualling Yard	8RV 1
4.	Exterior. General view	
5.	archt.: Sir John Rennie, 1826-35	

Line 1:   100 for architecture; 077 for Great Britain
Line 2:   location; name of building; St 72 for Cutter number for Stonehouse
Line 3:   name of building; 8 for governmental and municipal buildings, etc.;
            RV for Royal Victualling Yard; 1 for exterior view
Line 4:   view of building
Line 5:   name of architect; construction date for building

Figure 12–Lantern Slide Shelflist Card, Harvard University (3x5-inches)

```
                                        neg.

  177      Stonehouse (Devon), The Royal Victualling Yard
  St 72
  8RV 1         Exterior.  General view
                  Archt.:  Sir John Rennie
                  1826-35


  Turnor, 19th Century Architecture in Britain, pl. 39
```

The following added entries are prepared for this slide: ARCHITECTURE, ENGLISH, 19TH CENTURY; and RENNIE, SIR JOHN, 1794-1874. These entries are placed above "Stonehouse (Devon), . . . " with additional cards placed in the general card catalog to the slide and photograph collections. Typed in the upper right-hand corner of the shelflist card, "neg." is abbreviated to indicate that a negative is available for this slide. At the bottom of the shelflist card is an abbreviated citation for the following source: Reginald Turnor, *19th Century Architecture in Britain*, London: B. T. Batsford, Ltd., 1950. This slide was made from plate 39 in Turnor's book.

Princeton University has a classification system similar in complexity to that used at Harvard and Michigan. A decimal notation system is used, accompanied by Cutter numbers for cities and for artists' names. The summaries of these systems are identical, e.g., medium, period, country, artist or site.

The following institutions base their systems upon the Harvard and/or Michigan classification: Skidmore College, Syracuse University, University of California at Los Angeles, University of California at Riverside, University of New Mexico, University of Pennsylvania, University of Rochester (New York), University of Texas, and Vassar College. The Ringling School of Art uses some features of the Harvard/Michigan system in combination with the Santa Cruz classification schedule for art and an alphabetical notation scheme used to classify art books at the Ringling Library (Straight, 1975, pp. 4-5). Cards for both books and slides are interfiled in the library's main catalog. The Cleveland Museum of Art also uses a modified version of the Harvard/Michigan system, depending primarily upon the nine major classes with substantial modification of the various chronological and geographical divisions and subdivisions (Cleveland Museum of Art, 1977). With its extensive holdings in Oriental and other non-Western arts, the Cleveland schedule provides useful outlines for African tribes, for Chinese dynasties, and for Japanese, Indian, and Southeast Asian chronologies. The University of Wisconsin–Madison uses a classification similar to Harvard/Michigan in its organizational pattern by medium, cultural, or geographical area, and by subject. The Wisconsin classification also includes chronological and tribal outlines for non-Western arts, e.g., for North, Middle and South American chronologies or tribes (*Slide Classification* . . . , 1978, pp. 9-11). Refer to the directory of slide libraries for departmental locations at these various institutions.

The Metropolitan Museum of Art

A two-page outline of the Metropolitan Museum of Art slide classification system is available upon request. The Metropolitan does not use a notation system for slides. Accession numbers are used only as an inventory check. The Western arts are classified by medium or what the Metropolitan Slide Library refers to as "art form," then by country, and finally by chronological period for architecture and sculpture. Standard subdivisions follow the main classes and divisions. For Ancient arts and other than Western arts (such as Far Eastern, Near Eastern, and so forth), the divisions under geographical areas are first by country and then by medium. The primitive arts of Africa, Oceania, and North America are classified by geographical or cultural area, tribe, and medium. One of the unique features of the Metropolitan system is the use of museum locations as a filing device. For example, a collection of paintings by a single artist might be filed by their museum locations rather than by subject content or by date, which in most instances are more commonly used for this purpose. Using the owning institution as a source for locating objects may not be the most practical method for academic institutions. However, for a museum, it is useful in consolidating the works of a particular artist in its own collection. Information about the historical evolution of the Metropolitan system has been documented by its chief slide cataloger, Priscilla Farah (1976). Ohio State University and Pennsylvania State University base their systems upon that of the Metropolitan. The Massachusetts Institute of Technology utilizes a combination of the Harvard, Metropolitan, and Yale University classification schedules.

National Collection of Fine Arts, Smithsonian Institution

The National Collection of Fine Arts Slide and Photograph Archive (NCFA/ SAPA) is a specialized visual resource library within the Smithsonian Institution. The 40,000 slides in this collection consist primarily of American art from the seventeenth to the twentieth century. A handbook entitled *NCFA Slide and Photograph Archive* (1978) provides a general description of the SAPA organization and operations and outlines their information storage and retrieval system, which utilizes the Smithsonian Institution SELGEM (Self Generating Master) System for information management. Developed under the direction of Eleanor E. Fink (Chief, Office of Visual Resources), SAPA operates with a fully automated classification and indexing system. The notation system is based upon the Santa Cruz classification code, which is used for period designations (seventeenth-twentieth centuries), for medium (architecture, sculpture, painting, drawing, graphic arts, photography, ceramics and glassware, and fabric and design), and for part of the SAPA *Thesaurus*, which includes forty primary descriptors, with sixteen derived from Santa Cruz (e.g., A for Abstract, C for Animal) (Palmer, 1978).

Cataloging and classification information is entered manually on a data collection sheet having twenty tagged descriptors and a total of thirty lines possible for computer input; e.g., for the tag "Subjects," six lines or subject headings may be entered (*NCFA . . .* , 1978). A computer index could be produced for each line, for as many subject headings entered, or for any combination of these headings. The following list identifies the twenty descriptors, their corresponding tag numbers, and the number of lines allowed per tag (if more than one):

001	Serial No.	(a ten-digit field, which includes a source code)
010	Negative No.	(used primarily for photographs)
040,040 02	Title 1	(two lines for title)
041,041 02	Title 2	(two lines for second title)
050-050 06	Subjects	(six lines for subject headings)
081	Source	(NCFA, private or commercial)
110,115	Attribution	(two lines, first line for name of artist)
116,117	Life Dates	(two lines, first line for artist's dates)
120	Birthplace	
130	Country	
140	Ex. & Cat. No.	(exhibition name and checklist number for NCFA exhibition works)
150	Registrar	(museum registration number)
204	Date of Execution	
205	Period	(century, e.g., 17th century)
300	Medium	(general medium, e.g., painting)
301	Medium Remarks	(specific form of medium, e.g., oil on canvas)
305	Dimensions	
310,310 03	Location	(two lines, first for full name of museum, collection or dealer, second for abbreviated location code for computer generated slide label)
320	Remarks	(varied data, e.g., filing of slide in public lending collection)
330	Classification	(a twenty-digit field for the call number)

Most slide collections would not require a descriptor list as extensive as that prepared for SAPA; however, this identification model provides input for a data bank that is "reasonably compatible with those of many other similar collections within the Smithsonian Museums, or with those of non-Smithsonian SELGEM museum clients, making information transfer possible" (Palmer, 1978).

After the data is entered for each of the tagged descriptors on the data collection sheet, it is typed on OCR (optical character recognition) paper using an IBM Selectric typewriter. With the OCR method, the paper is scanned by machine, and data is transposed directly onto computer tape for storage in either entry or serial number order. OCR makes it unnecessary to have direct access to a computer terminal or to keypunch machines. Figure 13 is a sample OCR page prepared by SAPA.

Prior to 1979, SAPA had used manually typed slide labels. Use of a Centronics terminal has made it possible to generate slide labels via computer. Earlier efforts to produce computer labels were not considered successful, because the size of the typeface severely limited the amount of information that could be entered on each label. The sample label in Figure 14 (see page 85) was manually prepared.

Figure 13–OCR Page, NCFA/SAPA

```
MALLOS

ᗅ12345

001    08582457

040    WAR DANCE

050    FIGURE{S} IN EXTERIOR

05002  ETHNIC-INDIAN-SIOUX, WESTERN {DAKOTA, TETON}

05003  CEREMONY-DANCE

05004  ARCH EXTERIOR-DOMESTIC-TEEPEE

05005  LANDSCAPE-NIGHT

081    NCFA

110    CATLIN, GEORGE

116    1796-1872

120    USA/PA/WILKES-BARRE

130    USA

150    NCFA/L 1965.1.457

204    1832

205    19TH C

300    PAINTING

301    O/C

305    19 1/2 X 26 1/2

310    NCFA, WASH DC

320    PUBLIC; PHOTO

330    F630N    C365M    W256A.1

001    858412994

040    BARBER SHOP, THE

050    CITYSCAPE

05002  ARCH EXTERIOR-COMMERICAL
```

Figure 14—Slide Label, NCFA/SAPA

1.	F630N	CATLIN, GEORGE
2.	C365M	WAR DANCE
3.	W256A.1	1832

4.	O/C	
5.	NCFA	
6.	08582457	NCFA/SAPA

Line 1:   F for painting; 630 for U.S.; N for 19th century; name of artist
Line 2:   C365 for Cutter number for Catlin; M for figure(s) in exterior; title of painting
Line 3:   W256 for Cutter number for title; A.1 for detail number
Line 4:   O/C for oil on canvas
Line 5:   location
Line 6:   serial number; source

Computer-produced indexes are regularly prepared for SAPA and include the following: 1) master index having complete descriptor tagging data, 2) artist index, 3) subject index, and 4) the artist authority index. In its final form, the *Thesaurus* or subject descriptors' list will also be computer generated. Figures 15, 16, and 17 (see pages 86-87) illustrate printouts for the master, subject and artist indexes.

Due to copyright restrictions, SAPA maintains two separately filed slide collections: 1) a staff collection, filed by artist and title, of slides produced at the NCFA photo lab and those purchased or received as gifts; and 2) a public lending collection filed by medium, century, artist, and subject of art slides from either the Smithsonian museums or commercial producers and/or distributors (Fink, 1979).

Figure 15—Master Index, NCFA/SAPA

```
                          NCFA SLIDE & PHOTO ARCHIVES UPDATE #21

                                    MASTER COPY

P: 085 ....2....V....3....V....4....V....5....V    ....2....V....3....V....4....V....5....V
09/26/78....6....V....7....V....                   ....6....V....7....V....

        03                                         CEREMONY-DANCE              RECREATION
        04                                         LANDSCAPE-WATER             LANDSCAPE
081 01  SOURCE                      NCFA                                       NCFA
110 01  ARTIST                      CATLIN, GEORGE                             CATLIN, GEORGE
116 01  LIFE DATES                  1796-1872                                  1796-1872
120 01  BIRTHPLACE                  U.S.A./PA./WILKES-BARRE                    U.S.A./PA./WILKES-BARRE
130 01  COUNTRY CLASSIFIED          U.S.A.                                     U.S.A.
150 01  REGISTRAR'S NO.             NCFA/L 1965.1.449                          NCFA/L 1965.1.455
204 01  DATE OF EXECUTION           1834                                       N.D.
205 01  CENTURY                     19TH C.                                    19TH. C.
300 01  MEDIUM                      PAINTING                                   PAINTING
301 01                              O.C.                                       O.C.
305 01  DIMENSIONS                  19 1/2 X 27 5/8                            19 5/8 X 27 5/8
310 01  LOCATION                    NCFA, WASH. D.C.                           NCFA, WASH. D.C.
320 01  REMARKS                     PUBLIC; PHOTO                              PUBLIC; PHOTO
330 01  CALL NUMBER                 F630N  C365M  E113A.1                      F630N  C365M  M272A.1

SERIAL 00000000 ************************************        08592458 ********** FOOT WAR PARTY IN COUNCIL, MANDAN
040 01  TITLE 1    08592457 ******** WAR DANCE             FOOT WAR PARTY IN COUNCIL, MANDAN
050 01  SUBJECTS            FIGURE(S) IN EXTERIOR          FIGURE(S) IN EXTERIOR
    02                      ETHNIC-INDIAN-SIOUX, WESTERN (DAKOTA, TE    ETHNIC-INDIAN-MANDAN
                            TON)
    03                      CEREMONY-DANCE                 LANDSCAPE-MOUNTAIN
    04                      ARCH EXTERIOR-DOMESTIC-TEEPEE  CEREMONY
```

Figure 16—Subject Index, NCFA/SAPA

```
02/14/77          NCFA SLIDE AND PHOTOGRAPH ARCHIVE    SUBJECT INDEX          PAGE  85

CEREMONY-DANCE (PAINTING)

CATLIN, GEORGE                          DANCE TO THE MEDICINE BAG OF THE BRAVE
  FIGURE(S) IN EXTERIOR / FIGURE GROUP / ETHNIC-INDIAN FOX /
  ETHNIC-INDIAN-SAUK / CEREMONY-DANCE                      F630N  C365M  D174A.1  PUBLIC; PHOTO  08582444  N
CATLIN, GEORGE                          EAGLE DANCE OF THE CHOCTAW
  FIGURE(S) IN EXTERIOR / ETHNIC-INDIAN-CHOCTAW / CEREMONY-DANCE
  LANDSCAPE-WATER                                          F630N  C365M  E113A.1  PUBLIC; PHOTO  08582449  N
CATLIN, GEORGE                          GROUP OF DANCERS (PROBABLY EASTERN MARGINAL GREAT PLAINS)
  FIGURE(S) IN EXTERIOR / ETHNIC-INDIAN / CEREMONY-DANCE /
  ARCH EXTERIOR-DOMESTIC-TEEPEE / EQUESTRIAN               F630N  C365M  G082A.1  PUBLIC; PHOTO  08582706  N
CATLIN, GEORGE                          MANDAN BUFFALO DANCE
  FIGURE GROUP-MALE / ETHNIC-INDIAN-MANDAN / CEREMONY-DANCE
                                        WAR DANCE          F630N  C365I  M273A.1  PUBLIC; PHOTO  08582440  N
CATLIN, GEORGE
  FIGURE(S) IN EXTERIOR / ETHNIC-INDIAN-SIOUX, WESTERN (DAKOTA, TE /
  CEREMONY-DANCE / ARCH EXTERIOR-DOMESTIC-TEEPEE / LANDSCAPE-NIGHT
                                        F630N  C365M  W256A.1  PUBLIC; PHOTO  08582457  N
```

Figure 17—Artist Index, NCFA/SAPA

```
12/06/76          NCFA SLIDE AND PHOTOGRAPH ARCHIVE   ARTIST INDEX                          PAGE  17

CATLIN, GEORGE (1796-1872) U.S.A./PA./WILKES-BARRE
   PAINTING    (CONT.)
      SAND BAR, WIFE OF TRADER FRANCOIS CHARDON              F630N  C365U  S213A.1   PUBLIC; PHOTO  08582089  N
      SELF-TORTURE IN SIOUX CEREMONY                         F630N  C365M  S465A.1   PUBLIC; PHOTO  08582460  N
      SHE WHO BATHES HER KNEES, WIFE OF WOLF ON THE HILL     F630N  C365U  S554A.1   PUBLIC; PHOTO  08582144  N
      SIOUX INDIANS ON SNOWSHOES LANCING BUFFALO             F630N  C365M  S618A.1   PUBLIC; PHOTO  08582565  N
      SIOUX VILLAGE, LAKE CALHOUN, NEAR FORT SNELLING        F630N  C365P  S618A.1   PUBLIC; PHOTO  08582335  N
      SMOKE, THE, CHIEF OF THE TRIBE                         F630N  C365W  S666A.1   PUBLIC; PHOTO  08582095  N
      SPEARING SALMON BY TORCHLIGHT                          F630N  C365M  S741A.1   PUBLIC; PHOTO  08582575  N
      STEEP WIND, A BRAVE OF THE "BAD ARROW POINTS" BAND     F630N  C365W  S814A.1   PUBLIC; PHOTO  08582086  N
      STRUTTING PIGEON, WIFE OF WHITE CLOUD                  F630N  C365T  S927A.1   PUBLIC; PHOTO  08582525  N
      STURGEON'S HEAD, A FOX WARRIOR                         F630N  C365W  S935A.1   PUBLIC; PHOTO  08582018  N
      SWAN-SCENE NEAR THE COTEAU DES PRAIRIES                F630N  C365P  S972A.1   PUBLIC; PHOTO  08582348  N
      SWEET-SCENTED GRASS, 12-YR.-OLD DAUGHTER OF BLOODY HAND F630N C365U  S974A.1   PUBLIC; PHOTO  08582125  N
      TCHOW-EE-PUT-O-KAW, A WOMAN                            F630N  C365U  T252A.1   PUBLIC; PHOTO  08582292  N
      TEL-MAZ-HA-ZA, A WARRIOR                               F630N  C365N  T277A.1   PUBLIC; PHOTO  08582293  N
      THIGHS, A WICHITA WOMAN                                F630N  C365U  T439A.1   PUBLIC; PHOTO  08582058  N
      TOW-EE-KA-WET, A CREE WOMAN                            F630N  C365U  T737A.1   PUBLIC; PHOTO  08582178  N
      TWO COMANCHE GIRLS                                     F630N  C365M  T974A.1   PUBLIC; PHOTO  08582053  N
      TWO CROWS, A BAND CHIEF                                F630N  C365W  T974A.1   PUBLIC; PHOTO  08582164  N
      UNIDENTIFIED MAN                                       F630N  C365U  U584A.1   PUBLIC; PHOTO  08582703  N
      UNIDENTIFIED MAN                                       F630N  C365U  U585A.1   PUBLIC; PHOTO  08582704  N
      UNIDENTIFIED MAN (PROBABLY S.E. INDIAN)                F630N  C365T  W136A.1   PUBLIC; PHOTO  08582030  N
      WAH-CHEE-TE, WIFE OF CLERMONT, & CHILD                 F630N  C365W  W255A.1   PUBLIC; PHOTO  08582106  N
      WAR CHIEF, A REPUBLICAN PAWNEE                         F630N  C365M  W256A.1   PUBLIC; PHOTO  08582457  N
      WAR DANCE                                              F630N  C365C  W362A.1   PUBLIC; PHOTO  08582563  N
      WEAPONS & APPEARANCE OF THE GRIZZLY BEAR               F630N  C365W  W399A.1   PUBLIC; PHOTO  08582055  N
      WEE-TA-RA-SHA-RO, HEAD CHIEF OF THE TRIBE              F63PN  C365W  W552A.1   PUBLIC; PHOTO  08582009  N
      WHALE, THE, ONE OF KEOKUK'S PRINCIPAL BRAVES           F630N  C365W  W575A.1   PUBLIC; PHOTO  08582003  N
      WHIRLING THUNDER, ELDEST SON OF BLACK HAWK             F630N  C365C  W583A.1   PUBLIC; PHOTO  08582460  N
      WHITE CLOUD, ADVISER TO BLACK HAWK                     F630N  C365C  W599A.1   PUBLIC; PHOTO  08582009  N
      WHITE WOLVES ATTACKING A BUFFALO BULL                  F630N  C365M  W776A.1   PUBLIC; PHOTO  08582347  N
      WINNEBAGO SHOOTING DUCKS ON WISCONSIN RIVE?            F630N  C365N  W059A.1   PUBLIC; PHOTO  08582143  N
      WOLF ON THE HILL, TRIBAL CHIEF                         F630N  C365I  W072A.1   PUBLIC; PHOTO  08502147  N
      WOMAN & CHILD, SHOWING HOW HEADS OF CHILDREN ARE FLATTENED

CATLIN, GEORGE, AFTER (1796-1872) U.S.A./PA./WILKESBARRE
   PAINTING
      OSCEOLA                                                F630P  GB19W.C OB12A.1  PUBLIC; PHOTO  08650595
```

National Gallery of Art, Washington, D.C., and the Art Institute of Chicago

The National Gallery of Art (NGA) uses a classification system that was developed by the Art Institute of Chicago (AIC) in 1943. The guide to this system contains 174 pages of explanation, which includes the outline of the system; alphabetical symbols for culture and country; cultural and chronological tables; subject content designations; an alphabetical list of art schools and centers; and a list of museums and libraries, with alphabetical code abbreviations. Cutter numbers are used for artists' names and for city names.

Primarily, the main classes, divisions, and subdivisions are represented in the following outline:

A   Architecture
        Country or cultural area
            Location (cite site) or century

D   Diagrams (only those that cannot be classified with specific objects or countries or cultures)

A	Architecture	M	Minor Arts
AE	Aesthetic Analysis	P	Painting
CO	Cosmology	PS	Psychology
CR	Criticism	S	Sculpture
D	Decoration	TH	Theater
LI	Literature		

(G)   Graphic Arts (G is always followed by a 2nd upper case letter to indicate the kind of Graphic Art)
        GD   Drawings
                Country or cultural area
                    Artist or country or century
        GP   Prints (same as drawings)

M   Maps (this section is arranged in two main divisions)
      1. General maps
          a. Maps of the *World* as a whole and those that include part of both hemispheres
          b. Maps of the *Eastern Hemisphere*
          c. Maps of the *Western Hemisphere*
          d. Maps of the *Northern Hemisphere* (used only when "Eastern" or "Western" hemispheres are not appropriate)
          e. Maps of the *Southern Hemisphere* (used only when "Eastern" or "Western" hemispheres are not appropriate)
      2. Maps of individual *countries*. Within this section the countries are alphabetically arranged, and disbanded countries, i.e., Flanders, etc., are included in this section under their original names.

(M)   Minor Arts (M is always followed by an Arabic number to indicate the specific Minor Art)
        Type of minor art, e.g., M1   Arms and Armour
            Country or cultural area
               Century or subculture

MU   Museum Techniques
      ED   Education
      EX   Exhibitions
      HA   Handling of objects
      LA   Laboratory processes

P   Painting
          Country or cultural area
              Artist (if known) or century (if artist unknown) or culture, subculture,
              site of discovery, or century (prehistoric, ancient, or primitive cultures)
                  Subject

PH   Photography
          Country or cultural area
              Photographer or century
              Subject

S   Sculpture (same as painting)

T   Techniques
          Type of art to which the technique belongs (major divisions used for type of
          art)
              Specific technique or material, the minor art division, the word *materials*,
              or the word *tools*.

This system has ten main classes and, with the exception of diagrams, maps, museum techniques, and techniques, can be summarized as follows:

Medium
      Country, geographical or cultural area
          Artist or century
             Subject

The following slide labels illustrate how this system is applied:

Figure 18–Slide Label, NGA

```
1.  |  A IT      ROME. S.AGNESE,
2.  |  R763 RC   FACADE(BY RAINAL-
3.  |  AG E 1    DI,1652-53;BORRO-


4.  |          MINI,1653-55;
5.  |          OTHERS,1655-66).

6.  |          EVANS TRIP 1966
```

Line 1:   A for architecture; IT for Italian; name of city; name of church
Line 2:   R763 for Cutter number for site or city of building; RC for cathedrals, churches, etc., or type of building; section of building illustrated; name of architect
Line 3:   AG for initials of building; E for exterior; 1 for sequence of slides dealing with a particular part or area of a single building; continuation of names of architects and periods during which they worked on construction of the building

(Slide label description continues on page 90)

Line 4:   continuation of architects' names and periods during which they worked on construction of the building

Line 5:   continuation of Line 4

Line 6:   source information for slide; slide made by a staff member in Rome in 1966

Figure 19—Slide Label, NGA

```
1.    P  DU      van Gogh.Self-
2.    G613  PM   Portrait at an Easel.
3.    GO  5      1888. Amsterdam,Stedelijk.
```

Line 1:   P for painting; DU for Dutch; name of artist; title of painting

Line 2:   G613 for Cutter number for artist; PM for portraits, male; continuation of title

Line 3:   GO for initials of subject; 5 for sequence of slides dealing with a particular subject; date; location

Figure 20—Slide Label, NGA

```
1.    M7  SP      Spanish.  11th c.(Catalan).
2.    AO11/ca     "Bible of Roda": page w.Daniel.
3.    PAN 1.66    1st ¼ 11th c. Paris,Bib.Nat.
4.                ms.lat.6,fol.66.
```

Line 1:   M for minor arts; 7 for manuscripts; SP for Spanish; country; century; school

Line 2:   AO11 for Cutter number for century; ca for initials of school; title of manuscript; title of specific page

Line 3:   PAN for initials of location; 1 for sequence of slides dealing with a particular subject; 66 for page number; date; location

Line 4:   ms.lat.6 for manuscript number; fol.66 for folio number

By 1976, the Art Institute had modified the main classes, divisions, and subdivisions of this system (Auchstetter, 1979). Four main classes were added (Biography, Customs, Decorative Arts, and Manuscripts) and four were dropped (Diagrams, Maps, Museum Techniques, and Techniques). The revised AIC system is summarized as follows:

A   Architecture (includes maps)
        Country
          City
            Building

B   Biography
        Country
          Artist

C   Customs*

D   Decorative Arts
        Type of decorative art, e.g., DC for Ceramics
        Country
          Sub-category for type of decorative art
            Century (for anonymous works)
            Name of craftsman

*Divided by country, then by artist or by century for anonymous works.

Gd   Graphic drawings*

Gp   Graphic prints*

M   Manuscripts*

P   Painting*

Ph   Photography*

S   Sculpture*

Subject categories and Cutter numbers are no longer used. Instead, access to individual slides is by date of the object rather than by subject, which has greatly expedited curatorial and faculty use of the collection (Auchstetter, 1979). The AIC slide collection is no longer open to the public. Figure 21 illustrates the use of the revised AIC schedule.

Figure 21—Slide Label, AIC

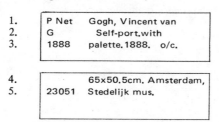

1.   P Net   Gogh, Vincent van
2.   G   Self-port.with
3.   1888   palette.1888.   o/c.

4.   65x50.5cm. Amsterdam,
5.   23051   Stedelijk mus.

Line 1:   P for painting; Net for Netherlands; name of artist
Line 2:   G for Gogh; title of painting
Line 3:   date of painting; continuation of title; date; o/c for oil on canvas
Line 4:   size of painting in centimeters; location
Line 5:   accession number; name of museum

Both the revised AIC and the NGA schedules include extensive treatment of the decorative arts, which is a relatively common feature of most museum slide classification systems. This section of most academic systems is not as thoroughly developed as museum schedules, because academic curriculums usually do not emphasize instruction in the decorative arts. However, the decorative arts tend to comprise the most complex section of many classification schedules and also pose the greatest number of problems relating to category identification and to the organizational arrangement of slides. The revised decorative arts section of the AIC system is particularly useful, because it encompasses a wide range of artforms while maintaining a relatively simple group of divisions and subdivisions that would be common both to academic and museum slide collections. Prepared by the AIC Slide Librarian, Rosann Auchstetter, the following outline lists all the divisions for type of decorative art and the subdivisions used within these groups:

DECORATIVE ARTS

DA	*Armor* (and arms)
DBA	*Basketry*
DBO	*Books* (covers and bindings)
DC	*Ceramics*
Por	Porcelain
PorS	Porcelain sculpture
Pot	Pottery
DCO	*Costume*
B	Body adornment
C	Costume
J	Jewelry
DE	*Enamel*
DF	*Furniture*
Fc	Case (Desks, chests, etc.)
Fd	Design
Ff	Fragments
Fs	Seating (chairs, beads, headrests, etc.)
Ft	Tables
L	Lighting
R	Rooms (model)
T	Timepieces
W	Wall decoration (screens, wallpaper, etc.)
DG	*Glass*
G	Glass
S	Stained glass
DH	*Heraldry, Emglems and Seals*
E	Emblems
H	Heraldry
S	Seals
DI	*Industrial Design* (machines, tools, and vehicles)
DIV	*Ivory and Related Organic Materials* (includes all objects of)
B	Bone
C	Coral
G	Gourds (not musical instruments)
I	Ivory
L	Leather
S	Shell
DL	*Lacquer*
DM	*Metal*
B	Brass
Br	Bronze
C	Copper
G	Gold
I	Iron
L	Lead
M	Metal (mixed metals, alloys, or metal unknown)
P	Pewter

S	Silver
St	Steel
T	Tin
DMO	*Mosaics* (not in situ)
DMU	*Musical instruments*
DN	*Numismatics*
DP	Paper
DSC	*Scenography*
DSI	*Signs, Symbols and Ornamental Motifs*
D	Designs (and ornamental motifs)
S	Signs
Sy	Symbols
DST	*Stone* (not sculptural)
	(subdivided in Asia and Latin America only)
J	Jade (includes all objects of)
S	Stone
DT	*Textiles, and Related Materials and Forms*
A	Applique (other than quilts)
B	Beadwork
C	Crochet
F	Featherwork
Fi	Fiberwork
K	Knitting
L	Lace (needlework not on a ground)
Ln	Netting (knotting and macrame)
Lt	Tatting
N	Needlework (needlework on a ground)
Nc	Crewel
Ne	Embroidery
Nn	Needlepoint (and petit point)
Nq	Quillwork
Np	Punch work (open work)
Q	Quilts
Qa	Quilts, applique
Qp	Quilts, pieced
R	Rugs
Rb	Rugs, braided
Rh	Rugs, hooked
Rk	Rugs, knotted
Rp	Rugs, pieced
Rs	Rugs, sewn
Rw	Rugs, woven
T	Textiles
Td	Textiles, dyed
Tn	Textiles, non-woven
Tp	Textiles, painted
Tpr	Textiles, printed
Tt	Textiles, tapestry
Tw	Textiles, woven

(Outline continues on page 94)

DTY   *Typography and Calligraphy* (not used in Asia)
C   Calligraphy
T   Typography

DW   *Wood* (not sculptural)
       (does not include musical instruments)

Figure 22 illustrates the application of this system for furniture.

Figure 22–Slide Label, AIC

1.	DF US Furniture.US.19thc.
2.	Fc 19 Case.Desk,slant top.
3.	1834 1834. Paint.wd. H.

4.	49 1/8". Winterthur, Del.
5.	73BB90 Winterthur mus.

Line 1:   DF for furniture; US for United States; type of decorative art; country; century
Line 2:   Fc for Case (Desks, chests, etc.); type of case
Line 3:   date; Paint.wd. for painted wood; H. for height
Line 4:   height of desk; location
Line 5:   accession number; museum

University of Minnesota

The University of Minnesota utilizes a classification system designed by Dimitri Tselos, formerly a member of the Department of Art History. In a paper published in the *College Art Journal* (1959), Tselos described the application of this schedule. The following institutions base their classification schemes on this system: Minneapolis Institute of Arts, Stanford University, University of Illinois at Chicago Circle, and the University of Washington (Seattle).

The Minnesota system uses art terms or alphabetical abbreviations rather than a numerical or decimal notation system such as that utilized in the Harvard/Michigan, NGA/AIC, or Princeton schedules. The following outline indicates the main classes and divisions of this system:

(A)   Primary Divisions:
       Aboriginal
       Far East
       Near East
       West
       XYZ

(B)   Eras:
       Ancient
       A-Mod (Ancient through Modern: Aboriginal, Far East)
       M-Mod (Medieval through Modern for Islamic)
       Medieval

15-16c
17-18c
19c
20c

(C)   Countries: constituent countries alphabetically.
(D)   Major Art Types:
        For all primary division except XYZ: Architecture, Painting, Sculpture,
        Varia (minor arts). For XYZ: Elements, Photography, Prints, Varia (20c
        minor arts)(ibid., p. 346).

Examples of abbreviations used include the following: 20c for twentieth
century; ARCH for architecture; FR for France; and ABOR for aboriginal. For
slide libraries not utilizing a decimal notation code in conjunction with their classification system, this type of abbreviated code is commonly used to expedite slide
filing. It is not necessary to read the entire label in order to determine where a
slide belongs within the classification scheme.

Two slide labels provided by the University of Minnesota illustrate application
of this system.

Figure 23–Slide Label, University of Minnesota

```
1.   | WEST GOGH   Port:man
2.   | 19    SELF PORTRAIT AT AN
3.   | FR           EASEL    1888
4.   | PTG          Amsterdam:Stedelijk Mus.

5.   |              78-79
```

Line 1:   WEST for primary geographical area; last name of artist; Port:man for
            the subject heading, portrait of a man
Line 2:   19 for 19th century; title of painting
Line 3:   FR for France; continuation of painting title; date
Line 4:   PTG for painting; location; museum
Line 5:   year of acquisition

Figure 24–Slide Label, University of Minnesota

```
1.   | ABOR NIGERIA   Benin
2.   | AFR   QUEEN MOTHER  16C
3.   | SC
4.   |       Bronze

5.   |       Philadelphia:Univ.Mus.
6.   |       77-78 191-1
```

Line 1:   ABOR for Aboriginal for primary cultural area; country; Benin for Benin
            culture or Bini tribe
Line 2:   AFR for Africa; title of image/subject; 16C for 16th century
Line 3:   SC for sculpture

(Slide label description continues on page 96)

Line 4:   type of material
Line 5:   location
Line 6:   year of acquisition; accession number

The following label was prepared by Stanford University to illustrate that institution's use of the Minnesota system.

Figure 25–Slide Label, Stanford University

1.	WEST MS 11thc BIBLE
2.	MED Roda Bible
3.	SP F.66: Daniel
4.	PTG

5.	Paris: BN Lat 6
6.	78Z.564

Line 1:   WEST for primary geographical area; MS for manuscript; date; BIBLE for form type
Line 2:   MED for medieval; manuscript title
Line 3:   SP for Spanish; F.66 for folio 66; title of image
Line 4:   PTG for painting (manuscripts are treated as a painting for type)
Line 5:   location and manuscript number
Line 6:   accession number (78 for 1978, Z for last name of professor requesting this slide, and 564 for the 564th slide made in 1978)

The Minnesota system can be summarized as follows:

Geographical or cultural area
   Period
      Country
         Medium
            Artist (if known)
            Architect (if known) or
            Architectural site
            Art Sub-types (chiefly for painting and sculpture, e.g., mosaics, murals, manuscripts, etc.)
               Form Types (chiefly for painting and sculpture, e.g., form types under manuscripts: Bible, Gospel, Psalter, etc.)
               Subject

As is apparent from the summary of this scheme, it varies from the majority of systems noted thus far in its main class emphasis on geographical or cultural areas rather than on medium, which has been moved to a section ranking in the overall system. Another distinctive feature of Minnesota's classification is the grouping of art sub-types under painting and sculpture. In most schedules, these sub-types are classed under the decorative arts or are considered as primary media divisions, e.g., manuscripts.

Yale University

The Metropolitan Museum of Art's classification system is used or modified by a significant number of academic institutions, so its broad outlines are not difficult to determine. A system similar to the Metropolitan's—if not actually derived from it—is Yale University's Slide and Photograph Collection classification schedule totaling 75 pages.

The four main classes are as follows:

Architecture
Painting (including Drawing)
Sculpture
Minor Arts

Each of these main classes is then arranged by the following divisions, subdivisions, sections, and subsections:

Periods (chronologically)
   Country (alphabetically—exceptions are noted)
      City (architecture)
         Building
      Artist (painting and sculpture)
         City
            Museum

The following periods are used:

General	Ancient world		Romanesque
Prehistoric	Early Christian		Gothic
Primitive	Byzantine	Early Medieval	Renaissance
Pre-Columbian	Merovingian	(alphabetical by city)	XIX-XX Centuries
Oriental	Carolingian		Latin America
Islamic	Ottonian		North America
Mudejar	Pre-Romanesque		

Figure 26 exemplifies Yale's preparation of cataloging data for 35mm slide labels for which the use of abbreviations is kept to a minimum:

Figure 26—Slide Label, Yale University

1.	Painting Holland
2.	Van Gogh, Vincent 1853-90
3.	Self-portrait at an easel,
4.	1888

5.	Amsterdam, Stedelijk Museum
6.	Yale Color 9.78.7892
7.	Purchase, direct

Line 1:   medium; country
Line 2:   name of artist, artist's dates

(Slide label description continues on page 98)

Line 3:	title of painting
Line 4:	date
Line 5:	location; museum
Line 6:	source information; color slide; date of acquisition combined with accession number
Line 7:	acquisition source (slide was purchased directly from the Stedelijk Museum)

Due to the complex origins of African visual arts, many institutions have devised systems especially suited to local needs. At Yale, African slides are classified first by area, then by tribe, then by medium. All African art forms are filed together except for architecture, which is maintained as a separate part of the African slide collection (Chillman, 1978).

A rapid perusal of this list indicates an integration of geographical, cultural, and chronological division designations, so Yale's use of the term "period" as applied to these terms is not totally consistent. Exceptions to the period, country, city, or artist classification are made for early medieval and manuscript slides. Early medieval is classified by city first rather than by country. Manuscripts are classified under Minor Arts and are divided by period, e.g., Early Christian, or by geographical area, e.g., Oriental, or by country. Within these divisions, the subdivisions of school, century, or artist are used.

Yale utilizes an abbreviated alphabetical code for their slide labels. The following slide label illustrates how the slides are cataloged:

Figure 27—Lantern Slide Label, Yale University

1.	Arch. XIX-XX U.S.
2.	North Dartmouth, Mass. Schools
3.	Southeastern Massachusetts Technical
4.	Institute,
5.	Paul Rudolph, Arch.

6.	Arts and Humanities Building, 1966-67
7.	Int: main hall
8.	Y67-094 A-V Center March 1967
9.	Architectural Record, March, 1967, p. 148

Line 1:	Arch. for architecture; XIX-XX for nineteenth through the twentieth century; U.S. for United States
Line 2:	name of city; name of state; subject or building type represented by Schools
Line 3:	name of academic institution in which the building is located
Line 4:	continuation of line 3
Line 5:	name of architect
Line 6:	name of building illustrated; building dates
Line 7:	view of building; int. for interior
Line 8:	Y67-094 is the negative or sequence number; A-V Center means that the slide was made by the Audio-Visual Center at Yale University; month and year when slide was made
Line 9:	source from which slide was made; name of the journal; date; plate number

As indicated by this label, Yale includes complete source information on all slide labels. The use of this type of information for slides will be discussed in Chapter 4.

The following label illustrates Yale's African cataloging.

Figure 28–Slide Label, Yale University

1.	Africa West Sculpture
2.	Dan tribe
3.	Go ge mask of Nya, wood
4.	Private collection

Line 1:   geographical area; medium
Line 2:   name of tribe
Line 3:   name of mask; type of material
Line 4:   source

Although limited information is available about African slide cataloging, the following institutions have prepared guides to their African systems: the Cleveland Museum of Art (1977), the University of California at Los Angeles (*The Black Book*, 1977), and the University of Wisconsin (*Slide Classification Scheme*, 1978). In 1976, the Mid-America College Art Association Research Committee on Special Classification Systems for Materials of the Third World Peoples issued a report (edited by Chester Cowen) that includes guidelines on classifying and cataloging African arts. Cowen has also prepared authority guides for geographical areas and tribal names (Cowen, 1974; Chillman, 1978). Another source that may be used to identify geographical divisions and tribes for African materials is *An Outline of African Art*, written as a supplement to the African art series of University Prints (Teel, 1970). See Chapter 4 for additional information on handling African slides.

Summary

In order to select the preceding classification systems, approximately twenty-five different schemes were examined, ranging from those devised for a slide collection of 15,000 slides to over 250,000 slides. The most salient aspect of all of these systems is their similarity. Whether developed for large or small collections, these classification systems all exhibit the basic utilization of medium, period, country or culture, artist or century, and subject format. The following outline of classes, divisions, subdivisions, sections, and subsections for the major art forms is representative of the classification systems utilized in most academic institutions:

Medium (architecture)
    Period
        Country, geographical or cultural area
            Site (city or geographical area)
                Type of building

>   Medium (painting or sculpture)
>   Period
>   Country, geographical or cultural area
>   Artist
>   Subject (or chronological order by date of work)
>
>   Medium (decorative arts)
>   Country, geographical or cultural area
>   Century

The major classes may have period preceding medium, but for the most part, the systems are all basically the same. Some use a decimal notation code (Harvard/Michigan, National Gallery of Art), while others do not (Metropolitan Museum of Art, University of Minnesota). One system is over 170 pages in length (National Gallery of Art), while another is less than fifteen pages long (Cornell University). The examination of these different classifications reveals several important patterns. First, the absence of a coordinated approach to classifying slides in one area—the arts—has been a predominant theme for these visual resource collections because of their relatively isolated beginnings throughout academic institutions. Second, each collection has been organized with the intention of satisfying individual institutional idiosyncracies and yet, at the same time, each has been repeating the work of the other. Although the Harvard/Michigan and Metropolitan systems have predominated as guides to other collections, in the majority of collections throughout the United States, the similarity is only coincidental and not planned. Finally, the literature on the classification and cataloging of slides has either been completely absent or so widely dispersed throughout periodicals, journals, or handbooks that it has not been readily accessible to slide library staffs.

University of California, Santa Cruz

A Slide Classification System for the Organization and Automatic Indexing of Interdisciplinary Collections of Slides and Pictures was developed at the University of California, Santa Cruz, by Wendell Simons (Associate Librarian) and Luraine Tansey (Slide Librarian) under grants from the Council on Library Resources (1970). This work represents a significant contribution to the consolidation and standardization of a classification system for art, history, and science slides. The difference between the concept of *visual* as opposed to *verbal* content was an essential component in the conception and realization of this system, and it was one of the reasons for not using systems such as the DDC or LC for classifying visual media. In the introduction to their system, the authors provided the following explanation of the dichotomy between unitary images and the book format:

> A picture is more analogous to a sentence or a single word than to a book. It makes a single statement on a single theme; a book can be encyclopedic in its coverage or very narrow. Book classifications provide for the very general, the very specific, and everything between. Classification of slides and pictures can make use of only the most specific (ibid., p. 2).

The possible range of visual content is simply not as broad as the range of verbal content in books—emotions, thoughts, concepts, imagination, speculations; these cannot become the visual content of a picture (ibid., p. 3).

A classification for visual phenomena must be cast in very concrete terms and this is why it appears necessary to create a separate and special classification system for slides and pictures (ibid., p. 4).

In addition, the Santa Cruz system was developed to fulfill four basic requirements:

1. The collection, and hence the classification, should be general, encompassing the subject matter of all academic disciplines.
2. The arrangement of the collection should reflect a broad historical, cultural approach to teaching.
3. The filing arrangement . . . should encourage and facilitate browsing, that is, visual inspection and comparison of the files.
4. . . . the collection should be fully cataloged or indexed, preferably by automated means (ibid., p. 2).

The preceding criteria would be useful for any slide collection classification being developed to meet diverse user needs in an effective manner.

The following outline is a summary of the classification schedule provided by Tansey:

HISTORY (Regional)
Field 1: Major time period
    2: Country (alphabetical)
    3: Major subject area
    4: Sub-category of subject area
    5: Person, place, or term Cuttered
    6: Format
    7: Subdivision
    8: Title of image in slide
    9: Detail or total image denotation
    10: Additional sequence of details

ART
Field 1: Major time period
    2: Country
    3: Art form
    4: Style
    5: Artist, place, or sub-period indicator
    6: Subject matter
    7: Optional subdivisions of Subject matter
    8: Title
    9: Total or part image
    10: Sequence code for details

(Outline continues on page 102)

SCIENCE
    Field 1: Scientific discipline
          2: Country
          3: Subject area
          4: Subdivision of Subject area
          5: Major category
          6: Subdivision of major category
          7: Additional subdivision of major categories
          8: Specific title of image on slide
          9: Total or detail code for sequence
         10: Additional sequencing code letter

Included within this system are chronological period tables for arts, country and geographical divisions, subject divisions and subdivisions, style designations, and a complete nomenclature for science divisions and subject subdivisions. An authority list giving artists' names, their Cutter number, nationality, medium, and birth and death dates is also provided. A numerical and alphabetical code is used to compose the call numbers.

In addition to the ten fields for each topic from which the call number is derived, five more fields are included for cataloging data. Fields 11 through 15 list the data in natural language rather than in coded alphabetical or numerical form:

    Field 11: Main entry or artist's name
          12: Title of image
          13: Date of work
          14: Present location (city and collection)
          15: Source of the slide

For each slide, a punch card is made that includes all fifteen fields. From these punch cards, it is then possible to generate machine-readable indexes to the collection by call number, by each of the ten fields represented by the call number, and by any of the remaining five fields. For example, if a patron wants to know which slides in the collection are from the National Gallery of Art in London, then an index by present location or museum could be generated or scanned. It is, of course, possible to utilize the system manually without ever producing machine automated indexes. The University of California at Santa Cruz annually produces automated indexes (with quarterly supplements) to the slide collection, which then updates the previous year's data base. A shelflist or call number index, an artist or place index, a subject matter index, an alphabetical title index, a date index, and a place name or location index comprise possible computer print-outs to the slide collection. As of 1978, approximately 85,000 slides (out of 120,000) had been classified, cataloged, and indexed using this system (Simons, 1978).

As is apparent from the summary schedule, this scheme draws heavily upon the inherently natural and visible order of artistic, historical, and scientific materials. The previous endeavors to classify pictorial materials have by no means been neglected, but instead, have been incorporated into the system and have refined it. Even if the entire system is not used by a collection, aspects of it such as the subject divisions or the artist authority file may be practical for integration into a previously established collection. In order to make the system function both as an indexing and retrieval device, slides could be placed on aperture cards and mechanically retrieved, but this approach is awkward for a large collection. The Medical School at the University of California at San Diego has used aperture cards as a master slide file from which they have duplicate slides made for faculty use. These cards are retrieved according to a keyword system based upon the publication *Standard Nomenclature of Diseases and Operations* (National Conference on Medical Nomenclature, 1961), which is also recommended as a source for fields 5, 6, and 7 of the Santa Cruz system. Other published thesauri are also noted by Simons and Tansey in the section on the sciences.

Figure 29 illustrates the application of the Santa Cruz classification system:

Figure 29–Art Slide Label, UC/SC

1. N468F GOGH, VINCENT VAN
2. G613W Self Portrait at an
3. S470A Easel.Oil/Canvas
4.   1888

5. AMSTERDAM:STEDELIJK MUS.
6. 651.85.31   (Erpel)
7. Size: 25-1/2" x 20"

Line 1: N for 19th century; 468 for Holland, Netherlands; F for painting; name of artist
Line 2: G613 for Cutter number for Gogh; W for portraits; title of painting
Line 3: S470 for Cutter number for title; A for detail number; continuation of title; type of painting
Line 4: date
Line 5: location; museum
Line 6: accession number and source
Line 7: size of painting

Figure 30 provides this same information as it appears in printed form at the top of a punch card. The numbers above the card indicate the fifteen sort fields. Fields not used for the call number are blank, i.e., 4 and 7. All fields are fixed except 11 and 12, and 14 and 15; i.e., within fields 11 and 12, both the length of the artist's name and the title of the image may vary, depending upon which requires more space within this field of 32 characters. Eighty columns of data (or characters) can be keypunched on each card.

Figure 30–Punch Card, UC/SC

Figures 31 and 32 are sample labels from the history and science sections of the Santa Cruz system.

Figure 31—History Slide Label, UC/SC

```
1.    G630LJ    FORD, JOHN
2.    F699YM    Stagecoach.
3.    S7790     Ringo Kid
4.              1939

5.    JOHN WAYNE
6.    368.38.448      (R)
7.    Producer:   UNITED ARTISTS
```

Line 1:   G for 20th century; 630 for United States; L for "Recreation outside the Home, Sports"; J for motion pictures

Line 2:   F699 for Cutter number for Ford; Y for Western (subject content of film); M for live action (film technique); title of film

Line 3:   S779 for Cutter number for Stagecoach; O for sequencing detail; title of image

Line 4:   date of film

Line 5:   actor in this scene from motion picture slide (for most history slides, this line is used for the location of the image shown)

Line 6:   accession number and source code

Line 7:   producer

Figure 32—Science Slide Label, UC/SC

```
1.    V730G     LEGUMINOSAE
2.    L521      Lupinus Nanus
3.    L969B     Sky Lupine

4.    SANTA CRUZ:    UCSC
5.    RK1.2.8         (Kerrigan)
```

Line 1:   V for life sciences; 730 for Cutter number designating a state, local community or institution; G for Botany

Line 2:   L521 for Leguminosae which designates the arrangement for botany by taxonomic family

Line 3:   L969 for Cutter number for Lupinus Nanus (taxonomic binomial— genus species); B for detail number; Sky Lupine for common name

Line 4:   location (where photo of flower was taken)

Line 5:   accession number and source code

Maryellen LoPresti (former Catalog Slide Librarian, Georgia Institute of Technology) has documented one application of the Santa Cruz system in a paper published in *Special Libraries* (1973). As of 1978, about 8,890 slides had been classified at Georgia Institute of Technology, with the staff concluding that the Santa Cruz system is generally satisfactory and allows "for quick access and the continuing expansion and refinement of an art slide library" (Dunn, 1978).

Unfortunately, although a number of institutions are utilizing this system, no formal procedures exist for registering program modifications made by individual slide libraries, so even the application of this system may result in inconsistencies in the classification of art and architecture slides from one collection to another (ibid.). According to Georgia's slide cataloger, Edith M. Dunn, two punch cards are prepared per slide from data entered on a coding sheet. Card 1 is used for the artist and title fields and Card 2, for all remaining fields. By increasing the number of keypunch cards used for data input, more information can be provided in each of the sort fields, which is particularly useful for the artist and title entries. Figure 33 is a sample label for the minor arts prepared for the art section of the Santa Cruz system.

Figure 33–Minor Arts Slide Label, Georgia Institute of Technology

1.	P397X LOEWY
2.	L827W
3.	B863B

4.	BROADWAY LIMITED.
5.	BAR-LOUNGE CAR.
6.	INTERIOR. BAR.

7.	1938
8.	
9.	4.72.78

[Three labels are prepared per slide.]

Line 1:	P for 20th century; 397 for France; X for "Minor arts in other materials" (known artist); name of artist
Line 2:	L827 for Cutter number for Loewy; W for vehicles:land
Line 3:	B863 for Cutter number for title; B for detail number
Line 4:	title of image
Line 5:	general view of image
Line 6:	detailed view of image
Line 7:	date
Line 8:	blank
Line 9:	accession number and source code

Other institutions that use the Santa Cruz classification system include the following: Ball State University, Indiana; the California Institute of the Arts, Los Angeles; San Fernando State College; and the University of Houston.

SUMMARY

For the slide collection composed solely of sets, the Dewey Decimal, Library of Congress, or other formal classification schedules can be readily used. Application of a common system allows for complete integration of print and nonprint media in a central catalog, logical filing and/or shelving arrangements, and subject organization reflective of a single classification system. As a rule, unitary image collections of slides have not logically adapted to classification systems devised for printed materials; therefore, the application of an established scheme for visual media such as the Santa Cruz schedule is recommended. Moreover, the availability of the Santa Cruz system through the ERIC Document Reproduction Service makes it one of the most accessible schedules outlined.

As the most highly developed fine arts classification system, the Harvard/ Michigan schedule should be used to supplement sections of the Santa Cruz system that may require additional categories or subject definition. The preparation of cataloging data for card files should be consistent with the latest edition of the *AAC Rules*, which would also insure a consistent standard bibliographic description (ISBD(G)). When the application of automated keyword indexing systems is possible, this approach could be utilized with the Santa Cruz system. As the use of keyword indexing becomes more common, the arrangement of slides mandated by a formal classification schedule may become a less critical function of retrieval than it is for most unitary image collections at the present time. Ultimately, the function of the collection, the needs of the user, and the potential for expansion should affect the classification, cataloging, or retrieval method selected by each library. Within this framework, every attempt should be made to utilize standard approaches to the organization of slide libraries.

REFERENCES

Akers, Susan G. 1969. *Simple Library Cataloging.* 5th edition. Metuchen, New Jersey: Scarecrow Press.

The American Institute of Architects Filing System for Architectural Plates and Articles. 1956. Second edition, revised. Washington, D.C.: The American Institute of Architects. (AIA document 261).

American Library Color Slide Catalogue of World Art: Teachers Manual for the Study of Art History and Related Courses. 1964. New York: American Library Color Slides Co. (Sixth printing, 1970).

Anglo-American Cataloging Rules. 1967. North American Text. Chicago: American Library Association.

Anglo-American Cataloguing Rules. 1978. Second edition. Prepared by the American Library Association, the British Library, the Canadian Committee on Cataloguing, the Library Association, and the Library of Congress. Edited by Michael Gorman and Paul Winkler. Chicago: American Librarian Association and Canadian Library Association.

Anglo-American Cataloging Rules: Chapter 6. Separately Published Monographs. 1974. North American Text. Chicago: American Library Association.

Anglo-American Cataloging Rules: Chapter 12 Revised; Audiovisual Media and Special Instructional Materials. 1975. North American Text. Chicago: American Library Association.

Association for Educational Communications and Technology. Cataloging Committee. 1971. *Standards for Cataloging Nonprint Materials.* Revised edition. Washington, D.C.: Association for Educational Communications and Technology.

Association for Educational Communications and Technology. The Information
Science Committee. 1972. *Standards for Cataloging Nonprint Materials*.
Third edition. Washington, D.C.: Association for Educational Communica-
tions and Technology.

Auchstetter, Rosann M., Slide Librarian, Chicago Art Institute. Personal communication. January 11, 1979.

*The Black Book: A Cataloguing Handbook for the Slide and Photograph Collection
of the Art Department, UCLA*. 1977. Los Angeles: University of California.

Bogar, Candace S. 1975. "Classification for an Architecture and Art Slide Collection." *Special Libraries* 66 (December):570-74.

Chillman, Helen, Librarian, Slide and Photograph Collection, Yale University.
Personal communication. September 1978.

Chisholm, Margaret. 1975. "Problems and Directions in Bibliographic Organization
of Media." In *Reader in Media, Technology and Libraries*, edited by Margaret
Chisholm with Dennis D. McDonald, pp. 350-60. Englewood, Colorado:
Microcard Editions Books.

Clarke, Virginia. 1953. *Non-Book Library Materials; A Handbook of Procedures
for a Uniform and Simplified System of Handling Audio-Visual Aids, Vertical
File, and Other Non-Book Materials in the School Library*. Denton, Texas:
Laboratory School Library, North Texas State College and North Texas
State College Print Shop.

Clarke, Virginia. 1969. *The Organization of Nonbook Materials in the Laboratory
School Library*. Revised edition. Denton, Texas: Laboratory School Library.

*The Cleveland Museum of Art Slide Library Classification Scheme, Chronologies
and Subdivisions*. 1977. Edited by Dr. Sara Jane Pearman, Slide Librarian.
Cleveland: Cleveland Museum of Art.

Cowen, Chester R. 1974. "Systems for Arranging Resources on African Populations." Mimeographed. Norman, Oklahoma: University of Oklahoma.

Daily, Jay E. 1967. "Selection, Processing and Storage of Non-print Materials:
A Critique of the Anglo-American Cataloguing Rules as They Relate to Newer
Media." *Library Trends* 16 (October):283-89.

Daughtry, Bessie. 1948. *Cataloguing, Arrangement and Storage of Motion Pictures,
Filmstrips, and 2" x 2" Slides*. Master's Thesis. Florida State University.

Diamond, Robert M. 1969. *The Development of a Retrieval System for 35mm
Slides Utilized in Art and Humanities Instruction*. Washington, D.C.: Bureau
of Research, Office of Education, U.S. Department of Health, Education,
and Welfare. (Final Report, Project No. 8-B-080).

Diamond, Robert M. 1972. "A Retrieval System for 35mm Slides Utilized in Art
and Humanities Instruction." In *Bibliographic Control of Nonprint Media*,
edited by Pearce S. Grove and Evelyn G. Clement, pp. 346-59. Chicago:
American Library Association.

Dunn, Edith M., Library Assistant, Architecture Library, Georgia Institute of
Technology. Personal communication. August 1978.

Farah, Priscilla. 1976. "The Photograph and Slide Library of the Metropolitan
Museum of Art: A 68-Year View of Classification." In *Newsletter* supple-
ment, "Library Classification Systems and the Visual Arts," edited by
David J. Patten. 4 (Summer):S6-S7.

Fink, Eleanor E., Chief, Office of Visual Resources, National Collection of Fine
Arts. 1979. Personal communication.

Gorman, Michael. 1978. "The Anglo-American Cataloguing Rules, Second Edition."
   Library Resources 22 (Summer):209-226.

Grove, Pearce S., and Herman L. Totten. 1969. "Bibliographic Control of Media:
   The Librarian's Excedrin Headache." *Wilson Library Bulletin* 44 (November):
   299-311.

Hagler, Ronald. 1978. "Development of Cataloging Rules for Nonbook Materials."
   Library Resources and Technical Services 19 (Summer):268-78.

Harris, Evelyn J. 1968. *Instructional Materials Cataloguing Guide*. Tucson, Arizona:
   The University of Arizona, College of Education, Bureau of Educational
   Research and Service.

Harvard-Williams, P., and S. Watson. 1960. "Slide Collection at Liverpool School
   of Architecture." *Journal of Documentation* 16 (March):11-14.

Hicks, Warren B., and Alma M. Tillin. 1967. *The Organization of Nonbook Materials
   in School Libraries*. Sacramento, California: California State Department of
   Education.

Hicks, Warren B., and Alma M. Tillin. 1970. *Developing Multi-Media Libraries*.
   New York: Bowker.

Hopkinson, Shirley L. 1963. *The Descriptive Cataloging of Library Materials*.
   San Jose, California: San Jose State College, Claremont House.

*ISBD(G): General International Standard Bibliographic Description: Annotated
   Text*. 1977. Prepared by the Working Group on the General International
   Standard Bibliographic Description set up by the IFLA Committee on
   Cataloguing. London: International Federal of Library Associations and
   Institutions.

Johnson, Jean T., et al. 1971. *AV Cataloging and Processing Simplified*. Raleigh,
   North Carolina: Audiovisual Catalogers, Inc.

Keen, Eunice. 1955. *Manual for Use in the Cataloging and Classification of Audio-
   Visual Materials for a High School Library*. Lakeland, Florida: Lakeland
   High School.

Library of Congress. Catalog Publication Division. 1976. *Films and Other Materials
   for Projection, 1975*. Washington, D.C.: Library of Congress.

Library of Congress. MARC Development Office. 1970. *Films: A MARC Format*.
   Washington, D.C.: U.S. Government Printing Office. Addenda 1-7, 1972-
   1976.

Library of Congress Processing Department. Subject Cataloging Division. 1970.
   Outline of the Library of Congress Classification. Second edition. Washington, D.C.: Library of Congress.

Loertscher, David V. 1975. *A Nonbook Cataloging Sampler*. First edition. Austin,
   Texas: Armadillo Press.

LoPresti, Maryellen. 1973. "Automated Slide Classification System at Georgia
   Tech." *Special Libraries* 64 (November):509-513.

Maltby, Arthur. 1975. *Sayers' Manual of Classification for Librarians*. 5th edition.
   London: Andre Deutsch, Ltd.

Mason, Donald. 1958. *A Primer of Non-Book Materials in Libraries*. London:
   Association of Assistant Librarians.

Massonneau, Suzanne. 1977. "Developments in the Organization of AV Materials."
   Library Trends 25 (January):665-84.

Mid-America College Art Association. Research Committee on Special Classification Systems for Visual Materials of the Third World Peoples. 1976. *Report of the Research Committee . . . , 1974-1975.* Edited by Chester R. Cowen. Parts I and II. Norman, Oklahoma: The School of Art, University of Oklahoma.

NCFA Slide and Photograph Archive. Division of Office of Slides and Photography, National Collection of Fine Arts. 1978. Washington, D.C.: Smithsonian Institution.

National Conference on Medical Nomenclature. 1961. *Standard Nomenclature of Diseases and Operations.* 5th edition. New York: McGraw-Hill.

National Education Association. Department of Audiovisual Instruction. 1968. *Standards for Cataloging, Coding, and Scheduling Educational Media.* Washington, D.C.: National Education Association.

Non-Book Materials Cataloguing Rules: Integrated Code of Practice and Draft Revision of the Anglo-American Cataloguing Rules, British Text, Part III. 1974. Prepared by the Media Cataloguing Rules Committee, Library Association. Second edition. Great Britain: Council for the Educational Technology for the United Kingdom with the Library Association. (Working Paper No. 11).

Palmer, Marlene, Librarian, Slide and Photograph Archive, National Collection of Fine Arts. Personal communication. October 1978.

Perusse, L. F. 1954. "Classifying and Cataloguing Lantern Slides." *Journal of Cataloguing and Classification* X (April):77-83.

The Picture Collection Subject Headings. 1968. Prepared by William J. Dane. 6th edition. Hamden, Connecticut: Shoe String Press.

Quinly, W. J. 1967. "Selection, Processing, and Storage of Non-Print Materials: Aids, Indexes and Guidelines." *Library Trends* 16 (October):274-82.

Rogers, JoAnn V. 1979. "Nonprint Cataloging: A Call for Standardization." *American Libraries* 10 (January):46-48.

Rufsvold, Margaret I. 1949. *Audio-Visual School Library Service, A Handbook for Librarians.* Chicago: American Library Association.

Sayers, W. C. Berwick. 1955. *A Manual of Classification for Librarians and Bibliographers.* Third edition revised. London: Grafton and Co.

Sayers, W. C. Berwick. 1958. *An Introduction to Library Classification.* 9th edition. London: Grafton and Co.

Sayers, W. C. Berwick. 1967. *A Manual of Classification for Librarians.* Completely revised and partly re-written by Arthur Maltby. 4th edition. London: Andre Deutsch, Ltd.

Shores, Louis. 1960. *Instructional Materials.* New York: Ronald Press.

Shores, Louis. 1968. "The Medium Way; Librarians' Methods, and Media in the New Learning Mode." *The Library College Journal* 1 (Winter):10-17.

Silva, Manil. 1970. *Special Libraries.* London: Andre Deutsch Ltd.

Simons, Wendell. 1972. "Development of a Universal Classification System for Two-by-Two Inch Slide Collections." In *Bibliographic Control of Nonprint Media,* edited by Pearce S. Grove and Evelyn G. Clement, pp. 360-73. Chicago: American Library Association.

Simons, Wendell, Associate University Librarian, University of California, Santa Cruz. Personal communication. September 1978.

Simons, Wendell W., and Luraine C. Tansey. 1970. *A Slide Classification System for the Organization and Automatic Indexing of Interdisciplinary Collections of Slides and Pictures.* Santa Cruz, California: University of California.

Slide Classification Scheme: Department of Art History, University of Wisconsin— Madison. 1978. Prepared by Christine L. Sundt, Slide Curator. Mimeographed. Madison, Wisconsin: University of Wisconsin.

Stone, C. Walter. 1969. "Image for the Future." *California School Libraries* 41 (November):4-7, 37-40.

Straight, Elsie H. c. 1975. "The Slide Classification and Cataloging System Developed for the Ringling School of Art Library, Sarasota, Florida." Typescript.

Swan, E. 1960. "Problems Involved in Establishing a Slide Collection in the School of Architecture, School of Melbourne." *Australian Library Journal* 9 (July): 159-62.

Teel, William. 1970. *An Outline of African Art.* Cambridge, Massachusetts: University Prints.

Thompson, Dixie. 1952. *Organization of Audio-Visual Materials.* Tempe, Arizona: Arizona State College, Curriculum Laboratory.

Tillin, Alma M., and William J. Quinly. 1976. *Standards for Cataloging Nonprint Materials; An Interpretation and Practical Application.* 4th edition. Washington, D.C.: Association for Educational Communications and Technology.

Tselos, Dimitri. 1959. "A Simple Slide Classification System." *College Art Journal* 18 (Summer):344-49.

Tucker, B. R. 1975. "New Version of Chapter 12 of the AA Cataloging Rules." *Library Resources and Technical Services* 19 (Summer):260-67).

Weihs, Jean Riddle, Shirley Lewis, and Janet MacDonald. In consultation with the CLA/ALA/AECT/EMAC/CAML Advisory Committee on the Cataloguing of Nonbook Materials. 1973. *Non-Book Materials: The Organization of Integrated Collections.* First edition. Ottawa, Canada: The Canadian Library Association.

Wetmore, Rosamond B. 1969. *A Guide to the Organization of Library Collections.* Muncie, Indiana: Ball State University.

Wynar, Bohdan S. 1976. *Introduction to Cataloging and Classification.* 5th edition. Littleton, Colorado: Libraries Unlimited.

4−USE OF STANDARD LIBRARY
TECHNIQUES AND TOOLS

INTRODUCTION

Most slide curators and librarians are fairly sophisticated users of library techniques and tools. In fact, the title "slide library" might be a more informative and valid nomenclature than slide "collection." For the purposes of this chapter, a library tool is defined as a referral or reference device utilized by librarians to locate information. Those tools used heavily by both the library staff and the patron include author-title and classified card catalogs, various types of standard reference works such as dictionaries and encyclopedias, and a variety of indexing sources. Remaining are the tools restricted more frequently for the direct use of the library staff rather than for the general user (these include acquisition, accession, authority, circulation, and shelflist records). The library's maintenance of these latter records may indirectly affect the efficient use of the library by the patron, while the former provide immediate access to the library's reservoir of information. In addition to the use of manual library systems, increasing applications are being made of computer and data processing techniques. The chapter on cataloging and classification includes references to a number of such applications. This chapter focuses on how automated systems are being used to facilitate subject indexing, authority file development, and inventory and acquisitions control.

Whether or not the individual in charge of the slide library identifies the index to artists' names as an authority file, for all practical purposes, it is. The lack of standardized terminology has led to many variations of basic library techniques and tools for slide libraries because the majority of these academic collections were not begun under the direction of the library. In schools and museums, slides usually found their natural location for organization within the library, although they frequently received limited attention during their initial growth period. The relatively recent abundance of publications on the organization of audiovisual materials for school and public library systems is indicative of the rather late concern shown for the standardized organization of these materials within the library context.

For the benefit of those unfamiliar with the various terms used to define library organizational methods and tools, the purpose of this chapter is to clarify and to establish a basic nomenclature for slide libraries based upon that used by libraries in general. In most instances, the terminology is not new or original but instead represents a synthesis of methods and terms used at the present time in many slide libraries throughout the United States.

CARD CATALOGS/INDEXING SYSTEMS

Subject Catalog and Index File

As the majority of academic slide libraries are arranged in subject order based upon a classification system without notation, the use of a subject catalog is usually considered unnecessary because the collection is self-indexing. *Sears List of Subject Headings* (1977) and the *Library of Congress Subject Headings* (U.S. Library of Congress, 1975) are the standard sources of subject heading format for most libraries. How do these standard headings relate to the classed slide file? An individual who is looking for nineteenth century French painting books in a library should check under the heading, "Painting, Modern—19th century—France," which utilizes the following order:

> Medium (painting)
> > Period (modern, 19th century)
> > > Country (France)

The books entered under this subject heading would then be in main entry or title order depending upon the filing rules of the particular library. In the classed slide library, the patron would go directly to the slide files and check under "Painting, 19th century, France."

> Medium (painting)
> > Period (19th century)
> > > Country (France)

After country, however, the slides would be arranged alphabetically by artist. In contrast to the classed slide file, monographs on artists would be arranged separately in the subject catalog for book libraries directly under the artist's name. The slide file for a particular period would be arranged by the artists who defined the styles rather than by broad stylistic periods. Within each artist subsection, the slides would be classed by the subject orientation of a particular artist, e.g., portraits, landscapes, secular or religious works and so forth. This type of self-indexing arrangement, however, can present problems for the non-specialist who would not necessarily know by name and nationality, or by period, all the landscape artists whose work he would like to examine. The function provided by the general library card catalog heading, "Painting, Modern—19th century—France," is not possible for the classed slide file because of its internal class structure. A subject or classed slide file can operate fairly efficiently in a specialized academic departmental collection, in a museum, or in an art school context; but once a collection must provide multi-disciplinary access, then exhaustive reference service must be given to the user whose field is outside the subject orientation of the slide collection.

In the school, public library, and centralized academic library system, a collection of slides by individual artists or on any specific topic would necessitate the use of a subject catalog to locate materials. It is unfair to expect the non-specialist to utilize such a collection without the added expense of extra staff to accommodate this use pattern. The non-specialist should not be expected to know the country, medium, period, or style in which an artist worked or in which a given historical concept or trend was established. For example, the historian interested in the changing patterns of costume styles should be able to approach the topic directly from this subject rather than through given historical periods or incidents.

Utilization of a subject approach is mandatory for multi-disciplinary retrieval. For examples of the application of standard subject heading rules, consult audio-visual cataloging manuals (Clarke, 1969; Hicks and Tillin, 1967; Loertscher, 1975; Tillin and Quinly, 1976; Weihs, 1973; and Wetmore, 1969). Figures 34 and 35 illustrate subject cards for art and nature slides based upon *Sears List of Subject Headings* (1977) and the AECT *Standards for Cataloging Nonprint Materials* (Tillin and Quinly, 1976).

Figure 34—Art Slide Subject Card (3x5-inches)

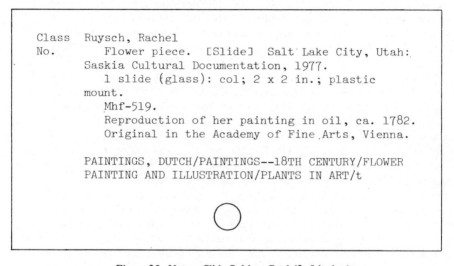

```
Class   Ruysch, Rachel
No.         Flower piece.  [Slide]  Salt Lake City, Utah:
        Saskia Cultural Documentation, 1977.
            1 slide (glass): col; 2 x 2 in.; plastic
        mount.
            Mhf-519.
            Reproduction of her painting in oil, ca. 1782.
            Original in the Academy of Fine Arts, Vienna.

        PAINTINGS, DUTCH/PAINTINGS--18TH CENTURY/FLOWER
        PAINTING AND ILLUSTRATION/PLANTS IN ART/t
```

Figure 35—Nature Slide Subject Card (3x5-inches)

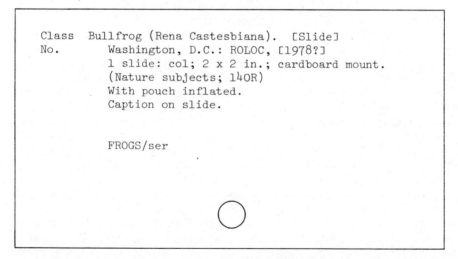

```
Class   Bullfrog (Rena Castesbiana).  [Slide]
No.         Washington, D.C.: ROLOC, [1978?]
            1 slide: col; 2 x 2 in.; cardboard mount.
            (Nature subjects; 140R)
            With pouch inflated.
            Caption on slide.



            FROGS/ser
```

In addition to using the Library of Congress and *Sears* lists of subject headings, guides designed for picture collections can be utilized for indexing slides. *The Picture Collection Subject Headings* is a published list of the headings used to index over one million pictures, postcards, slides, and other visual media in the Art and Music Department of the Newark (New Jersey) Public Library (1968). Based upon her experience with the New York Picture Collection and a Hunter College Library picture file, Donna Hill prepared *The Picture File: A Manual and a*

Curriculum-related Subject Heading List (1975). Most large newspapers or magazine publishers also maintain extensive clipping and picture files, which may be examined and which may offer varied approaches to specialized subject indexing. For example, the Time, Inc. Picture Collection (New York City) has over ten million images, adds about 600 to 700 pictures per week, and uses 10,000 subject headings and major divisions developed for indexing purposes. Other large picture collections are at the New York Public Library (over two million), the Queensborough Public Library (about one million), and the Westport Connecticut Public Library (750,000). The New York Public Library Picture Collection uses subject headings based upon the list prepared for the Newark Public Library.

When an instructional materials center is being developed so that a media collection can serve an entire campus, school or library system, it is impractical to devise a limited-use system. If such a collection is to have a central catalog, which is a necessity for the total media approach, the materials should be integrated in the subject catalog but not on the shelves, unless materials have been developed to be used only as packages or sets. To intershelve records, slides, and photographs is inefficient and wasteful of space. Storage for slides alone is quite complicated (see Chapter 6). What must be kept in mind is the difference between unitary image collections and packaged or set collections. For example, a set of slides (boxed), photographs (boxed), and records may conform enough in size to be intershelved without a loss of convenience. What happens, however, when an individual wants to mix various media from these sets? If the collection is indexed only by set, as it is shelved, then the ability of the user to integrate materials in novel ways might be seriously impeded, if not destroyed. The most desirable system would provide for machine indexing of all print and nonprint material so that sound, image, and word could be retrieved without regard to physical format.

Very few academic collections have subject catalogs to their slide collections, although this is the rule rather than the exception in school library systems. Harvard University once maintained a contact print catalog alphabetically by artist, school, or city for its lantern slide collection. It no longer does so for 35mm slides because of the time and labor involved in its development. Moreover, the self-indexing nature of the collection does not encourage use of such catalogs except by users outside the particular subject discipline of the collection. The Art Institute of Chicago maintains a dictionary catalog for painters, architects, buildings, and subjects in its collection. At Pratt Institute, where the collection is housed in the general library rather than in a departmental one, an attempt is being made to index the collection on a limited basis.

Other collections having subject indexes to their slides include the Cleveland Museum of Art; Cornell University College of Architecture, Art and Planning; and the University of Washington. In the Philadelphia College of Art Slide Library, slides are organized by medium, including painting, sculpture, architecture, photography, crafts, and other main classes. In order to provide access to painters by historical period, and by style and movement, a style index has been developed. This collection also has a portrait catalog, which indexes individuals represented in the various media; however, as is noted in their guide to the collection: "Although the collection is designed for browsing, there is no provision for generalized thematic approaches. It is advisable to do your homework and have a clear idea of the specific artists you want to look up" ("Slide Library," 1976). This statement exemplifies the problems faced by the uninitiated user of subject-specialty slide collections.

Fortunately, individuals working in slide libraries are becoming increasingly innovative regarding the problem of subject access to slides.

When a collection is used by individuals from a variety of disciplines, subject access must be provided to insure the greatest possible access to discrete images. The Evergreen State College Library offers a useful example of how a campus-wide slide collection (about 21,000) attempts to meet the needs of interdisciplinary users (Crawford, 1978). At Evergreen, Library of Congress classification and subject headings, and the *Anglo-American Cataloguing Rules* are used for all types of print and nonprint media. Cards for all materials are interfiled in the Library's central catalog. Nonprint materials are usually housed separately from the book collection. Like the books, the slides are shelved in call number order. Figure 36 illustrates how the cards appear in the central catalog.

Figure 36–Art Slide Catalog Card, The Evergreen State College Library (3x5-inches)

```
SLID    Kabuki theatre. [Slide]. -- Long Ditton,
NE         England : Miniature Gallery, [1974?]
1318          24 slides : color ; 2 x 2 in. -- (Japa-
.E6        nese popular prints 1700-1900)
S65
            Slide index for contents.
      For works by artist see artist index.
      CREDITS: Slides selected from prints owned by the
Victoria and Albert Museum, England, and arranged
into a 1973 exhibit, "The Floating World."
      SUMMARY: Prints depict scenes and actors from Ka-
buki theatre.
                                  (continued)
                                  EVG77-0091
```

```
SLID    Kabuki theatre. [Slide].
NE                                     (card 2)
1318
.E6
S65


Includes works by Toyokuni, among others.
      1. Prints, Japanese.  I. Victoria and Albert Muse-
um, South Kensington.  II.  Miniature Gallery.  III.
Series. [Slide]
```

Both the solutions and the problems regarding subject access to slides are exemplified by these catalog cards. The 24 slides are cataloged as a single set of illustrations on Kabuki Theatre and are given the subject heading, "Prints, Japanese." Both the "CREDITS" and "SUMMARY" notes explain the use of this heading. Added entries are provided for the museum owning the original prints from which the slides were made and for the commercial slide producer (Miniature Gallery) that made the slides. Fourteen different artists are represented within this set of slides. The notes area of the card also includes references to the "Slide index for contents" and to an "artist index." The "Slide index for contents" is a typed listing in shelflist order of all the sets in the Evergreen collection and includes the title and a brief description of the contents in each set. This index assists users as they browse through the slides, which are in call number order and filed in visual display rack cabinets (see Photograph 9, p. 181). Accompanying the "Slide index to contents" is a "Slide Set List," which individually lists all the slides in each set. This latter list is alphabetical by artist or by title, depending upon the image cataloged. The "artist index" was developed to facilitate access by artist to individual slides, which is not a function of the central card catalog cards. Obvious advantages to Evergreen's handling of the slide collection include centralized user access to print and nonprint media via a single card catalog, and consistent classification, cataloging, and shelving patterns for all materials in a general library facility. At the same time, the need for additional subject access to a unitary image collection mandated the development of supplemental indexing guides, which were prepared by an industrious slide curator.

The Educational Materials Center at Marycrest College offers another example of a slide collection (15,422) that serves interdisciplinary needs and functions as part of a central library facility. The nonprint collections are shelved separately from the books and have their own "Media Catalog," which is based on the AECT *Standards for Cataloging Nonprint Materials*, third edition (1972). For shelving purposes, each slide is assigned an accession number and letter symbol, e.g., SL 15179. See Figure 37.

**Figure 37—Medical Sciences Slide Card, Media Catalog, Marycrest
College Educational Materials Center (3x5-inches)**

```
SL
15179-    Calculating Ambient gas tensions by Arnold
15211        Sladen.  National Audio Visual Center, 1974.
             S-2629-X

          33 slides with cassette.  Workbook script.

          1.  Blood, Gases in.  2.  Oxygen in the
          body-Measurement.
```

Unlike Evergreen's Library, the Marycrest Educational Materials Center maintains two separate catalogs for the book and media collections, but subject cards for all nonprint materials are interfiled in the library's central subject catalog in addition to being in the "Media Catalog." The division of catalogs at Marycrest alleviated what had become an unwieldy central catalog for library materials, while it still provided a combined subject catalog that facilitates user access both to print and nonprint media.

Additional variations on the theme of subject access to slides include opportunities both for manual and/or machine indexing. The Santa Cruz classification system can be implemented to generate its own indexes either via computer or manually (see Chapter 3). Although its is a classed and structured system, Santa Cruz incorporates aspects of the keyword or uniterm method of subject indexing. Each keyword or term designated by the numbers that compose a given field has an indexing potential; consequently, it is possible to retrieve a slide by the first term of any of the sort fields, e.g., artist's last name, chronological period, first word of the title of an image, date of execution, and so forth.

Usually keyword indexing is not dependent upon a classification system such as the Santa Cruz scheme but is derived from the use of permuted title indexes or thesaurus construction. To permute a title is to rearrange the words or keywords within the title, so that the title itself can be used for subject access to a given work. Such rearrangement of terms readily adapts to computer manipulation and also can be utilized with subject headings (Smith and Treese, 1975). At the University of Wisconsin—Stout, a permuted title index is used for nonprint media retrieval (Schwarz, 1974). Elizabeth Lewis (formerly Fine Arts Librarian at the U.S. Military Academy) developed a computer-based permuted title and artist or object index to their slide collection. Instead of using keywords within a given title, thesaurus construction is based on the development of descriptors or keywords selected specifically for a collection requiring indexing. A number of publications record the application of this retrieval system for nonprint media (Chouraqui, 1973; Daily, 1973, pp. 19-36; Fleischer, 1969; Lamy-Rousseau, 1974). Several studies have treated descriptor indexing for slides (Diamond, 1972; Lewis, 1976; Motley, 1970; Nacke and Murza, 1977; *NCFA Slide and Photograph Archive*, 1978; Ohlgren, 1977 and 1978; Ohrn, 1975; Rahn, 1975; Sedgley and Merrett, 1974; *SLIDEX*, 1978; Strohlein, 1975; and Tansey, 1975).

The distinctive feature of thesaurus construction is the selection of descriptors by one or more subject specialists as they examine the slides for visual content. Diamond's work describes this process of descriptor selection as does the publication on SLIDEX, an automated indexing system developed at Howard University (1972; 1978). Such collections are usually filed by accession number and retrieved primarily by use of computer-generated print-outs arranged by descriptors, e.g., artist's name, geographical locations, medium or type of material, and so forth. The descriptor approach allows the user to retrieve slides without the constraints of a rigid classification schedule, which prescribes a linear approach to a single slide. For example, in most slide libraries, if a user wanted to examine all the slides of works in the Prado Museum, prior knowledge would be required of the art historical periods, countries, and individual artists represented in this museum's collections. If computer-generated indexes by keyword were available, one group of printouts would usually include a listing arranged by museum name, followed alphabetically by artist or title (if anonymous) of each image from the Prado

Museum that was in the slide collection. This direct retrieval approach to the individual slide is used with SLIDEX and with the automated classification and indexing system of the National Collection of Fine Arts Slide and Photograph Archive (1978; NCFA 1978). In addition to the use of standard printouts, a computer-produced catalog on microfilm (Computer Output Microfilm, or COM) can also be prepared. A COM catalog for art slides is used at the Royal Melbourne Institute of Technology (Sedgley and Merrett, 1974). At the Georgia Institute of Technology, where the Santa Cruz system is utilized, both standard printouts and a Computer Output Microfiche catalog are options for slide retrieval (LoPresti, 1973).

Several slide collections representing highly specialized subject areas or functions have benefitted from in-depth descriptor or keyword indexing (Ohlgren, 1977 and 1978; Ohrn, 1975; Rahn, 1975). *Illuminated Manuscripts: An Index to Selected Bodleian Library Color Reproductions* and *A Supplemental Index* provide access to 750 slide sets containing about 30,000 slides of over 1,100 manuscripts and books (1977; 1978). Compiled and edited by Dr. Thomas H. Ohlgren (Purdue University), these two volumes are computer-generated indexes to the Bodleian Library slide sets housed in the Medieval and Renaissance Photographic Archive at Purdue.

Eleven indexes have been produced to retrieve slides by the following categories: Bodleian negative references; slide set title; manuscript title; shelfmark; provenance; dates executed; languages of texts; artists or schools of illumination; authors of texts; types of manuscripts; and contents or subject matter. Rather than a keyword index to contents, this work is based on a "keyphrase" index so that the most significant term or descriptor is placed at the beginning of each phrase, thereby identifying the subject matter of a given illumination. For example, the phrase, "Expulsion of Adam and Eve from Paradise" is used to describe the subject contents of an illumination from a Book of Hours (1977, p. 449). With keyword indexing, each significant term in this phrase would be indexed, i.e., "Expulsion," "Adam," "Eve," and "Paradise"; however, keyphrase indexing permits indexing only by the first term, "Expulsion." Keyword indexing was considered for this project but was rejected because it "would have produced over 2,500 pages of data" (ibid., p. xxx).

According to Ohlgren (1978), keyword access is possible if the data base is used in an on-line mode via computer terminal. Ohlgren also considered use of the Santa Cruz classification scheme and ICONCLASS for the organization of the Bodleian contents. Developed at the University of Leiden (1973-1978), ICONCLASS is a classification system designed to enable the filing of art reproductions by their subject matter. Published in seven volumes, the ICONCLASS system is divided into nine main classes: 1 Supernatural; 2 Nature; 3 Man; 4 Society; 5 Abstracts; 6 History; 7 The Bible; 8 Sagas, Legends, and Tales; and 9 Classical Mythology and Antiquities. The seven volumes devoted to a description of the "system" are complemented by another seven volumes providing bibliographies prepared for each of the main classes and by three index volumes. Both the Santa Cruz and ICONCLASS systems are "designed primarily as shelving and retrieval schemes for *individual* photographic reproductions" and because the "Bodleian materials exist in roll and set form, they do not lend themselves to the shelving apparatus of these systems" or "to natural-language descriptions of iconographic content" (*Illuminated Manuscripts . . .* , 1978, p. xxiv). In his introduction to the second volume of the Bodleian index, Ohlgren also cited the following problems that compound the development of subject indexing in the arts:

> My task would have been greatly simplified if I had had access to a standard thesaurus of iconographic terms for Christian and secular iconography. Although several photographic archives, such as the Index to Christian Art at Princeton and the Warburg Institute in London, have developed their own classification schemes for internal use, no standard thesaurus of terms exists for general use. The Iconclass System, with its thousands of descriptors, could fill this need once the project is completed. . . . I recognized at once the seemingly impossible task of finding verbal equivalents for pictorial content. Verbal language is inadequate for expressing visual language. Words are only crude approximations for images. Ideally, any indexing and retrieval system should refer the user directly to the pictorial materials. The natural-language indexing terms and the verbal abstracts of the slide sets are simply intermediaries to get the user to the slides themselves. It is, of course, now technically feasible to use the computer to automatically retrieve coded microfiche cards containing pictorial images, and to display them on a remote terminal equipped with a cathode-ray tube. The user, instead of using a printed index and manually searching for the slides in the file, enters a search request to the data base and receives a list of keyphrases containing the search term as well as the numeric code for the fiche card and frame number. The user can then request the automated retrieval system to display the desired slide on the screen. Such an on-line system, however, is very expensive, and it would be difficult to justify the expenditure for an infrequently used slide file (ibid., 1978, pp. xxv-xxvi).

Additional information about the Bodleian project has been published in *Computers and the Humanities* and the *Transactions of the First International Conference on Automatic Processing of Art History Data and Documents* (Ohlgren, 1979 and 1978). (The Bodleian Library slides are available either on rental from Purdue University or by purchase as unmounted rolls of color microfilm from the Bodleian.)

Established in 1967, the African Studies Program Slide Archives at Indiana University has undergone a variety of changes to provide cultural, historical and contextual access to its collection. Fortunately, the evolution of the Slide Archives has been extensively documented by Steven Ohrn and William Siegmann (1973; 1974; 1975). This collection provides a useful case study on the selection of various indexing and organizational strategies to achieve maximum user access to a specialized subject archive. Initially, 27 subject categories were used to file and to locate images by subject. Filing within subject categories was by accession number. To facilitate access to individual slides within these subject headings, an index card file was maintained to record donors' names, ethnic groups, geographical locations, and subject matter. Although the 27 headings formed the basic organizational structure of the collection, additional subject terms were developed as needed within the index card file (ibid., 1973; 1974). By 1971, this system was no longer flexible enough for a growing collection of about 3,500 slides. At that time, parts of the Santa Cruz system were adapted and the original subject categories were either redefined or dropped. Forty major filing categories were developed, forming an organizational structure for new slides and allowing for similar slides to be grouped together. As in the first system, slides were filed numerically, as accessioned, within the major subject categories. *Africa, Its People and Their Culture History* was used as the authority for cultural or ethnic groups (Murdock, 1959).

Subject or descriptor access to slides was facilitated by use of the 6600 KWIC (Key Word In Context) computer program. A basic index card was prepared to be used for keypunching data, with five cards punched per index card. Although all data for each image was keypunched, only the title field was indexed for keyword access. The title field contained the following information: country; city, town or village; culture or ethnic group; subject categories, and source (Ohrn, 1974). Each index card included a description of the contents of an individual slide, and this information was included on the print-outs but not used for indexing purposes. Using the title field with KWIC indexing, each slide was listed on the print-outs by five to ten different terms (ibid., 1974).

From 1973 to 1977, the Archive used a manual retrieval system based upon the organization of slides by collection or source. This approach was based upon the fact that the majority of slides in the Archives represented "collections" taken by individual faculty, students, and/or amateur photographers who had shot their slides while doing fieldwork in Africa. Card catalog indexes were used to retrieve slides by geographical location, cultural or ethnic group, and by subject. After users had an opportunity to work with both a computer and a manual system, a decision was made to return to an automated system in 1978 (Lazar, 1979). The slides are still organized based upon the forty major filing categories or subject headings, and these are summarized in the following list (for descriptive information about these headings, see Ohrn, 1975, pp. 35-38):

AD	Domestic Animals	ME	Medical
AG	Agriculture	MI	Musical Instruments
AW	Wildlife	MK	Markets
BU	Business and Commerce	MR	Mineral Resources
CD	Civil Defense	MU	Manufacturing
CM	Communications Media	PA	Plastic Arts
CO	Construction	PO	Politics
DB	Death and Burial	RT	Research Techniques
DL	Domestic Life	RC	Recreation
ET	Ethnography	SC	Social Conditions
FI	Fishing	SL	Schools
FO	Forestry	SP	Settlement Patterns
FS	Festivals and Societies	TA	Traditional Architecture
GA	Graphic Arts	TC	Trades and Crafts
GC	Graphs and Charts	TP	Transportation
GE	Geography	TR	Traditional Religion
GO	Governmental Operations	UN	Universities
HG	Hunting and Gathering	UR	Urban
HI	History	XN	Christianity
IS	Islam	ZP	Maps

All cataloging data is being prepared on computer coding forms (COBOL), allowing five cards per slide for the following descriptor fields: 1) major subject category, 2) country, 3) town, 4) subject headings, 5) photographer or source code, 6) description of image (functions as a title), and 7) file code. The slides are filed and labeled using a "file code," which is formed by combining the major subject category abbreviation with an accession number. Computer-generated indexes can be produced for each of the descriptor fields. Figure 38 is a sample group of punch cards prepared for a single slide.

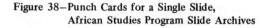

Figure 38–Punch Cards for a Single Slide,
African Studies Program Slide Archives

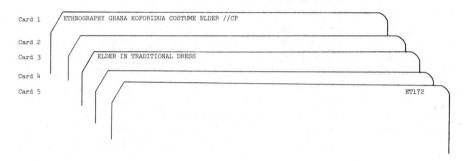

Card 1:   major subject category; country; town; subject headings ("Costume"
           and "Elder"); photographer or source code
Card 2:   blank (not needed for this slide)
Card 3:   description (or title)
Card 4:   blank (not needed for this slide)
Card 5:   ET for Ethnography; 172 for accession number

Even though all five cards were not needed for keypunching data for the slide
represented by Figure 38, blank cards would still be required for the card pack for
accurate computer processing. Only the file code (ET172) would be typed on the
slide label. At the University of Wisconsin–Madison, the African Studies Slide
Collection is organized by country, then by category or broad subject areas such
as those used at Indiana University. A published catalog listing the collection and
subject codes has been prepared for the Wisconsin collection ("Collection of 35mm
Slides," 1977). In addition, Chester Cowen (University of Oklahoma, Norman)
has prepared an alphabetical concordance of African tribal names keyed to geographical areas and related tribal clusters (Cowen, 1974; Mid-America College Art Association. Research Committee on Special Classification Systems for Visual Materials
of the Third World Peoples. *Report . . .* , 1976).

A keyword system for master paintings dating from 1430 to 1810 has been
developed for a private slide collection and published as *Rahn's Coloured Slide
Collection* (1975). This book includes a computer-generated list of 373 keywords
indexing about 5,000 slides by subject. Although a slide library may not have all
of the slides identified by Rahn's system, most collections would probably include
a representative sampling of these paintings; consequently, it would be possible to
retrieve slides by using his alphabetical indexes by artist, country, keyword (or
subject term), museum (including churches and private collections), and commercial slide producers.

The various options available for subject indexing of medical slide collections
are described in the book *The Management of 35mm Medical Slides*, by Alfred
Strohlein of the Media Resources Branch, National Medical Audiovisual Center,
Atlanta, Georgia (1975). One of the systems outlined by Strohlein is MeSH (Medical Subject Headings), which is composed of natural language terms developed for
the subject indexing of biomedical literature (ibid., pp. 17-20, 65-66). Used by
the National Library of Medicine (NLM), MeSH represents a national authority

for medical subject headings and is used for *Index Medicus* and for computer searching on MEDLINE terminals that are part of the national bibliographic data base established by NLM. The use of MeSH would combine subject access both to print and nonprint media.

According to a report in the *Bowker Annual of Library and Book Trade Information*, NLM has established a new data base with audiovisuals on-line, AVLINE, using a thesaurus of medical subject headings (1976, pp. 33-34). Included in AVLINE are biomedical films, videotapes, slide packages, and other nonprint materials. Using MeSH to retrieve slides has been cited in the literature for a number of medical slide collections: Cleveland Health Sciences Library (Moulton and Wood, 1975), Eccles Health Services Library (Bogen, 1976), the University of Missouri—Kansas City School of Medicine (Raymond and Algermissen, 1976), and the University of Connecticut Health Center Library (Brantz and Forsman, 1977).

Other commonly used systems of standardized terms include *Standard Nomenclature of Diseases and Operations, Current Medical Information and Terminology, Systematized Nomenclature of Pathology* and *International Classification of Diseases*. At the University of California at San Diego Medical School, the *Standard Nomenclature of Diseases and Operations* is used to retrieve images stored on aperture cards, which form a master slide file from which duplicate slides are made for faculty use. In addition, some institutions may develop their own subject headings for access to slide collections, e.g., the C-E Refractories' Research and Development Library at Valley Forge, Pennsylvania (Clawson and Rankowski, 1978) and the Stellenbosch University Medical Library (Visser, 1977). Ideally, when nationally recognized standards exist, these should receive first priority for the subject indexing of library collections and should be consistently applied both to print and nonprint collections.

Author-Title Catalog and Authority File

If a collection of slides is biographical, a standard author catalog is appropriate, using entry format consistent with the second edition of the *Anglo-American Cataloguing Rules* (1978). If the collection includes art, the author catalog would be an artist catalog—painter, sculptor, architect, craftsman, and so forth—leading the user to materials by the same artist under a uniform name, whether the art form or medium is of one type or a variety of types. For collections arranged by historical period or by medium, this catalog would provide invaluable access to all of the works by one artist. This is the same function that the author catalog provides for books.

Sets of slides can be assigned a title main entry card with added entry artist cards if appropriate. Locating slides solely by title, however, should be avoided and instead, combined with some form of subject, author, or artist catalog to insure a variety of access keys to an individual item or set of slides. The various manuals mentioned thus far provide adequate information on this catalog form and should be consulted if a title main entry approach to slides is used.

If the collection is small or if a consolidation of catalogs is desirable, the authority file can be combined with the author or artist catalog. The authority file gives the accepted format of an author's or artist's name, which will be used consistently throughout a single collection. Cross references are included for pseudonyms and for complicated name forms. For artists and architects, standard authorities include the following sources:

> *American Architects Directory.* New York: Bowker, 1955-62, 1970.
> *Art Design Photo.* Teaneck, New Jersey: Somerset House, 1972- .
> *Art Index.* New York: H. W. Wilson, 1930- .
> *ARTbibliographies MODERN.* Santa Barbara, California: American Bibliographical Center-Clio Press, 1969- .
> Bénézit, Emmanuel. *Dictionnaire critique et documentaire des peintres, sculpteurs, dessinateurs, et graveurs.* rev. and enl. ed. Paris: Librairie Gruend, 1976.
> Bryan, Michael. *Bryan's Dictionary of Painters and Engravers.* 1905, reprint ed., New York: Kennikat Press, 1971.
> *Catalog of the Avery Memorial Architectural Library of Columbia University.* 2nd ed. Boston: G. K. Hall, 1968. Supplements: 1972, 1976, and 1977.
> *Catalog of the Library of the Museum of Modern Art.* Boston: G. K. Hall, 1976.
> *Catalogue of the Harvard University Fine Arts Library. The Fogg Art Museum.* Boston: G. K. Hall, 1971. Supplement: 1976.
> *Contemporary Artists.* Edited by Colin Naylor and Genesis P-Orridge. London: St. James Press, 1977.
> Fletcher, Sir Bannister Flight. *A History of Architecture on the Comparative Method, for Students, Craftsmen, and Amateurs . . . .* 16th ed. London: Batsford, 1954.
> *Library Catalog of the Metropolitan Museum of Art.* Boston: G. K. Hall, 1960. Supplements: 1962, 1965, 1968, 1970, 1973, 1975, and 1977.
> *National Art Library Catalogue. Victoria and Albert Museum.* Boston: G. K. Hall, 1972.
> New York City, The Research Libraries, New York Public Library. *Dictionary Catalog of the Art and Architecture Division.* Boston: G. K. Hall, 1975. Supplement: *Bibliographic Guide to Art and Architecture,* 1975- .
> *RILA: Répertoire international de la littérature de l'art.* Williamstown, Massachusetts: Sterling and Francine Clark Art Institute, 1975- .
> Thieme, Ulrich, and Felix Becker. *Allgemeines Lexikon der bildenden Kuenstler von der antike bis zur Gegenwart.* Leipzig: E. A. Seeman, 1908-1954.
> Vollmer, Hans. *Allgemeines Lexikon der bildenden Kuenstler des XX. Jahrhunderts.* Leipzig: E. A. Seeman, 1953-1962.

For additional dictionary and encyclopedia authorities, consult the *Guide to Reference Books*, by Eugene Sheehy (1976), and *American Reference Books Annual*, edited by Bohdan S. Wynar (1970-), for general materials. Consult the following for art sources: *Guide to Art Reference Books*, by Mary Chamberlain (1959); *Fine Arts: A Bibliographic Guide*, 2nd ed., by Donald L. Ehresmann (1979); *Art Research Methods and Resources*, by Lois Swan Jones (1978); and *Guide to Basic Information Sources in the Visual Arts*, by Gerd Muehsam (1978).

The above-mentioned German work by Thieme and Becker is the most comprehensive dictionary of artists available. This basic source is supplemented and updated by Vollmer. Neither of these volumes, however, is particularly useful for contemporary artists. The *Art Index* or the Museum of Modern Art library catalog are valuable sources on contemporary artists. Library catalogs are helpful for name or entry verification; those of the Bibliothèque Nationale, the British Museum, and others cited above should be used when necessary. When the exact form of a name cannot be verified in such sources, strict adherence to the *Anglo-American Cataloguing Rules* (1978) is recommended.

When possible, the authority file card should, in addition to the standard name entry, provide birth and death dates, nationality, and the source of the name as used. Cross reference cards would also appear in this file. The mobility of the contemporary artist has posed nationality attribution problems for many collections. As a consequence, some collections file all artists in one alphabet without country divisions, while others follow the place of birth as the authority, even though the legal nationality of an artist may have changed. Included in the Santa Cruz system is an authority for approximately 4,000 artists that gives birth dates, Cutter numbers, and nationalities. This list is based upon the strict use of place of birth for all nationality attributions.

The major drawback to having the single integrated nationality arrangement for all artists is the size and awkwardness associated with using it. Another disadvantage of the integrated artist file is the fact that distinctions are not made with regard to period or chronology. It further divorces the user from a subject approach to the catalog because one cannot locate material by nationality or by historical alignment. Individuals who would normally be interested only in Renaissance slides would conflict with the user desiring to use only nineteenth and twentieth century materials. Moreover, unless a refined subject approach is available, the non-specialist would have a great deal of difficulty finding, for example, the religious art that dominated during the Renaissance. Historical or nationality divisions within the files yield more readily to browsing. For collections basing their system upon one similar to the Santa Cruz classification, where nationality divisions are integral to the system, an authority file is mandatory.

The authority file functions to prevent the entry of an artist or author under different name forms or nationalities in the files, which could cause dispersion of that person's works throughout the files. The following is a complete set of authority cards for a single artist including cross references:

Figure 39—Main Authority Card (3x5-inches)

```
Toeput, Lodewyk                      Netherlands

Also called:  Lodovico Pozzo da Treviso
              Lodovico Fiammingo; or
              Pozzoserrato


Born:  Antwerp, c.1550
Died:  Treviso, between 8/14/1603 and 11/9/1605


Thieme-Becker
```

Figure 40—Cross Reference Cards (3x5-inches)

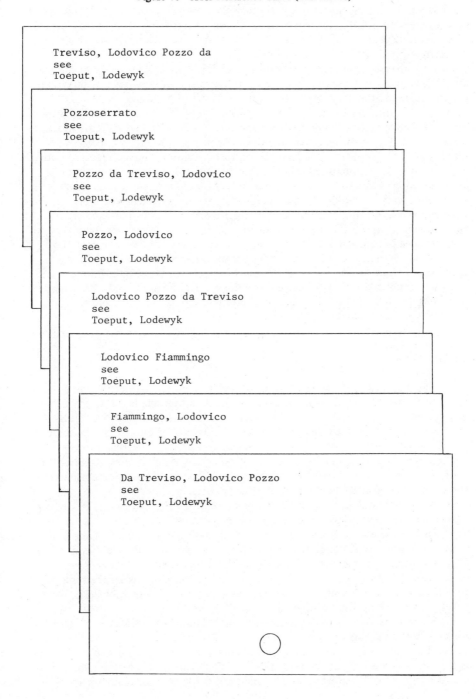

The use of authority files is relatively common in slide libraries. Among the many academic and museum collections that maintain authority files for painters, sculptors, architects or for all of these are the following institutions: Art Institute of Chicago; Elmhurst College, Illinois; Cleveland Museum of Art; Howard University; Indiana University; Rhode Island School of Design; School of Visual Arts, New York; Stanford University; University of California at Los Angeles; University of Illinois; and Yale University. Princeton and the State University of New York at Binghamton maintain additional authority files for the names of buildings.

The Sterling and Francine Clark Art Institute Slide Library shares the authority cards used for *RILA: Répertoire international de la littérature de l'art*, which is prepared at the Institute. Consequently, their files also include some decorative artists and photographers, in addition to painters, sculptors and architects. Another slide library that maintains extensive authority files is that at the Winterthur Museum, which has standard artist and architect files plus those for base-metal and pewter workers, building names, graphic artists, lighting manufacturers, photographers, and silversmiths. Computer-generated authority files are used at Howard University for the following categories: geographic locations; art historical periods; type of medium or subject category; artist/architect/designer; material; name of object, date, graphic representation; source; areas and details of images; and form of visual aid (SLIDEX, 1978, pp. 14-26). Other collections having computer-produced authority files include the Georgia Institute of Technology, the National Collection of Fine Arts Slide and Photograph Archive, and the University of California at Santa Cruz.

Shelflist Catalog

The majority of the slide libraries studied have either an interfiled or a separate shelflist. The California Institute of the Arts, Georgia Institute of Technology, the National Collection of Fine Arts, the University of California at Santa Cruz, and the U.S. Military Academy at West Point have machine-printed shelflists. As the use of computer indexing increases, the availability of shelflist print-outs for holdings should become relatively common among slide libraries. An inventory control system such as the shelflist is an invaluable aid for slide collections serving the same function as that provided for print libraries.

An interfiled shelflist refers to the placement of a shelflist card in front (the most common method) or behind each slide in a drawer storage file. This card is approximately the same size as the slide (2x2-inches) and has a copy of the slide label information typed directly upon the card. For example, the University of Illinois at Chicago Circle has an interfiled shelflist that is made by typing carbons of all labels (Figures 41 and 42). The sheets used for the carbons are the same label sheets used for the slides and are self-adhesive, so the identical label information typed on a label can be adhered to a shelflist card.

Some collections include additional source data on the shelflist card, although frequently the shelflist and slide label are the same. It is not immediately apparent on the University of Illinois at Chicago Circle label or shelflist card, but source data is indicated by the "599a2" code on the third line. This code refers to a job order number and the year during which this slide was made. As each slide is made, it is

Figure 41–Slide with Label   **Figure 42–Shelflist Card**

entered on a job order sheet, which has a discrete number. These sheets are kept in loose-leaf notebooks as both source and accession records.

An interfiled shelflist has both advantages and disadvantages. With the removal of a slide from the file that has an interfiled shelflist card for each slide, the staff and users immediately know that a particular slide is in the permanent collection but has been temporarily removed. With the separate shelflist, it is first necessary to check an auxiliary record to determine the existence of a given item within the collection. Circulation controls are also possible with an interfiled shelflist, and these will be discussed in the section on this topic in this chapter. The shelflist card also functions as a filing aid, making more precise the exact location which the slide must be correctly re-filed. Where group filing of slides is maintained without call number order, an individual slide will not have a discrete filing location except as part of a group of slides. The major disadvantage is the added time it takes to remove slides individually and to re-file them individually rather than by groups. Moreover, the removal of these cards by the patron may also present problems that can be overcome by using a rod within the drawers similar to standard card catalog drawer rods, with the slides resting above the rods. For example, if a standard card catalog, such as the Library Bureau catalog, is used for slide filing, a diagram for the internal design of the drawer might look like Diagram 1 (courtesy of the Winterthur Museum, Delaware; see page 128). Blocks a, b, c, d, and e have been inserted into a standard card file in order to accommodate slides, shelflist cards, and rods.

Various institutions that have interfiled shelflists do not use rods. Some of these include the following: Cincinnati Art Museum, the National Collection of Fine Arts, Syracuse University, University of Louisville, University of Michigan, University of New Mexico, Vassar College, and the Walker Art Center. The use of rods or the need for rods will depend upon each institution's ability and desire to use this system. (See Chapter 6 for further information on storage systems.)

Diagram 1—Cross-section of drawer showing shelflist cards, slide position, and location for drawer rods (designed by the Winterthur Museum, Delaware).

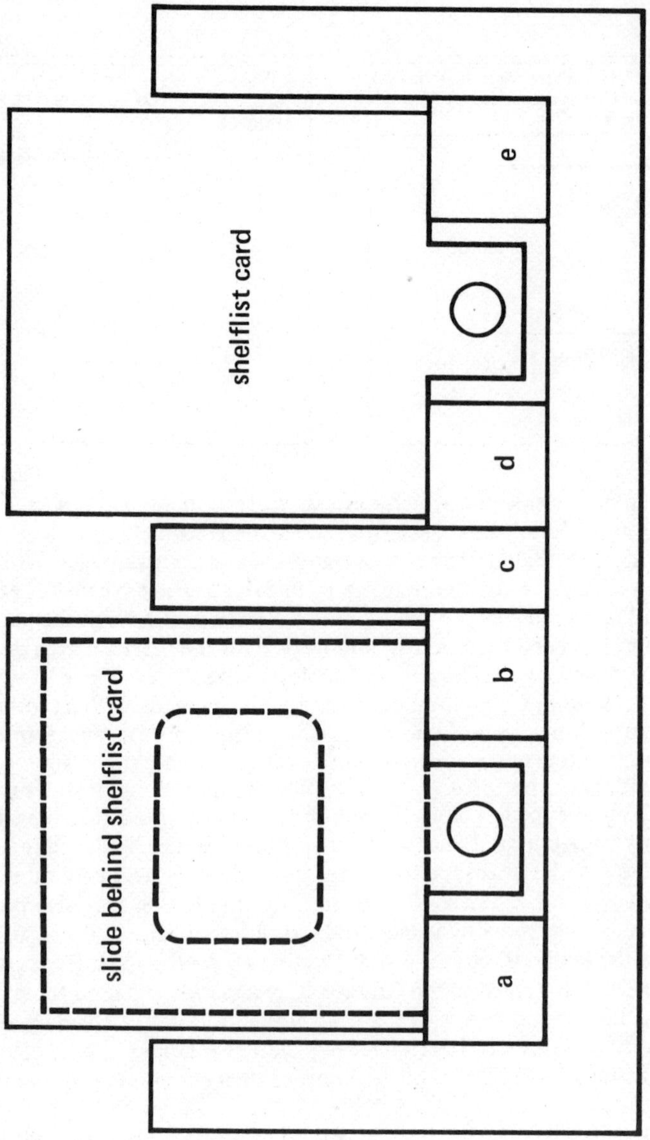

A separate shelflist is basically the same as a standard book shelflist, merely duplicating the shelf or file location for each item in card form. Frequently, when separate shelflists are used (standard library-size cards are used), additional information such as the type of film, size of slide, source, and whether or not it is the duplicate of another slide already in the collection is noted. The size of the interfiled shelflist card will somewhat restrict the amount of information that can be given supplementary to the label data in the format of the card. The following format is recommended for shelflist cards that are interfiled:

Figure 43–Interfiled Shelflist Card Format

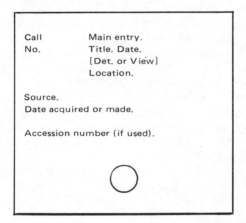

The main entry could be an artist, author, title, or a word or phrase that describes the content of the slide. "Detail" or "View" are bracketed because neither would appear on every shelflist card.

A shelflist filed apart from the slide file does not function as an immediate circulation aid, but it can still be used to provide information on the slide library's holdings in a given area or in general. If consolidation of files is desired, however, an integrated or interfiled shelflist can be useful in a collection not composed solely of slide sets. Slides filed by sets should have a separate shelflist.

Graphic Card Catalog

Library card catalogs typically represent print-based systems of documentation, reflecting the book format commonly associated with this tool. As visual documents, slides are capable of retrieval both by verbal description and by graphic representation. Distinctions between verbal and visual content and between print and pictorial images have been explored in the context of achieving maximum access to slides (Simons and Tansey, 1970; pp. 2-7; Freudenthal, 1974, pp. 114-15; Simons, 1972; Lewis, 1974 and 1976; and Ohrn, 1975). While the card catalog may meet the needs of the verbally literate, it is not usually associated with the relatively recent requirements for visual literacy (Dondis, 1973; Kepes, 1965).

As is apparent from the various efforts described in the preceding pages, access to the visual content of slides poses many problems that do not readily yield simple solutions; however, graphic card catalogs may provide alternatives to indexing systems based solely on a verbal mode of communication.

The idea of a catalog card having a graphic representation on it is not a new idea. A contact print catalog was developed for the Harvard University lantern slide collection established in the 1920s. More recently, the new technologies of color photography and xerography have been used to produce graphic card catalogs to index visual media. Boris Kuvshinoff (Applied Physics Laboratory, Johns Hopkins University) and Elizabeth Lewis (formerly at the U.S. Military Academy Library) prepared papers for *American Documentation* on the development of graphic card catalogs produced on keypunch cards and capable of both manual and computer retrieval (1967; 1969). Kuvshinoff discussed the use of the diazo process, and xerography (ibid., 1969).

Committed to the feasibility and utility of visual indexing of slides, Lewis also prepared a dissertation at Columbia University entitled "A Cost Study of Library Color Microimage Storage and Retrieval: Visual Indexing in Microfiche, Super-8 and Videotape" (1974). The five indexing methods studied by Lewis included three visual indexes (using color microfiche, Super-8 film, and videotape) and two verbal indexes (using a conventional card catalog and a permuted computer printed list). In a summary of her thesis published in *Special Libraries*, she noted that "it was a shock when the self-timed test results showed among all sets of users an overwhelming preference for the computer list by itself among the five methods, although the card catalog did come in a sorry last, as expected" (1976, p. 524). Working with a rather small and limited user group, Lewis indicated that different responses might have resulted if her sample structure had been increased (ibid., p. 526). The quality of the images used for visual indexing may also have affected her thesis conclusions.

Combining reasonable costs and high quality photographic reproduction are not often possible (Kuvshinoff, 1967; Lewis, 1969). However, a cost-effective system seems to have been developed for the C-E Refractories Research and Development Library, Valley Forge, Pennsylvania (Clawson and Rankowski, 1978). Using the color Xerox 6500 and self-adhesive paper made for photocopying, slides can be duplicated with the resulting image affixed to a catalog card. Figure 44 is a sample of a card prepared with this method. Although reproduced here in black and white, the image on the original card is in color. A slide adapter has been designed to improve the use of the Xerox 6500 color copier (Mailloux and Bollman, 1977).

Other collections that have a graphic card catalog include the Time, Inc., Picture Collection and the World Bank Photo Library. For the Time collection, a Recordak Model D camera is used to reduce an 8x10-inch print and its identifying information and print both on a 3x5-inch catalog card. The World Bank Photo Library uses color Xerox to produce a visual shelflist of their slide collection (World Bank Photo Library, 1977). At twenty slides per page, all of their slides are copied on 8½x11-inch sheets, including all labeling information. The sheets are then placed in plastic sleeves that are inserted into notebooks. Users can browse through these Xerox notebooks, which are arranged in the same order as the slides and function as modified card catalogs. The immediate advantage of this system is that the

Figure 44–Graphic Catalog Card, C-E Refractories (3x5-inches)

```
        1.  FIRECLAY      2.  MICROSTRUCTURES




MICRO    Fireclay brick. [Slide] / C-E
F5       Refractories, Research and
Fr. 2    Development Laboratory. --
M137     Valley Forge : The Laboratory.
           1 slide : col. ; 2 x 2 in.
           Slide as depicted on main entry
         under title. (M137)
```

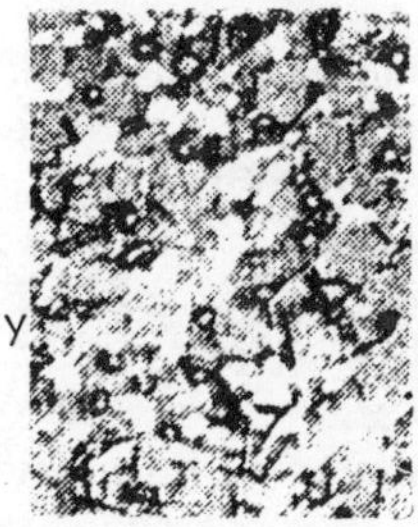

(Card courtesy of Catherine Clawson, C-E Refractories)

Xerox pages can be viewed without projection or additional illumination which is necessary for the slides.

Access to color Xerox is still quite limited and the author is only aware of two academic slide libraries that have investigated its application for preparing graphic card catalogs—the College of Architecture at the University of Houston, and the Fine Arts Department at the University of Rochester slide collections. Certainly, as this new technology becomes more common, it will yield many useful applications for visual indexing.

Summary

Slides may be considered expendable because of their low production and purchase costs and may not, according to some, merit the creation of a two or three-phase card catalog system. However, if the individual slide or set of slides is misplaced, and there is a convenient and complete record of that item or set within the library, it can be replaced and again be made available to the user. The replacement form may be in black and white rather than in color, or in 35mm rather than 3¼x4-inches, or a duplicate rather than an original slide, but these are minor points of differentiation. What is important is insuring the highest possible level of use and accessibility of information whether it is recorded orally, printed, or visualized as an image. Accomplishing this function efficiently is impossible without the use of the catalogs and indexing techniques described.

ACQUISITION RECORDS

The majority of the slide libraries studied utilize acquisition records. Acquisition records document the date of acquisition, the vendor or source of the slide, and basic entry information (which identifies the specific slide acquired), and a dealer code number or a reference to a book from which the slide was made. These records may be of a temporary nature or of a permanent one depending upon how they are used. For some collections, the acquisition or source records and the order forms are the same. If the majority of slides are being made from books, it is not unusual for the request form to be kept as a permanent record of all slides made with the slides having a code that refers back to its original order sheet. For slides commercially purchased, standard institutional order forms are usually utilized, and these may or may not provide the permanent record for slides purchased.

One of the most important aspects of the acquisition record is the notation of the vendor or source for each slide. This is critical for the replacement of slides and for supplementing the collection with similar types of material from a given source that has proven useful. A majority of slides made in academic institutions are copied directly from book plates, so an acquisition or source record can function as a bibliographic aid, referring a user to specific texts relating to the slide image. Frequently, the entire record of the source is included on the slide label, e.g., Yale University (see Chapter 3, Figure 27, page 98), so that it is not necessary to refer to a supplementary acquisition file to find this information. It is, however, rather time-consuming to include complete bibliographic citations or source data on each slide label, so some abbreviation or code may be more desirable. At the same time, a complete reference to the original source should be maintained in some form. The author has developed the following form, which is in use at Indiana University at the present time:

Figure 45–Acquisition or Source Record Format (3x5 or 4x6-inches)

```
    Author or vendor name.          Name of requester.
    Date acquired.                  Call number or book owner.
                                    [leave blank if vendor]

    Title of book.  Imprint [place, publisher, date].  [OR]
    Name and date of catalog.  Street address.  City.  State.
    Zip code.

    Plates, figures, or pages copied listed numerically.  [OR]
    Vendor number for each slide [if unavailable, the page and
    item number from vendor's catalog].
```

Figure 46—Sample from Book. Acquisition Card (3x5 or 4x6-inches)

```
Murdock, George Peter.              Professor R. Sieber.
12/1870.                           Personal Copy.

Africa:  Its Peoples and Their Culture.  New York:  McGraw-Hill,
1959.

Page (black and white):   353
```

The code on the slide label referring to this card (last line on label): 353.Murdock.12/1870.

The cards would be arranged alphabetically by author or vendor name; each slide would have a discrete code having the plate, page, or figure number first; author or vendor name second; and date of acquisition third. The year is abbreviated, using only the last two digits so that the slide (Figure 46, above) was made on December 18, 1970.

Figure 47—Sample from Vendor. Acquisition Card (3x5 or 4x6-inches)

```
Ward's.                            Mr. J. Whitehead.
7/1369.

Ward's Color Slides Identification List.  "Early Embryology
of the Frog (Rana Pipiens)."  Ward's Natural Science
Establishment, Inc.  P.O. Box 1712.  Rochester, New York.
14603.

171 W 1000 (Set of eight slides).  171 W 1011 - 171 W 1018.
```

The code on the slide label referring to this card (last line on label): 171 W 1011.Ward's. 7/1369.

The code 171 W 1011 (Figure 47, above) refers to the first slide's number in this set purchased from Ward's, July 13, 1969. For convenience, vendor and book sources should be interfiled. Either a 3x5-inch or 4x6-inch card is suitable for recording acquisition data.

There are numerous advantages to using this particular type of record as opposed to sheet, accession, or log books. First, the information is in a convenient format that demands a minimum of space and can be conveniently placed in standard-sized cabinets, while sheet records that may be kept in loose-leaf binders or in accession books become bulky and awkward to handle as they are amassed. In addition, the staff member or patron who needs to know the extent of purchases from a specific source or the number of plates copied from a book can go directly to the acquisition card, filed according to the author or vendor's name, without consulting the slide files. Unless an index to the accession or sheet records is kept, this is not possible. For inventory or accession records on an annual basis, the new acquisition cards for each year may be kept separate for that year, inventoried at the end according to the number of slides acquired, and then interfiled with the main file; or, as the new cards are added to the file, a note could be made of the number of slides acquired and then totaled at the end of the year. An accession card file would serve a similar purpose, although again, it would not integrate all slides being acquired from a given source.

For slides being added to the original source card at a later time, the new date would be placed after the original date on the second line, and a slash would be placed between the original page numbers and the second group or number acquired on the second date (Figure 48). If necessary, the notation of the person requesting slides could be continued on the reverse of the card. For the vendor card, a new card would be made since all of the slides in the particular set illustrated were purchased. More than one card for a single vendor would be arranged in date order, with the most recent acquisition card first.

Figure 48–Additions to Original Book Acquisition Card (3x5 or 4x6-inches)

```
Murdock, George Peter.            Professor R. Sieber. H. Smith
12/1870. 1/1371.                  Personal Copy. DT14.M97.

Africa:  Its Peoples and Their Culture.  New York:  McGraw-Hill,
1959.

Page (black and white):  353; / 272; 343
```

The code on the slide referring to this card's addition (last line on label): 272.Murdock. 1/1371.

Another possible method for keeping acquisition records is to type the source or acquisition data directly on the interfiled shelflist card or on a separate shelflist card. Unfortunately, the concept of maintaining an acquisition record arranged by the original source or vendor has not been commonly practiced in most academic collections, because the shelflist or accession record sheets have been the standard location for this information. As is apparent from the system suggested, however, such data need not be restricted to one location; e.g., a code may be typed on the label, or shelflist card, but it should be organized in the manner in which it will be needed, which is according to the name of the source.

Institutions recording their acquisition or source data directly upon the slide label include the following: Emory University, Georgia; San Jose State College; University of California at Berkeley; and the University of Florida. The following indicate source data on separate shelflist cards: Harvard University, University of Illinois, University of Oregon, and the University of Pennsylvania. Source data is indicated on interfiled shelflist cards by Toledo Museum of Art, University of Louisville, and the University of Michigan. Harvard University also provides abbreviated source data on the slide labels. Accession or log books are used at the following institutions: Art Institute of Chicago; Cleveland Museum of Art; Miami University, Ohio; Smith College; University of Chicago; University of Illinois at Chicago Circle; University of Iowa; University of New Mexico; University of North Carolina; University of Washington; and Wellesley College.

Order or acquisition records function for a slide library in the same manner as for book libraries and depend upon institutional formats in use at the time the order is placed. Book libraries like slide libraries also maintain vendor catalogs and, for a limited time, the original copies of order forms. These are used to check prices or identify vendors for the original purchases. In addition, if there are questions regarding the misplacement of an item when it is in the processing stage, the original order slip can be used to verify purchase. These same functions are provided by order or acquisition forms for slides ordered commercially and for those made from books. Indigenous, however, to the slide library—and to many photograph collections—where material frequently is made from book plates, is the need for bibliographic reference to the corresponding text and to the original book plate. The large number of commercial slide dealers specializing in specific topics also makes it advantageous to have direct reference to these sources. A formal acquisition record designed to perform this function is mandatory for the efficient use, replacement, and growth of the slide library in any type of institution.

CIRCULATION RECORDS

Over 80% of the academic collections in the United States and the majority of museums use some form of circulation control. The most common circulation system used is based on charge sheets on which a patron lists each slide individually, giving either a full subject description, call numbers, accession numbers, or an alphabetical code combined with descriptive data. These sheets generally require information similar to that written on standard book charge forms.

Standard 8½x11-inch pages are used rather than cards for charge sheets because an individual may charge out twenty or more slides at a single time. By using a sheet of a size corresponding to the number of entries or slides charged at one time, it is possible to determine all material charged to a single patron without checking an entire charge file. With this system, priority is placed on the name of the individual rather than on the item removed, as would be the case with book libraries. Consequently, it is necessary to know the name of the borrower before specific items can be traced for location. An example of the basic format of such a sheet is illustrated in Diagram 2.

The utilization of charge sheets for circulation control has obvious disadvantages, although the type of collection for which it is most commonly used must be considered if criticism of the method is to be valid. It functions fairly efficiently for those collections composed of one subject that is studied by a limited number of faculty members within the subject orientation of the collection. In the majority of art departments or schools where this system is applied, most users work according to specific areas of art history study, thereby automatically classifying their charged material by their area of specialization. For example, the medieval history professor would probably have the major portion of the Romanesque and Gothic architecture slides charged from the files. In order to locate specific slides in circulation, that person's charge sheet could be checked. As soon as a collection becomes widely used, however, this system collapses unless it is accompanied by a subject index to the slides charged out to each patron. Needless to say, this becomes a rather complicated and time-consuming effort, necessitating additional staff time to maintain such an index. In fact, when the charge sheet type of circulation control reaches or is beginning to reach the point when it is not feasible, an alternative method should be selected. The charge sheet method of circulation control is

Diagram 2—Slide Library Charge Sheet.

SLIDE LIBRARY CHARGE SHEET

Name: _____ Title: _____

Address: _____ Phone: _____

No. of 2″ x 2″ slides: _____   Date Charged: _____

No. of 3¼″ x 4″ slides: _____   Date Due: _____

Call No. or Access. No. or Abbreviated Code.	Artist or Subject.	Title.

commonly used by academic institutions for two reasons: it allows adequate space for recording information on individual slides, and most academic collections receive use by a limited number of subject specialists in a single discipline. This pattern is changing as academic collections become more in demand by other users.

For many academic collections, the application of rigid circulation controls is difficult because faculty use patterns may necessitate borrowing large numbers of slides at a single time. Such heavy use may prohibit the slide librarian from imposing complicated charging procedures for individual slides. Consequently, the faculty or staff may not be using the charge sheet method but a simpler charging process or, in some instances, none at all. The latter practice may apply when the collection and number of users is quite small, e.g., fewer than five users and fewer than 5,000 slides.

An example of a relatively simple method of circulation control is operative at the University of Michigan, where all of the faculty keep their slides in the slide library in trays or cases until they are removed for class presentation. Thus, all slides remain in the slide library unless they are in use, and all are available to all patrons, who may remove them temporarily. At Michigan, these trays or cases are kept on standard storage shelves in the workroom. As would be apparent, keeping all slides separated in lecture order ready for immediate use requires adequate space allotted for this function, based upon the total number of users or potential users of the slide library. This system works relatively well for users making slide presentations in the same building as the slide facility, but it presents transportation problems for individuals who may need their slides for a presentation outside the immediate building or institution. Again, as soon as slides are being used by a large number or individuals in various teaching stations and buildings, this procedure may become inadequate.

If the collection has been properly organized from its inception, then an interfiled shelflist has been developed. The interfiled shelflist can be an invaluable aid to circulation control. For collections used by a relatively constant group of patrons, each user is assigned color-coded cards or white cards with a person's name printed across the top of each card. A chart of names or of color codes could be posted in the slide library for everyone's use. As each patron removes a slide, a color card or card that identifies the user is placed in the slide's slot. These circulation cards should be ¼-inch to ½-inch higher than the interfiled shelflist cards. The circulation cards are visible above the interfiled shelflist cards and immediately show which slides have been removed from the file. The following illustrates how these cards would appear in the file:

Figure 49–Interfiled Circulation Cards

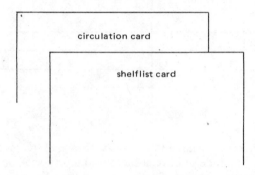

This method also informs the staff or user who has removed the slide. How is the irregular user handled? A single color-coded card may identify all outside (outside the immediate department) or irregular users, who then fill out a charge card or sheet indicating the total number of slides removed. Individual identification of each slide is not necessary, because each has already been identified within the slide file by the color card. The major disadvantage of this system is the need for a dual circulation system for inter-departmental or regular users and extra-departmental or irregular users. Another alternative available to the irregular user would involve signing each card that is inserted to replace each slide removed. That person's name would then refer to a charge card indicating the total number of slides charged, the person's address, and phone number. This latter method is a more precise means of distinguishing exactly which irregular user has charged out slides. In addition, the process of refiling slides is also simplified. The exact location of each missing slide is flagged by the circulation card.

How do large museums handle circulation control? Many, including the Boston Museum of Fine Arts, the Cleveland Museum of Art, and the St. Louis Art Museum use charge sheets or cards for circulation records. These are filed alphabetically by the name of the patron.

In the past, the Art Institute of Chicago and the Metropolitan Museum of Art used a Recordak microfilmer, which prepared microfilm copies of all slides that were charged out. At the present time, both these collections use photocopy machines to record loans. As noted by the staff at the Metropolitan Museum of Art:

An improvement over the Recordak microfilm method is the use of a flat bed photo-copy machine. This is recommended by The Metropolitan Museum of Art Slide Library because it provides an instant image of all the information on the slide labels. The Metropolitan Museum Slide Library requires its staff borrowers to attach the photocopy to the usual charge sheet which bears name, department, place and date of use, subject of lecture, number of slides and date of loan. Although more expensive than microfilm-ing, the photocopy method is more useful, and it provides the lecturers with complete records of the slides shown (Nolan, 1978).

The Art Institute of Chicago Slide Department has not been open to the public since 1973, but the advantages of using a Xerox machine for recording loans even for limited in-house use has also made this system their choice for circulation records. The top labels for forty to fifty slides or twenty complete slides can be duplicated all at one time on a single 8½x11-inch sheet of paper. By making two copies of each sheet, the lecturer can also have a complete list of slides used for a particular presentation. Such a list provides both a convenient record for immediate use and a reference source for future lectures, when these same slides may be needed again. Northern Illinois University is also using this system for faculty slide charges.

At the Evergreen State College Library, which has a computerized circulation system, slides are checked out in the same manner as books, with all media recorded both in manual keypunch card files and on computer print-outs. When a standard-ized classification and indexing system is used, slides (and especially slide sets) also offer possibilities for interlibrary loan arrangements, because recording loan charges represents a relatively simple process similar to that for books. For example, the Newark Public Library, which has about 15,000 slides classified by the Dewey sys-tem, participates in interlibrary loan through their state library network.

If slides are to be charged out in sets, standard book cards can be used and interfiled in the circulation file for books. Interfiling of all media and book circula-tion records, however, is based on the assumption that all materials have been classi-fied according to the same system. If this is not the case, separate files should be maintained and labeled so that there is no confusion regarding each file's function. Charging by slide set refers only to those slides that have been classified as a set. Sets of slides or individual slides that have been assigned discrete classification num-bers or an alphabetical code system combined with numbers such as the Dewey, Library of Congress, or Santa Cruz schedules can be charged on standard library charge cards and filed according to notation system used. Figure 50 (see page 140) is an example of a library charge card used for charging out a slide classified accord-ing to the Santa Cruz system.

Using a circulation system that readily conforms to standard library proce-dures and materials is a convenient method if the collection has been developed to adapt to this type of circulation pattern. Most collections, however, do not have a classification system that relies on the use of discrete call numbers for each slide, or they use an accession number that could also be used as a charge number. The disadvantages of maintaining only a file according to the name of the patron who has charged out the slides have already been noted. The dual system of circulation control, using an interfiled shelflist charge or circulation card and a charge card filed alphabetically by the name of the patron, is certainly the most efficient method for a unitary image collection. The charge card used could be a standard library card. The microfilm record, although an efficient method for maintaining

Figure 50—Charge Card

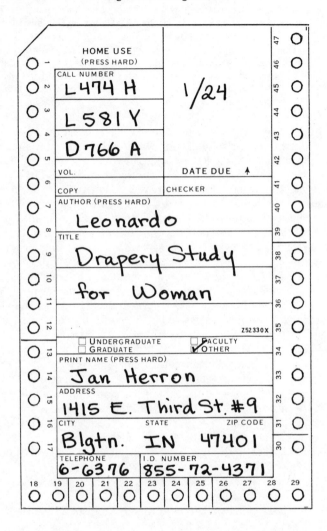

accurate circulation records, would be awkward for patrons and staff to use on a regular basis in order to identify individual slides that have been charged out.

Whether the slide library is an independent one developed for the use of a single academic department, for the use of more than one department or school, for the use of a museum curatorial staff, for the public, or for an instructional materials center designed for multi-disciplinary use, the user patterns will affect the type of circulation system selected. The circulation system chosen for a given institution can be flexible, depending upon the function of the collection, but it should be as consistent as possible for all users in order to avoid confusion. A combination interfiled shelflist and charge card system is recommended for academic collections having inter- and extra-departmental use. A standard library charge card should be used by collections of classified slide sets. For a unitary image collection of slides in a museum, public library or school, either the combination interfiled shelflist and charge card system, a photocopying system, or a standard library charge card system with each slide charged out individually (one per card) can be used.

SUMMARY

Standard library tools and techniques should be utilized in the slide library as frequently as possible. This basic principle will decrease arbitrary standards and procedures, will allow for the logical expansion of the collection, and will provide consistency and standardization in the use of all library materials. Most standard library procedures and tools have already benefitted from a great deal of reform and revision. If such procedures or tools can be directly adopted by the slide library with a minimal amount of change, then the general maintenance and organization of the collection should benefit by the adoption process.

REFERENCES

Anglo-American Cataloguing Rules. 1978. Second edition. Prepared by the American Library Association, the British Library, the Canadian Committee on Cataloguing, the Library Association, and the Library of Congress. Edited by Michael Gorman and Paul Winkler. Chicago: American Librarian Association and Canadian Library Association.

Association for Educational Communications and Technology. The Information Science Committee. 1972. *Standards for Cataloging Nonprint Materials.* Third edition. Washington, D.C.: Association for Educational Communications and Technology.

Bogen, Betty. 1976. "Computer-generated Catalog of Audiovisuals." *Medical Library Association Bulletin* 64 (April):224-27.

Bowker Annual of Library and Book Trade Information. 1976. 21st edition. New York: R. R. Bowker.

Brantz, Malcolm H., and Rick Forsman. 1977. "Classifications and Audiovisuals." *Medical Library Association Bulletin* 65 (April):261-64.

Chamberlain, Mary. 1959. *Guide to Art Reference Books.* Chicago: American Library Association.

Chouraqui, Eugene. 1973. "The Index and Filing System Used by the 'Inventaire General des Monument et des Richesses Artistiques de la France.' " *Computers and the Humanities* 7 (May):273-85.

Clarke, Virginia. 1969. *The Organization of Nonbook Materials in the Laboratory School Library.* Rev. edition. Denton, Texas: Laboratory School Library.

Clawson, Catherine R., and Charles A. Rankowski. 1978. "Classification and Cataloging of Slides Using Color Photography." *Special Libraries* 69 (August): 281-85.

"Collection of 35mm Slides." 1977. Rev. edition. Madison, Wisconsin: African Studies Program, University of Wisconsin–Madison.

Cowen, Chester R. [1974?] . "Systems for Arranging Resources on African Populations." Mimeographed. Norman, Oklahoma: University of Oklahoma.

Crawford, Melanie Ann, Slide Curator, The Evergreen State College. Personal communication. October 12, 1978.

Daily, Jay E. 1972. *Organizing Nonprint Materials; A Guide for Librarians.* New York: Marcel Dekker.

Diamond, Robert M. 1972. "A Retrieval System for 35mm Slides Utilized in Art and Humanities Instruction." In *Bibliographic Control of Nonprint Media.* Edited by Pearce S. Grove and Evelyn G. Clement. Chicago: American Library Association.

Dondis, Donis A. 1973. *A Primer of Visual Literacy.* Boston: MIT Press.

Ehresmann, Donald L. 2nd ed. 1979. *Fine Arts: A Bibliographic Guide.* Littleton, Colorado: Libraries Unlimited.

Fleischer, Eugene B. 1969. "Uniterm Your A-V Library." *Audiovisual Instruction* 14 (February):76-78.

Freudenthal, Juan R. 1974. "The Slide as a Communication Tool: A State-of-the-Art Survey." *School Media Quarterly* 2 (Winter):109-115.

Hicks, Warren B., and Alma M. Tillin. 1967. *The Organization of Nonbook Materials in School Libraries.* Sacramento, California: California State Department of Education.

Hill, Donna. 1975. *The Picture File: A Manual and a Curriculum-related Subject Heading List.* Hamden, Connecticut: Linnet Books.

ICONCLASS: An Iconographic Classification System. 1973-78. Prepared by Henri Van De Waal. Completed and edited by L. D. Couprie, with R. H. Fuchs and E. Tholen. 17 vols. Amsterdam: North-Holland Publishing.

Illuminated Manuscripts: An Index to Selected Bodleian Library Color Reproductions. 1977. Compiled and edited by Thomas H. Ohlgren. New York: Garland Publishing, Inc.

Illuminated Manuscripts and Books in the Bodleian Library: A Supplemental Index. 1978. Compiled and edited by Thomas H. Ohlgren. New York: Garland Publishing, Inc.

Jones, Lois Swan. 1978. *Art Research Methods and Resources: A Guide to Finding Art Information.* Dubuque, Iowa: Kendall/Hunt Publishing.

Kepes, Gyorgy. 1965. *Education of Vision.* New York: George Braziller.

Kuvshinoff, B. W. 1967. "A Graphic Graphics Card Catalog and Computer Index." *American Documentation* 18 (January):3-9.

Lamy-Rousseau, Francoise. 1974. *Traitement antomise des documents multimedia avec les systemes ISBD unifie.* Quebec: Ministere de l'education du Quebec, Service general des moyens d'enseignement.

Lazar, Paul, African Studies Program Slide Archives, Indiana University. Personal communication. January 1979.

Lewis, Elizabeth M. 1969. "A Graphic Catalog Card Index." *American Documentation* 20 (July):238-46.

Lewis, Elizabeth M. 1974. "A Cost Study of Library Color Microimage Storage and Retrieval: Visual Indexing in Microfiche, Super-8, and Videotape." Ed.D. dissertation. New York: Columbia University.

Lewis, Elizabeth M. 1976. "Visual Indexing of Graphic Material." *Special Libraries* 67 (November):518-27.

LoPresti, Maryellen. 1973. "Automated Slide Classification System at Georgia Tech." *Special Libraries* 64 (November):509-513.

Loertscher, David W. 1975. *A Nonbook Cataloging Sampler*. First edition. Austin, Texas: Armadillo Press.

Mailloux, L. D., and J. E. Bollman. 1977. "Xerox 6500 Slide Printer." *Journal of Applied Photographic Engineering* 3:230-34.

Mid-America College Art Association. Research Committee on Special Classification Systems for Visual Materials of the Third World Peoples. *Report of the Research Committee . . .* , 1974-1975. Edited by Chester R. Cowen. Parts I and II. Norman, Oklahoma: The School of Art, University of Oklahoma.

Motley, Drucilla. 1970. "How to Find Your Slides Fast!" *Educational Screen and AV Guide* 49 (May):18-20, 31.

Moulton, Bethe L., and William I. Woods. 1975. "Computer-produced Catalog for Non-Print Materials: Its Application in a Health Sciences Library." *Special Libraries* 66 (April):357-62.

Muehsam, Gerd. 1978. *Guide to Basic Information Sources in the Visual Arts*. Santa Barbara, California: Jeffrey Norton Publishers.

Murdock, George P. 1959. *Africa: Its Peoples and Their Culture*. New York: McGraw-Hill.

Nacke, Otto, and Gerhard Murza. 1977. "Ein einfaches Dokumentationssystem für Diapositive [A Simple Slide Documentation System]." *Nachrichten für Dokumentation* 28 (February):26-28.

NCFA Slide and Photograph Archives. Division of Office of Slides and Photography, National Collection of Fine Arts. 1978. Washington, D.C.: Smithsonian Institution.

Nolan, Margaret P. Personal communication. November 1978.

Ohlgren, Thomas H. 1978. "The Bodleian Project: Computer Cataloguing and Indexing of Illuminated Medieval Manuscripts." In *Transactions of the First International Conference on Automatic Processing of Art History Data and Documents*, pp. 290-318. Pisa, Italy: Scuola Normale Superiore.

Ohlgren, Thomas H. [1979]. "Computer Indexing of Illuminated Manuscripts for Use in Medieval Studies." In *Computers and the Humanities*. In press.

Ohrn, Steven, and Siegmann, William. 1973. "An Indexing System for African Slides." Mimeographed. Bloomington, Indiana: African Studies Program, Indiana University.

Ohrn, Steven G. 1974. *Cataloging the African Studies Film and Slide Collections*. Bloomington, Indiana:African Studies Program, Indiana University.

Ohrn, Steven G. 1975. *Cataloguing in Context: The African Studies Program Slide Archives*. Bloomington, Indiana: African Studies Program, Indiana University.

Rahn, Hans C. 1975. *Rahn'sche Fabdiapositivsammlung: eine ikonographische Klassifizierung von Meisterwerken der Malerei von 1430-1810 [Rahn's Coloured Slide Collection: An Iconographical Classification of Masterpaintings from 1430-1810]* . (In German and English). Bern: H. Lang.

Raymond, Sue L., and Virginia L. Algermissen. 1976. "Retrieval System for Biomedical Slides Using MeSH." *Medical Library Association Bulletin* 64 (April):233-35.

Schwartz, Philip J. 1974. "Keyword Indexing of Non-book Media." *Audiovisual Instruction* 19 (November):84-87.

Sears List of Subject Headings. 1977. 11th edition. Edited by Barbara M. Westby. New York: H. W. Wilson Co.

Sedgley, Anne, and Bronwen Merrett. 1974. "Cataloguing Slide Collections: Art and Architecture Slides at RMIT [Royal Melbourne Institute of Technology]." *Australian Library Journal* 23 (May):146-52.

Sheehy, Eugene P. 1976. *Guide to Reference Books*. Chicago: American Library Association.

Simons, Wendell. 1972. "Development of a Universal Classification System for Two-by-Two-Inch Slide Collections." In *Bibliographic Control of Nonprint Media*. Edited by Pearce S. Grove and Evelyn G. Clement, pp. 360-73. Chicago: American Library Association.

Simons, Wendell W., and Luraine C. Tansey. 1970. *A Slide Classification System for the Organization and Automatic Indexing of Interdisciplinary Collections of Slides and Pictures*. Santa Cruz, California: University of California.

"Slide Library. Philadelphia College of Art." 1976. Arco Building, Room 223.

SLIDEX: A System for Indexing, Filing, and Retrieving Slides and Other Visual Aids. 1978. Prepared by Mod Mekkawi, Laura H. Palmer, and Woodrow W. Lons, Jr. Washington, D.C.: Howard University. 38pp.

Smith, Virginia C., and William R. Treese. 1975. "A Computerized Approach to Art Exhibition Catalogs." *Library Trends* 23 (January):471-81.

Strohlein, Alfred. 1975. *The Management of 35mm Medical Slides*. New York: United Business Publications.

Tansey, Luraine C. 1975. "Classification of Research Photographs and Slides." *Library Trends* 23 (January):417-26.

Tillin, Alma M., and William J. Quinly. 1976. *Standards for Cataloging Nonprint Materials; An Interpretation and Practical Application*. 4th edition. Washington, D.C.: Association for Educational Communications and Technology.

U.S. Library of Congress. Subject Cataloging Division. 1975. *Library of Congress Subject Headings*. 8th edition. Washington, D.C.: The Division.

Visser, Ora. 1977. "Stellenbosch University Medical Library Slide Classification, Storage, Retrieval, and Issue System." *Medical Library Association Bulletin* 65 (July):377-79.

Weihs, Jean Riddle, Shirley Lewis, and Janet MacDonald. In consultation with the CLA/ALA/AECT/EMAC/CAML Advisory Committee on the Cataloguing of Nonbook Materials. 1973. *Non-Book Materials: The Organization of Integrated Collections*. First edition. Ottawa, Canada: The Canadian Library Association.

Wetmore, Rosamond B. 1969. *A Guide to the Organization of Library Collections*. Muncie, Indiana: Ball State University.

World Bank Photo Library. 1977. "The Organization of the World Bank Photo Library." By Susan Watters, Photo Librarian, Information and Public Affairs. Mimeographed. Washington, D.C.: The World Bank.

Wynar, Bohdan S. 1970- . *American Reference Books Annual*. Littleton, Colorado: Libraries Unlimited.

5—ACQUISITION, PRODUCTION METHODS, AND EQUIPMENT

INTRODUCTION

Most academic institutions and museums in the United States are engaged both in making and purchasing slides. It is possible to make slides institutionally for a relatively small expenditure per slide, while commercially acquired slides may be double or triple the cost. Although the majority of academic institutions both purchase and make their own slides, the budget allotment for commercial purchasing is usually smaller than that for internal production on a cost-per-slide basis; i.e., even if the budgets are the same, fewer slides can be acquired commercially because of the higher costs. At the same time, however, the cost range varies so radically (from about $0.30 to $3.00 per slide) that in many instances, even the cost factor is not significant enough to prevent commercial purchasing. Moreover, an institution may prefer not to invest in the staff, cameras, film, copystands, and processing materials and equipment necessary to make slides. For some institutions, it is less expensive to purchase slides mounted, labeled, and ready to use from commercial sources than to make them locally.

Under a Ford Foundation Grant in 1961-1962, the College Art Association undertook a study that touched on every aspect of visual arts education in academic institutions and museums. Andrew C. Ritchie's study, *The Visual Arts in Higher Education* (1966), briefly notes the problems of supplying quality slides for lectures and also the vast sums expended in this area in 1961-1962:

> In 1961-62 the total slide budget for 264 departments, our questionnaire revealed, came to $172,600, to meet an annual demand of 233,000 slides. Since by no means all departments answered our questionnaire it is conservative to estimate that at least a quarter of a million dollars is being spent annually in America by art departments for slides alone (Ritchie, p. 43).

In the author's 1969 study, with 91 institutions supplying information on slide production rates, a total of 572,643 slides were produced and purchased, with a range of from 500 to 16,000 slides acquired per year. The 1974 report of the Professional Status Subcommittee of the CAA Visual Resources Committee documented that of 182 institutions, total annual acquisitions numbered 949,939, with nearly 60% of this total representing in-house or local production (DeLaurier, 1979). The average annual acquisition rate of these 182 institutions was 5,220 slides—more than five times that of the 1961-1962 CAA survey. The earlier CAA figures reveal an average cost for slide acquisition of $0.74 per slide in 1961-1962. If this same figure were used today to determine the total budgets for 182 institutions, the resultant expenditure would be $702,955. A more realistic cost per slide of $1.00, still very conservative, gives a current annual expenditure of nearly one million dollars by 182 institutions for slides in the art and architecture fields alone. Although all of these surveys are now dated, their results are provided to illustrate the fact that the acquisition of slides by academic institutions and museums is a major undertaking involving vast expenditures. Budgets necessary to acquire slides are rarely understood because of the relatively low per unit cost of slides in relation to that of other media, i.e., filmstrips, phonorecordings, tapes, and so forth.

Certainly, on the academic level, the commercial distributor and producer plays an important role in collection building even though significant quantities of slides are produced institutionally.

The figures discussed apply only to colleges, universities, and a small number of museums, and to only one or two subject areas. A large number of institutions, particularly on the public school level, have not been identified in terms of the extent of their acquisition of slides. As is apparent from the directory of slide distributors and producers outside of the art field (at the back of the book), this is not an insignificant market for either business or educational institutions.

There are obvious advantages and disadvantages to both methods of acquisition. Each institution should decide which method or combination of acquisition methods is most economical and efficient based upon its needs and budget.

TYPES OF SLIDES

The most common slide used in slide libraries is the 2x2-inch slide produced by using a 35mm camera. In addition to this format, there are "super slides" or square 2x2-inch slides, 2¼x2¼-inch slides, and 3¼x4-inch or lantern slides. The square 2x2-inch slide (which uses 126 film) results from using the Instamatic cameras and are frequently called Instamatic slides. All of the standard 2x2-inch size slides can be used in 2x2-inch slide-filmstrip projectors. Lantern or 3¼x4-inch projectors can project the lantern slide, 2x2-inch (all formats), and 2¼x2¼-inch slides with appropriate slide carriers or masks. The general range of sizes derived from 2¼x3¼-inch film is 2½x2¼-inch, 2-3/4x2-3/4-inch, and 3¼x4-inch slides.

Slide collections that were established before 1940 still have relatively large quantities of lantern slides. Many of these collections have withdrawn lantern slides from daily use, while others maintain them as part of their active library. Large lantern slide collections are still actively used at Harvard University (80,000 lantern slides), University of Michigan (61,000 lantern slides), and Princeton University (105,000 lantern slides). Although academic institutions often maintain large lantern slide collections, very few are still actively engaged in producing them, as are Harvard University and Smith College. Many more have been or are currently converting their lantern slide collections to a 2x2-inch format, as are Princeton University, University of Iowa, SUNY—Buffalo, and the University of Wisconsin. Smaller lantern slide collections exist, often in obscurity, throughout the country, and these frequently contain material that can provide valuable documentation for art, architecture, and cultural historians as well as for local historical and preservation societies. All collections of lantern slides should be evaluated carefully and stored, even if they are no longer actively used. Archival storage of lantern slides is discussed in Chapter 6.

The lantern slide may not enjoy the widespread use that it did at the turn of the century and for the first three decades of the twentieth century, but the "handmade" lantern slide is still noteworthy particularly for schoolroom use and for production by both students and teachers. A publication useful in this area by Holland, Hartsell, and Davidson describes five different types of handmade 3¼x4-inch slides: cellophane typewritten slides; frosted cellophane or plastic slides; etched or ground glass slides; gelatin slides; and silhouette slides (1958, pp. 60-63). Using 2x2-inch cover glass, miniature slides can be made from laboratory

Diagram 3—Slide Sizes.

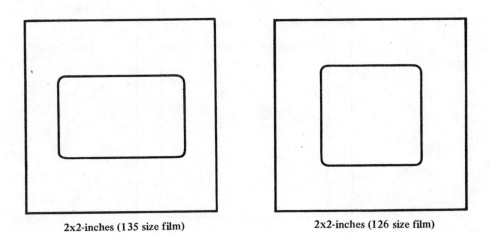

2x2-inches (135 size film)   2x2-inches (126 size film)

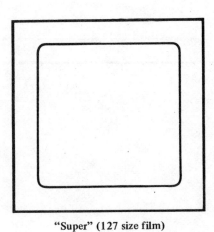

"Super" (127 size film)

(Diagram continues on page 148)

Diagram 3—Slide Sizes (cont'd)

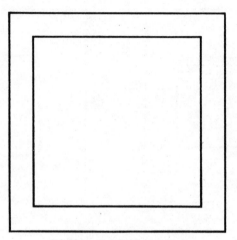

2¼x2¼-inches (120 size film)

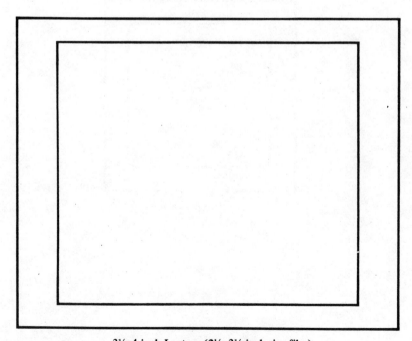

3¼x4-inch Lantern (2¼x3¼-inch size film)

specimens such as hair or wood slivers. Students can also make their own slides, using paints and felt markers. Several articles have appeared on various types of 2x2-inch handmade slides in *Arts and Activities* (Cyr, 1977; Scott, 1972). For additional literature on this topic, see the bibliography on "Slides Made without Film" in the Selected Bibliography.

Until the advent of Polaroid Land film within the last ten years, the lantern slide played a less prominent role in slide library collection building because of its cost, fragility, size, and weight as compared with 2x2-inch slides. As indicated earlier, these slides were printed upon glass plates and bound with another glass plate of the same size covering the emulsion side of the slide to protect it from damage. Even with standard photographic processing and film available, the lantern slide has not held its own with the miniature slide. Now, using a Polaroid Land camera with 46L (for continuous tone) or 146L (for line copy), a Polaroid process can be used for 3¼x4-inch or 2¼x2¼-inch slides, providing rapid projection material for less than $0.75 per slide (Wiesinger, 1964; Minor, 1977).

MAKING SLIDES FROM REPRODUCTIONS AND PHOTOGRAPHS

Although there is an adequate amount of literature on various types of slides and basic production methods, an area that has not enjoyed widespread publication is the copying of slides from reproductions or book plates and from photographs. Most reproductions in books have been produced by offset or letterpress, with offset being the less expensive process for the printing of large quantities of plate material. Several books have been published on the photographic processes involved in the reproduction of works of art, and the reader is advised to examine this material, some of which is included in the bibliography on the "Photography of Art and Architecture."

Notwithstanding the complexity of the techniques of photographic reproduction, a slide librarian should become familiar with the basic principles for judging the quality of a reproduction or photograph in order to insure that slides made from such reproductions are of the highest quality possible. The majority of academic collections make their own slides from book plates or photographs, so it is imperative to establish selection standards for these reproductions in order to control slide quality. Some schools may have large photograph collections that provide a source for slides along with picture and vertical file materials. Photograph collections (whether archival or for student study) and picture or vertical file materials are also useful for slides if the same quality criteria are applied.

Black and White Slides

Whether the slide library has its own photographic equipment for making slides or the campus audiovisual center or museum photography department is responsible for this task, the slide librarian always should examine critically any material submitted for copy work. A poor-quality reproduction or photograph will result in a low quality slide. The following questions should be asked when judging the quality of black and white reproductions or photographs.

1. **Is the image in focus, or are the edges of objects fuzzy?**

2. **Is there a wide range of contrasts, including darks, middle tones or greys, and whites; or is the image "washed" out?** If it is a high contrast reproduction or photograph, it will have limited or negligible middle tones or greys. Detail is frequently lost entirely during the copying process. If it is low contrast, the entire reproduction will have a grey or faded quality.

3. **Does the reproduction have an overall grey cast, and if so, is it characteristic of the original image?** Many graphic reproductions of drawings or prints may actually have this monotone quality from the outset, so it is indicative of the original image and not of inferior photographic techniques. Frequently, the immediate response to this question is, "How can I know the quality of the original if I have never seen it?" Unfortunately, this is the case for many individuals who are faced with copy work of this type. A good source of expertise is teachers or persons who have had the opportunity to travel and to examine firsthand paintings, drawings, prints, and other objets d'art. The other method for judging is provided by this outline.

4. **Is the reproduction or photograph too small to be copied and projected successfully?** If the image is small and of inferior quality, it is doubtful that, if projected on a large scale, original quality will be retained. In *Planning and Producing Slide Programs*, the Eastman Kodak Company recommends a simple technique for determining whether an image to be copied for projection is of adequate size (1978). Rooms designed for projection usually have a maximum viewing distance that is about eight times the width of the screen image: "if the projected material is legible for the farthest viewer, who is seated 8 times the projected image height from the screen, it will be legible for all other members of the audience. . . . For 8H viewing, legibility can be judged by an average viewer by looking at the material to be copied from a distance of 8 times its height" (ibid., p. 36). Using this formula, take a reproduction in a book that is four inches wide; multiply four times eight, which equals 32; and examine the image from a distance of 32 inches. If the image and relevant details are visible, the reproduction size should be adequate for copying and projection. This technique is particularly useful for judging projection clarity of highly detailed monochromatic images.

5. **What is the general quality level of the rest of the plates in the book?** Most publications are fairly consistent in their reproduction qualities, as this has been predetermined by the process used and papers selected for optimal printing of black and white plates. Many books having the highest quality plates will require the use of different papers and printing methods for color, black and white, and line reproductions such as maps or fine drawings or prints. This added expense of plate reproduction is indicative of the generally high cost of "picture" books. If the book demonstrates relatively high quality throughout, then the plate in question is probably fairly accurate, at least in terms of reproduction potentials. From the beginning, it should be remembered that any reproduction is automatically removed from the fidelity of the object itself and therefore will minimally suffer from distortion of one form or another. What needs to be determined is the severity of that distortion.

6. **If the item reproduced has been placed against a backdrop, e.g., a cloth, paper, or board, does the background detract from the object itself?** If so, an attempt should be made to find another reproduction which has a simpler background.

Many researchers and teachers prefer monochrome or black and white slides or reproductions to color ones, because monochrome plates can be better controlled in terms of their quality; i.e., color processing is less flexible than black and white (Lewis and Smith, 1969). There are also cases where color slides are simply not necessary or do not satisfy the demands of a given image or user. For line drawings, topographical maps, or architectural diagrams, the black and white slide is preferred because of the greater resolving power of black and white film. An excellent explanation of this concept is provided in a book on the history of photographic research by C. E. K. Mees in a chapter entitled, "The Structure of the Developed Image" (1961, pp. 87-98). The relative instability of color films has also made the use of black and white preferable in archival situations. The archival treatment of both black and white and color slides is discussed in Chapter 6.

Color Slides

Whether the image projected is a painting, a butterfly, or a scene of the Grand Canyon, the reality of the projection is heightened with color slides. Certainly, if the color slide is of high quality, even the most demanding user would prefer it to a monochrome one, depending upon the subject matter illustrated. Criteria for judging photographs using supplementary equipment other than direct visual examination are discussed by Mees (ibid.). For the purposes of this chapter, however, criteria based solely upon direct eye-to-image evaluation are elucidated. In the majority of slide libraries, this type of direct examination of film and images will be the only available guide for qualitative judgments. In order to determine the quality of color plates or slides, some basic information on the color theory of photography is necessary. Again, if the reader is interested in a detailed discussion of this topic, Mees' book, *The Encyclopedia of Photography* (1965), and other publications are readily available.

The three primary colors in photography are red, green, and blue as compared to red, yellow, and blue in color theory. The three complementary colors are cyan, magenta, and yellow in photography as compared to orange, green and purple in color theory.

Photography	Color Theory
Primary Colors	
red	red
green	yellow
blue	blue
Complementary Colors	
cyan	orange
magenta	green
yellow	purple

In order to judge the accuracy of the standard photographic image, e.g., an indoor or outdoor scene with people, the skin tones and whites should be examined, as they are good indicators of the faithfulness of the overall photograph to the original color scheme—this assumes that color filters were not used intentionally to distort the colors of the original scene. If the skin tones or whites have a red, green, blue, cyan, magenta, or yellow cast, then the remainder of the picture probably demonstrates corresponding levels of color error.

Light is an important factor affecting the potential for color error or accuracy of a photograph, as are background and foreground colors for a given subject. Mid-morning or mid-afternoon lighting is preferred for making color slides using only natural light, because at these times, the distortion level caused by early morning, noon, or late afternoon lighting is lowest. Using only natural light, a copy stand and camera, it is possible to make good slides from color reproductions. As it is rather awkward to do such work outside, a table placed near a window that is receiving adequate natural lighting will prove satisfactory. Needless to say, this type of set-up is not desirable for copying large quantities of material on a regular basis, but it is offered simply as an alternative method for irregular copy work when proper artificial lighting is not available. Using natural light does, however, avoid some of the problems encountered by the inexperienced and occasional slide producer who is not familiar with how to use appropriate color filters and artificial lighting to insure maximum color fidelity.

In photography, the range of color accuracy or error is based upon the relationship of the primary and complementary colors. For example, in order to correct for an image having a red cast, a cyan filter is used, for green, a magenta filter, and for blue, a yellow filter. The cyan filter is actually absorbing the red, and this is referred to as additive color mixture. The reverse also applies—if an image has a cyan cast, a red filter is used; for magenta, a green filter; and for yellow, a blue filter. The latter process is called subtractive color mixture.

Additive Color Mixture	Subtractive Color Mixture
red ◄—— cyan	red ——► cyan
green ◄— magenta	green ——► magenta
blue ◄—— yellow	blue ——► yellow

Different filter intensities can be used, depending upon the intensity of the color error. Combinations of different filters can also be used for color correction, e.g., for a magenta cast, a yellow plus cyan filter; for yellow, a cyan plus magenta filter; and for cyan, a magenta plus yellow filter. This is a highly simplified explanation of the actual photographic changes occurring, but the reader needs to recognize this color range to understand a basic explanation of color correction.

When examining color photographs or reproductions from books, the following questions should be asked:

1. **Is the image in focus or are the edges of objects fuzzy?**

2. **Do whites or skin tones appear to be unnatural?**

3. **Does the entire image have a red, green, blue, cyan, magenta, or yellow cast? If so, is this in keeping with the fidelity of the original image, or is it a distortion of**

the image? This question can be particularly problematic with regard to contemporary art, as the likeness of the image to reality is no longer a valid criterion for color accuracy. Instead, the image must be judged in terms of the artist's style and general use of colors. The same may apply to geological or scientific studies where comparisons with the original image are not possible, so the quality of the image must be judged as it appears and not based upon preconceptions.

4. **If the reproduction is in a book, do all the plates exhibit the same color cast? If so, are all the plates by the same artist or of the same object? Or, are all the plates of different objects or works of art?** If all the reproduced works in a book or magazine are of different art objects, images, or scenes, then they should not have the same color cast. If it is still impossible to judge the quality of a plate, a teacher or individual having experience with the subject matter illustrated should be consulted.

5. **What is the general quality of the publication? Is poor quality paper used, e.g., paper having the quality of newsprint? Does the quality of paper vary for color plates as compared with text pages?** It is not always necessary to print the text and plates on different types of paper if, for example, plates make up the major content of the publication and very little text is reproduced, or if quality paper is used throughout. Under these circumstances, it is rare to find different types of paper due to the added expense. Sierra Club publications have excellent quality nature studies and frequently utilize only one paper type, which is highly conducive to quality plate production. Magazines such as *Apollo, National Geographic*, and *Scientific American* use the same paper throughout while maintaining high reproduction standards. Art publications by the Abrams Company and scientific publications by C. V. Mosby and Freeman also provide excellent slide copy. Abrams, Mosby, and Freeman frequently use different paper types for text and plate material. Museum-issued publications also provide sources for quality slides, as most museums are prepared to produce high quality photographic copies of their holdings under controlled conditions because they can make original photographs directly from the objects themselves. Each field has its quality publishers, and a slide librarian should become familiar with these to insure maximum copy standards for slides.

6. **If the item has been reproduced against a backdrop, does the background detract from the object itself?** A fine scientific specimen or an art object can be greatly enhanced by the proper background; or conversely, its true coloration can be distorted by the color of the backdrop against which it was photographed.

Whether color or black and white slides are being made from reproductions or photographs, some loss in quality from the original is to be expected as part of the copying process, resulting in increased contrast, a loss in sharpness, and changes in color value. If precautions are taken as outlined, quality loss should be minimized.

EQUIPMENT FOR SLIDE PRODUCTION

Basically, there are four different methods by which slides can be institutionally produced:

1. Purchase the necessary equipment and supplies and hire a part- or full-time photographer.
2. Purchase the necessary equipment and supplies and have the slide library staff shoot and process the slides or send the film to a commercial film processor.
3. Hire a professional photographer who already has the equipment and can purchase supplies and pay that person by the slide or by the hour.
4. Have the institutional audiovisual center or museum photography division make the slides and pay the center by the slide or by the hour, whichever is customary in that institution.

Any of these approaches will vary greatly in cost, with any of the three systems being capable of ranges from less than $100 to more than $1,000 for supplies and equipment purchases, or for labor costs. If the decision is made not to purchase supplies and equipment for institutional slide production, a Polaroid set-up for quick slide copy or equipment for slide duplication may be desirable to have in the slide library.

Each institution will have budget and production schedules that will form the parameters for experimentation and acquisition of slide copying and duplicating equipment. Unless the slide librarian has had previous photographic experience, the nomenclature alone will prevent her or him from making valid equipment choices for this aspect of slide production. It is true in this area, as in others, that a little background can hinder selection more than none at all. The individual with limited background frequently will purchase equipment thinking that he or she knows all that is necessary, while the individual without any previous experience will consult a specialist in photography or photographic equipment. In either case, consultation with a specialist should be mandatory before costly and irreversible errors are made.

Those institutions having media centers or museums having photographic facilities should have built-in sources of information on this topic. If an institution has a photography department, the staff or faculty should be consulted about copying set-ups. A good overview of the equipment and facilities necessary for copy work is provided in the *Encyclopedia of Photography* under the heading "Copying and Close-up Photography" (1965, vol. 6, pp. 964-982). If a particular institution does not offer the various possibilities for information cited, then those that do should be consulted. At the present time, more than half of the academic collections in the United States employ a photographer on a part-time basis to make their slides, while relatively few utilize the services of a full-time photographer. The improved quality of the new Ektachrome films, which can be processed locally in short periods of time, has made the use of campus audiovisual services more attractive to many schools.

Available film types—both black and white and color—have changed significantly in the last five years. Some films, such as Kodachrome II Type A professional film were removed from the market, and new types, such as the E-6 family of Ektachromes were introduced. With these new films, or replacements for withdrawn

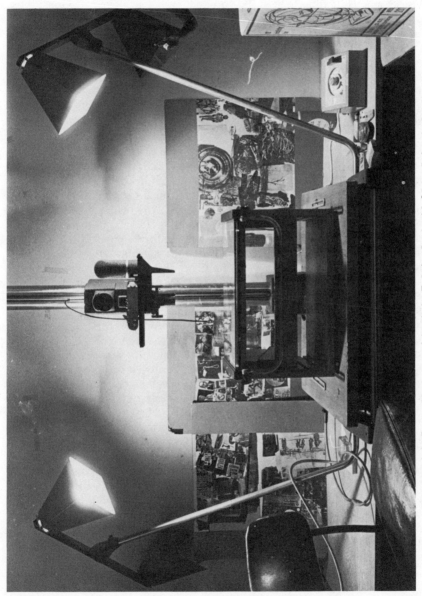

Photograph 1. Reprovit copy stand (made by E. Leitz, Inc.) with 35mm Leica single-lens reflex camera. Department of Art History. Cornell University.

films, have come changes in stability, length of processing time, chemistry, and image quality. Changes and innovations are continual in the photographic industry, and a regular check of the literature and of local photographic suppliers is advised.

Black and white films used in slide production fall into two categories: those that produce negatives, from which positives are then made, and those that produce an initial positive image. The second group is more widely used in slide production for academic collections, but for those institutions desiring negatives, a process utilizing Eastman Fine Grain Release Positive Film No. 5302 is possible (Churney, 1975). Much has been written in recent years on methods of producing direct positive black and white slides, both on new types of film that may be used for this purpose and on simpler and more efficient processing methods. Procedures for using Kodak Direct Positive Film No. 402 and Panatomic X film are outlined by Arnold Gassan (1977, pp. 151-52). Producing slides from Kodak Precision Line Film LPD4 has also been discussed in two papers published in the MACAA *Newsletter* ("Black White Slide Film," 1977; "Film and Photography," 1978). New innovations in black and white slide production include Kodak Rapid Processing Copy film No. SO-185, originally marketed as a 35mm X-ray film (Hollander, 1974), and Kodak Super Speed Duplicating film No. 2251, which makes it possible to obtain black and white slides in less than 45 minutes (Jones, 1976). For further information on black and white slide production, the forthcoming MACAA guide on slide production, and Kodak's *Planning and Producing Slide Programs* (1978) are recommended.

Of the major systems of color film available for slide production, Kodak, AGFA-Gavaert, Polaroid, Cibachrome ("The Four Most Important Colour-systems . . . ," 1977), the Kodak Kodachrome and Ektachrome families of films are most commonly used by institutions in this country. Although color fidelity and stability are important considerations in the choice of a film type for slide production, the availability and speed of the processing required may often be the deciding factor. The ease of processing and improved color and stability of the new E-6 family of Ektachromes are making this film popular with institutions and commercial producers alike, as Ektachrome processing is often available within a 24-hour period.

Those schools wishing to retain the excellent color range and image quality of the old Kodachrome II Professional Film will find that the replacement for this 3400° film, Kodachrome 40 Type A, offers the advantages of the former with a greatly shortened processing time—a notable improvement as all Kodachrome film must be commercially processed. Although the difficulties of obtaining comparable speed and control of processing have limited the use of AGFA films by American slide collections, its excellent color qualities have made it popular with many European institutions and dealers. Revised information on Kodak color films and their use appears frequently and is available from Kodak or from most photographic stores. Also useful for keeping abreast of color information, particularly on stability and longevity, are photographic magazines such as *Peterson's Photographic Magazine, Technical Photography*, and *Industrial Photography*.

The *PMI Products and Services Directory* includes a listing of "Still Color Lab Services and Filmstrip Services" in their annual publication. This listing also gives sources that make slides "From Color Negatives" and "From Artwork." The *Professional Photographic Catalog* issued yearly by Standard Photo Supply in

Chicago includes guides to different film types from motion picture films to 35mm films. Both of these directories should be readily available to the slide library.

For copy photography from books, special supplies are required to compensate for the distortion of the image caused by book bindings. Merely opening the book and placing it on a stand without flattening the pages is insufficient preparation for shooting book plates. There are several solutions to this problem—many of which are not satisfactory. For example, weighted boards could be placed across the book, providing for an awkward and time-consuming process. The least expensive, yet relatively practical solution is the use of a piece of optically treated glass, which will both flatten the pages and prevent distortion of the image. Optimally, a framing box (e.g., Leitz) that handles books up to 11½x14-inches should be used, because it provides greater pressure than a sheet of glass and is more efficient to use. For books larger than this size, however, the optical glass will be necessary. An added benefit provided by the framing box is that by placing the surface of a page perpendicular to the image cone of the camera lens and that by proper arrangement of the lighting, a reduction in glare from shiny pages is minimized; i.e., the light is polarized. If polarization is a problem, several publications are available which explain this concept and how to manipulate it. In its pamphlet, *Using Polarized Light for Copying* (1975), Kodak explains the use of polarizing screens and lights. The *Encyclopedia of Photography* has a thorough explanation of polarization under the heading "Polarized Light in Photography" (1965, vol. 16, pp. 2926-32).

Equipment for slide production from books and other printed sources ranges from simple self-made units (such as that outlined by Siddall in "Making Slides from Printed Materials" [1969]) to inexpensive commercial apparatus (such as the Kodak Ektagraphic Visual Maker [Gardner, 1976]) to costly, precision-designed systems such as the Leitz Reprovit. The costs and capabilities of many types of copystand systems are discussed in *Audiovisual Marketplace* (1978), the *Professional Photographic Catalog*, and the forthcoming MACAA guide on slide production. Specifically written to explain the problems confronted by museums preparing slides for sale to educational institutions, a 1968 article by Brian N. Rushton (Manager of the Publication Department of the Tate Gallery in London) provides a description of the costs, equipment, facilities and procedures used at the Tate Gallery.

Duplication is a convenient process for having multiple copies of slides readily available for teaching. In fact, Carlton Erickson (Director of the Audiovisual Center and Professor of Education, the University of Connecticut) has said that drawer filing of slides is becoming a phenomenon of the past and that once a teacher's use patterns are established, the slides should be copied and placed in magazines for that teacher's use (1968, p. 319). Large scale production of duplicate slides is also necessary for schools engaged in systematic student slide study and review, such as that at the University of Illinois, Urbana, shown in Photograph 11 (see page 191).

Two factors mitigate against wide-spread adoption of these practices in favor of individual drawer filing: 1) the substantially reduced image and color quality of mass or rapidly produced duplicate slides; and 2) the 1978 Copyright Law, which is discussed at the end of this chapter. Slide duplication requires specific types of films, and in the past, these films have not offered the color fidelity and stability of 35mm Kodachrome, Agfachrome, and Ektachrome. Recent evidence indicates that Kodak E-6 duplicating film has color stability that may equal that of comparable Kodachrome film (Hershenson, 1978); and sophisticated duplicating equipment can produce slides that improve, rather than decrease, the quality of the original. Quality duplicates require time, patience, and professional expertise, as outlined by commercial producer John Rosenthal (1978) and by slide curator Nancy DeLaurier (1977). In-house or locally produced duplicates are more often marked by strong color shifts and notable loss of sharpness.

If an institution does decide to produce its own duplicate slides, various systems are available for this process, ranging in cost from less than $50 for a bellows extension unit to more than $10,000 for sophisticated professional equipment. Examples of various set-ups available for this purpose include the Bowens Illumitran, the Honeywell Repronar, the Forox Slide Duplicator, and the Sickles 3300 Optical Printer. For further information, the reader should refer to the bibliography on production methods and to the equipment directory at the end of this book. In order to keep abreast of equipment changes, new products, and prices, the *Audio-Visual Equipment Directory, Audiovisual Marketplace*, the *PMI Catalog and Directory of products and Services*, and the *Professional Photographic Catalog* should be consulted regularly. Local audiovisual and media specialists can also be of use in evaluation of slide production equipment and methods. In addition, periodicals such as *Audio Visual, Audiovisual Instruction, Arts and Activities, Educational Product Report, AV Guide, Nation's Schools*, and *Previews* are useful sources of information on new equipment and media production methods.

BUYING SLIDES FROM COMMERCIAL SOURCES

Whether slides are being instituionally produced or commercially purchased, high quality levels should still prevail. As frequently as possible, slides should be purchased on approval, so that after careful examination, they can be returned to the source if unsatisfactory. If, out of a purchase of fifty slides, fewer than five are unsatisfactory, it may not be worth the effort and added expense to return so few slides; but, if 20% or more of a single order does not meet satisfactory quality standards as outlined in this chapter, the slides should be returned. Many academic institutions try not to purchase from those companies that do not allow for preview of orders. This policy favors those companies that base their reputations on quality slides and who can therefore allow such preview conditions. Abuse of this privilege by institutions that duplicate slides received on approval and then return them is making this time-consuming and expensive courtesy on the part of slide suppliers all but a thing of the past.

Commercial slides range in price from less than $0.50 to more than $3.00, depending on a variety of considerations. Slides can be purchased bound or unbound, labeled or unlabeled, singly or in sets, and as originals or duplicates. Of these, the production of the slide as an "original" (i.e., a slide shot on location in the camera) or as a "duplicate" (i.e., a slide produced by one of several means from an original, from a negative, or from an inter-negative) is the single greatest factor in the determination of its price. An original slide can frequently be priced at twice the amount of a duplicate slide of the same image. Accurate description of slides as "originals" or "duplicates" is a debated issue, however, with some "duplicates" being considered more "original" than others. Perhaps the most concise discussion of this complicated terminology is that contained in the introduction to the *Slide Buyer's Guide* (1976).

Life expectancy of film will vary greatly depending upon humidity, temperature, and storage conditions, but some films are not as stable as others and are
therefore more prone to deviations in quality. Differences in film brands and processing procedures can affect the overall quality in originals and particularly in
duplicates. For example, a wide range of duplicate slide quality is possible among
the numerous European film distributors and producers from one country to the
next because of local production methods.

Primarily due to the pioneering efforts of Nancy DeLaurier in making slide
quality a concern of both slide librarians and commercial slide suppliers, information
on film types and production methods used is becoming increasingly common in
slide catalogs; and the reliability of slide sources can to some extent be related to
their willingness to explain in detail their sources and processes. However, it is
up to the purchaser to solicit more information if it is not indicated in the catalogs.
In 1976, the Visual Resources Committees of the Art Libraries Society of North
America and the College Art Association issued the following joint statement on
slide quality standards:

> We feel that slide suppliers should be informed of those factors which are most impor-
> tant to us in considering the quality of slides purchased for our slide collections. The
> following are our standards for evaluating slides:
> COLOR: The color should be as true as possible to the original work of art, neither
> over- nor under-exposed, nor off-color due to the lighting or the film-type.
> FILM: The film should have fine-grained resolution, and color should be stable with a
> minimum shelf-life of ten years. Duplicate slides should be newly-printed as far as
> possible to maximize their shelf-life. High contrast in duplicate slides should be con-
> trolled. The film should be clean with no dirt or scratches on the surface nor duplicated
> onto the film from the master transparency or negative. The size 24x36mm is preferable;
> the supplier should indicate other sizes if used.
> PHOTOGRAPHY: The slides must be in focus and full-frame as far as possible without
> being cropped. Lighting should be adequate and even throughout, and without glare
> or reflections. In photographing paintings and buildings, distortion should be avoided.
> INFORMATION: Accurate and complete information is necessary: Artist's full name,
> nationality and dates, title of the work, medium, date and dimensions if known, and
> location. Cropped slides should be identified as such, and details should be described.
> An indication of the orientation is important, especially on details and abstract works
> of art. It should be clear which is the front of the slide.
> It is important to indicate whether the slide will be an original or a duplicate; specific
> information on the source of the slide, film type and processing would be appreciated.
> Return and replacement policies should be spelled out.
> PRICE: The price of the slide should fairly reflect the costs of production and distribu-
> tion ("Statement on Slide Quality Standards," 1978).

All commercial slide purchases should be evaluated against these standards
and notations made for future reference. The criteria enumerated previously for
evaluation of reproductions as sources for slides (most of which are applicable to
the evaluation of commercial slides), the section "On Buying Slides" from the
Slide Buyer's Guide, the MACAA *Newsletter*, and the *ARLIS/NA Newsletter*
are also recommended to the individual wishing to become an astute slide purchaser.

Along with the quality of the slide to be purchased, considerations of cost
should also take into account the usefulness of the slide's format to the collection.
Most producers and distributors will provide slides in cardboard mounts, with the

producer's catalog number on the slide plus descriptive information, or with a brief description printed or written directly on the mount or paper label. Slides purchased with only the cardboard mount and minimal pre-cataloging data are usually less expensive than those supplied fully glass-mounted with a completed label; and unless the collection's cataloging system differs radically from the supplier's, many of the slides in the second category are ready to be filed upon receipt after a quality check is made. Such pre-labeled slides do frequently require changes in the cataloging data, if only to rearrange the information into a given collection's entry format and filing order or to assign a classification number. Some dealers now supply printed labels with their ready-mounted slides, so an institution may apply the label to the slide mount of its choice.

Commercial slides, in almost all cases, are more expensive than the basic cost of an in-house product. The superficial comparison of $1.75 for a typical commercial slide with $0.25 or less for a single Kodachrome slide produced by the institution is very deceptive. Many factors—such as the photographer's time, the initial equipment investment, postage, chemicals, and dark room facilities—must also be added into the total in-house costs. In addition, if one must add the cost of a permanent binder, i.e., $0.15, and the labor and expense of labeling the slide, the commercially bound and labeled slide is certainly a viable alternative for many institutional situations. Institutions with available dark room facilities, audiovisual services, and large annual acquisition rates, however, can greatly reduce the cost of in-house slides by means of bulk purchasing and processing. Costs can also be cut by not having slides that are commercially processed placed in ready-mounts. These costs will vary from one institution to another depending upon local price and wage variances.

A choice between commercial and institutional slide production is a difficult one to make, and in most instances it should not be made at all. Instead, a coordination between commercial and institutional slide production should be considered. Much material, particularly that required for graduate instruction, will only be available in scholarly publications. Conversely, many European producers offer slides of art objects that are not reproduced in publications, or if published, are of such poor quality that good slides cannot be made from them. A new collection not having slide production facilities will rely heavily upon commercial suppliers; but as the collection expands and its budget and usage increase, the addition of production facilities should be studied.

The growth of academic use of non-print media in the last ten years has brought with it sources of supply for commercial slides, filmstrips, video formats, and other audiovisuals so extensive and diversified that it is difficult for the slide librarian to know what is available on a given topic; who it is available from; whether it can be bought or rented, what quality, film type, format, and cost can be expected; and even the current address of the company. Fortunately, with the burgeoning market have come many indexes and guides to slides on both general and specific topics. General indexes include the NICEM *Index to Educational Slides* (1977) (which lists over 28,000 titles on 26 subjects available from over 300 companies) and NICEM *Index to Producers and Distributors* (which lists the names and addresses of c. 9,000 media producers and distributors), the *Bowker AV Guide: A Subject Guide to Audio-Visual Educational Material* (1975), *GEMS, Guides to Educational Software* (Mirwis, 1977), *Multi-Media Review Digest* (1973-), and the National Audiovisual Center's *Catalog of U.S. Government Produced Audiovisual*

Materials (1974). Journals such as *Booklist* and *Previews* also contain regular columns on slide sources.

Guides and indexes to sources of art and art-related slides are also numerous. The *Slide Buyer's Guide* (1976) includes annotated listings for both United States and foreign commercial, museum, and institutional producers. Over half of the entries in the NICEM *Index to Educational Slides* (1977) are art related, but this coverage does not include major art museums. Museum sources specifically are indexed in *Museum Media: A Biennial Directory and Index of Publications and Audiovisuals Available from United States and Canadian Institutions* (1973), in *A Handlist of Museum Sources for Slides and Photographs* (1972), and in *Sources of Slides: The History of Art* (1970), published by the Metropolitan Museum of Art. Sources for slides in specific subject areas, such as African art, are also becoming available. One of the most recent developments in source indexing is the computer-generated *Sources for Commercial Slides of the Illustrations in Gardner's Art through the Ages, Sixth Edition*, which identifies slide suppliers on an image-by-image basis. Extensive indexes to both general and specific sources of slides are included at the end of this book.

Another innovation in slide production and acquisition is microfiche. Although use of microfiche for compact or archival storage of information has become common in most library systems, their potential as complementary or alternative materials for slide libraries is a recent development. Fiche may offer an inexpensive means of supplying students with images to study that match the slides used in classroom lectures or as a basis for auto-tutorial instruction (Schwarz, 1978). Custom-made fiche may be produced by sending pre-arranged slides to Kodak, at a cost in 1974 of approximately $1.50 per fiche when ordered in lots of 100 or more (Chandler, 1974).

Of potentially greater import to slide libraries and their users are the ambitious publishing ventures that are using fiche as a means of providing visual documentation in quantities that would be prohibitive if done as conventional black and white or color book illustrations. These "text-fiche" range from single volumes on specific topics, such as the publications of the Dunlap Society and the University of Chicago Press, to such monumental documentations as the *Index of American Design* (published by Chadwick-Healey/Somerset House), the *Photographic Record of the Victoria and Albert Museum, London* (published by Mindata, Ltd.), and the *Marburger Index* (published by K. G. Saur).

Whereas the Dunlap, Mindata, and Saur publications are traditional black and white fiche documentations, the University of Chicago Press and Chadwick-Healey/ Somerset House are engaged in color fiche production. The introduction of color microfiche has raised new problems, because the desirability of having large numbers of color images available to students and researchers has been offset, to some extent, by the initial expense of major color fiche documentation projects and by the possibilities of poor color, blurred edges, and fading. The archival qualities of black and white and color fiche approximate those of black and white and color film, respectively. And the producers of color fiche are careful to point out that "all film color dyes are subject to change over time," and that changes in color are not grounds for replacement (Irvine, 1978). A new technique for producing color fiche, employed by Chadwick-Healey/Somerset House, permits photographing the original object directly on the master fiche, thus eliminating the intermediate step of the color slide, and produces excellent results (Lewis, 1979).

Improvements in microfiche readers and the availability of readers that have classroom projection capabilities (such as the Bell & Howell PMR and the National Cash Register 456-200 Universal) are also key points in the increasing acceptance of this new format and its ability to make available visual images for library and classroom use that would otherwise be difficult to obtain.

COPYRIGHT CONSIDERATIONS

The matter of copyright protection is posed in making slides from book plates in the same manner as it is in reproducing pages of books with copying machines. When reviewing the question of "fair use," the issues of partial copying that does not interfere with the commercial value of the original item and copying for nonprofit purposes have been, in the past, important criteria for determining whether use is indeed "fair" (Siebert, 1964, pp. 26-27). The implications of the 1978 Copyright Law are still in the process of being clarified and will not be fully interpreted until actual court decisions have been reached; but duplication of copyrighted slides—whether from commercial, museum, institutional, or private sources—*without express permission* seems to emerge as the area in which institutional slide collections are most clearly violating the sense of the new copyright law. In the case of duplicating such slides, not a single page or sentence is being removed from the original item, but instead the total item itself is being plagiarized. Whether the educational intent is pure or not in this situation, a case for copyright infringement has been made. Many commercial distributors and producers have been indicating copyright protection on each slide or in their catalogs. Discretion should be exercised against indiscriminate copying of commercially produced slides, particularly if copyright is indicated. As a courtesy to the commercial producer and in order to avoid conflicts with copyright restrictions, consultation with the producer is advised.

The legality of producing slides from reproductions in copyrighted books, journals, calendars, etc., is a more difficult and more far-reaching problem than duplicating copyrighted slides. Figures from the 1974 CAA Professional Status Survey indicate that 182 institutions produce a combined total of 619,814 slides by in-house copy-photography from published sources (DeLaurier, 1974). Some sections of the new copyright law seem to allow for such reproduction, while others seem to clearly prohibit it. For collections engaged in substantial production of slides by either duplication or copy-photography, only two activities presently raise serious questions of legality: 1) the duplication of copyrighted slides, even if the copyright notice has been removed in the binding process; and 2) the systematic production of slides from every, or nearly every illustration in a given book, article, or other copyrighted work. If faculty members or other patrons insist on either of these two activities, the slide librarian should request that the patron secure written permission for such duplication. For a listing of all major documents relating to applications of the new law, see "Primary Sources for Understanding the New Copyright Law," by Hardy Carroll (1977). Slides are classified under 17:USCA §202.11 of the *United States Code Annotated*. For further information, see the references on copyright in the bibliography.

SUMMARY

One of the primary advantages of institutionally producing slides is that they can be more quickly available for classroom use than commercially produced slides. If Polaroid copy facilities are available, a slide can be ready for use within a matter of minutes. If black and white or color slides are needed, the shooting and processing may be completed within one day. If commercial processing is required for color slides, several days might be needed before the slides can be ready for use. Frequently, institutional expense per slide may be lower than that for commercial slides. At the same time, however, ordering commercial slides in bulk orders often lowers their cost to a rate commensurate with institutional production.

A department or library may not have to purchase its own copying facilities if an audiovisual center is available. Museums usually have a photographic set-up, which may include copying equipment. Commercial slides that are labeled, cataloged, and mounted offer advantages to slide libraries, particularly those with a small or inadequate staff. The precise method of collection building is an institutional prerogative based upon the needs and demands of each school or museum.

Unfortunately, many still approach slide production rather lightly, assuming that the size of the object is in direct proportion to its importance and acquisition requirements. In the past, the mere absence of a title page relegated a great deal of material to discard piles—and in some cases, it still does. The fact that it is extraordinarily easy to produce or purchase slides at a relatively low per item cost should not overshadow the necessity for adequate funds for cataloging, classifying, record keeping, and staffing. A total program for slide production and processing should be realized from the outset of collection building.

REFERENCES

The Audio-Visual Equipment Directory: A Guide to Current Models of A-V Equipment. 1977-78. 23rd edition. Fairfax, Virginia: National Audio-Visual Association.

Audiovisual Marketplace. A Multimedia Guide. 1978. New York: R. R. Bowker Company. Biennial publication.

"Black and White Slide Film in Use at the University of Missouri—Kansas City." 1977. *Mid-America College Art Association Slides and Photographs Newsletter* 4 (Fall):6.

Bowker AV Guide: A Subject Guide to Audio-Visual Educational Material. 1975. Edited by Marion Koenig. New York: Bowker.

Carroll, Hardy. 1977. "Primary Sources for Understanding the New Copyright Law." *College and Research Libraries News* 1 (January):1-2.

Chandler, Devon. 1975. "Transparency Microfiche: A New Dimension." *Audiovisual Instruction* 20 (December):45-46.

Churney, Marie. 1975. "Making Slides from Black-and-White Negatives." *Science Teacher* 42 (Fall):54+ .

Cyr, J. 1977. "Making Color Slides without a Camera." *Arts and Activities* 82 (November):41-43, 61.

DeLaurier, Nancy. 1975. "Slide Curators Professional Status Survey: Additional Statistical Report." Mimeographed. Kansas City, Missouri: Department of Art and Art History, University of Missouri.

DeLaurier, Nancy. 1977. "More on Slide Film." *Mid-America College Art Association Slides and Photographs Newsletter* 4 (Spring):10-11.

DeLaurier, Nancy. 1979. Personal communication.

The Encyclopedia of Photography. 1965. 20 vols. New York: Greystone Press.

Erickson, Carlton W. H. 1968. *Administering Instructional Media Programs*. New York: The Macmillan Company.

"Film and Photography." 1978. *Mid-America College Art Association Slides and Photographs Newsletter* 5 (Summer):7.

"The Four Most Important Colour-Systems in Colour-Photography Now: I. Kodak; II. AGFA-Gavaert; III. Polaroid; IV. Cibachrome." 1977. *Camera* 56 (July): 39-43.

Gardner, C. Hugh. 1976. "Making the Most of Your Visual Maker." *Audiovisual Instruction* 21 (March):48-49, 51-53.

Gassan, Arnold. 1977. *Handbook for Contemporary Photography*. 4th edition. Rochester, New York: Light Impressions.

A Handlist of Museum Sources for Slides and Photographs. 1972. Prepared by Sharon Petrini and Troy-Jjohn Bromberger. Santa Barbara, California: The Slide Library, the Art Department, University of California at Santa Barbara.

Hershenson, Martin. 1978. "Permanence." *Technical Photography* 10 (August): 14-15, 48.

Holland, Ben F., Horace C. Hartsell, and Raymond L. Davidson. 1958. *Audio-Visual Materials and Devices*. Lubbock, Texas: Rodgers Litho.

Hollander, Steven. 1974. "Better, Faster 35mm Black and White Transparencies." *Audiovisual Instruction* 19 (November):83-84.

Index to Educational Slides. 1977. Los Angeles: National Information Center for Educational Media (NICEM), University of Southern California.

Index to Producers and Distributors. 1977. 4th edition. Los Angeles: National Information Center for Educational Media (NICEM), University of Southern California.

Jones, R. B. 1976. "Black and White Slides from Super Speed Duplicating Film." *Audiovisual Instruction* 21 (September):61.

Lewis, Elizabeth. 1979. "The Marburger Index." *Microforms Review* [in press].

Lewis, John N. C., and Edwin Smith. 1969. *The Graphic Reproduction and Photography of Works of Art*. London: W. S. Cowell, Ltd.

Media Review Digest: The Only Complete Guide to Reviews of Non-book Media. 1973- . Ann Arbor, Michigan: The Pierian Press.

Mess, C. E. K. 1961. *From Dry Plates to Ektachrome: A Film Story of Photographic Research*. New York: Ziff-Davis.

Minor, Ed., and Harvey R. Frye. 1977. *Techniques for Producing Visual Instructional Media*. 2nd edition. New York: McGraw-Hill.

Mirwis, Allan. 1977. *GEMS, Guides to Educational Media Software*. Brooklyn: Educational Media Information Service.

Museum Media; A Biennial Directory and Index of Publications and Audiovisuals Available from United States and Canadian Institutions. 1973. Edited by Paul Wasserman and Esther Herman. Detroit, Michigan: Gale Research.

National Audiovisual Center. 1974. *A Catalog of U.S. Government Produced AV Materials, 1974.* Washington, D.C.: NAVC, National Archives and Records Service, General Services Administration.

Planning and Producing Slide Programs. 1978. Rochester, New York: Eastman Kodak. (Kodak Publication No. S-30).

PMI Photo Methods for Industry Catalog and Directory of Products and Services. New York: Gellert Publishing Corp. Published annually.

Professional Photographic Catalog. Chicago: Standard Photo Supply. Published annually.

Ritchie, Andrew C. 1966. *The Visual Arts in Higher Education.* New York: College Arts Association.

Rosenthal, John W. 1978. "Helpful Hints for Color Correction." *Mid-America College Art Association Slides and Photographs Newsletter* 5 (Summer):6-7.

Schwarz, Philip J. 1978. "Use of Color Microfiche as a Replacement for Slides in a University Elementary Accounting Course." *The Journal of Micrographics* 11 (Jan./Feb.):217-19.

Scott, E. 1972. "Hand-made Slide: Whetstone for Perceptual Acuity." *Arts and Activities* 71 (April):30-31.

Siddall, William R. 1969. "Making Slides from Printed Materials." *Journal of Geography* 68 (October):430-32.

Siebert, Fred S. 1964. *Copyrights, Clearances, and Rights of Teachers in the New Educational Media.* Washington, D.C.: American Council on Education.

Slide Buyer's Guide. 1976. Prepared by Nancy DeLaurier. New York: College Art Association.

Sources for Commercial Slides of the Illustrations in Gardner's Art Through the Ages. 1976. Sixth edition. Compiled by Luraine Tansey with Melody Barch and Linda Burton. New York: Harcourt Brace Jovanovich, Inc.

Sources of Slides. The History of Art. 1970. New York: The Slide Library, The Metropolitan Museum of Art.

"Statement on Slide Quality Standards." 1978. Prepared by the Joint ARLIS/VRSIG-CAA/VR Subcommittee. *Mid-America College Arts Association Slides and Photographs Newsletter* 5 (June):5.

Using Polarized Light for Copying. 1975. Rochester, New York: Eastman Kodak Company. (Kodak Publication No. S-70-1-2).

Wiesinger, Robert. 1964. "Instant 35mm Slides." *Educational Screen and AV Guide* 43 (February):88.

6–STORAGE AND ACCESS SYSTEMS

INTRODUCTION

Storage for any type of information—whether it is in book, microfiche, micro-film, magnetic tape, or slide format—is constantly changing depending upon the technology available. In the future, it is possible that traditional book libraries as they exist today may only be rare book archives or found in history museums, because the common information medium may be microfiche combined with audio systems or else computer data banks accessible by on-line consoles in homes, offices, or educational institutions. Many of these changes are occurring at the present time. Ultimately, visual data may be electronically stored and retrievable through display consoles in each classroom, so teacher and student would never become involved in the physical removal of slides from a drawer or file. At the present time, automated carrels on the market offer the student unlimited possi-bilities for independent learning situations, combining audio-tape, filmstrip, 16mm projectors, and slide systems. However, until the complete storage and retrieval of visual data is a standard procedure, manual slide storage and access systems will prevail for lack of a better solution.

HOW TO SELECT A STORAGE FACILITY

In order to select a suitable facility for filing slides, both the storage and the accessibility function of that facility should be considered. Ten questions should be asked and answered in a satisfactory manner to determine which type of facility will be best suited to institutional needs.

1. **How are the slides to be used?** This is one of the most critical questions asked to determine the type of housing needed. Slides filed and used either by set or individually should have a storage system that reflects this use pattern. Slide libraries based upon a set rather than an individual slide arrangement will also tend to have different acquisition, cataloging, and classification systems. Slides used by set can be stored directly in the projector trays or magazines, which can then be stored on open shelves, in cabinets, or in one of the multi-media units on the market designed to handle slides, filmstrips, tape, 16mm films, and other media. If slides are used by set, any of the unitary image methods of storage would prove cumbersome and inconvenient, while the opposite would apply to slides utilized individually. Groups of slides that are constantly needed for visual reference are inconvenient to the user if housed in drawers. Even tray or magazine storage may be undesirable if immediate visual study is necessary. Filing the slides on visual display racks or in plastic sleeves—holding twenty slides; four horizontally and five vertically—provides immediate visual access to the files without the aid of auxiliary equipment such as projectors.

2. **Who is to use the slides?** Different types of users will demand various storage systems. For teachers working in a given subject area who need immediate access to slides on a daily basis, slides filed together by sets will probably be most

convenient. For individuals requiring a multi-disciplinary approach, it may be more desirable to file slides individually by subject categories and to allow each user maximum flexibility to integrate different areas. Whatever system is used, it should be relatively consistent throughout the collection. Too many methods of organization and storage within a single collection will tend to disperse materials and confuse the user. There is, of course, the possibility of duplicating or making multiple copies of slides so that a single image might be available in more than one place in the collection. Using multiple copies, a single image could be filed individually, by set, or in different subject categories at the same time.

3. **How frequently will the slides be used?** If users are constantly demanding the use of single slides that are normally kept in sets, it may be more efficient to begin a slide filing and storage system that is better suited to these requirements. Or, if users are continually frustrated by the individual filing system because they must always rearrange their slides by set for presentation purposes, a storage system should be adapted for this use pattern. If the collection is rarely used or is archival in nature, a storage system that provides maximum protection from handling, humidity, and temperature fluctuations should be selected.

4. **How many individuals will the collection serve?** If a great many users are served by the collection, congestion may occur at the files if the slides have not been stored to allow access by more than one user at a time. Single vertical cabinets having a capacity of 7,000 to 8,000 slides may be undesirable, because only one user at a time can have access to the files. Because drawers in large capacity cabinets are usually quite cumbersome, they are awkward to remove for consultation. Some vertical cabinets, however, can be designed with removable trays that fit inside the drawers. There are also small cabinets available for housing about 2,500 mounted slides or fewer; these have easily removable drawers and can be stacked or placed on table tops throughout the slide library. In selecting proper storage equipment, it is important to know the number of people who use the files at one time. Photographs in this chapter illustrating various housing types will assist in decision-making on this subject.

5. **What type of expansion schedule will the collection have?** Some storage systems are not conducive to rapid expansion rates, while others are. If the slides are filed by set within trays or magazines, acquisition will not affect those slides already filed; but if constant interfiling of new slides is required for visual display rack cabinets, then moving and readjusting slides on these racks can be quite time-consuming and impractical with this housing system. It is most convenient when entire drawers or trays of slides can be moved in groups to allow for expansion, which is possible in many standard drawer-type cabinets.

6. **How will the collection be filed?** Flexibility and user requirements should dictate multiple types of storage when necessary. Even in a predominantly unitary image collection, there may be a select number of slide sets for standard lectures. Slide sets can be filed in projector trays if they are consistently utilized in the same lecture pattern. Unitary image collections can utilize a variety of filing patterns depending upon how the slides are organized. For example, a collection having an interfiled shelflist may be filed with the cards in front of the slides, behind the slides, and with or without rods holding the cards. Filing can also be affected by color coding the top of the slide; by glancing through a drawer, it is immediately

apparent if any slide is not in the correct section of the collection (i.e., each medium would have a distinct color band across the top of the mount, thereby identifying all architecture, sculpture, painting slides). Another variation of this form of coding is the typing of brief label identification on the top edge of a label that has been designed to extend over the top of the slide mount. The Winterthur Museum uses *both* color and label coding on the top of their slide labels to facilitate filing. Further discussion of the effects of filing on storage will be included with the various types of storage systems.

7.   **How will the collection be circulated?** If it is to be circulated in sets, then it should be housed and filed in sets if at all feasible. A collection that is not circulated and used only for visual access will demand a storage system conducive to visual examination without necessarily involving the removal of slides from their housing. For example, visual display rack or plastic sleeve filing in loose-leaf notebooks may be practical in this case. Or, the core or basic collection may never circulate, because duplicates are automatically made for lecture purposes and for research use of slides.

8.   **How much time can be allowed for slide presentation preparation?** In some instances, faculty or lecturers may prefer not to rummage through drawers locating slides individually for slide presentations, but would rather have access to slides by tray, magazine, or set so that the entire slide show is ready as soon as the set or tray is removed from the shelf or cabinet in the slide library. This method of storage, however, is neither recommended nor advisable for all institutions or individuals utilizing slides. Visual display housing may aid in the convenient and more rapid selection of slides depending upon the user's needs. In other instances, drawer housing may prove adequate.

9.   **How much care should be taken to prevent handling of individual slides?** In the past, adequate slide mounts have not been readily available or economically feasible for many collections. With the advent of plastic and aluminum slide mounts, the problems previously associated with handling are not as critical as they have been. Staff time and expense for mounting slides and for protecting them properly from damage may still be prohibitive for some collections, although many of the new mounts—particularly the plastic ones—require a minimal amount of time for binding. Such mounts are reusable. If the slides are kept in cardboard mounts without the protection of glass, they should be handled as little as possible to avoid marring the film with fingerprints, scratches, or dirt. The visual display rack method of storage is more viable for slides not protected by glass mounts than a drawer system, because the user is less likely to handle or remove the slides from the cabinet unless intending to use them. Visual display storage allows study and examination of slides with minimal slide handling, because the slides do not have to be removed from their housing for viewing.

10.   **What are the budget limitations for the collection?** Storage systems will range in cost from less than $10 for a box, tray, or magazine to over $500 for a wooden or metal cabinet. Some cabinets may be as high as $1,000 depending upon whether they are wood or metal, have custom-made drawer interiors, or visual display racks. The most expensive cabinet is not necessarily the most efficient or best solution for slide housing in a given institution. If all the factors of use and collection building do not influence cabinet choice, an extremely costly and unfortunate error may result.

TYPES OF STORAGE

There are four basic types of slide storage:

1. Filing drawer cabinets for individual slides or slide sets. Slides must be removed from the drawers for viewing.
2. Visual display rack cabinets. Slides are filed on metal frames, which pull out for immediate visual access.
3. Tray or magazine storage. Trays designed for projector viewing and boxed slide sets are placed in boxes, which can be stacked or shelved.
4. Plastic sleeve storage. Slides inserted into plastic sleeves held in loose-leaf binders are easily accessible for viewing.

Filing Drawer Cabinets—The majority of academic collections in the United States utilize a metal filing drawer cabinet, allowing for individual slide filing. This method of storage is indicative of the cataloging, circulation, and filing patterns used in most academic institutions. These collections have relatively heavy use patterns and need a system whereby large quantities of individual slides may be frequently removed from the drawers. Each slide is individually filed, cataloged, and circulated as a single unit rather than as part of a predetermined subject set. Moreover, most of these collections exhibit extensive expansion patterns, so storage must be readily adaptable to continual interfiling of new slides.

Within the range of filing drawer cabinets, there are various cabinet types. Cabinets may be either metal or wood, have a fixed filing slot for each slide or for a group of slides, or have an expansive system using some form of backstop to keep the slides in an upright position. Some cabinets can be supplied with either fixed single slide or group filing inserts—often supplied with the cabinets—so that variable filing arrangements are possible. Neumade, Luxor, and Wilson slide cabinets can accommodate either group or single slide filing systems (see Photograph 2, page 170). Neumade cabinets can be stacked or individually placed on tables or desks (see Photograph 8, page 179) or can be stored within a floor model console cabinet (see Photograph 10, page 182). The Neumade metal console cabinet can be purchased with or without lockable doors. Similar in design to Neumade cabinets, Wallach cabinets are designed only for group filing.

One of the most common group filing systems is a standard wooden card catalog modified as a slide cabinet. This type of cabinet is a stock item made by Library Bureau Division of Mohawk Valley Community Corporation and is referred to as a 2x2-inch file cabinet (Photographs 4, page 172; 5, page 173; 17, page 234). An added feature of these cabinets is the availability of sliding reference shelves, such as those used with standard library card cabinets, which provide flat workspace at the file. Each drawer has a fixed wooden panel placed down the center; this has slots that correspond to those on wooden panels placed down the sides of each drawer. Within these slots, either cardboard, plastic, or fibreboard cards may be inserted to hold the slides in an upright position. The height of the insert cards is the same height as—or slightly higher than—the wooden drawer panels that correspond to the interior height of the drawer. Diagrams 4 and 5 (see pages 174-75) illustrate how these different interiors appear in perspective and provide overhead views of a single row. Drawers may vary from two to seven or more rows. The filing slots for either single or group slide filing may be the same height as the top of the drawers

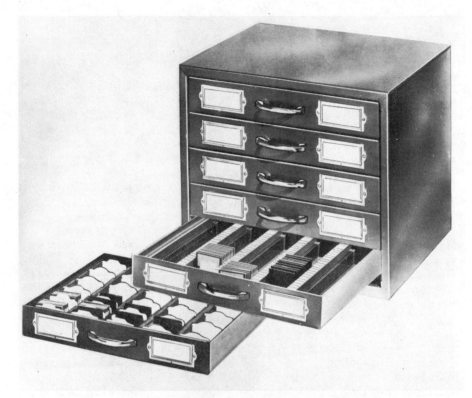

Photograph 2. Neumade 2x2-inch slide cabinet shown with drawers for single
slide filing and for group filing (bottom). (Photograph
courtesy of Neumade Products Corporation.)

or as low as ½-inches above the drawer bottom. The panels placed inside card catalog drawers for slide storage conversion may be designed for single or group filing
of slides. Backstops similar to those used in standard card catalog cabinets may be
used for slides.

User preferences play an important role in drawer selection. Some may consider it an inconvenience to have to remove each slide individually, as would be the
case with fixed single slide filing slots. In this case, group filing is preferred. The backstop drawer also allows for more flexibility within each filing row, because new groups
of slides may be added to the row without moving slides from one fixed group or
single unit location to another. A drawer designed for group filing will usually accommodate twice as many slides as one for single filing because of the amount of space
required to section the interior of the drawer for single slide filing slots (Photograph
2, above, and Diagram 5, page 175). Slides in cardboard mounts require about half
the filing space of those with plastic, metal or glass mounts. Some slide drawers
are designed to hold only cardboard mounted slides—this is only true of drawers for
fixed slot single slide filing. Regular mounted slides can be filed eight per inch;
cardboard mounted slides can be filed sixteen per inch. Cardboard or fibreboard

inserts spaced every inch support eight slides. Seven of the eight slides can be removed without having the remaining slides fall to the bottom of the drawer. With any group or sequence filing system, the slides should be grouped so that a user may withdraw most of the slides from a single group without having the remaining slides dependent upon the removed slides for their support within the drawer—this is the function of the fibreboard inserts.

Another factor affecting cabinet choice is the user preference for cabinets having easily removable and relatively lightweight individual drawers. For example, the small lightweight metal Neumade, the wooden Nega-File, and the Library Bureau wooden slide cabinets have drawers that can be removed from the cabinets and used throughout the slide library (see Photographs 2, page 170; 3, below; 4, page 172; 5, page 173; 7, page 178; 8, page 179).

Photograph 3. Nega-File slide cabinets and custom-made light tables in foreground; Library Bureau 3¼x4-inch cabinets in rear. Department of Art and Archaeology. Princeton University.

Photograph 4. Library Bureau 2x2-inch wooden slide cabinets with custom-made illuminators and work areas in foreground. Graduate School of Fine Arts. The University of Pennsylvania.

Such stacking units are usually a convenient size, have lightweight drawers, and have either single or group filing slots for slides. The large single-unit metal filing cabinet will hold up to 11,500 slides, and it requires less space than the stacking units for an equivalent number of slides. Because of the size of individual drawers and their storage capacity, which may be as high as 1,000 slides per drawer, these drawers are too bulky and heavy for removal for daily use by patrons. The drawers are usually the width and depth of standard metal filing cabinets, while the height of the cabinet may vary from four to five feet or more, depending upon the type of base used. Photograph 13 (see page 193) shows vertical metal slide cabinets utilized at the University of Illinois at Chicago Circle and the Walker Art Center. In order to allow the patron to remove sections of a drawer conveniently, it is possible to have removable trays built for the drawers of metal files as has been done at the University of Illinois at Chicago Circle and the Walker Art Center. The cabinets used

(Text continues on page 176)

Photograph 5. Library Bureau wooden slide cabinets and carrels for slide viewing (adapted from Model No. 65901 made by Herman Miller, New York). The Metropolitan Museum of Art. (Photograph courtesy of the Metropolitan Museum of Art.)

Diagram 4—Wooden panels that change card catalog drawers into slide
files—perspective view.

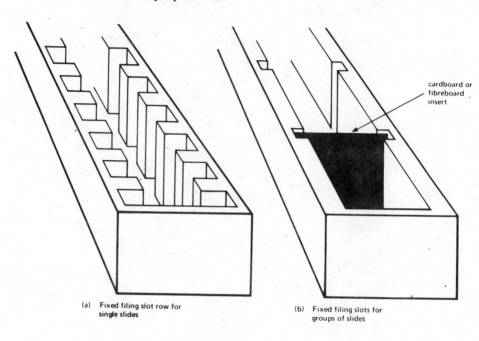

cardboard or
fibreboard
insert

(a) Fixed filing slot row for
single slides

(b) Fixed filing slots for
groups of slides

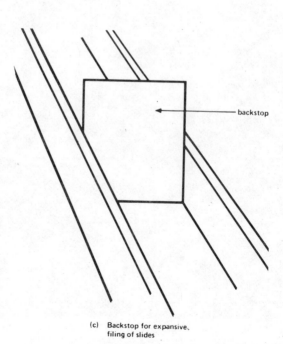

backstop

(c) Backstop for expansive,
filing of slides

Diagram 5—Wooden panels that change card catalog drawers into slide files—overhead view.

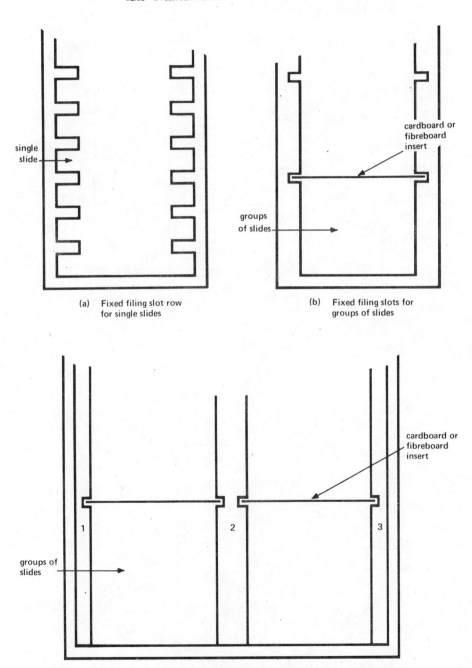

(a) Fixed filing slot row
for single slides

(b) Fixed filing slots for
groups of slides

(c) Converted card catalog drawer with panel inserts
(1, 2, 3) with fixed filing slots for groups of slides

are ten-drawer Steelcase metal files. Diagrams 6 and 7 illustrate how such trays may be designed and placed in the drawers. (The Walker Art Center slide trays are custom made by Lauderdale Industries.)

Diagram 6–One of eight trays designed to be placed in a Steelcase metal filing cabinet.

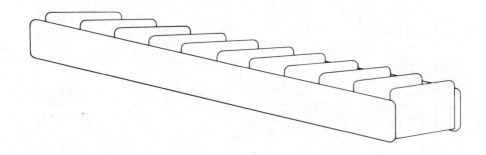

Diagram 7–Overhead view showing eight trays per drawer.

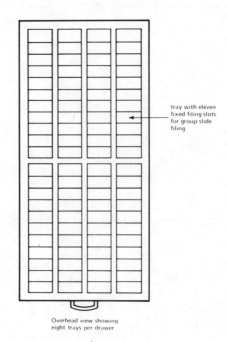

tray with eleven fixed filing slots for group slide filing

Overhead view showing eight trays per drawer

The metal cabinets illustrated thus far have been designed for slides, although interior alterations may have been made. The Philadelphia College of Art (Photograph 6) demonstrates how an imaginative conversion of a filing system can be made to adapt to slide storage. A custom-made tray has been designed to fit on the six levels of a metal horizontal filing cabinet. There are eight trays per level: each cabinet holds 48 trays, for a total slide capacity of about 6,500 slides. Each tray holds two rows of slides without the use of fixed filing slots or a backstop. The trays may be removed and set on top the cabinets for slide examination. These cabinets can be stacked if they are bolted together and then fastened to the wall.

Photograph 6. Conserva Files (made by Supreme Steel Equipment Corporation) with custom-made illuminators for slide preparation and viewing in foreground. The Conserva File is a waist-high cabinet with pull-out racks for which custom-made trays have been made which are shelved 8 per rack, a 48-tray capacity per cabinet. Each cabinet holds from 6,000 to 7,000 slides. Philadelphia College of Art.

If it is necessary to take precautions against the indiscriminate or accidental removal of guide or shelflist cards from the drawers, rods may be installed in metal or wooden filing cabinets (see Diagram 1, page 128). In cabinets designed for metal rods, the rod may not have been set low enough for this particular function, but the amount of tipping may be so slight that it may not present a problem, depending upon the height of the rod from the dropped portion of the drawer. If the cabinets do not come equipped with rods, standard metal slide files such as those by Steelcase could be altered to hold rods.

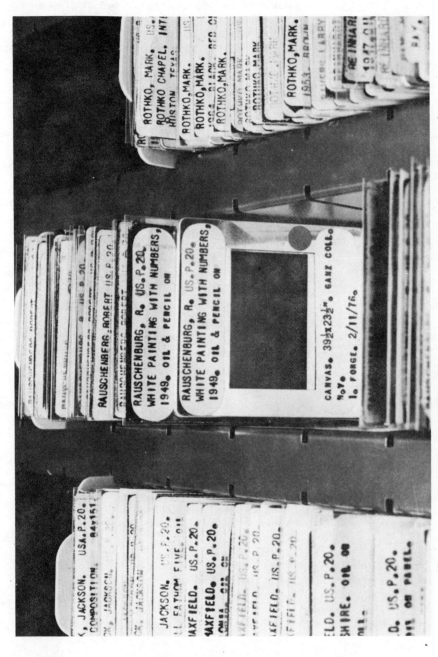

Photograph 7. Neumade metal 2x2-inch slide drawer. Interior view showing Mylar shelflist cards placed behind slides. Fine Arts Department, Indiana University.

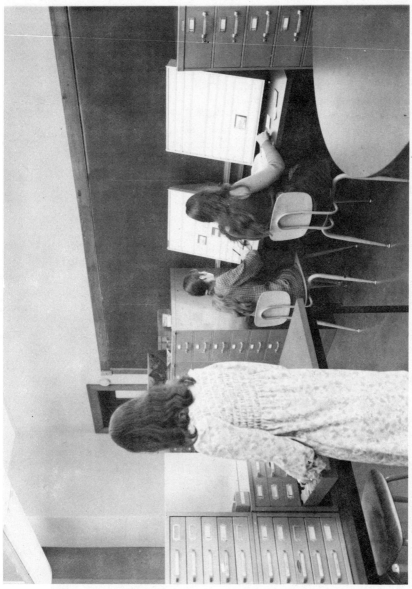

Photograph 8. Neumade stacking slide cabinets, Steelcase cabinets modified for 3¼x4-inch slides (against wall at right), and Ednalite Transviewer being used for slide preview. Department of the History of Art. The University of Michigan. (Photograph courtesy of Robert Williams, Photographic Services, The University of Michigan.)

A small number of collections have custom-made cabinets that campus or private workshops build to their specifications. Others purchase standard filing cabinets, then fit them with trays designed and built within the institution (Diagram 6, page 176). Commercially available cabinets vary in price from less than $100 per unit to more than $500 per unit. If custom-made trays are used, the additional cost may be $200 or more, depending upon the size of the cabinet and the number of trays needed. Whether a great deal of money is saved by custom-designing the entire cabinet is questionable. The efficiency of custom-made systems varies from one institution to another. Before embarking upon the task of custom-designing cabinet storage systems, those available commercially should be studied and examined.

Portable slide storage cases could be used as temporary housing for slides (see Chapter 9), but they are not recommended as permanent storage. They are not designed to stack or to be shelved vertically. The primary function of these cases is for carrying slides and not for storing them.

Visual Display Rack Cabinets—The second type of storage system uses display racks that support slides on metal frames. This system allows slides to be examined without removing them from the cabinet (see Photograph 9). Visual display rack storage is particularly well suited to laboratory or studio use where comparison and examination of slides is desirable. However, a supplementary index to the slides stored in display racks is necessary. It is not possible to include guide cards on the racks unless they are the exact dimensions of the slide—2x2-inches or 3x4-inches—including surface and density dimensions. The cost of guides equivalent in size to slides would be prohibitive and the additional space required for them would substantially decrease the filing capacity of the cabinet. Frequently, these cabinets are supplied with an indexing card, which allows for listing slides by rack and frame. Because of the large amount of time required to rearrange and refile slides in display racks, this type of storage system is not well suited to rapidly expanding collections or those with extensive acquisition programs. If, however, slides are arranged by accession order, or if the growth pattern is low, these cabinets may provide adequate storage for slides.

An interfiled shelflist for slides stored in display racks is most difficult to implement although a separate shelflist is quite functional. If a circulation system is necessary, charge-sheets or cards arranged by call number, accession number, or the name of the user are the most viable systems.

A single slide rack may hold up to 100 or more slides depending upon the type of cabinet. As is shown in Photograph 9, these cabinets usually come equipped with their own viewing equipment, such as a lightbox built-in behind the racks to illuminate the slides for convenient viewing. Another variation of visual display rack storage is based upon horizontal rather than vertical slide racks, e.g., Visual Horizons Slide Storage Cabinet. The horizontal rack slides out in the same manner as a drawer so that the viewer looks down at the slides. These cabinets also include a light box that automatically turns on when a slide rack is pulled out for viewing. Visual display rack storage is used at the following institutions: California State University, Northridge; C-E Refractories (Clawson and Rankowski, 1978); Evergreen State College; Ringling School of Art; University of Missouri—Kansas City School of Medicine (Raymond and Algermissen, 1976); and the University of Oregon. Multiplex Display Fixture Co. also makes this type of cabinet.

Photograph 9. ABODIA 5000-Visual slide storage cabinet (made by Elden Enterprises, Inc.). The slides can be locked behind plexiglas doors, with access to each rack possible from the top of the cabinet. Fifty metal racks hold 100 slides each. The racks pull out from both sides of the cabinet. Each base drawer can hold up to 3,250 cardboard mounted slides. (Photograph courtesy of Elden Enterprises, Inc.)

The storage system can affect the way in which a collection may be utilized and organized. Visual display rack cabinets adapt best to situations that demand immediate visual access, avoid complicated interfiling arrangements, file slides by accession order, or closely limit expansion within the main body of the collection.

Tray or Magazine Storage—For storage of formal presentations on a single subject or topic, slides can be stored in trays or magazines for immediate classroom use. Both the teacher and the students can enjoy the convenience of slides previously selected and arranged for them on a specific topic. A large number of companies have slide sets available (see Directory of Slide Sources), and such sets should be kept together if they are consistently used as sets. The boxes in which commercially produced slide sets are sold can be used as permanent storage. These boxes, however, will tend to vary greatly in durability and general quality, so they may not be satisfactory for long-term storage. For heavily used sets, storage directly in projector trays is recommended. Trays or magazines of the circular or rectangular box type vary in size and capacity, depending upon the projector for which they are designed. The use of this type of storage is based on the following prerequisites: 1) the institution is using automatic slide-changing projectors or projectors equipped with slide-changing trays; 2) only 2x2-inch slides are purchased and used; 3) the institution has an adequate indexing system to insure maximum utility of slides; 4) as

Photograph 10. Neumade 2x2-inch stacking slide cabinets against wall at left and in center. Custom-made light tables at right. E. S. Bird Library. Syracuse University. (Photograph courtesy of Ramona Roters, Slide Librarian.)

the slides will receive no handling, or at least, minimal handling, they will probably not require heavy-duty mounts (glass, plastic, or metal binders with glass) to protect them. Slide mounts, however, do serve more functions than merely protection from handling and these will be discussed in Chapter 9.

Circulation is relatively simple, as each box rather than each individual slide can be charged out by call number or accession number. Magazines or trays are usually supplied with cardboard or plastic boxes that provide the permanent housing for the slide trays. The filing arrangement of the slides within magazines or trays is predetermined by the slide distributor or manufacturer, or by the individual who developed the sets. These boxes of magazines or trays can be shelved on standard library shelves, in cabinets, or on projection stands. Using this system, the slides may be satisfactorily intershelved with the book collection. Both the trays or magazines and the boxes are relatively inexpensive, usually costing less than $10.

Plastic Sleeve Storage—The fourth type of storage system files groups or sets of slides in plastic or vinyl holders. Each sleeve contains twenty pockets for slides. The holders can be purchased in standard sheet size, 8½x11-inches, to fit in loose-leaf binders. This system also allows for immediate visual access and has the same limitations and advantages as the visual display rack cabinets. These holders are designed for cardboard mounted slides only. Vinyl sleeves cost less than $0.50 each and are stocked by most photography stores. Whether this method of storage is advisable for a large collection of slide sets is questionable, unless the slides are rarely removed for projector viewing and are only used in the holders either for direct visual examination or with overhead projectors.

Plastic sleeve storage is used for the circulating collection (15,422 slides) in the Educational Materials Center at Marycrest College, Iowa, and for teaching slide sets in the Pathology Department at the University of California, San Diego (Strohlein, 1975, p. 35). However, use of plastic sleeves has not been commonly documented for U.S. slide libraries. The following institutions in the United Kingdom and South Africa have recorded their use of this storage technique: Design Council Slide Library (Murton, 1976); Edinburgh College of Art (Viles, 1973); Preston Polytechnic School of Art and Design (Pacey, 1977); and the Stellenbosch University Medical Library, South Africa (Visser, 1977).

A major disadvantage of plastic sleeves is that moisture tends to collect between the film and the plastic, and this condensation may cause permanent damage to the film. In addition, most plastics are made with polyvinyl chloride (PVC), which emits chlorine (HCL) gases that attack the silver in black and white film and the dyes in color film. Mylar and cellulose tri-acetate sleeves are recommended for storing negatives and transparencies (Kach, 1978, p. 47). These sleeves are available from Kodak and Talas Library Services, New York. In order to combat problems associated with moisture and PVC, the Franklin Distributors Corporation developed an archival storage system for slides based upon the use of a "firm, lightweight plastic that provides a protective backing for slides, and at the same time offer enough defused light to skan-view the slides" ("Safe Slide Filing," 1976). Rather than placing slides in pockets, as is typical of plastic sleeves, the slide is placed in a fixed slot having raised edges to secure the slide. Each molded page has twenty slots to hold slides and may be stored upright in filing cabinets or flat in loose-leaf binders. These sleeves and those from the Kimac Corporation are made from translucent polypropylene (Kach, 1978). Other sources for plastic sleeves and molded plastic pages are listed in the directory under "Plastic Album Pages."

ENVIRONMENT CONTROLS IN THE SLIDE LIBRARY

Automated retrieval systems, expensive cabinets, and thousands of dollars allocated to purchase and produce slides will be of little value if there are no provisions for proper humidity and temperature controls in the slide library. High humidity will cause fungal growth and film base degeneration. Low humidity will cause film to become brittle. High temperatures will cause rapid fading of color dyes. Both the temperature and the relative humidity should be properly controlled to maximize short- and long-term storage and use of slide films. The American National Standards Institute (ANSI), the British Standards Institution, Eastman Kodak, and the International Standard Organization (ISO) have documented preferred conditions of climate control for films for temporary and archival storage. The following ANSI recommendations provide guidelines for minimum and maximum ranges for humidity and temperature that are applicable to slide film:

HUMIDITY

Short-term storage shall not exceed 60% rh and should not be lower than 30% rh (ANSI 1976, p. 8).
Prolonged exposure to conditions above 60% relative humidity will tend to destroy the gelatin emulsion layer due to the growth of fungus.
Relative humidity of greater than 90% can lead to degradation of the film base.
To store at low humidity avoids fungal growth as well as reduces the rate of chemical degradation (p. 13).

TEMPERATURE

Ideally, a maximum temperature for extended periods should not exceed 24°C (75°F) and temperature below 21°C (70°F) is preferable (p. 8).
Continuous temperatures above about 38°C (100°F) may permanently reduce the pliability of some film bases and may accelerate fading of dye images and vesicular images (p. 13).

According to Kodak, slides should be stored where it is "dry, dark, and cool" with a relative humidity in the range of 25 to 50% and a temperature of 70°F or less (*Proper Care . . .* , 1978, p. 67). While the life of black and white film may be extended for considerable periods of time if stored under these conditions (about 30-40% rh and 70°F), color dyes are not stable and will fade even in dark, cool storage. "For optimum dye stability," Kodak recommends that negatives be stored in "a freezer at -18° to -23°C (0° to -10°F)" and that for archival storage of color images, it is necessary to "make three color-separation negatives on black-and-white film and process for permanence" (*Kodak Color Dataguide*, 1978, p. 11).

The widespread use of color films since the 1950s has created a vast pool of recorded information in a form that, unfortunately, appears to have a relatively short life span. While various standards organizations have been primarily concerned with black and white film, Henry Wilhelm (head of the East Street Gallery, Grinnell, Iowa) has been engaged in research to develop guidelines for storing color films to maximize their usable life. In order to document his work, he has written

Preservation of Contemporary Photography Materials (1978). A summary of Wilhelm's conclusions (excerpted from his book) and a related paper by David Kach were published in *Industrial Photography* and provide an excellent overview of problems and solutions related to storing color film (1978). Wilhelm delineates very precise storage configurations based upon the use of a "modern frost-free refrigerator/freezer," which maintains a "temperature of about 1.5°C (35°F) and relative humidity levels between 25 and 35 percent all year around, regardless of the ambient humidity and temperature levels" (1978, p. 32). Before installing a refrigerator in a slide library, Wilhelm's guidelines should be carefully studied, as they require strict conformity to rigid specifications for humidity and temperature controls that are not necessarily met by most refrigerators. For slides that are used regularly and do not represent material of archival or research value, refrigerated storage is not practical. Collections of slides used for instruction or for public loan and stored where people regularly work should conform to the following environmental controls:

1) temperature range of 70°F to 75°F with 70°F preferred;
2) humidity range of 30 to 40%;
3) storage on a main floor of a building with basements and attics as the least desirable locations; and
4) filtered air to minimize dust and dirt particles.

If a slide collection is maintained in an especially humid climate, additional controls may be necessary. The University of Houston College of Architecture Slide Library provides a useful example of how to deal with humidity control (Tannenbaum, 1978). First, wooden cabinets are not used to store slides, as they tend to absorb and retain moisture. Neumade metal slide files house the collection and provide adequate air circulation among stored slides. Second, in addition to having air-conditioning, a room-sized dehumidifier is run in the slide library. Third, film cans filled with silica gel are placed in the back of each *drawer* of the slide cabinets. Fourth, containerized silica gel is placed in the bottom of each slide storage *case* used to carry slides to and from classes. Unfortunately, Houston still has problems with fungus despite all these measures. Reported in the *Journal of Micrographics*, a "new method of simple, inexpensive film protection, ethylene oxide, dry color sterilization" may offer some future solutions to fungus growth (Dorfman, 1978, p. 257). Individuals working with slide film should periodically check the literature to keep abreast of such studies and review data issued by the American Society for Testing and Materials for research on fungus testing. (Manufacturers and/or distributors of products used for film care and for humidity control are listed in the directory under "Materials for Film Care/Preservation.")
     The slide librarian should be alerted to the fact that images that seem relatively insignificant or ephemeral today may indeed become the research artifacts for later generations of historians. In fact, such a situation does exist regarding the preservation of lantern slides, which, in some instances, record architecture, monuments, paintings, sculpture and other artforms that have since been lost or destroyed by wars, their environment, or careless handling. Archival collections of lantern slides are maintained in institutions such as the Library of Congress and the Eastman House in Rochester, New York. For those seeking information on the care and storage of lantern slides, guidelines are provided in *Collection, Use, and Care of*

Historical Photographs (Weinstein and Booth, 1977). Many academic institutions that still have large lantern slide collections have begun to transfer these rather fragile images to 35mm slides, e.g., Columbia University Graduate School of Architecture, Princeton University, SUNY at Buffalo, the University of Colorado, and the University of Wisconsin. National attention was called to the dilemma of lantern slide preservation versus conversion at a recent workshop held by slide curators and librarians during a meeting of the College Art Association (Scott, 1978, p. 28). The concept of regional conservation centers or of a national lantern slide depository has also been discussed among those concerned with the care and handling of these collections ("Visual Resources SIG . . . ," 1977). During the last ten years, the increasing awareness of the need to preserve photographic documents will surely promote future action to preserve lantern slides. (See also section V, "Care and Preservation of Films and Slides" in the Selected Bibliography.)

REFERENCES

American National Standards Institute. 1976. "Practice for Storage of Processed Safety Photographic Film." New York: American National Standards Institute. ANSI PH1.43-1976.

Clawson, Datherine R., and Charles A. Rankowski. 1978. "Classification and Cataloging of Slides Using Color Photocopying." *Special Libraries* 69 (August): 281-85.

Dorfman, Harold H. 1978. "The Effect of Fungus on Silver Gelatin, Diazo and Vesicular Films." *Journal of Micrographics* 11 (March):257-60.

Kach, David. 1978. "Photographic Dilemma: Stability and Storage of Color Materials." *Industrial Photography* 27 (August):28-29, 46-50.

Kodak Color Dataguide. 1978. Sixth edition. Rochester, New York: Eastman Kodak. (Kodak Publication No. R-19).

Murton, Jan. 1976. "Design Council Slide Library." *Art Libraries Journal* 1 (Winter):26-32.

Pacey, Philip. 1977. "Handling Slides Single Handed." *Art Libraries Journal* 2 (April):22-30.

"Proper Care of Slide Film" and "Handling, Care and Preservation of Mounted Transparencies." 1978. In *Planning and Producing Slide Programs*, pp. 65-67. Rochester, New York: Eastman Kodak. (Kodak Publication No. S-30).

Raymond, Sue L., and Virginia L. Algermissen. 1976. "Retrieval System for Biomedical Slides Using MeSH." *Medical Library Association Bulletin* 64 (April): 233-35.

"Safe Slide Filing." 1976. *American Archivist* 39 (April):230.

Scott, Gillian M. "Report on the Visual Resources Committee Sessions at CAA Annual Meeting—New York, January 25-27, 1978." *ARLIS/NA Newsletter* 6 (February):26-28.

Strohlein, Alfred. 1975. *The Management of 35mm Medical Slides*. New York: United Business Publications.

Tannenbaum, Charlotte, Reference Assistant, College of Architecture Slide Library, University of Houston. Personal communication. August 1978.

Viles, Meta. 1973. "Slide Collection, Edinburgh College of Art." *ARLIS/NA Newsletter* 17 (December):19-20.

Visser, Ora. 1977. "Stellenbosch University Medical Library Slide Classification, Storage, Retrieval, and Issue System." *Medical Library Association Bulletin* 65 (July):377-79.

"Visual Resources SIG [Special Interest Group] Business Meeting." 1977. *ARLIS/NA Newsletter* 5 (February):49.

Weinstein, Robert A., and Larry Booth. 1977. *Collection, Use and Care of Historical Photographs*. Nashville, Tennessee: American Association for State and Local History.

Wilhelm, Henry. 1978. *Preservation of Contemporary Photographic Materials*. Grinnell, Iowa: East Street Gallery, 723 State Street, Box 68, in press. 75-9136.0-916268-00-4.

Wilhelm, Henry. 1978. "Storing Color Materials: Frost-Free Refrigerators Offer a Low-Cost Solution." *Industrial Photography* 27 (October):32-33, 55-60.

7–PLANNING FOR PHYSICAL FACILITIES

INTRODUCTION

Of the limited number of publications on slides and slide libraries, none have provided recommendations on spatial requirements for slide library facilities. Certainly, there is a multitude of general media facility literature, but slide facilities are only considered as a small part of such planning, if at all. Many of the books on media center planning do include sections on space and building requirements, but they do not satisfy the needs of a comprehensive slide library facility.

The following are typical observations made after a direct study of more than 25 slide libraries that were evaluated on the basis of functional layout, planning, and space allocations:

spacious but not well planned—office and work areas have inadequate space allocations;

entire facility crowded—no space for expansion or proper space allocations;

moderately allocated space in terms of collection needs but too diffused for efficient administration and staffing;

spacious new facility with inadequate lighting, storage, and work spaces;

work area large though poorly planned; inconvenient for staff.

More often than not, even if the slide library had been allocated an area large enough for efficient operation, improper internal allocations or layout of areas negated the benefits derived by the amount of space acquired. This chapter will examine the requirements of a total slide library facility with any facet capable of integration into a general media facility.

FUNCTIONS DEFINED

In order to determine the spatial requirements of a slide library, the functions that it performs must be outlined and defined. The following represent the major functional spaces with their respective requirements indicated:

1. Storage
   slide housing
   user catalogs

2. Viewing
   tables with sloped wooden or metal illuminators and/or
   carrels with built-in illumination and/or
   light tables
   previewers providing magnification and/or
   rear screen projection viewer
   front screen projection (room or space)

3. Circulation and Reference
   desk for charging out slides
   area for slide return
   reference desk

4. Administration and Operation
   slide librarian's office
   general operation or work area
   > typing spaces for a specified number of supportive staff
   > cataloging desk(s)
   > filing cabinet(s) for correspondence and commercial catalogs
   > cabinets for authority, shelflist and source files (if applicable)
   > tables for slide mounting and wall shelving for supplies
   > storage cabinets for projectors, office and slide supplies, and extra previewers, miscellaneous equipment
   > book cases for internal library and for books from which slides are made and booktruck (optional)
   > slide sorting table(s) for preparing slides for refiling
   > sink

5. Storage for Slides Prepared for Classroom Use
   tables for slide cases, trays or magazines and/or
   wall or free-standing shelving to hold cases, trays or magazines

6. Photography and Processing (optional)
   copystand and camera
   slide duplicator
   storage for photography supplies

Storage—The storage area should encompass the slide housing and catalogs such as author, artist, title, and/or subject. This space will vary in total dimensions based upon the type of cabinet selected. Space for opening drawers, for the user standing in front of an opened drawer, and for aisles or traffic patterns should be included.

Diagram 8—Space requirements for cabinets.

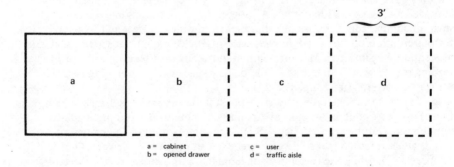

a = cabinet
b = opened drawer
c = user
d = traffic aisle

Total dimensions for each cabinet space would be a + b + c + d. Depending upon the location of the cabinet, space for traffic aisles on either side of the cabinet may be necessary. This combination of spaces would also apply to user catalogs. Space "a" is equivalent to "b," varying according to the depth of the cabinet and corresponding depth of each drawer. The amount of space for the user, "c," and traffic aisle, "d" (average aisle width is three feet), will vary according to whether or not the slides are examined only at the cabinets or have drawers or trays that may be easily removed for use at tables. Keyes Metcalf, a nationally recognized authority on library buildings, recommends space allocations for card catalogs that are also useful for determining slide storage space (1965, pp. 335-40).

A metal vertical slide cabinet such as those made by Library Bureau and Steelcase will house from 7,000 to 11,000 slides. These cabinets range in size from four feet to five feet high, approximately 13 inches wide by 28 inches deep and contain eight to ten drawers. Card catalog cabinets modified for slide storage are usually five drawers wide (approximately 33 inches), nine drawers high (approximately five inches), and approximately 18 inches deep. Each cabinet is usually composed of three 15-drawer stacking units, with a total slide capacity of about 6,500 slides. Although a modified card catalog cabinet has a smaller capacity than a vertical slide cabinet, a modified cabinet requires nearly one-half square foot more floor space than a vertical cabinet. The slide capacity of the modified cabinet can be made equal to that of the vertical cabinet by the addition of a fourth 15-drawer unit. However, this added height may make the cabinets inconvenient for the user. For a comparison of cabinet heights, see Photographs 4 (page 172) and 5 (page 173) (University of Pennsylvania, and the Metropolitan Museum of Art). The height of the drawer units plus the base determine the total base height of the cabinets. Obviously, bases from one foot to 1½ feet high, will allow more units to be stacked, resulting in larger filing capacity. Vertical cabinets having a large capacity can usually be purchased with low bases for more convenient access. File drawers placed 1½ feet to two feet above the floor are functional if low seating is supplied for the users. However, a base lower than 18 inches is not recommended.

Viewing—The slide viewing areas are frequently one of the most inadequately allocated areas in the slide library. Although the size of slides may be relatively small in comparison to books or other media, in order to view and to arrange them for presentation purposes, a *minimal* space of 3x4-feet of surface area per regular user should be allocated. Metcalf recommends 25 square feet per user for library reading rooms, which includes table and chair space and surrounding aisle widths for traffic patterns (ibid., pp. 128-29).

There are various types and sizes of illuminators available for slide examination. The Metropolitan Museum of Art has a combination of sloped table-top illuminators (Photograph 12, page 192), illuminators built in to custom-made carrels (Photograph 5, page 173), and rear-screen projection viewers (Photograph 12, page 192). While the carrel or light table has a predefined space, the table-top illuminators may be placed on 3x5-foot desk tops or grouped on large tables. In order to determine spatial requirements for viewing, the variety, size, and quantity of viewing devices must be resolved.

Another requirement for viewing is the allocation of an area, ideally a room adjoining the slide library, that allows for projector preview of slides by users and staff. This area provides the staff with the proper facilities for evaluating the quality of institutionally produced and commercially purchased slides and the teacher an opportunity to simulate classroom presentation.

Increasing need for student viewing areas for slides can also affect space utilization in the slide library. The University of Illinois–Urbana Slide Library, Architecture Building, provides the student with two options for slide review. The first, called the "Slide Reviewer," can either be free-standing or built into a wall and is illustrated in Photograph 18 (page 237) and discussed in Chapter 9. Although Photograph 18 shows this unit as free standing, at Illinois, the "Slide Reviewer" is installed within a wall so that students only have access to the control panel and viewing screen. When the Slide Library at Illinois was expanded recently, the staff sought a second solution to student access to slides, which is illustrated in Photograph 11. The slide viewing wall illustrated extends over twenty feet along a hallway outside the Slide Library. The back of the viewing wall (which is covered in semi-opaque plexiglass) opens into the Slide Library, so the staff can easily remove and insert slides along the plastic ledges. From the viewing side of the wall, clear glass windows protect the slides and provide convenient student access for image review after seeing slides projected in the classroom. Light sources are built into the viewing wall to expedite both daytime and evening slide viewing.

Photograph 11. Slide viewing wall. Slide Library, Architecture Building. University of Illinois–Urbana.

Photograph 12. Kodak Carousel projectors, used with two Caritels (made by Hudson-Photographic Industries, Inc.), and a sloped illuminator (made by the Stacor Corporation). The Metropolitan Museum of Art. (Photograph courtesy of the Metropolitan Museum of Art.)

Electrical fixtures and outlets for viewers, light tables, illuminators, or projectors must be planned for the viewing area. Viewing equipment is not always placed directly against walls, so adequate outlets located throughout the viewing area may be necessary. Consultation with electrical and building planning specialists should be sought.

The viewing area may surround the slide housing, be in the center of the slide housing, or be integrated with storage. If slide cabinets and facilities are completely separated from one another, use of the slide collection may be impaired. Ideally, space should be allotted within the slide storage sections for limited and multiple viewing areas. Viewing facilities should be easily accessible from the slide files. Examples of viewing areas placed centrally to the slide housing are shown in Photographs 4 (page 172) and 13 (below), University of Pennsylvania and the University of Illinois at Chicago Circle; integrated storage and viewing in Photograph 5 (page 173), the Metropolitan Museum of Art; and of the viewing area on the perimeters of the storage space in Photograph 10 (page 182), Syracuse University.

Photograph 13. Steelcase 2x2-inch slide cabinets, custom-made light tables, circulation table against wall (left), and reference library in rear. College of Architecture and Art. University of Illinois at Chicago Circle.

Circulation and Reference—A specified space is necessary for the charging and discharging or return of slides whether a simple charge-card, sheet, or microfilming set-up such as the Recordak system is used. Proper storage facilities are necessary to hold returned slides in an upright rather than flat position. This decreases the possibility of damage or breakage and makes sorting easier if the slides are kept in an orderly arrangement when returned. In some institutions, the individual returning slides places them in pre-sorting trays by historical topic, medium, or subject. Consequently, these items are immediately accessible on a limited basis without having to shuffle through a large quantity of randomly grouped slides. This particular type of pre-sorting device is only feasible with unitary image collections. Slide collections arranged in sets may handle the returned slides in the same manner as books or other media.

Slide drawers may be used as pre-sorting or slide return trays; custom-made wooden boxes may be designed using the basic format of a slide drawer. The width and length of the return tray may vary depending upon the use of the collection. Wooden trays may be stacked inside a shell made for this purpose (see Diagram 9).

Diagram 9—A wooden portable stacking tray for returned slides.

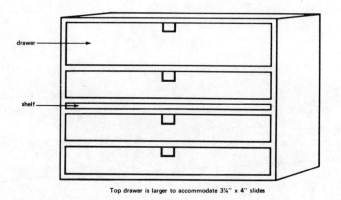

Top drawer is larger to accommodate 3¼" x 4" slides

(a) Stacking box

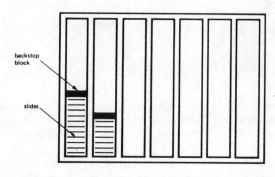

(b) Drawer interior

The bottom of each drawer may be of metal or have a metal insert, so a magnetic backstop block device may be used. The custom-made circulation desk at the Metropolitan Museum of Art has slide return boxes designed to accommodate magnetic backstops. A 3x5-foot desk or table would represent a minimal space allocation for slide charging and return. Again, the amount of space necessary for this function will vary depending upon how many users the collection serves.

Administration and Operation—The supervisor of the slide library (a slide librarian) should have adequate space for staff and user consultation without disturbing the other operations of the collection. A separate office is recommended. If the slide collection is part of a general media collection, the media specialist supervising these collections should have an area allocated for administrative functions. Visiting guests, dealers, and manufacturers should have an opportunity to speak with the slide librarian or media specialist without disturbing the users and staff. A preview room should also be available for this purpose.

Whether the library handles books, records, photographs, slides, or any other media, the generous allocation of space to the operational or work areas is critical for the efficient preparation of materials for the user. Acquisition includes those procedures related to the purchasing, ordering, and preparation of slides apart from the actual filming and processing. This area would include files for catalogs of dealers, equipment manufacturers, and commercial sources for slides, typing facilities, and desks for label preparation, cataloging and classification, correspondence, and order preparation. In addition, tables for the mounting and repair of slides (allowing approximately 3x4-feet of surface area per worker) are necessary. Space is required for cataloging aids, which includes a small reference library, shelflist, and authority files. Adequate wall shelving and portable book shelving, e.g., book-trucks, should be provided for the reference materials, books being held in the library for slide production, and slide binding supplies.

The work area should also include a large sorting table—a minimum of 3x5-feet—for the slide filing or refiling process. If the slides are kept as sets, then minimal space will be required for this procedure. Within academic slide libraries having over 100,000 slides, as many as 2,000 or more may be circulated and refiled in a single week. Appropriate spaces will vary according to the arrangement and use of the collection. A table or desk-top having a white or off-white surface is recommended. If a great deal of slide masking is done, an illuminator such as the one made by the Stacor Corporation (Photograph 12, page 192) will be needed. Several illuminators should also be available for staff use within the work area. Adequate electrical wiring and outlets to accommodate this equipment should also be included in the work area.

Ideally, each slide library should have a separate staff workroom separated from the circulation, reference and viewing areas, e.g., see Diagrams 11 (page 203), 14 (page 206), and 15 (page 207). In order to have efficient work spaces for slide mounting, cleaning, repair, and related functions, a combination of table surfaces, upright viewers, and light tables having built-in illumination is required. The use of cantilevered shelving placed by the work surfaces provides efficient access to the variety of materials and equipment needed for slide preparation. Photograph 14 (page 196) exemplifies this type of workroom, which is part of the slide library facility at Columbia University.

Photograph 14. Slide preparation and general workroom, with cantilevered shelving (back and left) and custom-made light tables (foreground). Department of Art History and Archaeology. Columbia University.

Storage for Slides Prepared for Classroom Use—Depending upon the circulation procedures of each institution, a large number of slides that are ready for classroom presentation may need storage space in the slide library. For example, many institutions require that slides only be removed from the library when they are in actual classroom use. Consequently, an area must be allocated within the slide library to accommodate cases or trays of slides previously selected and arranged for presentation. At the University of Michigan, vertical wall shelving along a wall approximately twelve feet long and five shelves high in the cataloging and work room serves this function. It holds cases, boxes, or trays of slides. When a teacher or user is preparing a slide presentation over a period of time, that person may prefer to keep the slides in the library. By leaving slides in the library until they are to be used for presentation purposes, other users and staff may have access to the slides. The location of a shelving unit may be in the storage, circulation, or work areas, depending upon where the least user inconvenience occurs.

Photography and Processing—A room large enough to accommodate a copystand, duplicator, processing facilities (tanks, sinks and so forth) plus refrigerated storage for film and other photographic supplies should be provided. Approximately 75 square feet should be allocated but this will vary depending upon the number of functions actually performed by the slide library. If the slide library purchases slides only and does not produce them for the collection, this area will be unnecessary. Space for a duplicator could be allowed within the work or operational area.

PREPARING A BUILDING PROGRAM

Planning for a slide library should begin with the preparation of a building program. Even though a new building *per se* is not being planned, a building program represents a systematic approach to outlining functions and their corresponding functional spaces and to determining the dimensions required for given areas. If a building is being planned, the building program is the guide used by the architect to prepare the building plans. For comprehensive information on building programs, user requirements, office and general work space, and other areas of library planning, see Metcalf's *Planning Academic and Research Library Buildings* (1965).

In order to illustrate how a building program would be written for a slide library, a sample program is included (see page 198). This particular program has been excerpted from an art library building program prepared for a combined museum and library building being constructed at Indiana University (Irvine, 1973). When preparing a building program, spatial requirements must be based upon projections of the size of a given collection. Both present and ultimate size is included in the program. Such projections can be determined by current growth rates and by the desired length of time that the new facility should provide for adequate housing and use of the library. Although the sample program provides for the needs of a rather sizeable slide library, the figures and types of calculations given may be extrapolated for either larger or smaller collections. Dimensions for aisles, users, and staff are based upon standard allocations provided in Metcalf's book.

Four basic elements of a building program are given: statement of general objectives and requirements; functional areas with square footage allocations; summary of space estimates; and a diagram showing the spatial relationships of the staff and public areas.

* * *

BUILDING PROGRAM FOR A SLIDE LIBRARY
AT INDIANA UNIVERSITY

Note: Sections I and V have been specially prepared by the author while the remaining sections are excerpted from the "Fine Arts Pavilion Library. Preliminary Building Program." Indiana University (ibid.). The information in Sections I and V is incorporated into the general material about the total library facility in the original building program.

I. GENERAL OBJECTIVES AND REQUIREMENTS

Enhancing and facilitating the study and teaching of art history and the fine and applied arts at Indiana University is the primary objective of the planned Slide Library. The general design of the Slide Library should be conducive to sustained periods of user preparation of lecture material. The slide collection is primarily a teaching collection utilized for classroom instruction; consequently, use is limited to faculty and staff with only occasional student access for the preparation of special or seminar reports. The Slide Library should be readily accessible to all users. Proximity to faculty offices and to the art library is desirable.

II. SLIDE STORAGE/VIEWING

a. Present collection: 220,000 slides (includes 5,000 3" x 4½" slides)
b. Ultimate collection: 350,000 slides, 35mm
c. Storage: 1 file unit 13" w x 28" d x 46.5" h holds 7,000 35mm slides = + 8 sq. ft. per cabinet. **Note:** Dimensions are for a metal Library Bureau slide file. Eight square foot per cabinet was derived from the following: + 2 sq. ft. per cabinet plus + 2 sq. ft. for opening drawer plus 4 sq. ft. for aisle = 8 sq. ft. per cabinet.

1 file unit 33" w x 17" d x 55" h holds 555 3" x 4½" slides = + 18 sq. ft. per cabinet. **Note:** Dimensions are for a wooden Library Bureau lantern slide file. Eighteen square foot per cabinet was derived from the following: + 4.5 sq. ft. per cabinet plus + 4.5 sq. ft. for opening drawer plus 9 sq. ft. for aisle = 18 sq. ft. per cabinet.

350,000 35mm slides = 50 units = 400 sq. ft.
5,000 3" x 4½" slides = 10 units = 180 sq. ft.

d. Viewing area: in storage space; should allow for 20 people working concurrently @ 25 sq. ft. ea. or 500 sq. ft.
e. Circulation desk: 50 sq. ft.
f. Storage for lecture slides: 120 linear ft. of 12" deep shelving, 3 shelves high or 40 sq. ft.
g. Space for slide sorting desk: 50 sq. ft. or 2 workers @ 25 sq. ft. ea.
h. Space for slide viewing by projector equipped with a screen: 100 sq. ft. (small room without windows).

Special Requirements

a. Viewing tables: flat, with a vertical or sloped translucent backlighted viewing surface at rear.
b. Size of viewing surface: arranged for standard flourescent 4 ft. long tube size.
c. Table size: 3' deep x 5' long tables if tables are used. **Alternative:** adjoining carrels with built-in viewing facilities.

III. SLIDE WORK SPACE

Location: contiguous to slide storage and viewing area.

Work Space for Staff:

1 slide librarian's office . . . . 150 sq. ft.
2 non-professionals (@ 100 sq. ft. ea.). . . . . 200 sq. ft.
General work space: 10 student assistants (6 working concurrently @
    50 sq. ft. ea.). . . . . 300 sq. ft.

                                                           650 sq. ft.

                                 Growth allowance. . . . . 150 sq. ft.

                                       Total . . . . 800 sq. ft.

Special Requirements

a. Sink
b. General electric service for slide mounting equipment, and viewing equipment.
c. Office and workspace shelving for books, slides and photographs.

General Comments

The following functions will be performed in the slide workroom: cataloguing of all slide orders (+ 300 per week); typing of all slide labels and file guidecards; preparation for filing of slides daily (+ 500 to 1,000); maintenance of source and authority files; preparation of all commercial orders and maintenance of dealer catalogs; development and typing of interfiled shelflist; preparation of all orders of commercial equipment and materials; receipt of all equipment and materials; maintenance and storage of charge-out equipment which includes + 15 projectors and several vertical portable viewing screens, and opaque projector, etc., and preparation of general office and correspondence records.

IV. SUMMARY OF SPACE ESTIMATES

Storage . . . . 580 sq. ft.
Viewing area. 500
Circulation 50
Storage/lecture slides 40
Slide sorting area 50
Viewing room. 100
Work space:
    Slide librarian's office 150
    Non-professional staff. 200
    General work space 300
Growth allowance. 150

                          Total . . . . 2,120 sq. ft.

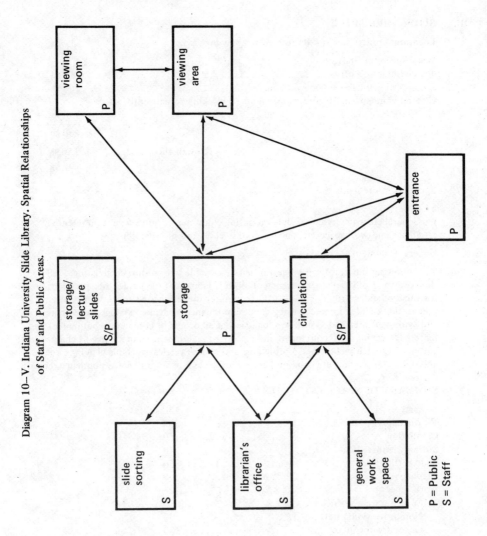

Diagram 10–V. Indiana University Slide Library. Spatial Relationships of Staff and Public Areas.

***

FLOOR PLANS

Few slide librarians will assert that their facilities are exemplary models of design and planning. Depending upon use, the size of the collection, number of staff, and functions to be performed within the library, each slide library will exhibit overall layout characteristics that have been adapted to suit institutional demands and requirements. In order to appreciate and understand some of the approaches used for slide library planning, a select number of floor plans are included. The plans illustrated are of slide libraries in relatively new buildings or in newly designed facilities. The Metropolitan Museum of Art facility was designed in 1968, Indiana University, in 1972. New buildings were constructed at the following institutions: Syracuse University, Ernest Stevenson Bird Library, 1972; University of Pennsylvania, Graduate School of Fine Arts, 1968, the University of California at Santa Cruz Library, 1966; and the University of Wisconsin, Elvehjem Art Center, 1970. The slide libraries at Syracuse University and at the University of California at Santa Cruz are both within central university library buildings. The Santa Cruz facility is especially noteworthy because it incorporates a slide viewing room equipped with speakers, so both audio and visual effects can be produced simultaneously. These speakers are connected to an audio system in an adjoining room, which is the location for recordings and tape playback in the library. Established in 1959, the Philadelphia College of Art Slide Library is a relatively new collection and provides an example of facilities design for an art school. For additional floor plans illustrating general slide library design options and listings of functional requirements, see the *Guide for Management of Visual Resources Collections* (1978, pp. 5-27).

With the exception of the Metropolitan Museum of Art, each plan represents a slide library designed for limited use restricted to faculty and staff only. Most academic institutions, however, do allow for student preparation of special or seminar reports using slides. As is readily apparent from a comparison of the Metropolitan plan with that of the academic institutions, general circulation and viewing areas require a great deal of space when public access to a collection must be accommodated. As slide libraries become generally available to faculty throughout an entire campus, rather than only to those within a single department, careful planning will be required to allow ample space for the selection and viewing of slides. At the present time, most academic slide libraries limit use of the collection to the faculty within the department or school in which the collection originated.

Unfortunately, the slide librarian is rarely consulted about the design of the spaces that will house and provide use of the collection. As a consequence, many facilities are ill-equipped to meet the variety of demands placed upon them. Such lack of consultation typifies the planning for new buildings, although the slide librarian is usually free to make decisions about how predetermined spaces will be used once the facility is built. The plans illustrated conform to this pattern with one exception—the Metropolitan Museum of Art Slide Library. In terms of circulation, storage, viewing, and general office and work areas, the Metropolitan has a model slide library. The staff of the Slide Library played a major role in the design of this facility. While studying the Metropolitan plan, the reader should keep in mind the size of the collection and its functional requirements to one of the largest museum curatorial staffs in the United States, and to the general public of a metropolis. While the basic layout of the Metropolitan's Slide Library remains the same in 1978, additional files for expansion have been added, so the physical space shown in Diagram 11 now houses 227,000 35mm slides and 150,000 lantern slides. (For further information on the Metropolitan facility, see an essay by Margaret P. Nolan, Chief Librarian of the Slide Library, in *Planning the Special Library* [1972, pp. 101-103].)

As a general rule for the design and planning of any slide library facility, the slide librarian should be required to prepare a building program and to offer assistance for the design of special facilities (e.g., work space for mounting slides, slide preview rooms) needed in a slide library. Both the staff and the users will enjoy the benefits of a properly planned facility.

(Text continues on page 210)

Diagram 11–The Metropolitan Museum of Art (150,000 lantern slides (1974), 227,000 35mm slides). (Diagram photograph courtesy of the Metropolitan Museum of Art.)

The METROPOLITAN MUSEUM of ART
SLIDE LIBRARY

S	2x2(35mm)Files
L	3x4 Files
C	Carrels With Viewers
T	Table for Viewers
M	Microfilm Machine
W	Work Cabinets

U	Supply Cabinets
R	Reserve Cabinets
F	File Trucks
Y	Typewriters
⊕	Electrical Outlets

feet 5 10 15 20
Scale

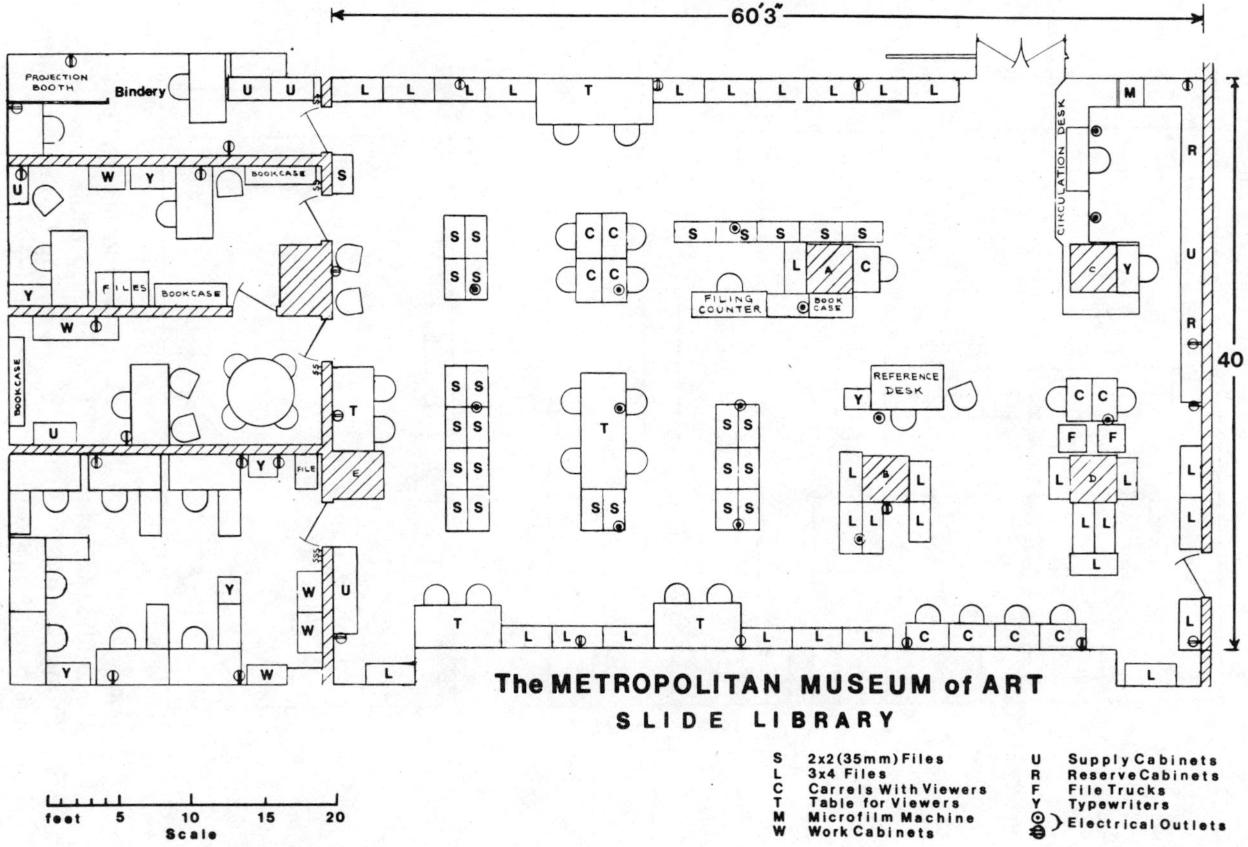

Diagram 12—Indiana University (5,000 lantern slides, 220,000 35mm slides)

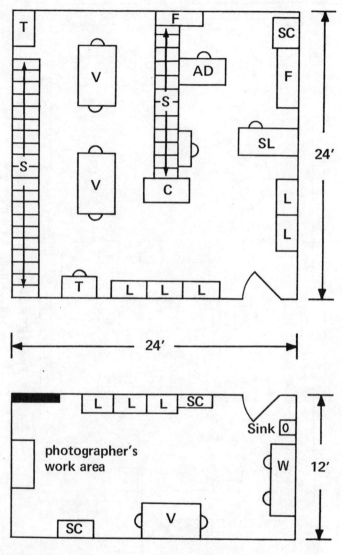

AD	Aid's Desk	SL	Slide Librarian's Desk
C	Circulation Desk	T	Typing Table
F	Filing Cabinet	V	Viewing Tables with Sloped
L	Lantern Slide Cabinets		Illuminators
S	2″ x 2″ Slide Cabinets	W	Work Table for Slide
SC	Supply Cabinets		Preparation

Scale: 1/8″ = 1′

Diagram 13—Philadelphia College of Art (140,000 35mm slides).

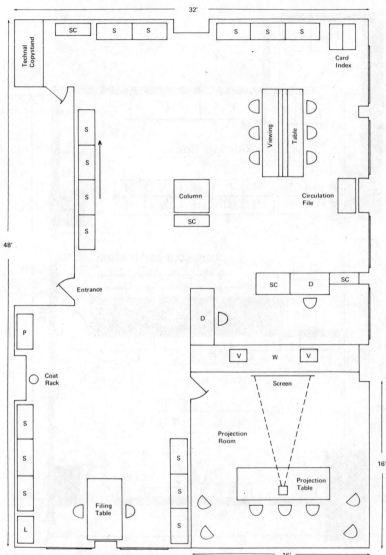

Scale ¼″ = 1′0″

D	Desk	SC	Storage Cabinets
L	Lantern Slide Cabinet	V	Viewer
P	Photograph Cabinet	W	Work Table for Slide Preparation
S	2x2-inch Slide Cabinet		

Diagram 14—Syracuse University (144,000 slides—includes lantern and 35mm slides).

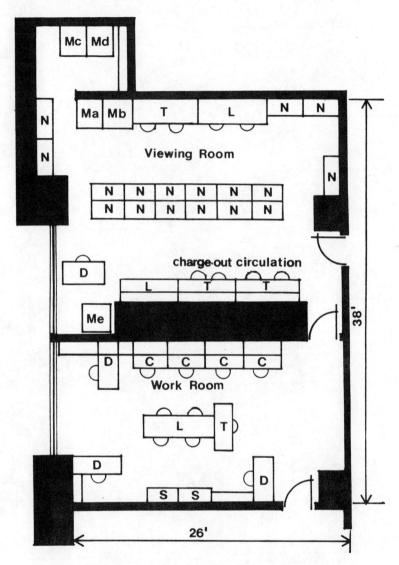

Scale 1/8"= 1'0"

C	Hanging Carrels with shelves and tables	M	Multiplex Slide Cabinets
D	Desks	N	Neumade Slide Cabinets
G	General Supplies	S	Steelcase (Slide Backlog)
L	Light Tables	T	Work Tables

Diagram 15–University of California, Santa Cruz (120,000 35mm slides).

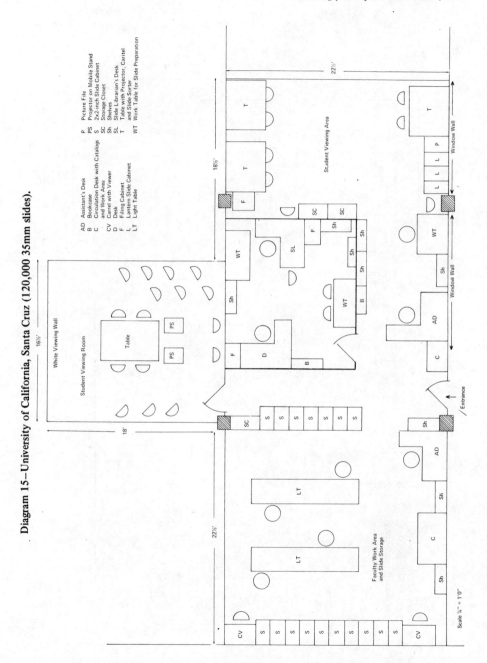

AD Assistant's Desk
B   Bookcase
C   Circulation Desk with Catalogs and Work Area
CV Carrel with Viewer
D   Desk
F   Filing Cabinet
L   Lantern Slide Cabinet
LT Light Table

P   Picture File
PS Projector on Mobile Stand
S   2x2-inch Slide Cabinet
SC Storage Closet
Sh Shelves
SL Slide Librarian's Desk
T   Table with Projector, Carrel and Slide Sorter
WT Work Table for Slide Preparation

White Viewing Wall

Student Viewing Room

Table

Student Viewing Area

Faculty Work Area and Slide Storage

Entrance

Window Wall

Scale ¼" = 1'0"

Diagram 16—University of Pennsylvania (114,000 35mm slides).

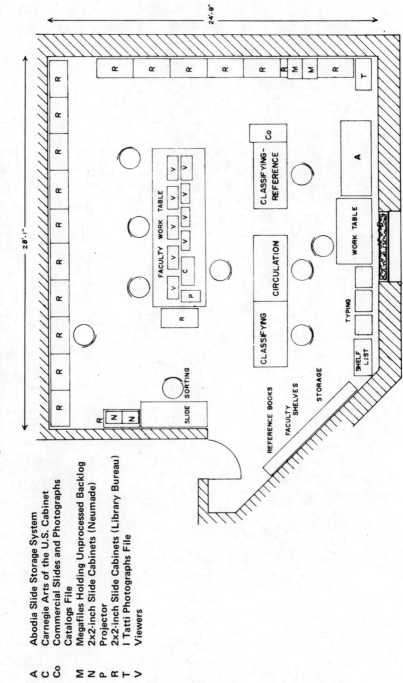

DRAWN BY C.A. EVERS

A   Abodia Slide Storage System
C   Carnegie Arts of the U.S. Cabinet
Co Commercial Slides and Photographs
    Catalogs File
M   Megafiles Holding Unprocessed Backlog
N   2x2-inch Slide Cabinets (Neumade)
P   Projector
R   2x2-inch Slide Cabinets (Library Bureau)
T   I Tatti Photographs File
V   Viewers

Diagram 17—University of Wisconsin—Madison (64,600 lantern slides, 189,000 35mm slides).

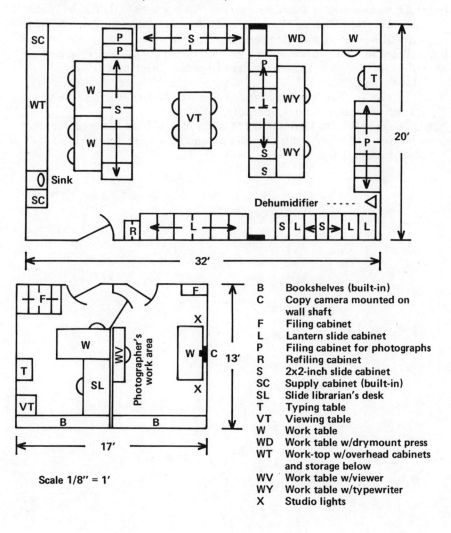

Scale 1/8″ = 1′

B   Bookshelves (built-in)
C   Copy camera mounted on wall shaft
F   Filing cabinet
L   Lantern slide cabinet
P   Filing cabinet for photographs
R   Refiling cabinet
S   2x2-inch slide cabinet
SC Supply cabinet (built-in)
SL Slide librarian's desk
T   Typing table
VT Viewing table
W   Work table
WD Work table w/drymount press
WT Work-top w/overhead cabinets and storage below
WV Work table w/viewer
WY Work table w/typewriter
X   Studio lights

REFERENCES

Guide for Management of Visual Resources Collections. 1978. Edited by Nancy S. Schuller. New Mexico: Mid-America College Art Association and the University of New Mexico at Albuquerque.

Irvine, Betty Jo. "Fine Arts Pavilion Library. Preliminary Building Program." Rev. Bloomington, Indiana: Indiana University, September 1973. (Mimeographed).

Metcalf, Keyes D. *Planning Academic and Research Library Buildings.* New York: McGraw-Hill Book Company, 1965.

Nolan, Margaret P. "The Metropolitan Museum of Art—Slide Library." *Planning the Special Library.* Edited by Ellis Mount. New York: Special Libraries Association, 1972.

8–PROJECTION SYSTEMS

INTRODUCTION

Projectors, stands, screens, and general facilities for the use of this equipment have received a great deal of attention in the past ten years in both the book and periodical literature. As a consequence of the ready availability of information on this topic—certainly not a common phenomenon for slides—it is unnecessary to dwell at length on this subject. Instead, a bibliography dealing with projection systems is appended. A directory of manufacturers and distributors of equipment is also provided. Therefore, this chapter functions only as an outline of the kinds of information available. When relevant, suggestions and recommendations are offered regarding problem areas in which conflicting ideas may prevail.

TYPES OF PROJECTORS

Projectors have changed in some respects, while in others they have remained similar to the seventeenth-century "magic lantern." Today, the magic lantern proto-type survives in manual projectors for 3¼x4-inch lantern slides and 2x2-inch slides, the latter being more common as this size often adapted for film strips. Innovations in the development of projectors with automatic or remote control slide changing and focusing mechanisms revolutionized the audiovisual world and most classroom and lecture use of slides as well. Still more recent has been the development of sophisticated multi-projector dissolve systems for smooth transitions from image to image, and combination sound-slide equipment. At the present time, most coordinated sound-slide systems depend upon use of a programming unit that con-nects to both an automatic slide-changing projector and to a tape recorder. The sound-slide system made by the Kalart Victor Corporation incorporates a slide and tape into a single cassette. With this system, as each slide is projected a coordinated audio presentation is also made. Sound-slide units such as the Singer Caramate and the Bell and Howell Ringmaster are compact and adaptable to a variety of student study situations.

Random access projectors eliminate viewing of slides in a strictly sequential format, as well as viewing a blank screen with no image projected upon it. Random access projectors are available from several companies, including Decision Systems, Inc., Kodak, GAF, Hoppmann, Mast Development Company, and Spindler and Sauppe, Inc. Another projector concept, developed by the Fordham Equipment Co., is a miniature projector complete with adapters for microfiche, aperture cards, filmstrips, and slides. These programming units and projector systems are illustrated and annotated in the *Audio Visual Equipment Directory* (1979). The *Photo Methods for Industry Catalog* and the *Professional Photographic Catalog* (issued by Standard Photo Supply and distributed by local photographic dealers) are annual publications that provide information on types of projection equipment with illustrations and prices.

The overhead slide projector, such as the one made by the Buhl Projector Co., Inc., offers the same advantages as an overhead transparency machine; however, it can be used only for short-throw projections. This projector can also be used with slides stored in plastic sleeve holders. Descriptions of this projector can be found in Eboch and Cochern's book on audiovisual equipment (1968, p. 41), and in Erickson's *Fundamentals of Teaching with Audiovisual Technology* (1965, p. 334). Projectors can be equipped to handle not only standard visual images but also microscope slides. Projection of microscope slides with 2x2-inch projectors requires the use of lens adapters such as those produced by the Leitz Company. Microscopic projections are particularly useful in chemistry and biology classes (ibid., pp. 64-68; Wittich, 1973, pp. 414-15). Projectors especially designed for microscopic projection are listed in *The Audio-Visual Equipment Directory* as "Micro-projectors" and are available from several companies, including Bausch and Lomb, Inc., and Ken-A-Vision Manufacturing Co., Inc.

Although most standard 2x2-inch slide projectors do come with adapters for filmstrips and slides, "A Plea for TWO Projectors" was made in an *Audiovisual Instruction* article pointing out the inconvenience of constantly switching back and forth from filmstrip to slide projection in the same machine and pointing to the obvious advantages of having separate automatic slide and automatic filmstrip projectors (Ruark, 1968). Certainly, each institution should study the use pattern of its equipment and should allow for adequate varieties of projectors for each type of teaching situation.

For complete discussions on the use and care of projectors, the following chapters or sections of various books are recommended: Brown, Lewis and Harcleroad, "Projection-equipment Principles" (1977, pp. 386-89), and "2-by-2 inch Slide Projectors" (ibid., pp. 390-93); Cabeceiras, "Projection Equipment" (1978, pp. 120-24); Davidson, "Slide Projectors" (1969, pp. 22-49); De Kieffer, "Slides and Slide Projectors" (1962, pp. 116-24); Eboch and Cochern, "Still-Picture Projection" (1968, Chapter III, pp. 35-48); Erickson, "The Filmstrip and 2-inch by 2-inch Slide Projector" (1965, pp. 325-30); Oates, "Filmstrip-Slide Projectors" (1975, pp. 1-53); Rosenberg, "Slide Projectors" (1976, pp. 23, 26-30), including a "Checklist for Evaluating Slide Projectors" (ibid., pp. 28-29); and Wittich and Schuller, "Still Projection" (1973, pp. 391-445).

With the present rate of technology, the reader is urged to keep abreast of innovations through the various publications available on the market including those already mentioned and the following periodicals: *Audiovisual Instruction*; *Consumer Bulletin*; *Consumer Reports*; *Educational Product Report*; *AV Guide* (formerly *Educational Screen and AV Guide*); *Indiana Arts and Vocational Education*; *The Nation's Schools*; and *Previews*. Part of the slide librarian's responsibilities is to keep informed of equipment innovations and changes. This can be accomplished by monthly sessions in an academic or comprehensive public library audiovisual collection or by consulting media specialists.

PROJECTION BOOTHS AND STANDS

Deciding upon the proper projector and then placing it in the classroom or lecture hall are frequently considered two separate procedures having little relationship to one another. At least this appears to be the case upon examining a number of academic classroom projection set-ups, although lecture halls or auditoriums also have had surprisingly little planning for projection booth facilities. Ignorance of alternatives and solutions has contributed to this unfortunate situation. Media specialists and the literature should not be overlooked when an institution is planning a new or remodeled facility. Unfortunately, far too many academic buildings constructed for the teaching of art have not been designed with projection booths as part of the building plan. Rather, at some date after completion of the building, a custom-made, frequently inadequate booth, table, or stand is acquired to serve this need. There are basically four set-ups for accommodating projectors:

1. Tables or any other flat-surfaced furniture, e.g., a desk.
2. Mobile metal projection tables or stands equipped with wheels.
3. Fixed, partially enclosed sound-proofed booths.
4. Enclosed sound-proofed projection booths built into a classroom or auditorium having remote control facilities.

Tables and Flat-Surfaced Furniture—The first set-up relies upon the use of whatever surfaces may be available and is rarely satisfactory. If the projector table is too low, some people have to move out of the way of the projected image, or the projector has to be radically tilted (above a 9 degree angle), which may cause a keystoning effect (Culclasure, 1969, pp. 39-40). Standard projection tables or stands can be purchased for less than $100, thereby denying the validity of inadequate set-ups for economic reasons alone. If, however, the table has been specifically designed to accommodate a given viewing room and allows for proper projection height and convenient use, a table may adequately serve its function. The projector table is an integral part of the viewing room and functions in conjunction with the other furniture and equipment in the room—chairs, speakers, and projectors—to perform a specific function in a specific location. This latter utilization of furniture and equipment is not commensurate to the haphazard selection of any available table-top for slide projection.

Mobile Projection Stands—If one or two projectors are regularly used throughout a building in different classrooms, the second type of projection facility would probably be the most convenient for transporting and using projectors. Metal projection tables or stands, usually equipped with wheels, are expressly designed for holding a variety of projection equipment and are recommended for teaching situations that do not demand daily use of projectors for a given classroom. The primary advantage of these stands is their mobility and height, which easily adjust to various locations. In situations requiring daily use of projectors within a given classroom or group of classrooms, as is necessary for the teaching of art history on the academic level, a mobile stand that is not equipped with acoustical controls or remote controls is inadequate. A disturbance is created by the noise of the projectors—two or more are usually used for comparative purposes in the majority of academic institutions teaching art history—and by the need to signal the projectionist every time a slide should be changed. Companies making these stands include Luxor, Neumade Products Corp., Wallach and Associates, Inc., and H. Wilson. An entire section in *The Audio-Visual Equipment Directory* is devoted to "Projection Tables and Stands."

Partially Enclosed Sound-Proofed Booths—An example of the third type of facility is illustrated in Diagram 18 (see page 214). This particular booth was designed specifically for classroom use in the University of Missouri—Kansas City Department

Diagram 18– Enclosed projection booth. University of Missouri–Kansas City.
(Designed by Nancy and Jacques DeLaurier.)

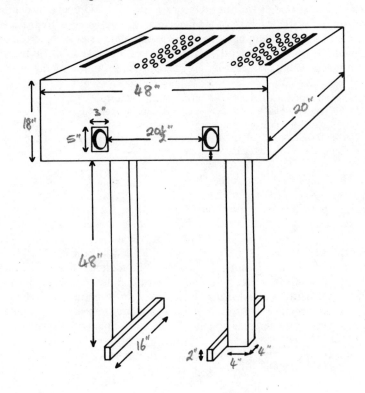

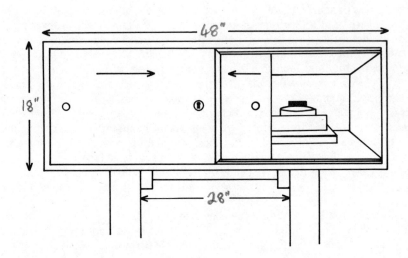

Errata sheet for Irvine, *Slide Libraries*, 2nd ed., page 214.

Diagram 18 — Enclosed projection booth. University of Missouri — Kansas City. (Designed by Dr. George Ehrlich)

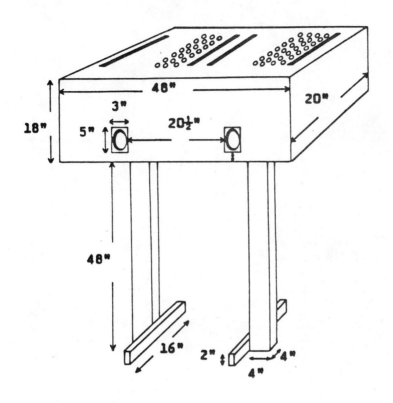

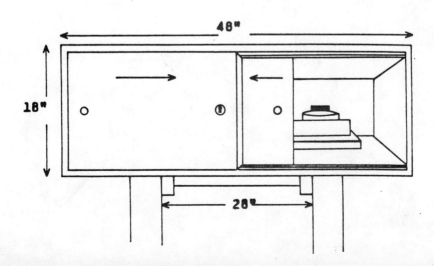

of Art and Art History. Booths of this type, which vary greatly from one institution to another because of custom-made modifications, may appear to be more trouble than they are worth in terms of design and cost, but in the majority of academic departments that regularly use projectors, at least two if not four (two 2x2-inch projectors and two 3¼x4-inch projectors) are used in every classroom for the teaching of art history. Many institutions with lantern slide collections retain dual projection set-ups (two 2x2-inch and/or 3¼x4-inch projectors), while others may maintain manual or combinations of automatic and manual projectors.

If nothing is done to eliminate some of the noise created by the projector motors and slide changers, a high level of distraction can be created. The booth in Diagram 18 represents an attempt by one school to relieve some of this distraction.

If they are properly designed, projection booths and stands can also provide a means of security control. Audiovisual equipment is expensive and highly subject to theft. Therefore, the selection of a particular booth or stand should include consideration of its potential for securing one or more projectors.

The custom-designed projection booth in use at the University of Missouri—Kansas City performs several functions in addition to positioning the projectors at a proper height and distance from the screen. It is a free-standing, enclosed unit with sliding doors, openings for two projectors, and ventilation holes on both top and bottom. Electrical power is provided by fixed sockets within the unit that are connected to a power source through the hollow metal legs, as are the remote control cables. The legs are doubly braced, stable, and the unit can be either stationary or moved from room to room. The unit measures 66x48-inches, and thus requires relatively little space within the classroom. The noise from the projectors is lessoned by their being enclosed, and the nuisance and potential danger of multiple cords and cables is eliminated. The sliding doors, which are lockable, provide a means of securing the projectors when not in use. Although by no means suited to every classroom situation, this unit does demonstrate that a simple well-designed projection booth can provide efficient noise and security control.

If manual or a combination of automatic and manual projectors are used, booths must be designed so that front openings will accommodate differing heights of projectors and lenses. A stand for the projectionist must also be provided in order to raise this individual above the hood so that the slide-changing instructions given by the teacher can be heard.

In a 1965 article, "Choosing Audio-Visual Equipment," Wendell Simons (Assistant University Librarian at the University of California at Santa Cruz) comments that enclosed projection booths are unnecessary and an inconvenience until used in a room having a 200 or more than 300 person capacity (ibid., p. 513). However, quite frequently, the problem of noise and distraction is the most critical in small rooms in which several projectors are in use. If there are thirty students in a small classroom (25 student capacity) and the noise from the projectors is noticeably audible in the back two to three rows, then one-third or more of the students may be affected by the noise levels of the projectors. Simons was also referring to the classroom in which projectors are moved in and out on a daily or weekly basis for use throughout a building or a system. Where projectors are used on a daily basis for lectures within a given classroom, any facility not having a partially or completely enclosed booth should not be considered conducive to a satisfactory teaching and learning environment.

Enclosed Sound-Proofed Booths—The fourth facility is based upon a completely enclosed projection booth, such as the one designed for the Department of Art History at Cornell University for a 200-student lecture hall. Photograph 15 shows the front exterior of the booth and Photograph 16 illustrates the interior and the multiple projection systems. This booth houses six projectors—two for automatic projection (Kodak Carousels) and four for manual projection (two Leitz Prado 500 and two Beseler Slide King 3¼x4-inch projectors). Although this booth is free-standing, it is permanently fixed to the floor. More common are the projection rooms for auditorium or large lecture halls that are built as an integral part of the auditorium. In contrast to the limited internal space of the booth at Cornell, full-scale projection rooms may be quite large, providing space for several people to work simultaneously under acoustically controlled conditions. Such facilities should allow for remote control access of the projectors by the speaker at the front of the lecture room.

A great deal of attention is directed in the literature toward the development of multi-media rooms or centers, including those at the following institutions: Colgate University (Morgan, 1963); Evergreen State College ("Not Just a Library . . . ," 1973); Ithaca College Instructional Resources Center ("College Core," 1969); Kent State University Audiovisual Center (Mitchell, 1967); Pennsylvania State University Instructional Learning Systems and Research Center (Carpenter, 1965); State University of New York four-year campuses ("SUNY . . . ," 1970); University of Texas at Austin Undergraduate Library (Colbert, 1961); and the University of Wisconsin Multimedia Instructional Laboratory ("AV Practices . . . ," 1964). "Designing Multimedia Rooms for Teaching or, The Instructor as the Forgotten User!" is a useful article on this subject by David S. Haviland (1970), Director of the Center for Architectural Research, Rensselaer Polytechnic Institute, Troy, New York. Haviland also helped to develop the latest edition of the AECT/NEA publication, *Educational Facilities with New Media*. Another AECT/NEA publication, *College Learning Resources Programs*, contains an equally informative chapter on facilities planning (McVey, 1977, pp. 49-70).

PROJECTION SCREENS AND OTHER VIEWING ROOM FACILITIES

In addition to the consideration of various projector models and their housing, acoustical control, lighting, ventilation, the location and number of electrical outlets, and viewing surfaces such as screens or walls should receive the attention of the individual maintaining, planning, or involved in the use of classrooms for slide presentations. If the slide librarian is not directly responsible for the viewing rooms, it may never be necessary for that person to be concerned with this area. However, it is not uncommon for this responsibility to fall within the jurisdiction of the slide library.

Of the 182 collections surveyed in the 1974 CAA Professional Status Survey (DeLaurier, 1974), less than 25% indicated that the slide librarian was not responsible for the classrooms' projection equipment. As is frequently the case, if an individual is responsible for even a single aspect of the classroom projection facility, it is quite possible to be called upon for advice regarding stands, booths, screens, pointers, and any other problem related to furnishing a classroom with viewing equipment. Such responsibility, however, should not necessarily be demanded

Photograph 15. Projection booth. Exterior. History of Art
Department. Cornell University.

Photograph 16. Projection booth. Interior showing two Kodak Carousel, two Leitz Prado 500
and two Beseler Slide King 3¼x4-inch projectors. Speaker at right for slide
projectionist to hear instructions for slide changing. History of Art
Department. Cornell University.

of the slide librarian. When it is feasible, the proper source for providing this service should be the institutional audiovisual or media center. In institutions where slide collections are located within the immediate jurisdiction of a media facility, this function is integral to the media center or program facility. If the slide librarian is called upon for advice in this area, unless that person has had a thorough training and background, a media specialist should be consulted. The information presented in this chapter only provides a skeletal structure from which a slide librarian may devise questions and seek further guidance from media specialists, technicians, and the literature.

Projection screens are categorized as either for front or rear projection. Front projection systems include both flat and curved screens with one of four basic types of surfaces: aluminum-painted or aluminized; glass beaded; matte white; and silver lenticular. *The Audio Visual Equipment Directory* includes comprehensive coverage of screen types, with separate sections for front, rear, and cabinet or table-top rear projection screens. Each of these types of screens has different levels of light reflection, angles of reflection or diffusion properties, and distances of reflection. The amount of light reflected is judged according to the amount of light reflected along the projection axis, which is the center line perpendicular from the projector to the midpoint of the screen.

Diagram 19–Projection axis.

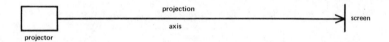

Light diffusion varies among screens because each has different angles of reflection. Diagram 20 illustrates how the angle of reflection or diffusion principle works.

Diagram 20–Angle of reflection.

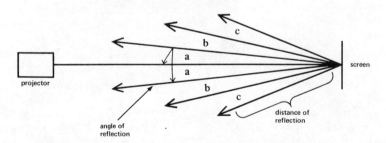

The distance between letters a, b, and c represent angles of reflection off the screen. If a screen has a small angle of reflection, as in "a," viewers sitting in the range of "b" or "c" would be unable to see the projected image satisfactorily. For example, with many of the daylight screens, the audience must be in direct alignment along the projection axis or only slightly to either side of it; otherwise the projected image will not be readily visible.

David James and George Nichols (1967; 1968) of Texas A&M University have written two excellent articles describing their testing of the four screen types and how each compared in their angles and distance of reflection. In the course of their research, they found that the aluminum-painted screen has the greatest distance and least wide angle of reflection, and that the matte screen has the greatest angle of reflection and the least amount of distance for reflection—compare "a" and "c," respectively, in Diagram 20 for an analogous example of how the screens differ in their reflection patterns. More recent studies have examined the brightness qualities of flat front, flat rear, and curved projection screens (Wadsworth, 1971a), and the effects such variables as viewing angle, contrast, and size of image can have on the viewer (Wilkinson, 1976).

The matte screen has the greatest angle for diffused light or reflection, but it does not permit the same intense level of brilliance of light reflection for as long a distance as does the aluminum-painted screen. The matte white screen is most conducive to a room that is wide but not very deep, while the aluminum-painted screen is best suited to a long narrow room. The silver lenticular and glass beaded screens, respectively, fall between the ranges of the matte white and aluminum-painted screens. A wall can be utilized for screening purposes, with reflection comparable to that of matte screens, if it is painted with "Super White" screen paint (Frederick, 1974, p. 238).

A new concept in screens is the black screen, which is distributed in the United States by International Audio Visual, Inc. Like the daylight screens, the black screen can be viewed under normal light conditions without darkening a room; but it reflects light equally over a wide viewing angle which cannot be achieved with most daylight screens. This screen is supposed to provide a greater brilliance and clarity of image than most screens. Certainly, the reader should take note of this projection screen innovation, read the literature regarding its use, and consult a media specialist for further information.

Two inter-related areas of increasing use are those of rear-projection systems and integrated multi-media classroom facilities. In rear projection systems, the image is projected onto a translucent screen *from behind*, rather than onto a reflective surface from in front. Rear projection makes possible use of slides, films, and other media in an undarkened room, and it also provides for good security and maintenance arrangements. If not properly designed for a particular classroom environment, however, a rear-projection facility can result in loss of image quality on the screen. In an article that has become a standard for planning projection facilities ("1W, 2W, 3W, 4W, 5W, 6W, Law for Audiovisual Presentations"), Ray Wadsworth itemizes the considerations crucial to rear screen projection areas: adequate space for proper lens focal length, adequate height to prevent "keystoning," adequate workspace behind the projector area, and reduced incident light and sound (1971b, pp. 21-22).

Academic use of rear-screen projection in multi-media classrooms is widespread in institutions throughout the country, including the following: Indiana State University, Terre Haute; Ithaca High School, New York ("New Buildings...," 1966); Kent State University (Mitchell, 1967); University of Wisconsin—Madison (McVey, 1975); North Division of Niles Township Community High Schools, Skokie, Illinois (Cress and Stowe, 1967); Pennsylvania State University (Carpenter,

1965); University of Miami (Simons, 1965); and the University of Texas at Austin (Colbert, 1961).

As indicated earlier, acoustical control plays an important role in classroom or auditorium environments. Wall and floor surfaces in addition to the type of projection stand or booth should be considered as integral parts of media room planning based upon each institution's use patterns. When rooms without windows are designed for projection, careful attention should be given to the development of an adequate ventilation system and to proper lighting controls, such as dimmer switches. A classroom designed for students who will be taking notes while viewing slides should have controlled lighting to allow for different light levels that compensate for satisfactory viewing of the projected image and for note-taking. The teacher should also have control of the lighting both at the back and at the front of the classroom to make adjustments without distracting the class. There should also be a suitable pointer for use with front and rear-screen projections. Ednalite, Spindler and Sauppe, Visual Horizons, and other companies listed in the directory supply pointers for every need and budget. Some projector remote control units (e.g., Leitz) are available with built-in pointers. In a small classroom, the teacher may not consider such a device necessary, but for auditorium or large-screen projections, it is essential to clearly indicate details of the visual image. A simple wooden pointer may suffice in the average classroom, but an illuminated pointer that projects a beam of light onto the screen satisfies the demands of lecture hall or auditorium presentations.

For more thorough discussions on the development of media rooms, the following publications are recommended: Cable, *Audio-Visual Handbook* (1970); Culclasure, "Film and Filmstrip Media" (1969, pp. 35-51; De Bernardis, *Planning Schools for New Media* (1961); Erickson, "The Physical Environment for Media Utilization" (1968, Chapter 6, pp. 175-225); Lewis, "What to Watch When You Select Projection Screens" (1967); Oldham, "Chalkboards and Beyond; Audiovisual Design of the Thirty-seat Classroom" (1972); Patrie, "How Does It Look from Where You Sit?" (1966); and Wadsworth, "Divisible Auditoriums: A Challenge to AV Systems" (1975).

REFERENCES

"AV Practices among Colleges and Universities." 1964. *American School and University* 36 (July):26.

The Audio-Visual Equipment Directory. 1979. 24th edition. Fairfax, Virginia: National Audio-Visual Association.

Brown, James W., Richard Lewis, and Fred F. Harcleroad. 1977. *A-V Instruction: Technology, Media, and Methods*. 5th edition. New York: McGraw-Hill.

Cabeceiras, James. 1978. *The Multimedia Library, Materials Selection and Use*. New York: Academic Press.

Carpenter, C. Ray. 1965. "The Pennsylvania State University; the Instructional Learning Systems and Research Center." *Audiovisual Instruction* 10 (February):134-35.

Colbert, Charles R. 1961. "Researching an Auditorium-teaching Centre." *American School and University* H1-H6.

"College Core; Ithaca's Instructional Resources Center Includes a Dial-Access-Information-Retrieval-System for Students." 1969. *College Management* 4 (November):23-26.

Cress, Hal J., and Richard Stowe. 1967. "We Designed and Constructed a Remote Control Classroom." *Audiovisual Instruction* 12 (October):830-35.

Culclasure, David. 1969. *Effective Use of Audiovisual Media.* Englewood Cliffs, N.J.: Prentice-Hall.

Davidson, Raymond L. 1969. *Audiovisual Machines.* 2nd edition. Scranton, Pennsylvania: International Textbook Company.

De Kieffer, R. E., and Lee Cochran. 1962. *Manual of Audiovisual Techniques.* 2nd edition. Englewood Cliffs, N.J.: Prentice-Hall.

DeLaurier, Nancy. 1974. "Slide Curators Professional Status Survey: Additional Statistical Report." Mimeographed. Kansas City, Missouri: Department of Art and Art History, University of Missouri.

Eboch, Sidney, and George W. Cochern. 1968. *Operating Audio-Visual Equipment.* 2nd edition. San Francisco, California: Chandler Publishing Co.

Educational Facilities with New Media. 1966. Edited by Alan C. Green. Washington, D.C.: Department of Audiovisual Instruction, National Education Association. (Stock No. 071-02302).

Erickson, Carlton W. H. 1965. *Fundamentals of Teaching with Audiovisual Technology.* New York: Macmillan. (Text edition, 1972).

Frederick, Franz J. 1974. "Minitutorial on Screening Facilities." *School Media Quarterly* 2 (Spring):237-44, 253-55. "Erratum," 1974 3 (Fall):29.

Haviland, David S. 1970. "Designing Multimedia Rooms for Teaching or, The Instructor as the Forgotten User!" *Audiovisual Instruction* 15 (October): 78-81.

James, David A., and George V. Nichols. 1968. "Adequate Slide Projection." *Indiana Arts and Vocational Education* 57 (March):90, 92, 94, 96, 98.

James, David A., and George V. Nichols. 1968. "Experimental Comparison of Projection Screens." *Indiana Arts and Vocational Education* 56 (November):44-46.

McVey, G. F. 1975. "Components of an Effective Multi-media System for College and University Instruction." *Audiovisual Instruction* 20 (April):42-45.

McVey, G. F. 1977. "Facilities." In *College Learning Resources Programs*, pp. 49-70. Washington, D.C.: Association of Educational Communications and Technology.

Mitchell, John W. 1967. "Viewing Wall Contains Complete Audiovisual System." *Nation's Schools* 79 (May):70.

Morgan, Kenneth W. 1963. "When Amateurs Make an Audiovisual Room." *Audiovisual Instruction* 8 (April):220-21.

"New Buildings Designed for A-V Use." 1966. *American School and University* 38 (April):39-41.

"Not Just a Library, A Generic Library." 1973. *College and University Business* 55 (October):29-36.

Oates, Stanton C. 1975. *Audiovisual Equipment; Self Instruction Manual.* 3rd edition. Dubuque, Iowa: W. C. Brown.

Oldham, R. 1972. "Chalkboards and Beyond; AV Design of the Thirty-Seat Classroom." *Educational Product Report*, No. 43, 5 (April):39-52.

PMI Photo Methods for Industry. Catalog and Directory of Products and Services. New York: Gellert Publishing Corporation. Published annually.

Professional Photographic Catalog. Chicago: Standard Photo Supply. Published annually.

Rosenberg, Kenyon C., and John S. Doskey. 1976. *Media Equipment: A Guide and Dictionary*. Littleton, Colorado: Libraries Unlimited.

Ruark, Gerald L. 1968. "A Plea for Two Projectors; Utilizing Filmstrips and Slides." *Audiovisual Instruction* 13 (May):500.

Simons, Wendell W. 1965. "Choosing Audio-Visual Equipment." *Library Trends* 13 (April):503-526.

"SUNY Learning Resources Focus on Multimedia Rooms." 1970. *College and University Business* 48 (January):68.

Wadsworth, Raymond. 1971a. "How to Determine Seating Area for Good Viewing of Projected Images." *American School and University* 43 (July):6, 8-9.

Wadsworth, Raymond. 1971b. "1W, 2W, 3W, 4W, 5W, 6W, Law for AV Presentations." *American School and University* 44 (October):18-22.

Wadsworth, Raymond. 1975. "Divisible Auditoriums: A Challenge to AV Systems." *American School and University* 48 (October; November):60-64, 66, 68; 41-43.

Wilkinson, G. L. 1976. "Projection Variables and Performances." *AV Communication Review* 24 (Winter):413-36.

Wittich, Walter Arno, and Charles F. Schuller. 1973. *Instructional Technology: Its Nature and Use*. 5th edition. New York: Harper & Row.

9–MISCELLANEOUS EQUIPMENT AND SUPPLIES

INTRODUCTION

A great deal of specialized equipment and supplies is necessary for the efficient operation of a slide library. Slide mounting materials, portable viewers, light tables, magnifiers, slide sorters, carrying cases, slide catalog filing cards, and typewriters with small type and variable line spacing will be described and discussed. The Directory of Distributors and Manufacturers of Equipment and Supplies lists sources for all items cited in this chapter.

MOUNTING MATERIALS

Mounting materials include slide mounts, masks, film cleaners, and labels. Optional equipment, dependent upon the type of slide mount used and the budget of the slide library, includes automatic film cutters and slide mounting machines. Both the *Professional Photographic Catalog* and the *Photo Methods for Industry Catalog* are useful aids, listing and illustrating all types of mounting materials.

The type of slide mount selected depends upon the following factors:

1. How frequently will the slides be used?
2. Who will use the slides? How many individuals?
3. How will slides be stored?
4. What types of projectors will be used?
5. What will be the average projection time per slide?
6. How much expense can be absorbed for mounting materials and for binding time?

If the slides will receive only occasional use, heavy-duty mounts may not be necessary; but if they are subjected to constant use and subsequently are handled frequently by a great many users, then to provide maximum film life, a mount giving adequate film protection both from smudging and from heat should be used. If slides are stored in trays or magazines as sets without being handled each time they are used, a less substantial mount, possibly without glass, may be adequate. Slides that are stored in cabinets from which they will be manually removed do need protection to prevent fingerprints and scratches on the film surface. In addition, a cardbound mount may not provide the durability desired for constant handling and use of slides. Slides that are projected for long periods of time—over five minutes per slide—should also have the protection that glass and heavy-duty mounts provide.

A heavy-duty mount is a slide mount with glass covering both sides of the film. The glass should have been treated to retard or prevent Newton rings. These rings are created by the diffraction of light that occurs when moisture is present as the slide comes in contact with glass. Anti-Newton-ring glass is uneven on one side, and this side is placed against the non-emulsion or smooth side of the film, thereby preventing a flat contact between the film and the glass. The emulsion side is uneven from the outset, so the glass resting against this side of the film need not be treated. Both light and heat reduces the lifetime of a slide; the added protection provided by glass is necessary to prolong the life of the film if subjected to rigorous classroom use, as well as to keep the film in a flat plane for sharp focusing (Tull, 1978a, p. 322).

When projected, slides should be used in projectors having an adequate cooling and ventilation system. The exact bulb wattage required for use in various projectors should also be closely observed, as the cooling and ventilation have usually been adjusted to compensate for the heat levels generated by the wattage recommended for a given projector. Projector maintenance should also be strictly monitored, as overheating can damage the projector, the film, and the binder.

Slide mounts may be classified by the following categories:

1. Cardboard or fibreboard
2. Glass
3. Plastic—with or without glass
4. Aluminum or metal—with or without glass

The different types of slide mounts vary in cost and in binding time. The least expensive is a cardbound mount without glass, while the metal mount with Anti-Newton-ring glass usually requires the highest expenditure per mount. With the exception of the cardboard or ready-mount slide binding, all other categories are considered heavy-duty if they fulfill the qualifications defining this type of mount.

Slides can be ordered in roll format. These slides are not pre-cut or mounted in cardboard or plastic, which usually decreases commercial processing costs and allows the institution to choose the binding best suited to its needs and budget. As more parts are required for binding—glass, masks, mounts, mounting equipment, and tape—binding time will increase in direct proportion to the complexity of the mount and the time required for masking. Evaluation of mounts should therefore include labor costs as well as the initial cost of the mount itself.

Cardboard or Fibreboard Mounts—The term "cardboard mount" refers to the type of mount used to bind slides that are commercially processed. Cardboard mounts can also be purchased separately by institutions making and processing their own slides. Cardboard mounts can be quickly bound and cost relatively little—less than $0.02 per slide. If slides are not handled regularly and are not used for prolonged periods of time, these mounts may suffice as permanent bindings. Slide protectors (sealed-edge sleeves) made of acetate can be purchased to provide temporary protection during projection.

Any mount dependent upon adhesive paper that requires moisture to make it adhere can present problems. Too much moisture may damage the film. Tapes used for binding or masking slides that are not self-adhesive and require added moisture also have the same disadvantage.

Glass Mounts—Glass mounts are composed of a mask 2x2-inch (or 2¼x2¼-inch or 3¼x4-inch) glass, and binding tape. The mask in this instance holds the film between the glass. A common use of the cardboard mount is as a mask between two cover glasses (2x2-inch), which are bound with narrow plastic, paper, self-adhesive, or electrical tape. Tapes of this type are available from stationary, hardware, or photographic shops. Scotch photographic and electrical, Erskine paper, and Leitz and 3M silver Mylar tapes are often used for this purpose, but as heat will cause many self-adhesive tapes to "bleed" and become gummy, paper tapes or those with inert bases such as Mylar are preferable.

Frequently, when cardboard mounts are used between two pieces of glass, the bound slide is too thick for projection in many of the automatic projectors. The slots in the trays or magazines of some projectors are not wide enough to hold bound slides. Consequently, the type of projectors utilized should affect the type of mount selected by the slide librarian. Glass used with masks or cardbound mounts can be purchased with or without Anti-Newton-ring treatment. Anti-Newton-ring glass will be slightly more expensive than plain binding glass, but the long-term benefits should make the small additional expenditure worthwhile.

Because the early lantern slides were glass slides which readily adapted to the use of an additional glass plate for protection of the emulsion of the image, glass mounts were the earliest used for 2x2-inch slides. According to recent, definitive articles by A. G. Tull, glass and tape binding may still be preferable to other methods for eliminating moisture damage to slides due to condensation (Tull, 1978a, 1978b).

Plastic Mounts—Plastic mounts may be purchased with or without glass with the option for either plain or Anti-Newton-ring glass. Usually, they are white plastic on one side with either blue or grey plastic on the other, e.g., Gepe, Agfacolor, and Kindermann mounts. The Lindia slide mount is grey plastic on both sides, and Kaiser mounts are white. Some mounts may be purchased without glass, e.g., Gepe and Kaiser. The reason for mounting slides in plastic mounts without glass is to prevent jamming in automatic projectors (possible from the frayed edges of cardboard mounts) and to provide a means of handling the slides without touching the film. Companies such as Kaiser, Seary, and Sickles also manufacture equipment that will automatically mount different types of plastic slides. Automatic mounting equipment ranges in price from about $150 to over $1,000 per machine.

Plastic mounts are available with pre-inserted glass (Agfacolor and Kindermann), with glass that is inserted separately during the binding process (Lindia), and as a single-hinged unit with pre-inserted glass (Kindermann). They also come in a variety of widths to fit automatic and manual projectors. For the extremely thin plastic mounts, additional masking of the film with tape may not be possible, because the added bulk of the tape may prevent the closing of the two sides of the plastic mount. This will vary, depending upon the density of the mount and the tape used. Manufacturers or distributors will send samples upon request in most cases. It is recommended that various types of mounts be examined first-hand in order to evaluate and select the mount best suited to a given institutional need.

Plastic mounts may be slightly more expensive than glass mounts, but with the purchase of Anti-Newton-ring glass for both mounts and tapes, and of masks for glass mounts, the price may vary only slightly, if at all. The plastic mount, however, will usually require less binding time, because a smaller number of operations is necessary than with the glass mount. For slides purchased commercially, which usually come pre-bound in cardboard mounts, a glass mount may be more convenient because the film is already masked and supported.

The primary difficulty encountered with using plastic mounts is the tendency of the plastic to melt after prolonged use or to warp from excessive heat. The white side of the mount, which faces the bulb, usually will reflect enough heat to retard this process, but mounts having a dark color on one side may be particularly susceptible to heat absorption. Depending upon each institution's use patterns, this characteristic may or may not be a problem, and testing of sample binders is recommended. Institutions having rear-screen projection systems, which reverse the normal front-to-back orientation of the slide in the projector, may need to use slide mounts that are white or light in color on both sides.

Aluminum or Metal Mounts—Aluminum mounts include Perrotcolor and Emde mounts. These mounts come equipped with either Anti-Newton-ring or plain glass. Some metal mounts also come without glass (e.g., Emde) and can be used to protect cardboard mounts. Metal mounts with Anti-Newton-ring glass cannot break or snap apart, come in the proper width to fit automatic projectors, and will withstand the heat and heavy use to which they may be subjected over long periods of time. Metal and plastic mounts that have the same type of glass are comparably priced, with metal mounts tending to be slightly more expensive. Actual costs of either plastic or metal mounts will vary, depending upon how much bulk ordering can be done by a given institution. According to the 1975-1977 MACAA surveys (Scott, 1978), Perrotcolor metal mounts and Gepe plastic mounts are favored by most academic slide collections. Schools using plastic binders include the Georgia Institute of Technology, Evergreen State College, Ohio State University, and the National Gallery of Fine Arts. Metal mounts are in use at the Art Institute of Chicago, the Metropolitan Museum of Art, Vassar College, the University of Texas—Austin, and the Winterthur Museum.

Masks and Masking Tape—Masking a slide can refer to the process of placing it in a holder or to placing tape along the edges of an image to block out an undesirable or distracting background or object. If the image has been masked while being photographed, then taped masking is not usually necessary. In this case, a standard metal, paper, or cardboard mask is adequate. Brands of masks include the Kodak Ready-mount, the Emde Readymount Binder, the Emde aluminum mask, and the Leitz and Kodak Masks. The Kodak Ready-mount and Emde Readymount Binder are equivalent to standard cardboard mounts and, therefore, can function as either a slide mount or a slide mask. The Leitz and Kodak masks are intended to be used with glass, not alone, because they are too thin to provide support to the film for projection. Diagrams 21-23 show a standard 2x2-inch slide mask—paper or metal—with a 35mm frame inserted into the mask. This type of mask is usually made with press-out flaps that hold the film in place while it is being bound. In Diagram 21, the film is inserted into section "a" of the mask and "b" is folded over, as shown in Diagram 22.

If additional masking is necessary, the tape is applied directly to the film, as shown in Diagram 23. Supplementary masking may be required for any slide mount, depending upon the image and the conditions under which it was

Diagram 21—Sample 35mm slide mask.

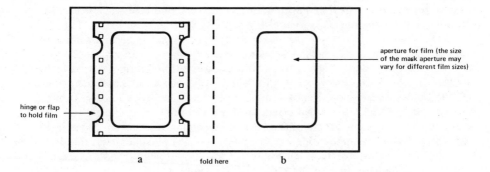

hinge or flap to hold film

aperture for film (the size of the mask aperture may vary for different film sizes)

a   fold here   b

Diagram 22—Slide mask closed with film in place.

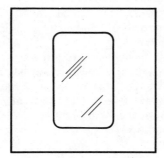

Diagram 23—Slide mask with additional masking tape.

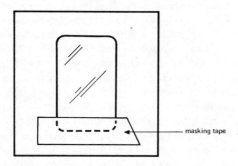

masking tape

photographed. For some types of mounts, such as Perrotcolor, precise trimming of excess masking tape is required. Most tapes used for binding glass slides can also be used for masking, but the importance of using inert, non-bleeding tapes is even more crucial in masking due to the direct contact of tape and film. The MACAA *Guide to Equipment for Slide Maintenance and Viewing* contains a lengthy discussion of the advantages and disadvantages of various tapes (1978, pp. 34-40). Black graphic tapes, such as those manufactured by Chartpak, are recommended for their opacity, while silver Mylar tapes, such as those manufactured by Leitz and 3M, offer extreme thinness and clean edges. A tape (not cited in the MACAA *Guide*) that offers the advantages of both complete opacity and thin, clean edges, is the aluminized sensing tape made for use on magnetic recordings. Scotch brand Sensing Tape comes in a dispenser that makes this product particularly easy to use. A slide librarian may find it helpful to keep several types of tape on hand for use in a variety of situations.

Film Cleaners and Glass—Additional mounting materials include film cleaners and labels. Before the film is bound in a closed mount such as plastic, metal, or glass, the film should be free of smudges and lint. This can be accomplished by using a camel's hair brush such as those made by Kodak or a Staticmaster brush made by Nuclear Products. As many of the glass and metal mounts cannot be easily taken apart for film cleaning without destroying part of the mount, the film should be cleaned before it is mounted. A small speck of lint may not seem of consequence during the mounting process, but once the slide is projected, it will present an annoying distraction to the viewers. Edwal Scientific Products makes cleaning fluids for films that will prevent the growth of fungus and make the film resistant to scratches, static, and color fading. Accidental smudging of the film surface can usually be corrected by use of this type of film cleaning fluid. An alcohol-and-water solution may be used to clean the glass before it is placed against the film. Standard glass cleaner without ammonia also may be used for this purpose. It is important that both the film and glass are clean before the slide is permanently mounted.

Labels—Labels that adhere to glass, paper, plastic or metal mounts and that do not curl up on the corners after long-term exposure to heat are necessary for permanent identification of each slide. Avery, Demco, Erskine, American Library Color Slide Company, Multiplex, and the Professional Tape Company make or distribute labels for slides. Slide labels may be gummed, require moisture to be applied, or may come in press-apply format. They also can be purchased in rolls or in sheets, or a self-adhesive paper or standard file folder label may be cut to fit a slide mount. This latter process, however, requires a prohibitive amount of staff time, and the resultant labels may not adhere as well as those specifically designed to be applied to glass, metal, or plastic surfaces.

Self-adhesive or press-apply marking dots that indicate how the slide is to be placed in the projector can be part of the label or purchased separately and applied directly to the label or to the mount. Most stationary and photography shops will have a variety of dots available. Alternatives to separate dots include the use of "magic markers" to indicate the projection or a thumbmark on each slide. The eraser tip of a pencil, inked on a stamp pad, can be used to print a dot on the slide label. This dot is sometimes referred to as a thumbmark because the projectionist holds the slide with thumb over the dot when placing it into the projector with the right hand. Whatever type of dot is used, it should be one that adheres readily and permanently to the slide mount or label. If the dot falls off the label or mount, slides may be placed in the projector incorrectly.

If the image is horizontal, the dot should be placed in the lower left-hand corner of the front of the slide, and if it is vertical, in the left-hand corner at the bottom of the image. When the slide is placed in the projector correctly, it is upside down and backwards, i.e., the slide is upside down and facing the projectionist rather than the screen. Labels can also be purchased with pre-printed dots or an institution may have them custom-designed with dots or thumbmarks of various colors that also indicate different subject areas (e.g., a red dot for geology, blue for architecture, and so forth). Color coding of this type can decrease the amount of time required for slide sorting before refiling (see Diagram 24).

Whatever thumbmark system is utilized, it should be consistently applied throughout the collection so that it is clear to the user how the slide is to be placed correctly into the projector, the tray, or magazine. Although this is a seemingly minor aspect of slide mounting, many patrons are discouraged from using slides because of the frequency of upside down projections, which create a disturbance in the classroom and a break in the continuity of a lecture. Distraction of this type is unnecessary if the slides are mounted and labeled correctly.

As noted above, particularly useful publications on mounting slides are the MACAA *Guide to Equipment for Slide Maintenance and Viewing* and the recent articles by A. G. Tull, two of which are reprinted in the *Guide*. In addition, the directory of dealers and/or manufacturers and the bibliography on the "Care and Preservation of Films and Slides" in the Selected Bibliography are recommended for further information on this specialized topic.

Diagram 24—Slide with dot or "thumbmark."

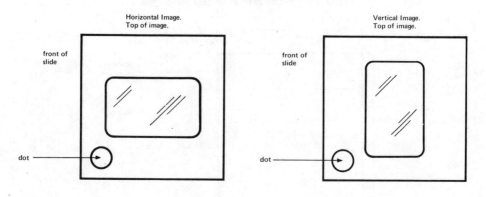

FILE GUIDES AND CARDS

A filing and storage system that is not based upon fixed tray or magazine housing and that does not use a visual display rack cabinet will need guide cards within the drawers to divide and subdivide slide categories. If durable guide cards or guides are not used, constant replacement is necessary, involving additional staff time and expense for materials. Moreover, sturdy and legible guides make the collection easier to use. Unfortunately, an efficient and economical solution has not been provided for most unitary image slide libraries.

The most common method for making slide guide cards is to cut them from bristol board, approximately 2x2½ inches. The identifying information is either typed across the top of the card or on adhesive papers or labels that can easily be inserted into the typewriter, moistened—if not self-adhesive—and attached to the top of the guide card. Fibreboard or lightweight cardboard can also be cut and used in a similar manner.

Another solution is to use fibreboard that has been cut to the correct size and attach a clear plastic tab to the top of the fibreboard. Plastic tabs are readily available in most stationery shops. This type of guide has the advantage of having a clear plastic tab through which paper labels may be inserted—those available in stationery shops come with pre-cut paper on which the identifying information can be typed. A guide prepared in this way is illustrated in Diagram 25. Clear plastic tabs of this type are commonly used as notebook guides. A modification of the fibreboard and plastic tab guide is used at the Boston Museum of Fine Arts, the Metropolitan Museum of Art, and Yale University, and can be custom-ordered from the Koller and Smith Co. The fibreboard is pre-cut by this company along with a clear plastic tab insert as shown in Diagram 26.

Diagram 25—Guide card with clear plastic tab.

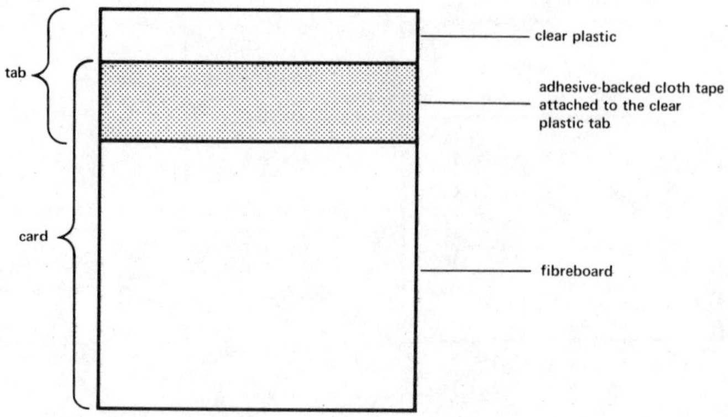

In both cases, a paper insert can be placed behind the clear plastic tab, so the typed information is protected from smearing and fading from handling. The primary advantages of this type of tab is that it is reusable, has a variable holder or tab into which a label may be inserted, allowing for at least three typed lines of information, and is relatively durable. With a collection that is heavily used,

Diagram 26–Modified guide card with clear plastic tab.

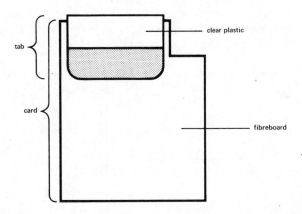

continual thumbing through the files will cause most bristol or cardboard guides to become dog-eared and bent within a year. Some institutions staple together two pieces of bristol board or cover the top edge with Scotch Magic Tape to make them wear longer. Even this practice is questionable as a means of providing heavy-duty guide cards and may consume an unnecessary amount of staff time.

In addition to the use of bristol board and fibreboard, standard library guides may be cut to fit slide drawers. At the University of California at Santa Cruz, 3x5-inch full-cut Demco Golden Guides are trimmed to the proper size for use as slide guide cards. These guides are made of durable plastic, are thinner than fibreboard guides, and have a clear plastic tab for inserting paper labels. Diagram 27 shows the original size guide cut to the correct size for slides, as indicated by the dotted lines.

Diagram 27–Demco Golden Guide card modified for slide files.

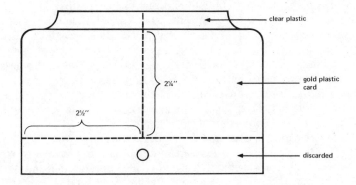

As is immediately apparent from the diagram, relatively little waste in materials occurs, with only a small fraction of the card being discarded; but staff time is still necessary in order to cut the cards. Using the above principle and the same plastic, Demco designed a slide guide card (with or without holes for rods) but has not marketed them as a standard item (see Diagram 28).

Diagram 28–Demco Golden Guide card designed for slide files.

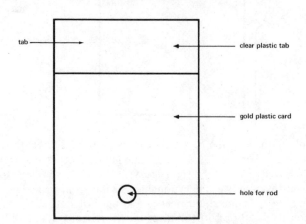

These guides can, however, be custom-ordered from Demco. In both diagrams illustrating modifications of a Demco Golden Guide, a clear plastic tab is available at the top of the card for paper label inserts. These cards are constructed as single sheets of plastic rather than as two separate types of material adhered to one another, as in the case of the fibreboard and plastic tab guide.

Plastic file guides made of Mylar may be custom-ordered from Demco and other plastics manufacturers. The Mylar guides used by the Slide Library at Indiana University are 2-3/4x2¼ inches (a size suited to the relatively deep drawers of their metal cabinets) and are designed so that lightweight paper or bristol board approximately 2¼x2 inches may be inserted into the guide (see Photograph 7, page 178). It has the same advantages as other plastic guides, including durability, flexibility, and minimal thickness that requires little space in the slide drawers as compared with fibreboard or cardboard guides. Unlike other guides, however, this design provides 75% of its surface for information and can accommodate xerox reproduction of labeled slides, making it particularly useful for collections with interfiled shelflists. Such guides may be tailored to an institution's unique needs (e.g., see Diagram 1, page 128, the Winterthur Museum).

The custom-ordered plastic or Mylar guides are usually more expensive than fibreboard or cardboard guides but they are more durable and have more space for typed information (see Diagram 29). As more slide libraries demand quality supplies and equipment for their collections, the cost necessitated by custom-ordering materials will hopefully decrease.

Diagram 29—Custom-ordered Mylar slide file guide

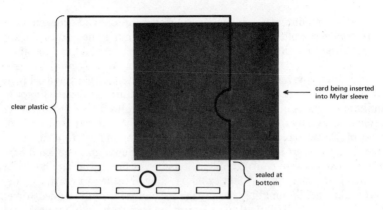

TYPEWRITERS

In order to provide adequate cataloging and classification data on each slide label and guide card, typewriters with small or "micro" print sizes are required. Companies supplying small type sizes include Adler, Facit, Olympia, and Olivetti. Although such typewriters may appear to be a luxury item, they most certainly are not. If the slide library does not have small print typewriters available, it is frequently forced to omit or abbreviate information to the degree that the label may be barely readable to anyone except the cataloging staff.

In addition to small type, some typewriters can be purchased with variable line spacers so that as many as four lines per 3/8-inch label may be typed (the average slide label is 3/8x1-7/8 inches). Caution should be exercised to avoid typing the lines too close together. Labels for 3¼x4-inch slides readily adapt to either pica or elite type.

Frequently, a new ribbon will cause smearing of the label, but if the label is handled carefully when removed from the typewriter and allowed to set for a few minutes, the problem should be somewhat alleviated. Carbon ribbons may also be used to prevent smearing, although most institutions do not find it necessary to take precautions of this type. Different label surfaces will also be affected by a new ribbon more readily than others, e.g., a coated or slick-surfaced paper will smear more easily than a flat-surfaced paper. If the problem is considered serious, either the ribbon or paper type should be changed. Another solution is to spray the labels immediately after typing with a clear plastic fixative or non-smear spray (available in most shops handling art supplies). Unless the slide library is well ventilated, however, this procedure may be uncomfortable and unsafe for both the staff and users. More commonly used is a mixture of water and white glue (e.g., Elmer's Glue), which is brushed over the labels immediately after typing. Smeared labels are difficult to read both by users and the staff and time wasted by retyping procedures are unnecessary if adequate precautions are taken in advance. Both typewriters and fixatives for labeling slides are discussed at length in the MACAA *Guide to Equipment for Slide Maintenance and Viewing* (1978, pp. 61-74).

LIGHT TABLES, VIEWERS, AND MAGNIFIERS

A viewing medium for preview, lecture preparation, and slide examination is necessary for every collection of slides. That medium may be part of the storage system, as with visual display rack cabinets; a plastic or metal hand or table-top viewer; an illuminator; a table-top light table that may or may not be an integrated part of the table; a portable rear projection screen used with a standard projector; or a standard screen used with a projector. Any medium having a light source that illuminates slides may be called an illuminator, although a distinction in terminology is usually made, based upon the size of the illuminated surface. A viewer or previewer has an illuminated surface ranging in size from slightly larger than the slide to about 6x6 inches. A viewer is small enough to be hand-held during use in most instances. In contrast, a light table gives the viewer an illuminated surface two feet square to 3x4 feet or larger. Screen projection varies greatly in size, but again, the illuminating device—the projector—is not intended to be held while used. The term "illuminator" is normally used to refer to vertical or sloped surface illumination ranging in size from 12x18 inches to 2x3 feet or larger. There are modifications of these various types, but a consistent application of the terms is desirable for explanatory purposes.

Hand or table-top viewers are commonly purchased by individuals and institutions using slides because they are easy to handle and operate, require minimal space, provide illumination, may be battery or electrically powered, and satisfy most demands for magnification of miniature slides. Photograph 17 shows

Photograph 17. Custom-made illuminators with Kindermann metal previewers placed on table-top in front of illuminators. Yale University.

a previewer used in conjunction with sloped illuminators, which are custom-made. GAF, Panavue, Bro-Dart, and other comapnies manufacture viewers of this type. Although made for miniature slides, not all of these viewers will accept slides bound in glass, metal, or plastic mounts. When selecting viewers for purchase, the brochures or distributor's guides should be carefully read to be sure that the viewer fulfills the qualifications required by a specific collection. The *Audio Visual Equipment Directory* and the MACAA *Guide* should also be consulted during the selection process.

A light table is a table having a built-in surface for illumination. The entire surface of the table may be capable of illumination or only a section of it. Photographs 3 (page 171), 10 (page 182), and 13 (page 193) include light tables that have been custom-designed having the entire surface of the table illuminated (Princeton University, Syracuse University, and the University of Illinois at Chicago Circle). Glass, plastic or plexiglass may be used for the illuminating surface. In the pamphlet *Audiovisual Planning Equipment*, Kodak recommends the use of cool white flourescent lamps for slide illumination (1978, p. 5). The problem frequently encountered with this type of light table is the amount of glare which occurs when an entire surface of a table is capable of illumination. The tables used at the University of Illinois at Chicago Circle, although having a relatively small surface area, approximately 2x3 feet, still present this problem. Some light tables have only a section of the table surface designed for illumination. Consequently, they do not create as much glare as an entirely illuminated surface might. Hamilton Manufacturing makes tracing tables that have glass working surfaces with flourescent lighting that can also be used for viewing slides. This type of product is listed as a "Transparency Illuminator" in the *Professional Photographic Catalog*.

More commonly used than a light table is the vertical or sloped metal or wood illuminator. The small illuminators that have only fixtures for light bulbs are called "slide sorters." Slide sorters usually have a viewing surface that is about 12x16 inches.

In the Kodak pamphlet, *Audiovisual Planning Equipment* (1978), the production of a wooden slide-sequence illuminator is explained. Placing slides in a specific viewing sequence often prompts the usage of the term "sequence" with various illuminators. Many eminent institutions have custom-made and designed variations of the type specified in the Kodak pamphlet, including the Metropolitan Museum of Art, Princeton University, the University of Pennsylvania, and Yale University. As is apparent in Photographs 4 (page 172), 5 (page 173), and 17 (page 234), all of these illuminators are quite similar. Princeton's, however, are particularly distinctive because they are built with wooden flaps that can be placed above the 2x2-inch slides to prevent glare and lifted for viewing larger or 3¼x4-inch slides. One of the most convenient aspects of the Kodak designed unit is the relative ease in changing bulbs, which can be accomplished by sliding out the vertical plastic viewing panel. Many of the custom-made versions require the removal and placement of bulbs from underneath or back of the illuminator, necessitating the movement of the illuminator. Moving such an illuminator can be quite cumbersome, inconvenient, and create a disturbance in the slide library.

Photograph 19 (see page 238) illustrates the use of an upright illuminator called Ednalite Sequential Editor/Transviewer made by the Ednalite Corporation. This illuminator is especially made for viewing slides, transparencies, x-rays, and other transparent or translucent film materials. The illumination surface is made of plexiglass and has eleven removable and adjustable metal channels for different size materials. This unit is also supplied with a magnifier made by Ednalite.

Many slide libraries provide several types of viewing devices to allow for individual viewing preferences and variations in viewing requirements. In Photograph 12 (page 192), two types of illuminators used at the Metropolitan Museum of Art are shown. The gently sloped metal table-top illuminator is made by the Stacor Corporation and the upright rear-projection screen cabinet called a Caritel is made by Hudson-Photographic Industries and distributed by Bro-Dart and other library suppliers. The Metropolitan also provides custom-made carrels by Herman Miller of New York for slide study and viewing by their curatorial staff and the general public. These carrels have been supplemented by vertical light viewers designed by a private contractor, according to the needs dictated by the Slide Library staff.

Another example of customized viewing equipment was designed by Ed Zagorski for use in the Architecture Building at the University of Illinois—Urbana (Photograph 18). It functions both to provide ease of student access to slide review materials and to protect the equipment from vandalism and theft (Zagorski, 1970, pp. 15-16). The "Slide Reviewer" is a lockable, rear-screen projection unit utilizing a Kodak Carousel Random Access Projector. Access to the control panel is provided by use of a key checked out from the library, and the projector and slide tray are controlled only by faculty and library staff. Identification of the slides in the Reviewer is posted above the control panel, which includes a table-top surface for writing.

Media carrels readily available that include facilities for front and rear projection screens for slides and filmstrips are illustrated in *The Audio Visual Equipment Directory*. Other preview set-ups for rear screen projections include the 3M Polacoat, and models by Lester A. Dine, Kindermann, and others. For additional references, see the Selected Bibliography under "Screens and Pointers" and "Rear Projection Screens—Table-Top Models."

As noted earlier, a magnifier is supplied with the Ednalite illuminator but it may also be purchased separately. Agfa, Bausch and Lomb, Logan, Visual Horizons, and other companies make hand magnifiers, which are listed in the *Professional Photographic Catalog*. Hand magnifiers are useful for rapid examination of slides for visual details and for preview of commercially purchased slides when other methods of viewing are not available or are inconvenient. Although it is desirable to have a preview room near the slide library for use by the staff and patrons of the slide library, this is not always feasible, so other types of magnified illumination should be available for this function. The Dazor Manufacturing Corporation makes a variety of Floating-Arm Magnifiers, which combine magnification with incandescent or flourescent lighting. These magnifiers may be attached to a table top or be purchased in free-standing pedestal models having iron bases; they are similar in principle to the standard floating-arm desk lamp.

**Photograph 18. "Slide Reviewer." University of Illinois–Urbana.
(Designed by Ed Zagorski. Photograph courtesy of
Jane Goldberg, Slide Curator.)**

CARRYING CASES

Whether a collection of slides is being circulated throughout an entire city
or within a given institution, it is necessary to have adequate cases or trays available for the transport of slides that will keep them in presentation order and prevent
their being broken or damaged. Smith-Victor, Nega-File, and Keystone Ferrule
handle ready-made metal or plastic cases for 2x2-inch up to 2-3/4x2-3/4-inch slides.
Other companies are listed in the Directory of Distributors and Manufacturers of
Equipment and Supplies. Projectors that have their own trays or magazines may be
used to transport slides, so long as the magazines are to be used in projectors into
which they fit. Carrying cases of this type are usually available in photography
stores and are frequently described as "storage cases." They may be used by

hobbyists or other individuals for slide housing, but they are not recommended as institutional storage.

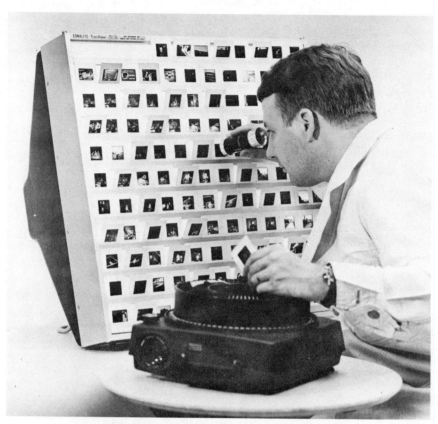

Photograph 19. Ednalite Sequential Editor/Transviewer with Ednalite magnifinder. (Photograph courtesy of the Ednalite Corporation.)

REFERENCES

Audiovisual Planning Equipment. 1978. Rochester, New York: Eastman Kodak. (Kodak Publication No. S-11.).

Guide to Equipment for Slide Maintenance and Viewing. 1978. Edited by Gillian Scott. Albuquerque, New Mexico: Mid-America College Art Association and the University of New Mexico at Albuquerque.

Minor, Ed, and Harvey R. Frye. 1977. *Techniques for Producing Visual Instructional Media.* Second edition. New York: McGraw-Hill.

Tull, A. G. 1978a. "Film Transparencies Between Glass, Part 1." *British Journal of Photography* 125:322-23.

Tull, A. G. 1978b. "Film Transparencies Between Glass, Parts 2 and 3." *British Journal of Photography* 125:349-51, 353.

Zagorski, Edward J., and Rob Fisher. 1970. "Undergraduate Instructional Award." Champaign, Illinois: University of Illinois. (Part II: The Slide Reviewer, pp. 15-24, Figures 1-10.).

SELECTED BIBLIOGRAPHY

Each citation in the following bibliography has been selected on the basis of its relevance to the management of slide libraries. The majority of all works cited provide either direct references to slides, equipment such as projectors, or to general principles involved in handling audiovisual materials that also apply to slides.

In order to facilitate use of the bibliography, which includes approximately 700 citations, the following outline of the classified headings is provided. Numbers in parentheses indicate pages where each section begins.

(X. Production continues on page 242)

I.   GENERAL WORKS

ALA Yearbook. Chicago: American Library Association, 1976- .
> See its section on "Multimedia Materials."

American Art Directory. Edited by Jacques Cattell Press. 47th ed. New York:
R. R. Bowker, 1978.

ARLIS Newsletter. [Art Libraries Society, United Kingdom]. 1969- .

ARLIS/NA Newsletter. [Art Libraries Society/North America]. Washington,
D.C.: ARLIS/NA, 1972- .
> Available from ARLIS/NA, Suite 4444, 7735 Old Georgetown Road,
> Washington, D.C., 20014.

Art Libraries Journal. Art Libraries Society in the United Kingdom and Republic
of Ireland, 1976- . Quarterly.
> Available from Dawne Leatherdale, 7 Rubens Court, Worle, Westonsuper-
> Mare, Avon, BS22 9PR, England.

ARTbibliographies Modern. Santa Barbara, Calif.: American Bibliographic Center,
1969- . Semi-annual.
> An indexing and abstracting service that provides abstracts of articles,
> books, and exhibition catalogs relating to nineteenth and twentieth century
> art; of special note are sections entitled "Theoretical Bibliography and Art
> Librarianship" and "Librarianship," which include citations on bibliography,
> picture and slide collections. Prior to volume 4 (1973), it was issued annually.

Bennett, Edna. *Pictures Unlimited: Sources of Pictorial Illustrations.* New York:
Photographic Trade News Corp., 1968.

Bowker Annual of Library and Book Trade Information. New York: R. R. Bowker,
1977. 22nd ed.

Contemporary Crafts Market Place. Compiled by American Crafts Council.
1977-1978 ed. New York: R. R. Bowker, 1977.
> Includes section on audiovisual materials, classified by subject area—e.g.,
> beadwork, clay, design, fiber, etc.; slide sources listed.

Cummings, Frederick. "Art Reference Library." *College and Research Libraries*
XXVII (May 1966):201-206.

Directory of Art Libraries and Visual Resource Collections in North America.
1978. Compiled by the Art Libraries Society of North America (ARLIS/NA).
Santa Barbara, Calif.: American Bibliographical Center—Clio Press, 1978.
> Listing of all art libraries by geographical area, and an inventory of art
> slide, photography, and other media resources.

Directory of Special Libraries and Information Centers. 4th ed. Detroit: Gale
Research, 1977.

Evans, Hilary, and Nelki, A. *Picture Researcher's Handbook: An International
Guide to Picture Sources—and How to Use Them.* Abbott, England: David
& Charles, 1975.

Freitag, Wolfgang M. "Art Libraries and Collections." In *Encyclopedia of Library
and Information Science,* vol. 1, pp. 571-621. New York: Marcel Dekker,
1968.

Library and Information Science Abstracts. Great Britain: Library Association,
1969- .

Picture Sources 3. Collections of Prints and Photographs in the U.S. and Canada.
Edited by Ann Novotny. New York: Special Libraries Association, 1975.

Shaw, Renata V. *Picture Searching Techniques and Tools.* New York: Special
Libraries Association, 1973.
A bibliography listing 500 printed sources that aid in the identification
or location of pictures.
Subject Collections. Edited by Lee Ash. 5th ed. New York: R. R. Bowker, 1978
Umbrella Glendale, Calif.: Umbrella Associates (P.O. Box 3692), 1978- .
A bimonthly newsletter of art news, reviews, and art information of
current trends.

II. GENERAL WORKS–AUDIOVISUAL

Bibliographic Control of Nonprint. Edited by Pearce S. Grove and Evelyn G.
Clement. Chicago: American Library Association, 1972.
Brown, James W., Lewis, Richard, and Harcleroad, Fred F. *A-V Instruction:
Technology, Media & Methods.* 5th ed. New York: McGraw-Hill, 1977.
Cabeceiras, James. *The Multimedia Library, Materials Selection and Use.* New
York: Academic Press, 1978.
Croghan, Anthony. *A Bibliographic System for Non-book Media: A Description
and List of Works.* London: Coburgh Publications, 1976.
De Kieffer, Robert E. *Audiovisual Instruction.* New York: The Center for Applied
Research in Education, Inc., 1965.
Educational Media Yearbook. Edited by James W. Brown. New York: R. R.
Bowker, 1973- .
Educational Technology: Definition and Glossary of Terms. Vol. 1. Prepared by
AECT Task Force on Definition and Terminology. Washington, D.C.: Asso-
ciation of Educational Communications and Technology, 1977.
Fleischer, Eugene B. *Bibliographic Citations for Nonprint Materials: A Manual
for Writers of Term Papers and Theses.* Preliminary ed. New Jersey Associa-
tion for Educational Communications & Technology, 1975.
Harcleroad, Fred F. "Learning Resources Approach to College and University
Library Development." *Library Trends* 16 (October 1967):228-40.
Hicks, Warren B., and Tillin, Alma. *Developing Multi-Media Libraries.* New York:
R. R. Bowker, 1970.
Lewis, Stanley T. "Experimentation with an Image Library." *Special Libraries*
56 (January 1965):35-38.
Line, Joyce. *Archival Collections of Non-book Materials: A Preliminary List
Indicating Policies for Preservation and Access.* London: British Library,
1977.
McNally, Paul T. *Non-book Materials: A Guide for Teachers and Librarians.*
Melbourne: Sun Books, 1973.
Merrill, Irving R., and Drob, Harold A. *Criteria for Planning the College and Univer-
sity Learning Resources Center.* Washington, D.C.: Association for Educational
Communications and Technology, 1977.
Nonprint Media in Academic Libraries. Edited by Pearce Grove. Chicago: American
Library Association, 1975.
Pessis-Pasternak, Guitta. *Dictionnaire de l'audio-visuel.* French-English, English-
French. Paris, France: Flammarion, 1976.
Reader in Media, Technology, and Libraries. Edited by Margaret Chisholm, with
Dennis D. McDonald. Englewood, Colo.: Microcard Editions Books, 1975.

Ritchie, Andrew C. *The Visual Arts in Higher Education.* New York: College Art
    Association, 1966.
Saettler, Paul. *A History of Instructional Technology.* New York: McGraw-Hill,
    1968.
Shores, Louis. *Audiovisual Librarianship: The Crusade for Media Unity (1946-1969).*
    Libraries Unlimited, 1973.
Shores, Louis. *Instructional Materials.* New York: Ronald Press, 1960.
Stone, C. Walter, ed. "Library Uses of the New Media of Communication." *Library
    Trends* 16 (October 1967).
Wellisch, Hans. *Nonbook Materials: A Bibliography of Recent Publications.*
    College Park, Md.: College of Library and Information Sciences, University
    of Maryland, 1975.
Wittich, Walter A., and Schuller, Charles F. *Instructional Technology: Its Nature
    and Use.* 5th ed. New York: Harper & Row, 1973.
Wynar, Christine L. *Guide to Reference Books for Media Centers.* Littleton, Colo.:
    Libraries Unlimited, 1973. *1974-75 Supplement,* 1976.

Administration and Staffing of Media Programs

American Association of School Librarians, ALA and Association for Educational
    Communications and Technology. *Media Programs: District and School.*
    Chicago: American Library Association, 1975.
Association for Educational Communications and Technology. *Jobs in Instruc-
    tional Media.* Washington, D.C.: Association for Educational Communications
    and Technology, 1970.
American Library Association (Association of College and Research Libraries),
    American Association of Community and Junior Colleges, Association for
    Educational Communications and Technology. (ALA-AACJC-AECT). "Guide-
    lines for Two-Year College Learning Resources Programs." *Audiovisual
    Instruction* 18 (January 1973):50-61.
Case, Robert N. "School Library Manpower Project Defines: Who Should Do What
    in the Media Center?" *Wilson Library Bulletin* 45 (May 1971):852-55.
Chisholm, Margaret E., and Ely, Donald P. *Media Personnel in Education: A
    Competency Approach.* Englewood Cliffs, N.J.: Prentice-Hall, 1976.
Christensen, R. M. "Junior College Library as an A-V Center." *College and Research
    Libraries* 26 (March 1965):121-28.
De Kieffer, Robert E., and De Kieffer, Melissa H. *Media Milestones in Teacher
    Training.* Washington, D.C.: Educational Media Council, 1970.
Erickson, Carlton W. H. *Administering Instructional Media Programs.* New York:
    The Macmillan Company, 1968.
Evans, Hilary. "How to Run a Picture Library for Pleasure (and Sometimes Profit)."
    Art Libraries Journal 2 (Spring 1977):18-32.
Fusaro, J. F. "Toward Library-College Media Centers; Proposal for the Nation's
    Community Colleges." *Junior College Journal* 40 (April 1970):40-44.
Goldstein, Harold. "The Importance of Newer Media in Library Training and the
    Education of Professional Personnel." *Library Trends* 16 (October 1967):
    259-65.
How to Start an Audiovisual Collection. Edited by Myra Nadler. Metuchen, N.J.:
    Scarecrow Press, 1978.

Hubbard, R. D. "AV and Library: Complement or Merge." *Audiovisual Instruction* 11 (June 1966):442-43.

"The Integration of Nonprint Media." Prepared by the Systems and Procedure Exchange Center (SPEC). Mimeographed. Washington, D.C.: Association of Research Libraries, Office of Management Studies, 1977. Kit 33.

Peltier, E. J. "Toward Total Media Librarianship: The Expanding Role of the Film Librarian." *Film Library Quarterly* 1 (Spring 1968): 19-21.

Public Library Association. Audiovisual Committee. *Guidelines for Audiovisual Materials and Services for Large Public Libraries.* Chicago: American Library Association, 1975.

Public Library Association. Audiovisual Committee. *Recommendations for Audiovisual Materials and Services for Small and Medium-sized Public Libraries.* Audiovisual Committee, Public Library Association. Chicago: American Library Association, 1975.

Shaw, Renata. "Picture Library Professionalism." *Picturescope* (U.S.A.) 22 (Summer 1974):25-28.

School Library Manpower Project. American Association of School Librarians. *Occupational Definitions for School Library Media Personnel.* Chicago: American Library Association, 1971.

"The Subprofessional or Technical Assistant: A Statement of Definition." *ALA Bulletin* 62 (April 1968):387-97.

Individual Media Programs

Bogan, Mary E., and White, William A. "Survey of AV Resources in Selected California Libraries and Library Systems." *California Librarian* 37 (October 1976):52-57.

Brown, James W. *New Media in Public Libraries: A Survey of Current Practices.* Syracuse, N.Y.: J. Norton, 1976.

"California State Library, Sacramento; Motion Picture Films, Filmstrips, Slides, and Microtext in California Public Libraries, 1972-73." *News Notes California Libraries* 69 (Winter 1974):90-96.

Carpenter, C. Ray. "The Pennsylvania State University; The Instructional Learning Systems and Research Center." *Audiovisual Instruction* 10 (February 1965): 134-35.

"College Core; Ithaca's Instructional Resources Center Includes a Dial-Access-Information-Retrieval-System for Students." *College Management* 4 (November 1969):23-26.

De Los Santos, A. "Role of the Multi-media Center in Meeting the Educational Needs of the Junior College Community." *Illinois Libraries* 51 (June 1969): 490-97.

LeClercq, Anne. "Organizing and Collecting Non-Print Materials in Academic Libraries." *North Carolina Libraries* 33 (Spring 1975):21-28.

Lenox, G. J. "Nonbook Materials, Recreational Reading and Faculty Reactions to Collections in the Center System Libraries." *Illinois Libraries* 49 (November 1967):827-50.

McVey, G. F. "Components of an Effective Multi-Media System for College and University Instruction." *Audiovisual Instruction* 29 (April 1975):42-45.

Moore, Everett LeRoy, ed. *Junior College Libraries: Development, Needs, and Perspectives.* Chicago: American Library Association, 1969.

"Not Just a Library, a Generic Library." *College and University Business* 55 (October 1973):29-36.

Snow, Carl E., et al. "Developing a Data Base for the Purdue Audiovisual Center." *Audiovisual Instruction* 20 (October 1975):20-21.

Stickney, Edith P., and Scherer, Henry. "Developing an AV Program in a Small College Library." *Library Journal* 84 (September 1, 1959):2457-59.

Veihman, Robert A. "Media Departments and Junior Colleges." *Illinois Libraries* 51 (April 1969):283-88.

III.   GENERAL WORKS–SLIDES

Bibler, Richard. "Make an Art Slide Library." *Design* 56 (January 1955):105-128.

Boerner, Susan Zee. "Fundamentals of the Slide Library." Mimeographed. 1977. ED 140-858.

     Available from ERIC, Document Reproduction Service, P.O. Box 190, Arlington, Virginia 22210.

Bradfield, Valerie. *Slide Collections: A User Requirements Survey.* Leicester: Leicester Polytechnic Library, 1976. 205pp. illus. 53 refs. (BLRD Report 5309).

Bradfield, Valerie. "Slides and Their Users: Thoughts Following a Survey of Some Slide Collections in Britain." *Art Libraries Journal* 2 (Autumn 1977):4-21.

Ellis, Shirley. "Thousand Words about the Slide." *ALA Bulletin* 53 (June 1959): 529-32.

Freitag, Wolfgang, and Irvine, Betty Jo. "Slides." In *Nonprint Media in Academic Libraries*, edited by Pearce Grove, pp. 102-121. Chicago: American Library Association, 1975.

Freudenthal, Juan R. "The Slide as a Communication Tool: A State-of-the-Art Survey." *School Media Quarterly* 2 (Winter 1974):109-115.

Guenther, Alfred. "Slides in Documentation." *Unesco Bulletin for Libraries* 17 (May/June 1963):157-62.

Guide for Management of Visual Resources Collections. Edited by Nancy S. Schuller. New Mexico: Mid-America College Art Association and the University of New Mexico at Albuquerque, 1978.

     Available from Zelda Richardson, Slide Library, Art Dept., University of New Mexico, Albuquerque, 87131.

Irvine, Betty Jo. "Organization and Management of Art Slide Collections." *Library Trends* 23 (January 1975):401-416.

Irvine, Betty Jo. "Slide Classification: A Historical Survey." *College and Research Libraries* 32 (January 1971):23-30.

Irvine, Betty Jo. "Slide Collections in Art Libraries." *College and Research Libraries* 30 (September 1969):443-45.

Irvine, Betty Jo. *Slide Libraries: A Guide for Academic Institutions and Museums.* Littleton, Colo.: Libraries Unlimited, 1974.

Leighton, Howard B. "The Lantern Slide and Art History." Mimeographed. New Jersey: The William Paterson College of New Jersey, 1975.

Mid-America College Art Association Slides and Photographs Newsletter. Edited by Nancy DeLaurier. Kansas City, Missouri: University of Missouri–Kansas City, 1974- .

Pacey, Philip. "Review of *Slide Libraries*, by Betty Jo Irvine." *ARLIS Newsletter* 22 (March 1975):24-25.

Pacey, Philip. "Slides and Filmstrips." In *Art Library Manual*, edited by Philip Pacey, pp. 272-84. New York: Bowker, 1977.

Positive: A Newsletter for Slide and Photograph Curators of Visual Arts in Canada. Edited by Brenda Messer. London, Ontario, Canada: Visual Arts Dept., University of Western Ontario, 1976- .

Reinhardt, Phyllis A. "Photograph and Slide Collections in Art Libraries." *Special Libraries* 50 (March 1959):97-102.

Rothschild, Norman, and Wright, George B. *Mounting, Projecting and Storing Slides*. 2nd ed. rev. New York: Universal Photo Books, 1961.

Schuller, Nancy. "Slide Collections." *Texas Library Journal* 47 (September 1971): 208-210, 242.

Simons, Wendell. "Review of *Slide Libraries*, by Betty Jo Irvine." *College and Research Libraries* 36 (January 1975):76.

Strohlein, Alfred. *The Management of 35mm Medical Slides*. New York: United Business Publications, 1975.
    Available from United Business Publications, Inc., 750 Third Avenue, New York, New York 10017.

Tselos, Dimitri. "Review of *Slide Libraries*, by Betty Jo Irvine." *Art Journal* 35 (Fall 1975):76.

"Visual Resources News." *ARLIS/NA Newsletter*.
    Regularly featured column beginning in 1974.

"Visual Resources SIG News/Special Interest Group." *ARLIS/NA Newsletter*.
    Irregularly featured column.

Walker, Lester C., Jr. "Slide Filing and Control." *College Art Journal* 16 (Summer 1957):325-29.

Bibliographies

Donnalley, Judith D. "The Organization of Slides: A Bibliography." *Picturescope* 22 (Winter 1974):76-80.

Freudenthal, Juan R. *The Slide as a Communication Tool: A Selective Bibliography*. 2nd rev. ed. Boston, Mass.: Simmons College, School of Library-Science, 1974.

Hess, Stanley, ed. *Annotated Bibliography of Slide Library Literature*. Syracuse, N.Y.: Syracuse University Press, 1978.

Lemke, Antje B., and Estabrook, Meg. "A Selective Bibliography of Recent Publications for the Slide Librarian." Mimeographed. New York: Syracuse University School of Information Studies, 1975.

Siegel, Diane E. "Bibliography on Slides." *Catholic Library World* 48 (May 1977): 448-50.

Sleeper, H. R. "Library of Color Slides." *American Institute of Architects Journal* 23 (Fall 1955):73-74.

Education for Slide Librarianship

"Continuing Education." *ARLIS/NA Newsletter* 1 (October 1973):30.
> Report of a one-day workshop, "The Slide as a Communication Tool,"
> directed by Dr. Juan R. Freudenthal, at Simmons College, Boston, September 15, 1973.

DeLaurier, Nancy. "Professional Status Survey of Slide Curators: A Report."
ARLIS/NA Newsletter 3 (October 1975):108.

DeLaurier, Nancy. "Report on the Professional Status Survey of Slide Curators."
Mimeographed. Kansas City, Missouri: Department of Art and Art History,
University of Missouri, 1975.

DeLaurier, Nancy. "Slide Curators Professional Status Survey: Additional Statistical Report." Mimeographed. Kansas City, Missouri: Department of Art and
Art History, University of Missouri, 1975.

Fry, P. Eileen. "Nonprint Media Training in Graduate Library Science Curriculums."
Mimeographed. Bloomington, Ind.: Indiana University, 1975. 4pp.

Holcomb, Alice T. "Basic Training for Slide Curators." *ARLIS/NA Newsletter* 4
(Summer 1976):119.
> Report of the "Workshop in Basic Training for Slide Curators," conducted
> by Nancy DeLaurier, at the Department of Art and Art History, University
> of Missouri–Kansas City, June 21-26, 1976.

Lemke, Antje B. "Slide Librarianship: A Contemporary Survey." *ARLIS/NA Newsletter* 3 (Summer 1975):85.
> Review of the institute sponsored by the School of Library Service, Columbia University, with the cooperation of the Metropolitan Museum of Art
> and ARLIS/NA, May 5-7, 1975.

"Professional Status." *Mid-America College Art Association Slides and Photographs
Newsletter* 4 (Winter 1977):1.

"Professional Status for Slide Curators." *CAA Newsletter* 2 (December 1977):9.
> Statement endorsed by ARLIS/NA and CAA.

"Seminar in Art Slide Librarianship." *ARLIS/NA Newsletter* 2 (October 1974):98.
> Report of the "Seminar in Art Slide Librarianship," conducted by
> Margaret P. Nolan, Metropolitan Museum of Art Photograph and Slide
> Library, and offered by the Department of Library Science, Queens College
> of the City University of New York.

"Slide Librarianship: Institute in May." *ARLIS/NA Newsletter* 3 (February 1975):
39.
> Report of institute on "Slide Librarianship: A Contemporary Survey,"
> sponsored by the School of Library Service, Columbia University, with the
> cooperation of the Metropolitan Museum of Art and ARLIS/NA, May 5-7,
> 1975.

"Statement on Professional Status for Slide Curators." *ARLIS/NA Newsletter* 3
(October 1975):108-109.

"Visual Resources News." *ARLIS/NA Newsletter* 4 (December 1975):7.
> Announcement that the Department of Art and Art History, University
> of Missouri–Kansas City, is to offer a continuing education workshop for
> one week, covering all aspects of slide library management, June 1976.

"Visual Resources News." *ARLIS/NA Newsletter* 4 (April 1976):91.
> Report on "Professional Status for Slide Curators," including a study by Eileen Fry on current offerings in library science for art slide curatorship.

"Visual Resources SIG [Special Interest Group] News." *ARLIS/NA Newsletter* 6 (Summer 1978):77.
> Formal training in slide librarianship available in courses offered by the University of Missouri–Kansas City, and the University of Texas–Austin.

Individual Slide Collections

Academic Collections

Conlon, J. E., and Kennedy, J. E. "An Afro-American Slide Project." *Art Journal* 30 (Winter 1970-71):164-65.
> Description of a program established at the University of South Alabama in 1969.

Curl, D. H. "University of Connecticut Slide Sets." *Audiovisual Instruction* 12 (May 1967):480.

Deal, Alice. "Slides and Catalogues at Virginia Commonwealth University School of the Arts Library." *Worldwide Art & Library Newsletter* 1 (April 1973): 1, 4.

Havard-Williams, P., and Watson, S. "Slide Collection at Liverpool School of Architecture." *Journal of Documentation* 16 (March 1960):11-14.

Maslen, Barbara. "Slide Loan Service for Hertfordshire." *ARLIS Newsletter* 10 (Fall 1972):7-9.

Matthews, J. "Slide Library of the Faculty of Art and Design at Bristol Polytechnica." *Art Libraries Journal* 1 (Winter 1976):20-25.

Napoli, Dolores. "Slide Collection Used at the Classics Department at Hunter College." *Picturescope* 22 (Fall 1974):45-51.

"Notre Dame University Library Gets Grant to Continue Work for a Design Slide Library." *BCLA Reporter* 17 (December 1973):21.

Pacey, Philip. "Handling Slides Single Handed." *Art Libraries Journal* 2 (April 1977):22-30.
> The library concerned is at Preston Polytechnic, England.

"The Power Research Library of Contemporary Art at Sydney University Has a Collection of 30,000 Slides . . . ." *ARLIS/NA Newsletter* 3 (February 1975): 42.

Roberts, Michael. "Slide Collections: Some Retrieval Problems and Their Solution." *CIIG Bulletin* [Construction Industry Information Group] 1 (October 1970): 5-12.

Solomon, Laurence. "An African Slide Center at New Paltz." *The Conch Newsletter* 1 (January/February 1973):3.

Sundt, Christine. "A Slide Collection for Students, University of Wisconsin, Madison." *Mid-America College Art Association Slides and Photographs Newsletter* 5 (December 1978):13.

Viles, Meta. "The Slide Collection, Edinburgh College of Art." *ARLIS Newsletter* 17 (December 1973):19-20.

Museum Collections

Farah, Priscilla. "The Photograph and Slide Library of The Metropolitan Museum of Art: A 68-Year View of Classification." 4 (Summer 1976):S6-S7. In *Newsletter* supplement, "Library Classification Systems and The Visual Arts," ed. by David J. Patten.

Gardner, H. "The Lending Collection of Slides of the Ryerson Library, Art Institute of Chicago." *Public Libraries* 24 (1919):312-14.

"Lantern Slide File and Loan System in Use at the Cleveland Museum of Natural History." *Museum News* 7 (May 1, 1929):7-8.

Moeller, P. L. "Slide and Photographic Services of the Museum of Modern Art." *Proceedings of Forty-first Conference*. Atlantic City, New Jersey: New York: Special Libraries Association, 1950.

"New Thomas J. Watson Library at the Metropolitan Museum of Art." *Special Libraries* 56 (July 1965):393-99.

Nolan, M. P. "Slides: History of Art (at the Metropolitan Museum of Art)." *Picturescope* 15 (1967):37.

Pederson, Jane. "Dias-biblioteket i the Metropolitan Museum of Art, New York [Slide Library in the Metropolitan Museum of Art]." *Bogens Verden* 52 (2/1970):120-23.

Public Library Collections

"Chicago Public Library Lantern Slide Collection." *Illinois Libraries* 17 (July 1935):108-109.

Fritzche, Hans-Joachim. "Über den Aufbau einer Diathek; Erfahrungen aus der Berliner Stadtbibliothek [To set up a collection of slides; experiences of the Berlin city library]." *Bibliothekar* 24 (October 1970):934-40.

"Lantern Slides and Stereographs in the Library." *ALA Bulletin* 23 (1929): S66-S67.
    Concerns the Chicago Public Library.

Mucharowski, Hans. "Anmerkungen zu Diaserien in öffentlichen Büchereien [Notations on slide series in public libraries]." *Buch und Bibliothek* 26 (July/August 1974):664-66.

Mucharowski, Hans. "Vorschläge für die Einrichtung einer Diathek in Stadtbüchereien [Proposals for the establishment of a slide collection in public libraries]." *Buch und Bibliothek* 24 (June 1972):703-705.

Page, Julie A. "Slides in the Public Library." *ARLIS/NA Newsletter* 4 (April 1976):84-86.

Pearson, E. "Birmingham Public Libraries: Visual Aids Department." *ARLIS Newsletter* 19 (June 1974):54-55.

"The Seattle Public Library is . . . Planning a Media Center." *ARLIS/NA Newsletter* 3 (February 1975):42.

"Umfrage-Ergebnis aus sieben Büchereien: Arbeit mit Dias [Questionnaire result from seven libraries: work with slides]." *Buch und Bibliothek* 24 (October 1972):989-93.

White, F. A., and Younger, J. "Slides and Filmstrips Add Service." *Wisconsin Library Bulletin* 62 (May 1966):162-63.

Special Collections

"American Artists Professional League Collection of Lantern Slides." *Art Digest* 13 (December 1938):33.

Bullard, Janet E., comp. "Slide Collection: A Catalogue of the 2" x 2" Slides in the Library Association." *Library Information Bulletin* 21 (1973):25-62.

Fennell, Yvonne. "Chester Photographic Survey." *Library Association Record* 72 (May 1970):197-99.

Goodstein, Jeanne. "Report on: The New York Zoological Society Photo Library." *Picturescope* 22 (Fall 1974):61-67.

"A Guide to Slide and Photograph Collections of Primitive Art from Boston to Washington, D.C." Compiled by June M. Axelrod. Art Libraries Society/ North America, 1976.

"A Guide to Slide and Photograph Collections of Primitive Art in Midwestern United States." Compiled by June M. Axelrod. Art Libraries Society/North America, 1976.

Lelieur, Anne-Claude. "Slides at the Bibliotheque Forney." *Art Libraries Journal* 2 (Autumn 1977):31-32.

Murton, Jan. "Design Council Slide Library." *Art Libraries Journal* 1 (Winter 1976):26-32.

World Bank Photo Library. Washington, D.C.: World Bank Audio Visual Division (1818 H Street, N.W.), 1978.

IV. CONFERENCE PROGRAMS ON SLIDES

Coulson, A. J. "Conference Report: Slides, Their Acquisition and Organization." *ARLIS Newsletter* 23 (June 1975):32-33.

Slides and Sound Recordings: Their Organization and Exploitation. London: Aslib Audio Visual Group, 1972.

"Southeastern College Art Conference: Slide Curators' Sessions." *ARLIS/NA Newsletter* 7 (February 1979):12-14.

ARLIS/NA (Art Libraries Society/North America)

"Circulating Slide Collections." *ARLIS/NA Newsletter* 5 (February 1977):57.
Program at the Fifth Annual ARLIS/NA Conference with panel members from the Cleveland Museum of Art, the Art Institute of Chicago, the National Gallery of Art (Washington, D.C.), and the State University of New York, Buffalo.

"Education for Art Librarianship." *ARLIS/NA Newsletter* 5 (February 1977): 52-53.

"Saturday Afternoon VRSIG [Visual Resources Special Interest Group] Workshops." *ARLIS/NA Newsletter* 4 (February 1976):40-41.

"VRSIG [Visual Resources Special Interest Group] Program on Hardware for New Visual Resources." *ARLIS/NA Newsletter* 5 (February 1977):50.

"VRSIG [Visual Resources Special Interest Group] Program on Organization and Access to New Media." *ARLIS/NA Newsletter* 5 (February 1977):53.

"Visual Resources Program of ARLIS/NA." *ARLIS/NA Newsletter* 6 (February 1978):22-24.

"Visual Resources News and Previews." Prepared by Carol Ulrich. *ARLIS/NA Newsletter* 5 (April 1977):100.

"Visual Resources SIG [Special Interest Group] Business Meeting." *ARLIS/NA Newsletter* 5 (February 1977):49.

CAA (College Art Association)

Abstracts of Papers Delivered in Art History Sessions. Annual Meeting. New York: College Art Association, January 24-27, 1973.
> See abstracts of the papers delivered at the Slides and Photographs Session, chaired by Margaret P. Nolan.

Donaldson, Dawn. "CAA Visual Resources Committee Sessions." *ARLIS/NA Newsletter* 4 (February 1976):55-57.
> Sessions reported include the following: "The Copyright Law: How Does It Affect the Visual Resources and Fine Arts Libraries?"; "Professional Status of Visual Resources Administrators"; and "The Slide Suppliers Meet the Buyers."

"CAA Annual Meeting, Slide and Photograph Sessions." *Art Journal* 32 (Summer 1973):422.

"CAA Slide and Photograph Session 1973." *Worldwide Art & Library Newsletter* 1 (December 1972):5.

Collins, Eleanor. "Slide Librarians and the College Art Association of America." *Worldwide Art & Library Newsletter* 1 (November 1972):1, 3.

Donaldson, Dawn. "CAA Visual Resources Sessions." *ARLIS/NA Newsletter* 5 (February 1977):67-68.

Grisé, Gail. "CAA Visual Resource Committee Sessions." *ARLIS/NA Newsletter* 3 (February 1975):40.

Grisé, Gail, and Holcomb, Alice T. "Visual Resources Committee Report [CAA]." *Art Journal* 34 (Summer 1975):340.

Irvine, Betty Jo. "Slides and Photographs Session." *Art Journal* 30 (Spring 1971): 306.

Jaenike, Edith M. "CAA Visual Documentation Sessions." *ARLIS/NA Newsletter* 1 (April 1974):43-45.

Jaenike, Edith M. "CAA Visual Documentation Sessions." *Art Journal* 34 (Fall 1974):40, 42.

Keaveney, Sydney Starr. "CAA Annual Meeting; Slide and Photographs Session." *Art Journal* 32 (Summer 1973):421-22.

Keaveney, Sydney S. "Report of the Slides and Photographs Session, CAA Annual Meeting, January, 1973." *Worldwide Art & Library Newsletter* 1 (February 1973):1-2.

Maxwell, Barbara B. "Slides and Photographs." *Art Journal* 31 (Spring 1972): 320-21.

Scott, Gillian M. "Report on the Visual Resources Committee Sessions at CAA Annual Meeting—New York, January 25-27, 1978." *ARLIS/NA Newsletter* 6 (February 1978):26-28.

"Slide and Photograph Librarians Committees." *Art Journal* 30 (Spring 1971): 306.

MACAA (Mid-America College Art Association)

Auchstetter, Rosann. "Visual Resources Sessions at MACAA." *ARLIS/NA Newsletter* 7 (February 1979):14-15.

"Conference Reports: Mid-America College Art Association Conference, October 25-28, 1978." *Mid-America College Art Association Slides and Photographs Newsletter* 5 (Winter 1978):1-2.

"MACAA Slide and Photograph Curators Meeting." *ARLIS/NA Newsletter* 2 (December 1973):12.

Schuller, Nancy S. "MACAA Slide and Photograph Curators Meeting. A Report." *Worldwide Art & Library Newsletter* 2 (January 1974):1.

"Slide/Photo Librarians Hold First Meeting." *Library Journal* 98 (February 1973): 379.

    MACAA meeting at the University of Notre Dame.

V. ACQUISITION AND SELECTION OF SLIDES

Booklist. Chicago: American Library Association, 1905- .

    Slides reviewed beginning in 1971.

Bowker AV Guide: A Subject Guide to Audio-visual Educational Materials. Edited by Marion Koenig. New York: R. R. Bowker, 1975.

Educator's Guide to Free Filmstrips. 29th ed. Randolph, Wisconsin: Educator's Progress Service, Inc., 1977.

    Includes slides.

Fetros, J. G. "Cooperative Picture Searching and Collection Development." *Special Libraries* 62 (May/June 1971):217-226.

    Lists wide variety of indexes to picture sources for use in copywork for the production of slides.

Index to Educational Slides. 3rd ed. Los Angeles: National Information Center for Educational Media (NICEM), 1977.

Index to Producers and Distributors. 4th ed. Los Angeles: National Information Center for Educational Media (NICEM), University of Southern California, 1977.

Kusnerz, P. A. "Acquisition of Slides and Photographs: Results of a Survey of Colleges, Museums and Libraries." *Picturescope* 20 (Summer 1972):66-77.

Lennox, Tom. "Slides Acquisitions: A Media Librarian's Problem." *Previews* 1 (November 1972):5-11.

Media Review Digest: The Only Complete Guide to Reviews of Non-book Media. Ann Arbor, Mich.: The Pierian Press, 1973- .

Mirwis, Allan. *GEMS, Guide to Educational Media Software*. Brooklyn: Educational Media Information Service, 1977.

NICEM Update of Nonbook Media. Los Angeles: National Information Center for Educational Media (NICEM), University of Southern California, 1977.

    Issued every other year in four bimonthly supplements to the fourteen NICEM *Indexes*.

National Audiovisual Center. *A Catalog of U.S. Government Produced AV Materials, 1974*. Washington, D.C.: National AV Center, National Archives and Records Service, General Services Administration, 1974.

Nottbrock, Anneliese. "Bezugsquellen für Diaserien [Sources of supply for slide series] ." In *Tontechnik und Mikrofilm in der Bibliothekspraxis*, ed. by Horst Ernestus. Berlin: Deutscher Bibliotheksverband [Federal Republic of Germany] , Arbeitsstelle für das Bibliothekswesen, 1973.

Previews; Nonprint Software and Hardware News and Reviews. New York: R. R.
    Bowker, 1972- . Monthly (September through May).
Rufsvold, Margaret I. *Guides to Educational Media: Films, Filmstrips, Multi-
    media Kits, Programmed Instruction Materials, Recordings on Discs and Tapes,
    Slides, Transparencies, Videotapes.* 4th ed. Chicago: American Library
    Association, 1977.
Sive, Mary Robinson. *Selecting Instructional Media.* Littleton, Colo.: Libraries
    Unlimited, 1978.
Slide Buyer's Guide. Edited by Nancy DeLaurier. 3rd ed. New York: College Art
    Association of America, 1976.
    Updated addenda for the *Guide* regularly appear in the *Mid-America
    College Art Association Slides and Photographs Newsletter,* edited by
    DeLaurier, Dept. of Art and Art History, University of Missouri–Kansas
    City, Missouri, 64110.
"Some Sources of 2 x 2-Inch Color Slides." Rochester, N.Y.: Eastman Kodak,
    1976. (Kodak Pamphlet No. S-2).
"Sources of Slides." *ARLIS Newsletter* 18 (March 1974):32-33.
"Where to Find Lantern Slides: A List of Distributors." *College Art Journal*
    V (January 1946):137-39.

Museum Guides

Dyer, Mary. "Here Comes the National Gallery: Programs Available Free from
    Its Extension Service: Films and Slides Programs." *American Education*
    11 (April 1975):6-10.
A Handlist of Museum Sources for Slides and Photographs. Prepared by Sharon
    Petrini and Troy-Jjohn Bromberger. Santa Barbara, Calif.: The Slide Library,
    The Art Department, University of California at Santa Barbara, 1972.
*Museum Media; A Biennial Directory and Index of Publications and Audiovisuals
    Available from United States and Canadian Institutions.* Edited by Paul
    Wasserman and Esther Herman. Detroit, Mich.: Gale Research, 1973.
Petrini, Sharon, and Bromberger, Troy-Jjohn. "Museums as Sources for Slides." *World-
    wide Art & Library Newsletter* 1 (February 1973):1, 4.

Subject Area Guides

Adshead, Shelagh. "The ICOGRADA Audio/Visual Archive." *Art Libraries Journal*
    1 (Autumn 1976):18-20.
Arts in the United States. A Pictorial Survey. Edited by Martha Davidson and
    William Pierson. New York: McGraw-Hill, 1960.
    Introduction and text accompanying the slide survey of the arts, sponsored
    by the Carnegie Foundation and distributed by the Sandak Co., New York.
*Color Slide Catalogue of World Painting. A Color Slide Listing of Major Paintings
    from the Paleolithic to the Present Day, with Explicit, Researched Data for
    the Study of Art and the Humanities.* New York: The American Library
    Color Slide Co., Inc., 1976.
Davidson, M., and Pierson, Jr., W. H. "Carnegie Survey of American Art." *College
    Art Journal* 17 (Winter 1958):171-80.
"Fourteenth Annual Survey of AV Materials. Slides." *The Classical World* 63
    (March 1970):227-29.

Hasbrouck, W. R. "Prairie School; The Domestic Architecture of Chicago."
    Prairie School Review 8 (1971):24.
Kocher, Sandra A. "2" x 2" Color Slides of Art." *Art Journal* 23 (Fall 1963):
    42, 44.
Lennox, Thomas. "Evaluation of Purchase Sources for 35mm Art-History Slides."
    Picturescope 19 (Spring 1971):10-49.
Maslen, Barbara. "Sources of Slides: Fine and Applied Arts." *ARLIS Newsletter*
    13 (December 1972):18-21.
"NCGE/GPN Slide Library [National Council for Geographic Education/Great
    Plains National]." *Journal of Geography* 77 (February 1978):77-78.
Powell, L. "Lambton Visual Aids." *ARLIS Newsletter* 24 (September 1975):
    26-28.
Pratt, Keith L., and Gray, D. W. S. *China: An Index to European Visual and Aural
    Materials, Including Hong Kong, Korea, Mongolia, Taiwan and Tibet.*
    Hamden, Conn.: Archon Books, 1973.
        See the "Slides" section, pp. 47-56.
Robbins, E. S. "Slide Evaluation." *Art Journal* 30 (Summer 1971):412.
"Slide Project." *Art Journal* 32 (Winter 1972-73):185.
*Sources for Commercial Slides of the Illustrations in Gardner's Art through the
    Ages, Sixth Edition.* Compiled by Luraine Tansey, with Melody Barch and
    Linda Burton. New York: Harcourt Brace Jovanovich, Inc., 1976.
Sources of Slides. The History of Art. New York: The Slide Library, The Metro-
    politan Museum of Art, 1970.
"Unesco World Art Series." *Unesco Bulletin for Libraries* 14 (March 1960):87-88.
"Unique Resources for the Study of Afro-American Art and Artists Has Recently
    Been Made Available in Six Southeastern States." *The Southeastern Librarian*
    27 (Summer 1977):141-42.
*Urban Outlook: A Selected Bibliography of Films, Filmstrips, Slides, and Audio
    Tapes.* Washington, D.C.: U.S. Department of Housing and Urban Develop-
    ment, June 1969.
"Visual Resources Available." *ARLIS/NA Newsletter* 5 (February 1977):83-84.
Willett, F. "Sources for Teaching about African Visual Art in American Schools
    and Colleges." *Africana Library Journal* 3 (Summer 1972):15-19.

VI.   CARE AND PRESERVATION OF FILMS AND SLIDES

American National Standards Institute. "Practice for Storage of Processed Safety
    Photographic Film." New York: American National Standards Institute,
    1976. (ANSI PH1.43-1976).
"Care of Processed Films and Archival Storage." *The Encyclopedia of Photography*,
    Vol. 19, pp. 3544-46. New York: Greystone Press, 1965.
"Color Slides Nibbled." *American Archivist* 31 (April 1968):207.
De la Vega, M. A., and Sauras, E. "Ageing of Colour Slides." (in Spanish). *Optica*
    9:185-91.
Dorfman, Harold H. "The Effect of Fungus on Silver Gelatin, Diazo and Vesicular
    Films." *Journal of Micrographics* 11 (March 1978):257-60.
"General Guidelines for the Care, Handling, and Storage of Film Media (Film-
    strips, Microforms, Motion Pictures, Slides, Transparencies)." In *Nonbook
    Materials: The Organization of Integrated Collections*, 1st ed., by Jean

Riddle Weihs, Shirley Lewis, and Janet Macdonald, p. 92. Ottawa: Canadian Library Association, 1973.

Hershenson, Martin. "Permanence." *Technical Photography* 10 (August 1978): 14-15, 48.

Hughes, T. "Conservation of Colour Photographic Records." *British Journal of Photography* 120 (1973):904-906.

Kach, David. "Photographic Dilemma: Stability and Storage of Color Materials." *Industrial Photography* 27 (August 1978):28-29, 46-50.

Langford, Michael J. "Play Cool, Keep Dark." *Industrial Photography* 23 (January 1974):8, 49.

"Preservation News" by Susan Swartzburg. *ARLIS/NA Newsletter* 6 (November 1978):116-17.

"Preservation of Slides and Photographs." *ARLIS/NA Newsletter* 4 (February 1976):38-40.

Prevention and Removal of Fungus on Prints and Films. Rochester, N.Y.: Eastman Kodak, 1971. (Kodak Pamphlet No. AE-22).

Procedures for Processing and Storing Black and White Photographs for Maximum Possible Permanence and Instructions for Set-Up and Use of: East Street Gallery Archival Print Washers, Film Washers, and Automatic Washer Controls. Grinnell, Iowa: East Street Gallery, 1970.

"Proper Care of Slide Film" and "Handling, Care and Preservation of Mounted Transparencies." In *Planning and Producing Slide Programs*, pp. 65-67. Rochester, N.Y.: Eastman Kodak, 1978. (Kodak Publication No. S-30).

Rothschild, Norman. "Fungus? Scratches? Dirt? Here's a Way to Preserve and Protect Your Slides." *Popular Photography* 76 (March 1975):16, 128.

Rothschild, Norman. "10 Ways to Save Bad Slides." *Popular Photography* 72 (February 1973):116-17.

Technology & Conservation. Magazine of Art, Architecture, and Antiquities. The Magazine for Analysis/Preservation/Restoration/Protection/Documentation. One Emerson Place, Boston, Mass., 02114.

Tull, A. G. *The Conservation of Colour Photographic Records*. London: Royal Photographic Society Publications, 1974.

Weinstein, Robert A., and Booth, Larry. *Collection, Use and Care of Historical Photographs*. Nashville, Tenn.: American Association for State and Local History, 1977.

Wilhelm, Henry. *Preservation of Contemporary Photographic Materials*. Grinnell, Iowa: East Street Gallery (723 State Street, Box 68, 50112), in press, 1978.

Wilhelm, Henry. "Storing Color Materials: Frost-Free Refrigerators Offer Low-Cost Solution." *Industrial Photography* 27 (October 1978):32-33, 55-60.

Slide Mounting

"The Conservation of Colour Photographic Records." *ARLIS Newsletter* 17 (December 1973):21-25.
    Symposium report, and "Bibliography," and "Dimensional Characteristics of Some Available Slide Mounts," by A. G. Tull.

Farber, Paul. "Mount Your Slides in Plastic—A Fast and Inexpensive Way." *U.S. Camera* 31 (April 1968):61.

Harrison, Howard. "Guide to Slide Mounts." *Camera 35* 9 (April/May 1965): 48-49, 62-63.
Smidt, Donna C. "On Slide Binding." *ARLIS/NA Newsletter* 1 (Summer 1973): 16.
Tull, A. G. "Film Transparencies between Glass, Part 1." *British Journal of Photography* 125 (1978):322-23.
Tull, A. G. "Film Transparencies between Glass, Parts 2 & 3." *British Journal of Photography* 125 (1978):349-51, 353.
Tull, A. G. "Hazards of Mounting Slides." *Photography Journal* 144 (1974):184, 232.
Tull, A. G. "Moisture and the Slide." *Journal of Photographic Science* 22 (1974): 107-110.

Storage Systems

Henning, Wolfram. "Möbel für die Aufbewahrung von Schallplatten, Tonband-kassetten und Dias [Furniture for Storing Records, Tape Cassettes and Slides]." *Buch und Bibliothek* 26 (October 1974):811-16, 818, 820-22.
Rothschild, Norman. "Are Slides Taking Up the Better Part of Your House? Start Filing and Sorting Now." *Popular Photography* 78 (April 1976): 20, 22, 94, 123.
"Safe Slide Filing." *American Archivist* 39 (April 1976):230.
Wyllie, Diana. "Slides and Filmstrips: Handling and Storage." In: Aslib A-V Group, A-V Workshop, May 7-8, 1970. London: Aslib, 1971. p. 20-23.

VII. CATALOGING AND CLASSIFICATION—AUDIOVISUAL

Akers, Susan G. *Akers' Simple Library Cataloging.* 6th ed. Completely revised and rewritten by Arthur Curley and Jana Varlejs. Metuchen, N.J.: Scarecrow Press, 1977.
Anglo-American Cataloguing Rules. 2nd ed. Prepared by the American Library Association, the British Library, the Canadian Committee on Cataloguing, the Library Association, and the Library of Congress. Edited by Michael Gorman and Paul Winkler. Chicago: American Librarian Association and Canadian Library Association, 1978.
Badten, J., and Motomatzu, N. "Commercial Media Cataloguing; What's Holding Us Up." *Library Journal* 93 (November 15, 1968):4352-53.
Brubaker, M. J. "A & P of A.V. Materials." *Illinois Libraries* 49 (Fall 1967): 129-40.
Chisholm, Margaret. "Problems and Directions in Bibliographic Organization of Media." In *Reader in Media, Technology and Libraries,* ed. by Margaret Chisholm with Dennis D. McDonald, pp. 350-60. Englewood, Colo.: Microcard Editions Books, 1975.
Clarke, Virginia. *The Organization of Nonbook Materials in the Laboratory School Library.* Rev. ed. Denton, Texas: Laboratory School Library, 1969.
"Commercial Media Cataloging—What's Around? An SLJ Survey of Available Services, Their Range of Materials, Cataloging Policies, and Marketing Patterns." *Library Journal* 93 (November 15, 1968):4345-51.
Daily, Jay E. *Organizing Nonprint Materials; A Guide for Librarians.* New York: Marcel Dekker, 1972.

Dunnington, D. B. "Integrating Media Services." *RQ* (ALA Reference Service Division) 9 (Winter 1969):116-18.

Foster, Donald L. *The Classification of Nonbook Materials in Academic Libraries: A Commentary and Bibliography.* Occasional Papers No. 104. Illinois: University of Illinois Graduate School of Library Science, September 1972.

Gambee, Budd L. *Non-book Materials as Library Resources.* Chapel Hill, N.C.: The Student Stores, University of North Carolina, 1967. (Bibliographies for Chapters 1, 2, 4 and 5 were revised June 1970).

Gorman, Michael. "The Anglo-American Cataloguing Rules, Second Edition." *Library Resources & Technical Services* 22 (Summer 1978):209-226.

Grove, Pearce S., and Totten, Herman L. "Bibliographic Control of Media: The Librarian's Excedrin Headache." *Wilson Library Bulletin* 44 (November 1969):299-311.

Hagler, Ronald. "Development of Cataloging Rules for Nonbook Materials." *Library Resources and Technical Services* 19 (Summer 1978):268-78.

Harris, Evelyn J. *Instructional Materials Cataloguing Guide.* Tucson, Ariz.: The University of Arizona, College of Education, Bureau of Educational Research and Service, 1968.

Hicks, Warren B., and Tillin, Alma M. *The Organization of Nonbook Materials in School Libraries.* Sacramento, Calif.: California State Department of Education, 1967.

ISBD (G): General International Standard Bibliographic Description: Annotated Text. Prepared by the Working Group on the General International Standard Bibliographic Description set up by the IFLA Committee on Cataloguing. London: International Federation of Library Associations and Institutions, 1977.

Johnson, Jean Thornton, et al. *AV Cataloging and Processing Simplified.* Raleigh, N.C.: Audiovisual Catalogers, Inc., 1971.

Johnson, Jean Thornton, et al. *AV Cataloging and Processing Simplified.* Morgantown, W. Virginia: Chateau Publishers, Inc., 1973.

Library of Congress. Catalog Publication Division. *Films and Other Materials for Projection, 1975.* Washington, D.C.: Library of Congress, 1976.

Loertscher, David W. *A Nonbook Cataloging Sampler.* 1st ed. Austin, Texas: Armadillo Press, 1975.

Massonneau, Suzanne. "Developments in the Organization of AV Materials." *Library Trends* 25 (January 1977):665-84.

Non-book Materials Cataloguing Rules: Integrated Code of Practice and Draft Revision of the Anglo-American Cataloguing Rules, British Text, Part III. Prepared by the Media Cataloguing Rules Committee, Library Association. 2nd ed. Great Britain: Council for the Educational Technology for the United Kingdom with the Library Association, 1974. (Working Paper No. 11).

Ravilious, C. P. *A Survey of Existing Systems and Current Proposals for the Cataloguing and Description of Non-book Materials Collected by Libraries: With Preliminary Suggestions for Their International Coordination.* Paris: Unesco, 1975.

Rogers, JoAnn V. "Nonprint Cataloging: A Call for Standardization." *American Libraries* 10 (January 1979):46-48.

Strout, Ruth French. *Organization of Library Materials II.* Madison, Wis.: University of Wisconsin, University Extension Division, 1966.

Tillin, Alma M., and Quinly, William J. *Standards for Cataloging Nonprint Materials; An Interpretation and Practical Application.* 4th ed. Washington, D.C.: Association for Educational Communications and Technology, 1976.

Tucker, B. R. "New Version of Chapter 12 of the AA Cataloging Rules." *Library Resources and Technical Services* 19 (Summer 1975):260-67.

Weihs, Jean Riddle, Lewis, Shirley, and MacDonald, Janet. In consultation with the CLA/ALA/AECT/EMAC/CAML Advisory Committee on the Cataloguing of Nonbook Materials. *Non-Book Materials: The Organization of Integrated Collections.* 1st ed. Ottawa, Canada: The Canadian Library Association, 1973.

Westhuis, Judith Loveys, and DeYoung, Julia M. *Cataloging Manual for Nonbook Materials in Learning Centers and School Libraries.* Rev. ed. Ann Arbor: Mich.: Michigan Association of School Librarians, The Bureau of School Services, The University of Michigan, 1967.

Wetmore, Rosamond B. *A Guide to the Organization of Library Collections.* Muncie, Ind.: Ball State University, 1969.

Computer and Data Processing Applications

Bogen, Betty. "Computer-Generated Catalog of Audiovisuals." *Medical Library Association Bulletin* 64 (April 1976):224-27.

Brantz, Malcolm H., and Forsman, Rick. "Classifications and Audiovisuals." *Medical Library Association Bulletin* 65 (April 1977):261-64.

Chouraqui, Eugene. "The Index and Filing System Used by the 'Inventaire General des Monuments et des Richesses Artistiques de la France.' " *Computers and the Humanities* 7 (May 1973):273-85.

Dome, J. E. "Automation of Media Cataloging." *AV Instruction* 11 (June 1966): 446.

Fleischer, Eugene B. "Uniterm Your A-V Library." *Audiovisual Instruction* 14 (February 1969):76-78.

Fox, Dexter L. "Art Terms Thesarus Project." *ARLIS/NA Newsletter* 2 (October 1974):92-93.

Lamy-Rousseau, Francoise. *Traitement automise des documents multi-media avec les systemes ISBD unifie.* Quebec: Ministere de l'education du Quebec, Service general des moyens d'enseignement, 1974.

Liao, R. C., and Sleeman, P. J. Inexpensive Computerized Cataloging of Educational Media; A Mini-System." *Audiovisual Instruction* 16 (Fall 1971):12-14.

Library of Congress. MARC Development Office. *Films: A MARC Format.* Washington, D.C.: U.S.G.P.O., 1970. Addenda 1-7, 1972-1976.

Lukas, Terrence. "Tap Your Computer's Negative Capability." *Audiovisual Instruction* 21 (October 1976):17.

Moulton, Bethe L., and Wood, William I. "Computer-Produced Catalog for Nonprint Materials: Its Application in a Health Sciences Library." *Special Libraries* 66 (April 1975):357-62.

Schwarz, Philip J. "Keyword Indexing of Non-book Media." *Audiovisual Instruction* 19 (November 1974):84-87.

"USC's Film Department Gets Grant for Automated Cataloging Project." *Library Journal* 90 (January 1, 1975):85.

Wasserman, M. N. "Computer-Prepared Book Catalog for Engineering Transparencies." *Special Libraries* 57 (February 1966):111-13.

Picture Collection Guides

The American Institute of Architects Filing System for Architectural Plates and Articles. 2nd ed. rev. Washington, D.C.: The American Institute of Architects, 1956. (AIA Document 261).

Cowen, Chester R. "Systems for Arranging Resources on African Populations." Mimeographed. Norman, Oklahoma: University of Oklahoma, 1974.

Gould, Geraldine N., and Wolfe, Ithmer C. *How to Organize and Maintain the Library Picture/Pamphlet File.* Dobbs Ferry, N.Y.: Oceana Publications, Inc., 1968.

Hill, Donna. *The Picture File: A Manual and a Curriculum-Related Subject Heading List.* Hamden, Conn.: Linnet Books, 1975.

ICONCLASS: An Iconographic Classification System. Prepared by Henri Van De Waal. Completed and edited by L. D. Couprie with R. H. Fuchs and E. Tholen. 17 vols. Amsterdam: North-Holland Publishing, 1973-1978.

McHenry, Nancy. *Subject Index.* Wilmette, Ill.: Encyclopaedia Britannica Films, Inc., 1965.

Mid-America College Art Association. Research Committee on Special Classification Systems for Visual Materials of the Third World Peoples. *Report of the Research Committee . . . , 1974-1975.* Edited by Chester R. Cowen. Parts I and II. Norman, Oklahoma: The School of Art, University of Oklahoma, 1976.

   Available from Mrs. Helena Tucker, School of Art, 520 Parrington Oval, University of Oklahoma, Norman, 73019.

The Picture Collection Subject Heading. Prepared by William J. Dane. 6th ed. Hamden, Conn.: Shoe String Press, 1968.

VIII. CATALOGING AND CLASSIFICATION—SLIDES

Babbitt, Katherine M. *Indexing Art Slides.* Term Paper. School of Library Science, New York State University at New Paltz, January 1968.

Bachmann, Barton. "Where's That Slide?" *U.S. Camera* 22 (February 1959): 78-79.

Bird, R. W. "Slides; The Cataloguing, Classification and Indexing of a Collection of Slides." *Catalogue and Index* 20 (October 1970):4.

The Black Book: A Cataloguing Handbook for the Slide and Photograph Collection of the Art Department, UCLA. Los Angeles: University of California, 1977.

   Supplements to *The Black Book* include the "Tribal African Art Classification" and the "Pre-Columbian Cataloging System."

Bogar, Candace S. "Classification for an Architecture and Art Slide Collection." *Special Libraries* 66 (December 1975):570-74.

Chez, R. A., and Kubiak, R. J. "Organizing a Medical School's Slide Collection." *Audiovisual Instruction* 14 (October 1969):121.

"Classification: The Key to Slide Collection Vigor." *Library Journal* 97 (March 15, 1972):965-66.

Clawson, Catherine R., and Rankowski, Charles A. "Classification and Cataloging of Slides Using Color Photocopying." *Special Libraries* 69 (August 1978): 281-85.

The Cleveland Museum of Art Slide Library Classification Scheme, Chronologies and Sub-Divisions. Edited by Dr. Sara Jane Pearman, Slide Librarian. Cleveland: Cleveland Museum of Art, 1977.

"Collection of 35mm Slides." Rev. ed. Madison, Wis.: African Studies Program, University of Wisconsin, 1977.

Daughtry, Bessie. "Cataloguing, Arrangement and Storage of Motion Pictures, Filmstrips, and 2" x 2" Slides." Master's Thesis. Florida State University, 1948.

Davis, Barbara. "Control and Storage of a Slide File Collection." Master's Thesis. Simmons College, School of Library Science, 1956.

Dyki, Judy. "Classification System for a Multi-Concept Slide Collection." Master's Thesis. Wayne State University, 1977. ED 158 754.
    Available from ERIC, Document Reproduction Service, P.O. Box 190, Arlington, Virginia 22210.

Gilley, Beulah. "Declassifying the Slide Secrets." *Museum News* (USA): 52 (March 1974):45-48.

Kohn, L. E. "A Photograph and Lantern Slide Catalog in the Making." *Library Journal* 57 (1932):941-45.

Ladewig, Adelheid G. "Routine for the Cataloging and Processing of Slides." *Journal of Cataloging and Classification* 6 (Summer 1950):67-68.

Lewis, Elizabeth M. "Control without Cards: The Organization of Color Slide Collections without Card Reference." *ARLIS/NA Newsletter* 1 (Summer 1973):17.

Lewis, Elizabeth M. "Control without Cards: The Organization of Color Slide Collections without Card Reference." *Unabashed Librarian* 9 (Fall 1973):7.

Lomer, G. R. "Lantern Slide Storing and Cataloguing." *Canadian Library Association Bulletin* 4 (March 1948):119-22.

Lucas, E. Louise. "The Classification and Care of Pictures and Slides." *A.L.A. Bulletin* 24 (1930):382-85.

McCord, Carey P., and Cook, Warren A. "A Classification System for Lantern Slides and Other Visual Aids in Occupational Health." *Industrial Medicine and Surgery* 27 (January 1958):46-49.

Miller, Ralph. "Skipper." "Where's That Slide?" *Camera 35* 7 (April/May 1963): 48-49, 54-55.

Nacke, Otto, and Murza, Gerhard. "Ein einfaches Dokumentationssystem für Diapositive [A simple slide documentation system]." *Nachrichten für Dokumentation* 28 (February 1977):26-28.

Perusse, L. F. "Classifying and Cataloguing Lantern Slides." *Journal of Cataloguing and Classification* 10 (April 1954):77-83.

"Photograph and Slide Library." New York: Slide Library, The Metropolitan Museum of Art, May 1968.

Rice, Mary Lois. "A System of Classification and Subject Headings for a Slide Collection in Architecture." Master's Thesis. University of Denver, February 1949.

Roberts, M. "Slide Collections: Some Retrieval Problems." *CIIG Bulletin* 1 (October 1970):5-12.

Sedgley, Anne, and Merrett, Bronwen. "Cataloguing Slide Collections: Art and Architecture Slides at RMIT [Royal Melbourne Institute of Technology]." *Australian Library Journal* 23 (May 1974):146-52.

Skoog, A. C., and Evans, G. "Slide Collection Classification." *Pennsylvania Library Association* 24 (January 1969):15-22.

Slide Classification Scheme: Department of Art History, University of Wisconsin— Madison. Prepared by Christine L. Sundt, Slide Curator. Mimeographed. Madison: University of Wisconsin, 1978.

"Slide Filing: Order from Chaos." *Audiovisual Notes from Kodak*, 71-1, pp. 4-5.

Straight, Elsie H. "The Slide Classification and Cataloging System Developed for the Ringling School of Art Library, Sarasota, Florida." Typewritten. c. 1975.

Swan, E. "Problems Involved in Establishing a Slide Collection in the School of Architecture, School of Melbourne." *Australian Library Journal* 9 (July 1960):159-62.

Tselos, Dimitri. "A Simple Slide Classification System." *College Art Journal* 18 (Summer 1959):344-49.

Visser, Ora. "Stellenbosch University Medical Library Slide Classification, Storage, Retrieval, and Issue System." *Medical Library Association Bulletin* 65 (July 1977):377-79.

White, Brenda. *Slide Collections. A Survey of Their Organisation in Libraries in the Feilds of Architecture, Building, and Planning.* Edinburgh: Author, 21 Morningside Gardens, November 1967.

World Bank Photo Library. "The Organization of the World Bank Photo Library." by Susan Watters, Photo Librarian, Information and Public Affairs. Mimeographed. Washington, D.C.: The World Bank, 1977.

Zahava, Irene. "Use of Extensive Subject Headings for an Art Slide Collection." *ARLIS/NA Newsletter* 6 (November 1978):97-100.

    Tompkins-Cortland Community College (Dryden, New York); 5,000 slides.

Computer and Data Processing Applications

Bogar, Candace W. "Computer Applications to the Classification of Slides." *Librarian* (The University of Michigan) 4 (May 24, 1973):8-9.

Davis, L. R. "Locate Your Slides and Negatives with This Punch Card File System." *U.S. Camera* 16 (September 1955):68-69.

Diamond, Robert M. *The Development of a Retrieval System for 35mm Slides Utilized in Art and Humanities Instruction.* Washington, D.C.: Bureau of Research, Office of Education, U.S. Department of Health, Education and Welfare, 1969. (Final Report, Project No. 8-B-080).

Diamond, Robert M. "A Retrieval System for 35mm Slides Utilized in Art and Humanities Instruction." In *Bibliographic Control of Nonprint Media*, ed. by Pearce S. Grove and Evelyn G. Clement, pp. 346-59. Chicago: American Library Association, 1972.

Illuminated Manuscripts and Books in the Bodleian Library: A Supplemental Index. Compiled and edited by Thomas H. Ohlgren. New York: Garland Publishing, 1978.

Illuminated Manuscripts: An Index to Selected Bodleian Library Color Reproductions. Compiled and edited by Thomas H. Ohlgren. New York: Garland Publishing, 1977.

Kuvshinoff, B. W. "A Graphic Graphics Card Catalog and Computer Index." *American Documentation* 18 (January 1967):3-9.

Lewis, Elizabeth M. "A Cost Study of Library Color Microimage Storage and
    Retrieval: Visual Indexing in Microfiche, Super-8, and Videotape." Ed.D.
    Dissertation. New York: Columbia University, 1974.
Lewis, Elizabeth M. "A Graphic Catalog Card Index." *American Documentation*
    20 (July 1969):238-46.
Lewis, Elizabeth M. "Visual Indexing of Graphic Material." *Special Libraries* 67
    (November 1976):518-27.
Motley, Drucilla. "How to Find Your Slides Fast!" *Educational Screen and AV
    Guide* 49 (May 1970):18-20, 31.
"NCFA Slide and Photograph Archive. Division of Office of Slides and Photography,
    National Collection of Fine Arts." Washington, D.C.: Smithsonian Institu-
    tion, 1978.
"NCFA Slide and Photograph Archive. Division of Office of Slides and Photography,
    National Collection of Fine Arts." Rev. ed. Washington, D.C.: Smithsonian
    Institution, 1979.
Ohlgren, Thomas H. "The Bodleian Project: Computer Cataloguing and Indexing
    of Illuminated Medieval Manuscripts." In *Transactions of the First Inter-
    national Conference on Automatic Processing of Art History Data and Docu-
    ments*, pp. 290-318. Pisa, Italy: Scuola Normale Superiore, 1978.
Ohlgren, Thomas H. "Computer Indexing of Illuminated Manuscripts for Use in
    Medieval Studies." *Computers and the Humanities* 12 (1978):189-99.
Ohrn, Steven G. *Cataloguing in Context: The African Studies Program Slide
    Archives*. Bloomington, Ind.: African Studies Program, Indiana University,
    1975.
Ohrn, Steven G. *Cataloging the African Studies Film and Slide Collections*. Bloom-
    ington, Ind.: African Studies Program, Indiana University, 1974.
Ohrn, Steven G., and Siegmann, William. "An Indexing System for African Slides."
    Mimeographed. Bloomington, Ind.: African Studies Program, Indiana Univer-
    sity, 1973.
Rahn, Hans C. *Rahn'sche Farbdiapositivsammlung: eine ikonographische Klassi-
    fizierung von Meisterwerken der Malerei von 1430-1810* [Rahn's Coloured
    Slide Collection: An Iconographical Classification of Masterpaintings from
    1430-1810]." (In German and English.). Bern: H. Lang, 1975.
Raymond, Sue L., and Algermissen, Virginia L. "Retrieval System for Biomedical
    Slides Using MeSH." *Medical Library Association Bulletin* 64 (April 1976):
    233-35.
*SLIDEX: A System for Indexing, Filing, and Retrieving Slides and Other Visual
    Aids*. Prepared by Mod Mekkawi, Laura H. Palmer, and Woodrow W. Lons,
    Jr. Washington, D.C.: Howard University, 1978.

Santa Cruz System

"Classification System for Slides." *Information Retrieval and Library Automation*
    III (February 1968):9.
Kazlauskas, Edward. "A Slide Classification System." In *The School Media Center:
    A Book of Readings*, ed. by Pearl L. Ward, and Robert Beacon, pp. 174-79.
    Metuchen, N.J.: Scarecrow Press, 1973.
LoPresti, Maryellen. "Automated Slide Classification System at Georgia Tech."
    Special Libraries 64 (November 1973):509-513.

LoPresti, Maryellen, and Lewis, Elizabeth M. "Letters to the Editors." *ARLIS/NA Newsletter* 1 (October 1973):31.

Simons, Wendell. "Development of a Universal Classification System for Two-by-Two Inch Slide Collections." In *Bibliographic Control of Nonprint Media*, ed. by Pearce S. Grove and Evelyn G. Clement, pp. 360-73. Chicago: American Library Association, 1972.

Simons, Wendell, and Tansey, Luraine. "The Computer at Santa Cruz: Slide Classification with Automated Cross-Indexing." *Picturescope* 18 (1970):64-75.

Simons, Wendell, and Tansey, Luraine C. *A Slide Classification System for the Organization and Automatic Indexing of Interdisciplinary Collections of Slides and Pictures*. Santa Cruz, Calif.: University of California, 1970. ERIC ED-048879.

   Available from ERIC, Document Reproduction Service, P.O. Box 190, Arlington, Virginia, 22210.

Simons, Wendell, and Tansey, Luraine C. *A Universal Slide Classification System with Automatic Indexing*. Santa Cruz, Calif.: The University Library, University of California, 1969. Preliminary edition.

Tansey, Luraine C. "Classification of Research Photographs and Slides." *Library Trends* 23 (January 1975):417-26.

Tansey, Luraine C. *Slide Collection Index Application*. University of California at Santa Cruz. New York: International Business Machines Corporation, Data Processing Division, 1972. (GE20-0402-0).

"Visual Media." In *A Bibliographic System for Non-Book Media*, by Antony Croghan, pp. 56-58. London: Coburgh Publications, 1976.

IX. EQUIPMENT

Audiovisual Planning Equipment. Rochester, N.Y.: Eastman Kodak, 1978. (Kodak Publication No. S-11).

Cable, Ralph. *Audio-Visual Handbook*. 3rd ed. London: University of London Press, Ltd., 1970.

Culclasure, David. *Effective Use of Audiovisual Media*. Englewood Cliffs, N.J.: Prentice-Hall, 1969.

Davidson, Raymond L. *Audiovisual Machines*. 2nd ed. Scranton, Pa.: International Textbook Company, 1969.

De Kieffer, R. E., and Cochran, Lee. *Manual of Audiovisual Techniques*. 2nd ed. Englewood Cliffs, N.J.: Prentice-Hall, 1962.

Eboch, Sidney, and Cochern, George W. *Operating Audio-Visual Equipment*. 2nd ed. San Francisco, Calif.:Chandler Publishing Co., 1968.

"Equipment Standards." *EPIEgram: Equipment* 6 (April 15, 1978):1-2.

Guide to Equipment for Slide Maintenance and Viewing. Edited by Gillian Scott. New Mexico: Mid-America College Art and the University of New Mexico at Albuquerque, 1978.

   Available from Zelda Richardson, Slide Library, Art Dept., University of New Mexico, Albuquerque, 87131.

Kaufman, Peter. *Guide to Basic and Miscellaneous Equipment Serving the Art Slide Curator or Librarian, Including Annotated Bibliographies on Art Slide Librarianship*. Washington, D.C.: Art Libraries Society/ North America, 1973.

Oates, Stanton C. *Audiovisual Equipment; Self Instruction Manual.* 3rd ed. Dubuque, Iowa: W. C. Brown, 1975.

Pula, Fred John. *Application and Operation of Audiovisual Equipment in Education.* New York: John Wiley, 1968.

Rosenberg, Kenyon C., and Doskey, John S. *Media Equipment: A Guide and Dictionary.* Littleton, Colo.: Libraries Unlimited, 1976.

Guides for Selection

AV Guide. 434 S. Wabash Ave., Chicago, Ill., 60605. Newsletter published monthly by Scranton Gillette Communications.

Audio Visual. Incorporating *Film User* and *Industrial Screen.* 1971- .

The Audio-Visual Equipment Directory. 1979. 24th ed. Fairfax, Va.: National Audio-Visual Association.

Audiovisual Instruction. Washington, D.C.: Association of Educational Communication and Technology. Monthly. 1955- .

Audiovisual Marketplace. A Multimedia Guide. New York: R. R. Bowker Company, 1978. Biennial publication.

Audio Visual Source Directory (MPE) for services and products. Tarrytown, N.Y.: Motion Picture Enterprises Publication, Inc., Spring/Summer 1978 edition. Published semi-annually.

BUHLetin. To keep you aware of the new ideas in lenses and projection devices from Buhl Optical Company. Pittsburgh: Buhl Optical, 1009 Beech Avenue, Summer 1978.

Educational Screen and AV Guide. Chicago, Ill.: Educational Screen, Inc., monthly. *Blue Book*, annual summer issue, is a comprehensive listing of the year's productions and directory of publishers.

EPIEgram: Equipment. EPIEgram: Materials. No. 1. October 1, 1972- . New York: EPIE Institute, 475 Riverside Drive, 10027.

Photographic Trade News. (PTN) *Master Buying Guide* [1978] and *Directory* [Issue Volume 41]. Hempstead, N.Y.: Photographic Trade News Corp.

PMI Photo Methods for Industry Catalog and Directory of Products and Services. New York: Gellert Publishing Corp., annual.

Professional Photographic Catalog. Chicago: Standard Photo Supply, annual.

Simons, Wendell W. "Choosing Audio-Visual Equipment." *Library Trends* 13 (April 1965):503-516.

Technical Photography. For Industrial, Military and Government Still, Cine & AV Professionals. Monthly. Hempstead, N.Y.: In-Plant Photography, Inc. (250 Fulton Avenue, 11550), 1968 (?)- .

Projectors and Projection Systems

"AV Practices among Colleges and Universities." *American School and University* 36 (July 1964):26.

Barnes, G. "Macro-projector from Slide Projector." *Science and Children* 12 (January 1975):6.

Designing for Projection. Rochester, N.Y.: Eastman Kodak Co., 1970. (V3-141).

Edgerton, W. D. "Simplified Synchronizing." *Educational Screen and AV Guide* 47 (September 1968):36.

Foss, H. A., and Pearce, G. L. "Liven Up Lab Learning with Synchronized 2 x 2 Sound Slide." *Audiovisual Instruction* 13 (March 1968):288, 290.

Freed, C. W. "Make Your Own Rear-Projection Screen." *School Shop* 27 (May 1968):54-56.

Gregory, John R. "Synchronization—1. Why You Need It, 2. What It Can Do, 3. How to Achieve It, 4. Latest Directory of Equipment." *U.S. Camera* 26 (October 1963):72-73.

"Kodak Ektagraphic and Carousel Slide Projectors." *EPIEgram: Equipment* 6 (October 1, 1977):2-3.

Kodak Sourcebook: Kodak Ektagraphic Slide Projectors. Rochester, N.Y.: Eastman Kodak, 1977. (Kodak Publication No. S-74).

Lewis, Philip. "Slide and Film Projectors Let Tapes Do the Talking." *Nations Schools* 86 (August 1970):44, 46.

Mannheim, L. A. "AV Projector with Integral Pointer." *Camera* 48 (August 1969): 47.

Mannheim, L. A. "Slide Projector with Dissolves." *Camera* 56 (January 1977): 42-45.

Mannheim, L. A. "Slide Projectors for Pocket Instamatic Slides, Automatic and AV Still Projectors." *Camera* 52 (February 1973):49-50.

Mutch, Kenneth L. "Slide Dissolve Unit." *Audiovisual Instruction* 18 (September 1973):49-51.

Patrie, M. "How Does It Look from Where You Sit?" *Audiovisual Instruction* 11 (March 1966):186-187.

"Problem of Slide-Tray Removal." *EPIEgram: Equipment* 6 (December 15, 1977):1; "Discussion." 6 (April 15, 1978):4.

"Question of the Frangible Filter: Slide Projector Heat Filters." *EPIEgram: Equipment* 6 (December 15, 1977):2.

Rothschild, Norman. "Slide Projectors: Where Do They Go from Here?" *Popular Photography* 65 (October 1969):84-85, 132.

Ruark, Gerald L. "A Plea for Two Projectors; Utilizing Filmstrips and Slides." *Audiovisual Instruction* 13 (May 1968):500.

"Telecture." *Journal of Health, Physical Education and Recreation* 41 (May 1970): 40.

"THD Halight Filmstrip/Slide Projector with Microfiche Attachment." *Reprographic Quarterly* 3 (1976):115-16.

Wadsworth, Raymond. "How to Determine Seating Area for Good Viewing of Projected Images." *American School and University* 43 (July 1971):6, 8-9.

Wadsworth, Raymond. "1W, 2W, 3W, 4W, 5W, 6W, Law for AV Presentations." *American School and University* 44 (October 1971):18-22.

Wilkinson, G. L. "Projection Variables and Performances." *AV Communication Review* 24 (Winter 1976):413-36.

Wyman, Raymond. "A Critical Look at Multimedia Rear-Screen Presentation Halls." *Audiovisual Instruction* 11 (May 1966):373-74.

Zagorski, Edward J., and Fisher, Rob. "Undergraduate Instructional Award." Champaign, Ill.: University of Illinois, 1970. (Part II: "The Slide Reviewer," pp. 15-24, Figures 1-10).

Screens

Carl, D. "Vision and Visual Comfort." *Audiovisual Instruction* 22 (September 1977):18-19.

"Eastman Kodak Ektalite Projection Screens." *EPIEgram: Equipment* 6 (February 1, 1978):4.

Edwards, Bernell J. "Front-Screen Projection for On-Camera Television—Color Slides." *Audiovisual Instruction* 20 (October 1975):43-44.

Frederick, Franz J. "Minitutorial on Screening Facilities." *School Media Quarterly* 2 (Spring 1974):237-44, 253-55; "Erratum" 3 (Fall 1974):29.

James, David A., and Nichols, George V. "Adequate Slide Projection." *Indiana Arts and Vocational Education* 57 (March 1968):90, 92, 94, 96, 98.

James, David A., and Nichols, George V. "Experimental Comparison of Projection Screens." *Indiana Arts and Vocational Education* 56 (November 1968):44-46.

Lewis, P. "What to Watch When You Select Projection Screens." *Nation's Schools* 79 (January 1967):88, 90, 92.

Olsen, Richard W., et al. "How to Build a Panoramic Screen for Your Classroom." *Audiovisual Instruction* 18 (May 1973):87-88.

Wadsworth, Raymond. "Front versus Rear Screen Projection." *American School and University* 45 (October 1972):12-13.

X.   PRODUCTION

Abrams, F. Russell. "Filmstrips Direct from Slides." *Audiovisual Instruction* 15 (April 1970):95.

Arnold, Rus. "The Nuisance of Newton Rings." *U.S. Camera* 30 (May 1967):12, 76-77.

Artwork Size Standards for Projected Visuals. Rochester, N.Y.: Eastman Kodak Co., 1968. (Kodak Pamphlet No. S-12).

Blatt, M. D. "Edges Rather Than Corners; Eliminating Backward or Upside Down Images." *Audiovisual Instruction* 15 (September 1970):83.

Bullough, Robert V., and Ellis, Barry. "Change of Pace for Slide Programs." *Audiovisual Instruction* 21 (October 1976):57.

Chang, Chi Kwong. "Projection of Stereoscopic Images by Ordinary Slide Projector." *Journal of Chemical Education* 53 (September 1976):601.

Hedin, Duane E. "Changing the Image of 35mm Slides." *Audiovisual Instruction* 20 (November 1975):40.

Jenkins, D. M. "Multiple Image Slides." *Audiovisual Instruction* 22 (January 1977): 41-43.

Kemp, Jerrold E. *Planning and Producing Audiovisual Materials.* With the assistance of Ron Carraher, Richard R. Szumski and Willard R. Card. 3rd ed. New York: Crowell, 1975.

Kirman, Joseph M. "Producing Your Own Social Studies Study Prints and Slides, or, Everything You Wanted to Know about 35mm Photography." *Audiovisual Instruction* 18 (April 1973):68-71.

Kurzweg, Lutz. "Inexpensive 35mm Slides Made Using a Xerox Machine." *Physics Teacher* 2 (March 1974):174, 180.

Laughlin, Mildred. "Action Activities: Holographic Slides." *Learning Today* 8 (Winter 1975):69-71.

Lewis, Philip. "Latest Slide-Making Aids Break Usage Bottleneck." *Nation's Schools* 82 (November 1968):80, 83, 85, 90.

"Local Production with 35mm Photography." *School Libraries* 20 (Winter 1971): 25-27.

Mailloux, L. D., and Bollman, J. E. "Xerox 6500 Slide Printer." *Journal of Applied Photographic Engineering* 3 (1977):230-34.

Miller, Ralph. "Skipper." "Slides to Prints." *U.S. Camera* 26 (August 1963):50-51, 84.

Minor, Ed., and Frye, Harvey R. *Techniques for Producing Visual Instructional Media*. 2nd ed. New York: McGraw-Hill, 1977.

Planning and Producing Slide Programs. Rochester, N.Y.: Eastman Kodak, 1978. (Kodak Publication No. S-30).

Reynolds, G. William, and Ward, Roger W. "2-inch x 2-inch Slide Series; Make 'em Yourself." *Physics Teacher* 9 (February 1971):93-94.

Shaver, Johnny M. "From Transparencies to Slides." *Audiovisual Instruction* 18 (December 1973):48-49.

Siddall, William R. "Making Slides from Printed Materials." *Journal of Geography* 68 (October 1969):430-32.

"Slide Duplicating." *Mid-America College Art Association Slides and Photographs Newsletter* 5 (Spring 1978):6.

Walker, Lester C., Jr. "Low Cost Slide Production for Teaching Aids." *College Art Journal* 13 (Fall 1953):39-41.

Wiesinger, Robert. "Instant 35mm Slides." *Educational Screen and AV Guide* 43 (February 1964):88.

General Photographic Guides

The Encyclopedia of Photography. 20 vols. New York: Greystone Press, 1965.

The Focal Encyclopedia of Photography. London: Focal Press, 1965.

Gassan, Arnold. *Handbook for Contemporary Photography*. 4th ed. Rochester, N.Y.: Light Impressions, 1977.

Mees, C. E. K. *From Dry Plates to Ektachrome: A Film Story of Photographic Research*. New York: Ziff-Davis, 1961.

Photo-Lab Index. 31st ed. New York: Morgan and Morgan, January 1973.

Photo Lab Index. Compact edition. 1st ed. Dobbs Ferry, N.Y.: Morgan and Morgan Inc., 1977- .

Photographic Abstracts. Abstracts of the World Literature of the Science, Technology and Applications of Photography. London: The Royal Photographic Society of Great Britain, 1922- .

    See abstracts under the following headings: "Preservation and Storage"; "Projection (other than cine)"; and "Colour Photography."

Publications Index. Motion Picture and Audiovisual Markets Division. Rochester, N.Y.: Eastman Kodak, 1978. (Kodak Publication No. S-4).

Black and White Film and Slides

Adler, Myles. "From Slide to Black and White Print . . . without a Negative." *U.S. Camera* 26 (October 1963):26, 100.

"Black and White Slide Film in Use at the University of Missouri–Kansas City." *Mid-America College Art Association Slides and Photographs Newsletter* 4 (Fall 1977):6.

Brooks, D. W., et al. "Some New Light on Black and White Slides." *Journal of Chemical Education* 50 (August 1973):566.

Churney, Marie. "Making Slides from Black-and-White Negatives." *Science Teacher* 42 (February 1975):54.

Eastman Kodak Company. *Kodak Films: Color and Black-and-White*. Rochester, N.Y.: Eastman Kodak Co., 1978. (Kodak Publication No. Af-1).

Gagnou, J. Marc. "Monochromatic Color with Black and White Slides." *Journal of Chemical Education* 53 (September 1976):604.

Hollander, Steven. "Better, Faster 35mm Black and White Transparencies." *Audiovisual Instruction* 19 (November 1974):83-84.

Jones, R. B. "Black and White Slides from Super Speed Duplicating Film." *Audiovisual Instruction* 21 (September 1976):61.

Mulvehill, Larry. "Black and White Slides from Black and White Negatives." *U.S. Camera* 29 (September 1966):26.

Color Film and Slides

Beam, P. C. "Color Slide Controversy." *College Art Journal* 2 (January 1943):35-38.

Bridaham, L. B. "On Making Color Slides in Art Museums." *Art Journal* 31 (Winter 1971-72):149.

Bridaham, L. B., and Mitchell, C. B. "Duplicating Color Slides; Research in Color Photography at the Art Institute of Chicago." *Museum News* 29 (December 15, 1951):6-7.

Bridaham, L. B., and Mitchell, C. B. "Successful Duplication of Color Slides; Results of Research at the Chicago Art Institute." *College Art Journal* 10 (Spring 1951):261-63.

Campbell, Charles E., and Trooien, Carl. "An Easy Production Method for Film-strips and 2 x 2 Slides." *Audiovisual Instruction* 15 (January 1970):81-83.

Carpenter, J. M. "Limitations of Color Slides." *College Art Journal* 2 (January 1943):38-40.

"Coloured Lantern Slides." *Bulletin of the Russell-Cotes Art Gallery and Museum* 17 (March 1938):10.

DeLaurier, Nancy. "More on Slide Film." *Mid-America College Art Association Slide and Photographs Newsletter* 4 (Spring 1977):10-11.

DeLaurier, Nancy. "Slide Quality." *ARLIS/NA Newsletter* 7 (February 1979):12-14.

"Directory of Color Films." *U.S. Camera* 30 (September 1967):52-53, 72.

E-4 Processing Errors with Kodak Ektachrome Film. Rochester, N.Y.: Eastman Kodak Co., 1966. (Kodak Pamphlet No. E-62).

Edelson, Mike. "The Kodachromes and Ektachromes." *U.S. Camera* 30 (August 1967):40-43, 64-65.

"Film and Photography." *Mid-America College Art Association Slides and Photographs Newsletter* 5 (Summer 1978):7.

"The Four Most Important Colour-Systems in Colour-Photography Now: I. Kodak; II. AGFA-Gravaert; III. Polaroid; IV. Cibachrome." *Camera* 56 (July 1977): 39-43.

Hall, Neal. "Adding Impact to 35mm Slides." *Audiovisual Instruction* 20 (May 1975):57.

Jasienski, S. "Colour Corrections to Transparencies Subsequent to Processing." *Camera* 44 (October 1965):37-38.

Kodak Color Dataguide. 6th ed. Rochester, N.Y.: Eastman Kodak, 1978. (Kodak Publication No. R-19).

"Kodak's New Slide Films . . . Better?" *Modern Photography* 40 (December 1976):106.

MacLaren, Grant E. "A Method for Producing 35mm Slides of Teacher-Authored Textual Materials." *Audiovisual Instruction* 15 (April 1970):101-103.

Marx, W. R. "How to Reduce Your Cost of Colored Slides." *Art Journal* 31 (Summer 1972):424, 427.

Moore, H. C. "Some Observations on the Preparation, Distribution and Use of Colour Slides Made by the Negative-Positive System." *Journal of Photographic Science* 22 (1974):117-18.

Perrenoud, F. "Copy Colour Slides." *Camera* 40 (April 1961):48.

Rosenthal, John W. "Helpful Hints for Color Correction." *Mid-America College Art Association Slides and Photographs Newsletter* 5 (Summer 1978):6-7.

Rushton, Brian N. "Producing and Selling a Quality Service to Education SLIDES." *Museum News* 46 (January 1968):27-32.

Seng, Mark W. "Color Slides and Filmstrips; An Easy Way." *Audiovisual Instruction* 14 (February 1969):54-55.

Spialter, Leonard, and Smith, Jonathon S., II. "Dye Solutions for the Preparation of Colored Slides." *Journal of Chemical Education* 38 (September 1961):473.

"Statement on Slide Quality Standards." Prepared by the Joint ARLIS/VRSIG-CAA/VR Subcommittee." *Mid-America College Art Association Slides and Photographs Newsletter* 5 (Summer 1978):5.

Tull, A. G. "Slide Materials—A Colour Quality Study: I." *British Journal of Photography* 124 (1977):637-41.

Tull, A. G. "Slide Materials—A Colour Quality Study: II." *British Journal of Photography* 124 (1977):648-49.

"U.S. Camera Tests—Kodachrome II." *U.S. Camera* 24 (May 1961):58-61, 76.

Zimmerman, Donald E., and Scherer, Cliff. "How to Get Colored Slides of Student Work for 2¢ Each." *Journalism Education* 32 (October 1977):63-65.

Copy Stands and Duplicators

Collins, J. S. "A Slide Production Module." *Forensic Photography* 3 (1973):12-14.

"A Cool Copy Cat." *U.S. Camera* 31 (July 1968):20, 88.

"Copy It." *Physics Teacher* 13 (April 1975):243.

"Duplicate Your Slides." *U.S. Camera* 24 (September 1961):72-73.

Erickson, D. G. "Easy, Inexpensive Slide Duplication." *Audiovisual Instruction* 17 (February 1972):76.

Gardner, C. Hugh. "Making the Most of Your Visualmaker." *Audiovisual Instruction* 21 (March 1976):48-49, 51-53.

"How to Make a Slide Copier." *U.S. Camera* 24 (November 1961):92-93.

Smith, Darrell L. "Make Your Own Slide Duplicating Unit." *School Shop* 27 (September 1967):52-53.

Spears, C. J. "The Rapid Copy Stand." *U.S. Camera* 31 (January 1968):50-51, 70.

Using Polarized Light for Copying. Rochester, N.Y.: Eastman Kodak Co., 1975.
(Kodak Publication No. S-70-1-2).

Lantern Slides

Ackerman, S. A. "Lightweight Lantern Slides." *Journal of Chemical Education*
40 (March 1965):151.
Allcott, J. "Hard-drawn Slides for Use with Photographic Slides." *College Art
Journal* 18 (Winter 1959):155-56.
Lantern Slides and How to Make Them. Rochester, N.Y.: Educational Sales Division, Bausch and Lomb Optical Co., 786 St. Paul St., 1949.
Shaw, William H. R., and Aronson, John N. "The Preparation of Inexpensive Lantern Slides." *Journal of Chemical Education* 40 (September 1963):483-84.

Microfiche

Bennett, Josiah, and Irvine, Betty Jo. "Review of *Victorian Bookbinding: A
Pictorial Survey*, by Sue Allen." *Journal of Academic Librarianship* 2 (May
1977):98-99.
    Critical review of the use of color microfiche to replace bookplates and
slides.
Chandler, Devon. "Transparency Microfiche: A New Dimension." *Audiovisual
Instruction* 20 (December 1975):45-46.
Lewis, Elizabeth. "The Marburger Index." *Microform Review* 8 (Winter 1979):40-42.
Schwarz, Philip J. "Use of Color Microfiche as a Replacement for Slides in a
University Elementary Accounting Course." *The Journal of Micrographics*
11 (January/February 1978):217-19.
Thomas, A. J. "Color Slides of Microfiche Save Space, Time, Money." *Journal
of Micrographics* 7 (May 1974):221-22.

Slide/Tape Sync

Bentley, Michael. "How to Publish Your Own Slide-Tape Presentation." *Audiovisual Instruction* 19 (March 1974):supplement 10-12.
Bohm, E. W. "MIOSW; Make Your Music Program Visible with an Audio-Slide
Presentation." *Music Education Journal* 63 (January 1977):68.
Clark, J. "Making Sound Filmstrips from 2" x 2" Slides." *Audiovisual Instruction*
10 (May 1965):402.
Francombe, A. "Production of Tape/Slide Sequences." *Educational Media International* 2 (1974):24-31.
Gaunt, J. H. "Developing Taped Narratives for Slide Presentations." *School
Libraries* 17 (Winter 1968):45-49.
Gould, Maurie. "Automated Slide Projector." *Physics Teacher* 13 (January 1975):
38-41.
"How to Make a Slide Show Click." *AIA Journal* 53 (April 1970):60. Reply:
Risse, E. M. 54 (November 1970):76.
Keel, John A. "Answers to 25 Basic Questions about . . . Adding Sound to Slides
and Movies." *U.S. Camera* 26 (October 1963):70-71, 106.
Lestingi, F. S. "Projection Pointers; Think Sync." *Physics Teacher* 15 (May 1977):
310-11.

Lukas, Terrence G. "Inexpensive, Easy to Build Slide-Tape Programmer." *Audiovisual Instruction* 20 (November 1975):46-48.

Lukas, Terrence G., et al. "Design an Automated 4 Slide, 2 Screen Projection System." *Audiovisual Instruction* 18 (September 1973):supplement 4-6.

McCarty, C., et al. "Multi-Projector Control Programmer." *Audiovisual Instruction* 15 (September 1970):84-85.

Mannheim, L. A. "Audio-Visual Automation—the Dynamic Still." *Camera* 50 (July, August 1971):43-44, 48, 50-51.

Miller, Ralph. "Skipper." "Cue-tips for Sound-Slide Shows." *U.S. Camera* 25 (April 1962):44, 65, 77.

Orgren, C. F. "Production of Slide-Tape Programs." *Unabashed Librarian* 16 (Summer 1975):25-28.

Ryan, Mack. "Preparing a Slide-Tape Program: A Step-by-Step Approach." *Audiovisual Instruction* 20 (September 1975):36-38, 42-43; (November 1975): 36-39.

Simpson, Robert. "Slide or Push? or Why Are There Two Ways of Making Slide-Sound Shows?" *Audio Visual* 7 (July 1978):30-31, 33-34.

Sleeman, Phillip J., and Adams, Sarah. "Planning and Producing a Tape-Slide Presentation." *School Activities* 38 (January 1967):14-15, 19.

Slides Made without Film

Bonid, J. D. "Making Slides without Cameras." *School Library Journal* 21 (April 1975):36.

Cyr, J. "Making Color Slides without a Camera." *Arts and Activities* 82 (November 1977):41-43, 61.

Eben, L. E. "Do-it-yourself Slides." *Grade Teacher* 87 (April 1970):96-97.

Gruber, M. T. "Make Your Own Slide Show." *Arts and Activities* 65 (March 1969): 38-39.

Hale, P., and Hale, J. "Use Write-on Slides to Bridge That Gap." *Instructor* 83 (October 1973):156.

Harper, G. "Making Transparent Slides." *Instructor* 76 (January 1967):115.

Moody, G. J. "Impressions Projected on Acetate Slides." *Arts and Activities* 59 (March 1966):28-30.

Movies and Slides without a Camera. Rochester, N.Y.: Eastman Kodak Co., Motion Picture and Education Markets Division, n.d. (Kodak Publication No. S-47).

Scott, E. "Hand-made Slide: Whetstone for Perceptual Acuity." *Arts and Activities* 71 (April 1972):30-31.

Wolf, Frank E. "Drosophila Holder and Multi-Purpose Chambered Slide." *The Science Teacher* 31 (September 1964):47.

Titling Slides

Collart, Marie E., and Wismar, Beth L. "Make Perfect Slide Captions Everytime." *Audiovisual Instruction* 21 (September 1976):13-15.

Cress, H. J., and Stowe, R. A. "Slide Captions Made Easier." *Audiovisual Instruction* 12 (January 1967):51-54.

Dayton, D. K. "How to Make Title Slides with High Contrast." *Audiovisual Instruction* 22 (April 1977):33-36; (May 1977):39-41.

Hutton, Deane W., and Lescohier, Jean A. "Making Title Slides; Superimposition Effect." *Audiovisual Instruction* 19 (May 1974):supplement 4-6.

Nye, R. Glenn. "Titling Your Slides." *U.S. Camera* 22 (November 1959):82-83.

Rutt, David. "Titling for Slide Presentations." *Audiovisual Instruction* 19 (May 1974):supplement 2-3.

Swenson, W. T. "Beam-Splitter: Your Answer to Professional Title Slides." *Man/ Society/Technology* 33 (May 1974):241-43.

Wilhelm, R. Dwight. "High Quality Superimposed Titles Inexpensively Produced." *Audiovisual Instruction* 11 (November 1966):758, 760, 762.

XI. COPYRIGHT

Bender, Ivan. "Copyright: Chaos or Compromise?" *Previews* 2 (November 1973): 3-5.

Carroll, Hardy. "Primary Sources for Understanding the New Copyright Law." *College and Research Libraries News* 1 (January 1977):1-2.

Copyright and Educational Media: A Guide to Fair Use and Permissions Procedures. Washington, D.C.: Association of Educational Communications and Technology, 1977.

"Copyright and the Nonprint Media." *Canadian Library Journal* 33 (April 1976): 109-112.

The Copyright Dilemma. Edited by Herbert S. White. Chicago: American Library Association, 1978.

"Copyright, Media, and the School Librarian; A Guide to Multimedia Copying in Schools. American Association of School Librarians." *School Media Quarterly* 6 (Spring 1978):192A-192P.

Copyright: New Law, New Directions. Filmstrip, Audiocassette, Script, and Information Booklet. Washington, D.C.: Association of Educational Communications and Technology, 1977.

"Copyright Today." *Audiovisual Instruction.* Regular column, October 1974- .

Golub, M. V. "Not by Books Alone: Library Copying of Nonprint, Copyrighted Material." *Law Library Journal* 70 (May 1977):153-70.

Johnston, Donald F. *Copyright Handbook.* New York: Bowker, 1978.

Kent, Allen, and Lancour, Harold. *Copyright. Current Viewpoints on History, Laws, and Legislation.* New York: R. R. Bowker, 1972.

Miller, Jerome K. *Copyright Guide for Educators and Librarians.* Chicago: American Library Association, 1979.

Siebert, Fred S. *Copyrights, Clearances, and Rights of Teachers in the New Educational Media.* Washington, D.C.: American Council on Education, 1964.

[United States Code Annotated], 17:U.S.C.A. § 101.
    Slides are classified under § 202.11 Photographs (Class J) of the United States Code Annotated.

XII. PLANNING PHYSICAL FACILITIES

American Library Association. Ad Hoc Committee on the Physical Facilities of Libraries. *Measurement and Comparison of Physical Facilities for Libraries.* Chicago: American Library Association, 1970.

De Bernardis, Amo; Doherty, Victor W.; Hummel, Errett; Brubaker, Charles
William. *Planning Schools for New Media*. Washington, D.C.: U.S. Department
of Health, Education and Welfare, Office of Education, 1961.

Educational Facilities with New Media. Edited by Alan C. Green. Washington,
D.C.: Department of Audiovisual Instruction, National Education Association, 1966. (Stock No. 071-02302).

Gilkey, R. "Designing Space for Use of Instructional Hardware." *The Clearing
House* 45 (December 1970):255-256.

Irvine, Betty Jo. "Fine Arts Pavilion Library. Preliminary Building Program."
Rev. Mimeographed. Bloomington, Ind.: Indiana University, September 1973.

McVey, G. F. "Facilities." In *College Learning Resources Programs*, pp. 49-70.
Washington, D.C.: Association of Educational Communications and Technology, 1977.

Media Center Facilities Design. Compiled and edited by Jane Anne Hannigan and
Glenn E. Estes. Chicago: American Library Association, 1978.

Metcalf, Keyes D. *Planning Academic and Research Library Buildings*. New York:
McGraw-Hill, 1965.

Moriarty, J. H. "New Media Facilities." *Library Trends* 16 (October 1967):251-58.

"New Buildings Designed for A-V Use." *American School and University* 38 (April
1966):39-41.

"New Community College Stresses A-V System." *American School and University*
44 (September 1971):42-43.

*New Spaces for Learning–Designing College Facilities to Utilize Instructional
Aids and Media*. New York: School of Architecture, Rensselaer Polytechnic
Institute, 1961.

Nolan, Margaret P. "The Metropolitan Museum of Art–Slide Library." In *Planning
the Special Library*, edited by Ellis Mount, pp. 101-103. New York: Special
Libraries Association, 1972.

Stone, C. W. "Planning for Media within University Library Buildings." *Library
Trends* 18 (October 1969):233-45.

Wadsworth, Raymond. "Integrated A-V Facilities for the Classroom; Audiovisual
System Concept." *American School and University* 44 (May 1972):83-84.

Classroom Design

Colbert, Charles R. "Researching an Auditorium-Teaching Centre." *American
School and University* 1961, H1-H6.

Cress, Hal J., and Stowe, Richard. "We Designed and Constructed a Remote Control
Classroom." *Audiovisual Instruction* 12 (October 1967):830-35.

Haviland, David S. "Designing Multimedia Rooms for Teaching or, The Instructor
as the Forgotten User!" *Audiovisual Instruction* 15 (October 1970):78-81.

McDougal, R., and Thompson, J. J. "Multi-Media Classroom: Planning and Operation." *Audiovisual Instruction* 12 (October 1967):826-29.

Mitchell, John W. "Viewing Wall Contains Complete Audiovisual System." *Nation's
Schools* 79 (May 1967):70.

Morgan, Kenneth W. "When Amateurs Make an Audiovisual Room." *Audiovisual
Instruction* 8 (April 1963):220-21.

Oldham, R. "Chalkboards and Beyond; AV Design of the Thirty-Seat Classroom."
Educational Product Report No. 43, 5 (April 1972):39-52.

"SUNY Learning Resources Focus on Multimedia Rooms." *College and University Business* 48 (January 1970):68.

Tanzman, J. "Media Starts with the Architect." *School Management* 14 (May 1970):50.

Wadsworth, Raymond H. "Divisible Auditoriums: A Challenge to AV Systems." *American School and University* 48 (October; November 1975):60-64, 66, 68; 41-43.

XIII. PHOTOGRAPHY OF ART AND ARCHITECTURE

Barsness, John C. *Photographing Crafts*. New York: American Crafts Council, 1974.

Conlon, V. M. *Camera Techniques in Archaeology*. New York: St. Martin Press, 1973.

Gernsheim, Helmut. *Focus on Architecture and Sculpture: An Original Approach to the Photography of Architecture and Sculpture*. London: The Fountain Press, 1949.

Lewis, John N. C., and Smith, Edwin. *The Graphic Reproduction and Photography of Works of Art*. London: W. S. Cowell, Ltd., 1969.

Lewis, John N. C., and Smith, Edwin. *Reproducing Art: The Photography, Graphic Reproduction and Printing of Works of Art*. New York: Praeger Co., 1969.

Matthews, Sydney K. *Photography in Archaeology and Art*. New York: Humanities Press, 1968.

Molitor, Joseph W. *Architectural Photography*. New York: Wiley-Interscience, 1976.

Nolan, Margaret P. "The Release of Photographic Reproductions of Art Objects." *Special Libraries* 56 (January 1965):42-46.

Shaw, Leslie. *Architectural Photography*. London: George Newnes, Ltd., 1949.

Shulman, Julius. *The Photography of Architecture and Design: Photographing Buildings, Interiors, and the Visual Arts*. New York: Whitney Library of Design, 1977.

Simmons, Harold G. *Archaeological Photography*. New York: University Press, 1969.

Veltri, John. *Architectural Photography*. New York: Amphoto, 1974.

XIV. USING SLIDES FOR INSTRUCTION

Blockhaus, W. "Slide/Sound Media in Basic Business Classes." *Business Education Forum* 27 (November 1972):55-57.

Burden, Ernest E. *Visual Presentation: A Practical Manual for Architects and Engineers*. New York: Big G Press, 1977.

Carithers, P. "Color Slides That Show Teaching." *Michigan Education Journal* 43 (May 1966):28-29.

Clark, F. E. "Good and the Not So Good for Three Common Teaching Resources: Audio Tapes, 2 by 2 Slides, and Narrated Slide Series." *Indiana Education* 66 (February 1977):66.

Cook, R. I., and McElhiney, D. S. "A-V Term Report." *Audiovisual Instruction* 12 (September 1967):696-98.

Cosgrove, L. "Use of Filmstrips and Slides." *Illinois Libraries* 42 (April 1960): 251-53.

Dennis, D. A. "Preproduction Planning: Key to Successful Slide Shows." *Audiovisual Instruction* 10 (May 1965):401.

Edgerton, W. D. "Europe on One Roll of Film a Day; Photographic Suggestions for Educator Traveling Abroad." *Audiovisual Instruction* 15 (March 1970): 99-101.

Erickson, Carlton W. H. *Fundamentals of Teaching with Audiovisual Technology.* New York: Macmillan, 1965. (Text edition, 1972).

Fadala, S. "Write On, Students, Write On and Produce a 35mm Slide Presentation." *Audiovisual Instruction* 18 (April 1973):supplement 16.

Freitag, Wolfgang. "Slides for Individual Use in the College Library." *Library Trends* 23 (January 1975):495-99.

Groneman, N. "How to Make Instructional Slide Presentations." *Business Education Forum* 29 (December 1974):8.

Hollis, R. "Your Own Slides." *Catholic School Journal* 70 (March 1970):30, 32.

Houser, R. L., et al. "Learning a Motion and a Nonmotion Concept by Motion Picture versus Slide Presentation." *AV Communication Review* 18 (Winter 1970):425-30.

"How Ten Top A-V Programs Compare." *Nation's Schools* 82 (October 1968): 74-78.

Jones, R. C. "Multicampus Instructional Resources Services; Three New Campuses in St. Louis." *Junior College Journal* 36 (March 1966):11-13.

Laughlin, M. "Action Activities: Photography." *Learning Today* 6 (Spring 1973): 85-88.

Maguire, James. "Who's Got Multi-Image? and What Are They Doing with It?" *Audiovisual Instruction* 22 (January 1977):54.

Oh, C. Y. "Student Preparation of Instructional Materials." *Audiovisual Instruction* 19 (January 1974):supplement 2-3.

"Oklahoma State University Library Will Loan Slides." *Kansas Library Bulletin* 37 (Winter 1968):12-13.

Orna, B. "Slides for Starters." *Times Educational Supplement* 3135 (July 4, 1975):48-49.

Patterson, D. D. "Facelift for Industrial Arts: Slide Show Featuring Women in Industrial Arts." *Man/Society/Technology* 34 (December 1974):85-86.

Pendered, N. C. "Field Trips Vicariously? Slide-Tape Presentation." *Man/Society/ Technology* 35 (September 1975):14-15.

Sharkey, Arthur P., Jr., and Emenecker, Richard H. "Rehearsing a Slide Presentation without a Projector!" *Audiovisual Instruction* 19 (May 1974):supplement 12-13.

Singer, Ira J. "Audio-Visual Dial Access Information Retrieval and the User." In *Audio Visual Media/Moyens Audio Visuals.* Vol. 4, pp. 17-23. Oxford, England: International Council for Educational Films, 1970.

Sister Gilmary. "Future Teachers Learn from Low Cost Methods." *Educational Screen and AV Guide* 44 (September 1965):24-25.

Sleeman, Phillip J., and Adams, Sarah. "Color Slides in Teaching and Learning." *School Activities* 37 (December 1965):13-15.

"Slides and Slide-Lectures Offered by the Library." *Library Journal* 94 (April 1969):1570.

Smith, Edgar, et al. *Techniques for Generating Instructional Slides*. Lowry AFB, Colo.: Air Force Human Resources Lab, Technical Training Division, 1975. ERIC Document ED 119 612.

Spector, A. "Writing the Slide-Essay." *English Journal* 65 (April 1976):74-75.

Stanger, B. N. "Slide Presentation Contributes to Maximum Learning." *Agricultural Education Magazine* 43 (October 1970):92.

Sullivan, H. W. "Don't Make a Slide Presentation." *Agricultural Education Magazine* 45 (April 1973):236-37.

"Teaching with Slides." *Classical World* 63 (January 1970):153-54.

"Using Film, Slides and Transparencies to Expand Daily Learning." *American School and University* 40 (April 1968):40-41, 61.

Wendt, P. R., and Butts, G. K. "A/V Materials: Filmstrips, Slides, and Transparencies." *Review of Educational Research* 32 (April 1962):144-46.

Art

Bass, R. E. "Color Slides for Beginning Graphic Arts Student." *Indiana Education* 64 (October 1975):62-63.

Burden, Ernest. "Slide Presentations [for architects]." *Architectural Record* 150 (July 1971):55-58.

Carleton, C. S. "Picasso = MC^2; Project CUE, an Experiment Designed to Integrate the Arts and Humanities into the School Curriculum." *American Education* 2 (March 1966):13-15.

Florian, V. L., and Novotny, D. F. "Enrich Art History with Sight and Sound." *Arts and Activities* 58 (September 1965):38-41.

Freitag, W. M. "Slides for Individual Use in the College Library." *Library Trends* 23 (January 1975):495-99.

Harwitz, A. "Turned-on Art." *American Education* 6 (March 1970):14-17.

Hess, H. L., and James, D. "Presenting a Conventional Drawing Concept in 35mm Slides." *Indiana Arts and Vocational Education* 56 (November 1967):51-53.

Hess, H. L., and Nystrom, D. C. "Using 35mm Slide Sets to Teach Pictorial Projection." *Indiana Arts and Vocational Education* 57 (December 1968):46-47.

Samuel, Evelyn. "Academic TOL [Type of Library] Article: Art Bibliography on Slides." *ARLIS/NA Newsletter* 6 (May 1978):47.

Sloane, Patricia. "Color Slides for Teaching Art History." *Art Journal* 31 (Spring 1972):276-80.

Geography

Connole, D. "Valuable Teaching Aid: The 35mm Slide Used in Conjunction with Topographic Maps." *Journal of Geography* 74 (February 1975):107-110.

Hall, V. S. "Access to Reference Tools of Geological Literature via the Carramate, an Individual Teaching Tool." *Kentucky Library Association Bulletin* 39 (Spec. Issue 1975):27-29.

Meyer, D. K. "Photographic Essay in Geographic Instruction." *Journal of Geography* 72 (September 1973):11-26.

Miller, E. Willard. "Use of Color Slides as a Geographic Teaching Aid." *Journal of Geography* 64 (October 1965):304-307.

Rafferty, M. D. "Field Techniques in the Classroom: The Use of Color Slides for Field Observations of Occupance Features." *Journal of Geography* 69 (February 1970):83-88.
White, Wayne R. "Slides; A Teaching Aid in Geography." *Audiovisual Instruction* 11 (May 1966):352-54.

Health Sciences

Diefenbach, Robert C. "Freezeframe: A New Way to Augment Motion Pictures with Tape/Slide." *Audiovisual Instruction* 19 (February 1974):48-50.
Lewis, E. M. "Color Miniatures for Medical Education." *Journal of Micrographics* 10 (November 1976):59-67.
Palgi, A., and Sheridan, T. B. "Nutrition Slide Show with Audience Participation." *Journal of Nutritional Education* 9 (July/September 1977):123-26.
Zollinger, R. M., and Howe, C. T. "The Illustration of Medical Lectures." *Medical and Biological Instruction* 14 (July 1964):154-62.

History

Fitzharris, J., et al. "Slide/Sound Projects in History Classes." *Audiovisual Instruction* 18 (November 1973):14-15.
Fritzche, H. J. "Die-Serien zur Geschichte der deutschen Arbeiterbewegung [Slide series on the history of the German working-class movement]." *Bibliothekar* 29 (February 1975):81-87.
Herbert, K. "Illustrated Lecture and Its Role in Classical Studies." *Classical Journal* 66 (February 1971):227-32.
Holmes, Charles W. "History Is Fragile . . . Save It! Greeley and Weld County, Colorado." *Audiovisual Instruction* 19 (May 1974):85.

Language

Burnett, E., and Thomason, S. "Casette-Slide Show in Required Composition." *College Composition and Communication* 25 (December 1974):426-30.
Busse, B. B. "Suggestions for Preparing Material to Use with Slides, Filmstrips and Motion Picture Films." *Hispania* 56 (March 1973):200-202.
"The Film, Slide, and Filmstrip Jungle." *Modern Language Journal* 54 (May 1970): 333-35.
Galt, Alan. *Slides and the Foreign Language Teacher: A Bibliography*. ED 135-213. Available from ERIC, Document Reproduction Service, P.O. Box 190, Arlington, Virginia, 22210.
"Gestaltungskriterien für Diareihen im Fremdsprachenunterricht [Criteria for the Preparation of Filmstrips and Slides for Use in Foreign Language Instruction]." *Contact* 13 (July 1969):19-22.
Hilbert, B. "Point and Shoot: Media Projects in Technical English; Miami-Dade Community College." *American Vocational Journal* 48 (October 1973):68.
Martinelli, J. "Bilingual Slide-Tape Library Orientation." *Audiovisual Instruction* 21 (January 1976):55-56.
Meyer, R. J., and Galle, B. W., Jr. "How to Build a Composition Slide File." *College Composition and Communication* 27 (October 1976):285-87.
Rees, A. W. L. "Tape and Slide: A Case for Caution." *English Language Teachers Journal* 28 (July 1974):325-30.

Walbruck, Harry A. "Films, Slides, or Tapes: German Instruction by Films."
 NALLD Journal 5 (October 1970):19-27.

Library Orientation

Allen, K. W. "Use of Slides for Teaching Reference." *Journal of Education for
 Librarianship* 6 (Fall 1965):137-39.
Barr, K. P. "SCONUL Tape/Slide Presentations for Library Instruction." In
 Exploitation of Library Resources: A Systems Approach; a workshop at
 the Hatfield Polytechnic, April 22, 1972, edited by R. J. P. Carey, pp. 25-30.
 England: Hatfield Polytechnic, 1972.
Biermann, J. "Library Orientation in Kodachrome." *Library Journal* 8 (September 15, 1958):2456-57.
Bolvin, B. "Libraries of the Future: A Multimedia Presentation." *Library News
 Bulletin* 34 (October 1967):286-88.
Donehue, B. K. " 'Sliding' Toward Progress." *School Libraries* 11 (March 1962):
 27, 57-58.
Earnshaw, F. "Cooperative Production of Tape/Slide Guides to Library Services."
 Library Association Record 73 (October 1971):192-93.
Evans, R. W. "Using Slides for Library Orientation." *Illinois Libraries* 51 (April
 1969):300-303.
Fjällbrant, N. "Use of Slide/Tape Guides in Library Instruction." *Tid Dok* 29
 (No. 5, 1973):116-21.
Hardesty, Larry L. "Use of Slide-Tape Presentations in Academic Libraries: A
 State-of-the-Art Survey." *Journal of Academic Librarianship* 3 (July 1977):
 137-40.
Hardesty, Larry L. *Use of Slide/Tape Presentations in Academic Libraries*. New
 York: Jeffrey Norton Publishers, Inc., 1978.
Hills, P. J. "The Production of Tape/Slide Guides to Library Service." *Visual
 Education* (June 1972):21-22.
Hills, P. J., Lincoln, L., and Turner, L. P. *Evaluation of Tape-Slide Guides for
 Library Instruction*. British Library Research and Development Reports,
 5378 HC. London: British Library, Research and Development Department,
 1978.
Keel, H. K. "Library Skills; Multimedia, Curriculum-Centered Presentation."
 Instructor 83 (November 1973):32.
Keller, C. W. "Monsanto Information Center's A-V Orientation Program." *Special
 Libraries* 57 (November 1966):548-51.
Kent, N. "Sliding into the High School Library." *Educational Screen and AV
 Guide* 43 (December 1964):700.
Palmer, M. C. "Creating Slide-Tape Library Instruction: The Librarian's Role."
 Drexel Library Quarterly 8 (July 1972):251-67.
Sanner, L. E. "Stillfilmer till hjälp i nyttjarut bildningen [Tape/Slide Presentations
 as a Help in Educating Users]." *Biblioteksbladet* 59 (No. 2, 1974):23-25.
Simons, Wendell W. "Slides Introduce the Library." *California Librarian* 19
 (April 1958):113.
"Slide Show to Save a Library." *LJ/SLJ Hotline* [Library Journal/School Library
 Journal] VII-32 (October 16, 1978):2.

Stevenson, M. B. "Evaluation of Tape/Slide Presentations." In *Exploitation of Library Resources: A Systems Approach*; a workshop at the Hatfield Polytechnic, April 22, 1972, edited by R. J. P. Carey, pp. 25-30. England: Hatfield Polytechnic, 1972.

Thompson, M. "AV Look at Library Skills; Slide Tape Show on Library Methodology." *Instructor* 84 (January 1975):110.

Science

Barry, R. D., et al. "General Chemistry Slide-Audio Tape Programs; Experience since 1971." *Journal of Chemical Education* 51 (August 1974):537-38.

Bledsoe, J. C., et al. "Use of Film Slides in Introductory Microbiology." *Journal of Educational Research* 63 (October 1969):86-93.

Fine, L. W., et al. "Lap-Dissolve Slides; Multiple-Use Formats for Pre-Laboratory Instruction." *Journal of Chemical Education* 54 (February 1977):72-74.

Foss, M. F. "Use Slides for Wood Identification." *Indiana Arts and Vocational Education* 57 (October 1968):330.

Greenslade, T. B., Jr. "Laboratory Notes on Slides." *Physics Teacher* 12 (October 1974):430-32. Reply: M. Iona 13 (March 1975):132.

Harpp, David N., and Snyder, James P. "Vitalizing the Lecture: Lap-Dissolve Projection." *Journal of Chemical Education* 54 (February 1977):68-71.

Harre, P. A. "Easy Way to Teach Soldering for Electronics: Slide Series Presentation." *Indiana Education* 63 (May 1974):26-27.

Hughson, R. C. "Illustrating and Pacing with Laboratory Slides: Electronic Instrumentation for Nursing Students." *Physics Teacher* 12 (October 1974): 429-30.

Kaye, J. "Biology Lab Final on 35mm Slides." *American Biology Teacher* 38 (September 1976):348-50.

Kowles, R. "Camera in Teaching High School Biology." *American Biology Teacher* 27 (November 1965):679-82.

Lanoux, S. "Practical Slides for Professional Meetings." *Journal of Chemical Education* 50 (July 1973):476.

O'Connor, P. J. "Comparison of Three Forms of A.V. Presentation in General Science Lessons." *Graduate Research in Education* 6 (Fall, 1970):67-82.

Rozenshtein, A. M. "Use of Slides to Study Flowering Plants." *Soviet Education* 18 (February 1976):38-43.

"Sound-on-Slide Projectors Help Science Students." *College Management* 7 (May 1972):32.

"Visual Aids for Teaching Biochemical Pathways." *American Biology Teacher* 31 (February 1969):83-85.

Wendlandt, W. W., et al. "Tape-Slide Freshman Chemistry Course for Non-Science Majors." *Journal of Chemical Education* 52 (February 1975):110-11.

DIRECTORY OF DISTRIBUTORS AND MANUFACTURERS OF EQUIPMENT AND SUPPLIES

"See also" references refer to the equipment and/or supplies listing under which the complete address of a distributor and/or manufacturer is provided.

GENERAL SOURCES

Bro-Dart, Inc., 744 Broad St., Newark, New Jersey 07101 / Cabinets, cardboard slide mounts, projectors, screens, stands, viewers.

Demco Educational Corporation, 2120 Fordem Ave., Madison, Wisconsin 53701 / Card stock for slide file guides, pointers, projectors, screens, viewers.

Highsmith Co., Inc., P.O. Box 25, Fort Atkinson, Wisconsin 53538 / Complete line of slide materials and equipment.

NASCO, 901 Janesville Ave., Fort Atkinson, Wisconsin 53538 / Complete line of slide materials and equipment.

Standard Photo Supply, 43 East Chicago Ave., Chicago, Illinois 60611 / Complete line of slide materials and equipment.

Visual Horizons, 208 Westfall Road, Rochester, New York 14620 / Cabinets, light tables, projection tables and stands, slide mounting supplies, viewers.

CARRYING CASES

Brumberger Co., Inc. / Carrying cases. *See also* Mounts/Binding Materials.

Keystone Ferrule and Nut Company, 909 Milwaukee Ave., Burlington, Wisconsin 53105 / Metal carrying cases, slide files, slide sorter.

Eastman Kodak Co. / Carrying cases. *See also* Projectors and Stands.

Logan Electric Specialty Manufacturing Co., 1431 West Hubbard St., Chicago, Illinois 60622 / Metal carrying cases and/or storage units.

Nega-File, Inc. / Carrying cases. *See also* Filing and Storage Cabinets.

Seary Manufacturing Corporation / Plastic slide boxes. *See also* Mounts/Binding Materials.

Smith-Victor Corporation, Griffith, Indiana 46319 / Projection stands, slide cases, slide sorters (metal and plastic).

DUPLICATORS

AMCAM International / Slide duplicator. *See also* Plastic Album Pages.

Bencher, Inc., 333 West Lake Street, Chicago, Illinois 60606 / Bencher M/M: multimedia copying system; movable copy stage; choice of three lighting systems; can illuminate from below for copying transparencies.

Bogen Photo Corporation, 232 South Van Brunt St., P.O. Box 448, Englewood, New Jersey 07631 / Bowens Illumitran (slide duplicator).

Honeywell, Inc. / Repronar (slide duplicator). *See also* Projectors and Stands.

E. Leitz, Inc. / Reprovit copy stand with camera, slide duplicator. *See also* Projectors and Stands.

Matrix Systems Ltd. / Slide duplicator. *See also* Viewers.

Sickles, Inc. / Slide duplicator. *See also* Mounts/Binding Materials.

FILING AND STORAGE CABINETS

Advance Products Co., Inc., P.O. Box 2178, 1101 East Central, Wichita, Kansas 67214 / "Pixmobile stacking cabinets." *See also* Projectors and Stands, and Screens and Pointers.

Art Steel Company, Inc., 170 West 233rd St., Bronx, New York 10463 / Metal slide file cabinets (modified "card file").

Brumberger, Co., Inc. / Metal six-drawer slide cabinet. *See also* Mounts/Binding Materials.

Jack C. Coffey Company, Inc., P.O. Box 131, 104 Lake View Ave., Waukegan, Illinois 60085 / Luxor metal slide filing cabinets, projectors, stands, viewers.

Elden Enterprises, Inc., P.O. Box 3201, Charleston, West Virginia 25332 / Metal visual display rack slide cabinets.

Gaylord Brothers, Inc., Library Supplies and Equipment, 7272 Morgan Rd., Liverpool, New York 13088 / Luxor metal slide filing cabinet.

Ideal Business Systems, Inc., 8565 Zionsville Rd., Indianapolis, Indiana 46268 / Distributor for Kardex Systems, Inc. (present owner of Reminton Rand Systems Division), 2x2-inch metal slide filing cabinets.

Lauderdale Industries, 2448 West Larpenter, St. Paul, Minnesota 55113 / Make custom-made, removable slide trays to fit a lockable file cabinet made by Steelcase, model no. 1821L, for the Walker Art Center.

Library Bureau, Division of Mohawk Valley Community Corporation, 801 Park Avenue, Herkimer, New York 13350 / Wood 2x2-inch slide filing cabinets (customized card catalog cabinets).

Luxor Corporation, Box 830, Waukegan, Illinois 60085 / *See* Projectors and Stands.

Matrix Systems Ltd. / Matrix retrieval storage cabinet. *See also* Viewers/Slide Sorters.

Multiplex Display Fixture Company, 1555 Larkin Williams Rd., Fenton (St. Louis County), Missouri 63026 / Metal visual display rack slide cabinets.

Nega-File, Inc., P.O. Box 78, Furlong, Pennsylvania 18925 / Carrying cases for 2x2-inch and 3¼x4-inch slides, wooden filing cabinets for 2x2-inch, 2¼x2¼-inch, and 3¼x4-inch slides.

Neumade Products Corporation, Box 568, 720 White Plains Rd., Scarsdale, New York 10583 / Metal slide filing cabinets.

Remington Rand, Inc. / *See* Library Bureau, and Ideal Business Systems, Inc.

Steelcase, Inc., 1120 39th St., SE, Grand Rapids, Michigan 49508 / Metal slide filing cabinets.

Supreme Equipment and Systems Corp., 170 53rd St., Brooklyn, New York 11120 / "Conserva File" (metal file modified for slide storage).

University Products, Inc. / Slide storage cabinets (Bretford). *See also* Materials for Film Care/Preservation.

Wallach and Associates, Inc., P.O. Box 18167, 1532 Hillcrest Blvd., Cleveland, Ohio 44118 / Metal slide filing cabinets.

H. Wilson Corporation, 555 West Taft Drive, South, Holland, Illinois 60473 / Metal slide filing cabinet.

FILE GUIDES

Demco Educational Corporation / Custom-ordered file guides, plastic card stock. *See also* General.

Koller and Smith Co., Inc., 532 5th Ave., Pelham, New York 11201 / Fibreboard with plastic file guides.

Library Bureau, Division of Sperry Rand Corp., 801 Park Ave., P.O. Box 271, Herkimer, New York 13350 / Mylar Slide File Guides; Remington Rand Kardex cards, cardboard, 2¼x2¼-inch (blue, buff, ecru, green, salmon, white).

LIGHT TABLES

Engstrom Enterprises / Light tables. *See also* Viewers/Slide Sorters.

Hamilton Industries, 1975 Evans St., Two Rivers, Wisconsin 54241 / Dial-A-Light tables; tracing tables.

Stacor Corporation, 285 Emmet St., Newark, New Jersey 07114 / Illuminated sorting tables.

MATERIALS FOR FILM CARE/PRESERVATION

Edwal Scientific Products Corporation, 12120 South Peoria, Chicago, Illinois 60643 / Anti-static slide cleaner; chemical product for preventing fungus on slides (Permafilm) and for dust and static control.

W. R. Grace & Co., Davison Chemical, Baltimore, Maryland 21226 / Silica Gel Air Dryer, (SW 0-6) K77-35-0022.

Multiform Desiccant Products, Inc., 1418 Niagara St., Buffalo, New York 14213 / Dri-Can producers (a dessicant material attracting water vapor, condensing it by holding it physically through surface absorption); useful to protect books, paintings, valuable art objects, and museum and historical artifacts from moisture and high humidity.

TALAS, Technical Library Service, 104 Fifth Avenue, New York, New York 10011 / Acid-free envelopes for photographs and film, chemicals for preservation purposes, plastic sleeves.

University Products, Inc., P.O. Box 101, South Canal Street, Holyoke, Massachusetts 01040 / Acid-free board and paper, Chartpak tape, plastic album pages, projection screens, slide storage cabinets (Bretford), and archival quality materials.

MOUNTS/BINDING MATERIALS

AGFA-Gevaert, Inc., Photographic Products, 275 North Street, Teterboro, New Jersey 07068 / Plastic slide mounts (Agfacolor Dia-Frames).

American Library Color Slide Company, Box 5810 Grand Central Station, New York, New York 10017 / Plastic slide mounts (Lindia, Titania), slide labels.

Audio-Visual Accessories & Supplies (AVAS), 196 Holt Street, Hackensack, New Jersey 07602 / Slide mounting supplies.

Avery Label Co., 1385 Livingston Ave., New Brunswick, New Jersey 08902 / Slide Labels.

Brumberger Co., Inc., 1948 Troutman Street, Brooklyn, New York 11237 / Binders, all-metal slide binder with glass.

Byers Photo Equipment Co., 6955 SW Sandburg, Portland, Oregon 97223 / Plastic slide mounts, presses, slide binding, heat sealing (for paper and plastic mounts).

Chartpak Rotex, Division Avery Products Corporation, 2620 South Susan St., Santa Ana, California 92704 / Masking tape.

Dazor Manufacturing Corporation, 4455-99 Duncan Ave., St. Louis, Missouri 63110 / High intensity lamps, illuminated magnifiers, incandescent and fluorescent portable lighting fixtures, magnifying lamps for binding slides.

Dot Line Corporation, 11916 Valerio St., North Hollywood, California 91605/ DL-3001 slide frames (glassless; use in manual or tray-fed projectors).

Edwal Scientific Products Corporation, 12120 South Peoria, Chicago, Illinois 60643 / Anti-stat cleaner; chemical product for preventing fungus on slides (Permafilm).

Emde Products, Inc., 2040 Stoner Ave., Los Angeles, California 90025 / Aluminum and glass mounts, slide binders and masks for 2x2-inch, 2-3/4x2-3/4-inch, and 3¼x4-inch slides, slide supplies.

HP Marketing Corporation, 216 Little Falls Road, Cedar Grove, New Jersey 07009 / Plastic slide binders (Gepe).

Heindl Masks 'n' Mounts, 200 St. Paul St., Rochester, New York 14604 / Slide mounting, mounting and storage equipment, viewers, projectors, and stands.

Karl Heitz, Inc., 979 Third Ave., New York, New York 10022 / Reader-projector for rapid evaluation of 35mm slides, projection stands, plastic slide mounts (Lindia), table viewers, viewers, zoom pocket microscopes.

Kaiser Corporation, 3555 North Prospect St., Colorado Springs, Colorado 80907 / Plastic slide mounts, slide mounting materials.

Kalt Corporation, P.O. Box 511, Santa Monica, California 90406 / Slide mounting supplies.

The Kimac Co., 478 Longhill Road, Guilford, Connecticut 06437 / Plastic slide covers, slide mounting supplies.

Kindermann, Division of EPOI International, Ltd., 623 Stewart Ave., Garden City, New York 11533 / Plastic slide mounts.

Eastman Kodak Co. / Slide masks (tape and paper strips), metal mount with glass. *See also* Projectors and Stands.

E. Leitz, Inc. / Slide masks, aluminum slide mounts (Perrotcolor). *See also* Projectors and Stands.

Multiplex Display Fixture Co. / Mounting supplies. *See also* Filing and Storage Cabinets.

Neumade Products Corporation / Mounting supplies. *See also* Filing and Storage Cabinets.

Nuclear Products Company, P.O. Box 5178, El Monte, California 91734 / Anti-static glass cleaning brush, mounting materials, static eliminators.

Pako Corporation, 6300 Olson Memorial Highway, Minneapolis, Minnesota 55440 / Slide mounting system and equipment.

Photo Plastic International, 1639A 12th St., Santa Monica, California 90404 / Clark plastic mounts.

Plastic Sealing Corporation / Mounting supplies. *See also* Plastic Album Pages.

Professional Tape Co., Inc., Time Products Co., 144 Tower Drive, Burr Ridge (Hinsdale), Illinois 60521 / "Time Labels," permanent adhesive slide labels.

Radio-Mat Slide Company, Inc., 444 North Peninsula Dr., Daytona Beach, Florida 32018 / Mounting materials (Radio Mat slides).

Seary Manufacturing Corporation, 19 Nebraska Ave., Endicott, New York 13760 / Slide mounting equipment (film cutters, mounting press, etc.), mounts without glass.

Sickles, Inc., Photo Equipment Division, P.O. Box 3396, Scottsdale, Arizona 85257 / Plastic slide mounts (Gepe), slide duplicators, slide production equipment.

Starex Inc., 655 Schuyler Ave., Kearny, New Jersey 07032 / Slide mounts (plastic and cardboard), "60 Second Slide Kit" (slide production procedures for making slides from a thermal copier [3M secretary] or paper copier [Xerox or IBM]).

3M Company / Photographic tape No. 235 for slide masking. *See also* Projectors and Stands.

University Products, Inc. / Slide labels, acid-free paper. *See also* Materials for Film Care/Preservation.

Wess Plastic Molds Company, 50 Schmitt Blvd., Farmingdale, New York 11735 / Wess plastic slide mounts.

PLASTIC ALBUM PAGES

AMCAM International, 813 North Franklin, Chicago, Illinois 60610 / Slide preservers, vinyl sheets.

Bardes Plastics, Inc., 5225 West Clinton Ave., Milwaukee, Wisconsin 53223 / Plastic holders for slides (for three-ring binder or file folder).

Erskine Co., 16-18 West 22nd St., New York, New York 10010 / Slide-Sho pages.

Franklin Distributors Corporation, P.O. Box 320, Denville, New Jersey 07834 / SAF-T-STOR slide filing system.

Arthur A. Kesler, 2204 Pattiglen Ave., La Verne, California 91750 / Hanging slide storage sheets.

Matrix Systems Ltd. / PVC Pages (Slidemaster System). *See also* Viewers/Slide Sorters.

Photo Plastic International / Vinyl slide storage sheets. *See also* Mounts/Binding Materials.

Plastic Sealing Corporation, 1507 North Gardner St., Hoolywood, California 90046 / VIS slide file folios for three-ring binders.

Plastican Corporation, 33 Laurel St., Butler, New Jersey 07405 / Plastic slide frames for three-ring binders.

Richard Manufacturing Company, 5914 Noble Ave., Van Nuys, California 91404 / Plastic "Album Pages" for three-ring binders for 2x2-inch and 2¼x2¼-inch slides.

TALAS / Plastic Album Pages. *See also* Materials for Film Care/Preservation.

20th Century Plastics, Inc., 3628 Crenshaw Boulevard, Los Angeles, California 90016 / Heavy duty vinyl pages for slides, prints, and negatives.

University Products, Inc. / Plastic pages. *See also* Materials for Film Care/Preservation.

PROJECTORS AND STANDS

Airequipt, Inc., 20 Jones St., New Rochelle, New York 10802 / Automatic slide projectors.

Applied Research and Engineering, Inc., 1475 Barnum Ave., Bridgeport, Connecticut 06610 / Rear projection screens, slide changers and controls, and projector dissolve units.

Berkey Technical, Division of Berkey Photo, Inc. / *See* Keystone, Division of Berkey Photo, Inc.

Charles Beseler Company, 216 South 18th St., East Orange, New Jersey 07018 / 3¼x4-inch projectors.

The Brewster Corporation, 50 River St., Old Saybrook, Connecticut 06475 / Projectors, screens (including Robo-Wall), viewers.

Brumberger Co., Inc. / Slide projectors. *See also* Mounts/Binding Materials.

Buhl Optical Company, 1009 Beech Ave., Pittsburgh, Pennsylvania 15233 / Projectors.

Buhl Projector Co., Division Bergen Laboratories, 60 Spruce St., Paterson, New Jersey 07501 / Overhead projectors.

Jack C. Coffey, Inc. / Projectors and stands. *See also* Filing and Storage Cabinets.

Compco Corporation, 1800 North Spaulding Ave., Chicago, Illinois 60647 / Projection stands, 3-D slide projectors.

Decision Systems, Inc., 200 Route 17, Mahwah, New Jersey 07430 / Dial-A-Slide random access projector.

Dot Line Corporation / Projectors and stands. *See also* Mounts/Binding Materials.

DuKane Corp., Audio-Visual Division, 2900 DuKane Dr., St. Charles, Illinois 60174 / Projectors, synchronizers.

Fordham Equipment, 3308 Edson Ave., Bronx, New York 10469 / Slide projectors.

Heindl Masks 'n' Mounts / Projectors and stands. *See also* Mounts/Binding Materials.

Karl Heitz, Inc. / Projection stands. *See also* Mounts/Binding Materials.

Honeywell, Inc., Photographic Products Division, P.O. Box 1010, Littleton, Colorado 80120 / Preview projectors (no screen required, preview area is part of projector), projectors, slide duplicators.

Hudson Photographic Industries, Inc. / *See* Prima Education Products Division.

International Audio Visual, Inc. / Projectors, stands. *See also* Screens and Pointers.

Jostens Library Services / Projectors and stands. *See also* Viewers/Slide Sorters.

Kalt Corporation / Projectors and stands. *See also* Mounts/Binding Materials.

Ken-A-Vision Manufacturing Company, Inc., 5615 Raytown Rd., Raytown, Missouri 64133 / Micro-projectors.

Keystone, Division of Berkey Photo Corporation, Keystone Place, Paramus, New Jersey 07652 / Projectors.

The Klitten Company, Inc., 1221 Ocean Ave., Santa Monica, California 90401 / Projectors, synchronizers and programmers.

Eastman Kodak Company, 343 State St., Rochester, New York 14650 / Projectors, stands.

E. Leitz, Inc., Link Drive, Rockleigh, New Jersey 07647 / Aluminum slide mounts (Perrot-Color binders and Per-O-Slide binders); 30mm x 30mm mounts for Minox slides; projectors; slide duplicators.

Luxor Corporation / Projection tables and stands. *See also* Filing and Storage Cabinets.

Neumade Products Corporation / Projection tables and stands. *See also* Filing and Storage Cabinets.

Optical Radiation Corporation, 6352 North Irwindale, Azusa, California 91702 /
Xenographic Model 500 high intensity slide projector.

Ludwig Pani, Kandlgasse 23, 1070 Wien, Austria/Pani projector.

Prima Education Products Division / Projectors. *See also* Screens and Pointers—
Rear Projection Screens.

Smith-Victor Corporation / Projection tables and stands. *See also* Carrying Cases.

George R. Snell, Associates, Inc. / Projectors, 2x2-inch and 3¼x4-inch, and stands.
See also Screens and Pointers.

Spindler and Sauppe, Inc., 13034 Saticoy St., North Hollywood, California 91605 /
A-V programmers, multi-speed dissolve controls, pointers (illuminated),
projectors.

Viewlex Audio-Visual, Inc., 1 Broadway Ave., Holbrook, Long Island, New York
11741 / Projectors.

H. Wilson Corporation / Projection tables and stands. *See also* Filing and Storage
Cabinets.

Sound Slide Projectors

Bell & Howell Co., Audio Visual Products Division, 7100 McCormick Road, Chicago,
Illinois 60645 / Sound slide projectors with built-in screen.

Creatron, Inc., 36 Cherry Lane, Floral Park, New York 11001 / Sound slide projectors with built-in screen.

Graflex Division / *See* The Singer Corporation.

Gruber Products Company / Sound slide projectors. *See also* Screens.

Hoppmann Corporation, 5410 Port Royal Rd., Springfield, Virginia 22151 /Sound
slide projectors, rear screen projection systems.

The Kalart Victor Corporation, P.O. Box 112, Hultenius St., Plainville, Connecticut
06062 / Sound slide projectors.

Montage Productions, Inc., 9 Industrial Drive, Rutherford, New Jersey 07070 /
Sound-slide projectors.

Pro-Gamo, Inc., 118 East 29th St., New York, New York 10016 / Sound slide
projectors (slide filmstrip sound synchronizer).

The Singer Corporation, 3750 Monroe Ave., Rochester, New York 14603 / Sound
slide projectors with built-in screen.

Standard Projector and Equipment Co., Inc., 3080 Lake Terrace, Glenview, Illinois
60025 / Sound slide projectors.

**3M Company (Minnesota Mining and Manufacturing Company), Visual Products
Division,** 3M Center, St. Paul, Minnesota 55101 / Sound-on-slide systems.

Victor Animatograph Corporation / *See* The Kalart Victor Corporation.

SCREENS AND POINTERS

Advance Products Co., Inc. / Screens (cabinet and table-top). *See also* Filing
and Storage Cabinets.

Applied Research and Engineering, Inc. / Screens. *See also* Projectors and Stands.

Brumberger Co., Inc. / Screens. *See also* Mounts/Binding Materials.

Buhl Optical Co. / Screens (cabinet-type table-top). *See also* Projectors and Stands.

Da-Lite Screen Company, Inc., P.O. Box 629, Warsaw, Indiana 46580 / Screens.

Dot Line Corporation / Screens. *See also* Mounts/Binding Materials.

Draper Shade and Screen Company, P.O. Box 108, Spiceland, Indiana 47385 / Screens, room darkening shades.

Ednalite Corporation / Pointers. *See also* Viewers/Slide Sorters.

Fordham Equipment Co. / Screens. *See also* Projectors and Stands.

International Audio Visual, Inc., 15818 Arminta St., Seattle, Washington 98121 / Black screens, pointers, projectors, screens, stands, xenon light sources.

Josten's Library Services / Screens. *See also* Viewers/Slide Sorters.

Kalt Corporation / Screens and pointers. *See also* Mounts/Binding Materials.

Eastman Kodak Co. / Screens. *See also* Projectors and Stands.

Montage Productions, Inc. / Screens. *See also* Sound/Slide Projectors.

Polacoat, Inc., 9750 Conklin Rd., Cincinnati, Ohio 45242 / Rear projection screens—table-top units, screens.

Raven Screen Corporation, 124 East 124th St., New York, New York 10035 / Screens.

The Singer Corporation / Screens. *See also* Sound Slide Projectors.

George R. Snell, Associates, Inc., 155 U.S. Route 22, Eastbound, Springfield, New Jersey 07081 / A-V systems (automatic sequential front and rear screen projection system), lecterns, pointers, projectors, screens, stands.

Spindler and Sauppe, Inc. / Pointers. *See also* Projectors and Stands.

Trans-Lux News-Sign Corporation, 625 Madison Ave., New York, New York 10022 / Rear projection screens.

University Products, Inc. / Screens. *See also* Film Care/Preservation Materials.

Rear Projection Screens—Table-Top Models

Lester A. Dine, Inc., 2080 Jericho Turnpike, New Hyde Park, New York 11042 / Projectors, rear projection screens, stands, viewers.

Elden Enterprises, Inc. / Rear projection screens and combination mobile projection table and screen cabinet. *See also* Filing and Storage Cabinets.

GAF Corporation / Rear projection screens. *See also* Viewers/Slide Sorters.

Gruber Products Company, 5254 Jackman Rd., Toledo, Ohio 43613 / Projection stands, screen unit (table-top), sound slide viewers, viewers with stands.

Hoppman Corporation / Rear projection systems. *See also* Sound Slide Projectors.

Polacoat, Inc. / Rear projection screens (table-top). *See also* Screens and Pointers.

Prima Education Products Division, Hudson Photographic Industries, Inc., 2 South Buckout Street, Irvington-On-Hudson, New York 10533 / Rear projection screens (Caritel, HPI Telescreen).

Seebamil Sales Corporation / *See* GAF Corporation.

VIEWERS/SLIDE SORTERS

AGFA-Gevaert, Inc., Camera-Werk, Tegernseer Landstrasse 161, 8000 Munich 90, Germany/Slide viewer.

Baia Corporation, 9353 Lee Rd., R7, Jackson, Michigan 49201 / Viewers.

The Brewster Corporation / *See* Projectors and Stands.

Brumberger Co., Inc. / Electrical slide viewer (up to 2¼-inch square). *See also* Mounts/Binding Materials.

Jack C. Coffey, Inc. / Viewers. *See also* Filing and Storage Cabinets.

Compco Corporation / Slide sorters. *See also* Projectors and Stands.

Ednalite Corporation, 210 North Water St., Peekskill, New York 10566 / Editor/ transviewer with magnifinder, electric projection pointer, magnifier.

Engstrom Enterprises, 1421 South Congress, Austin, Texas 78704 / Table-top viewers.

GAF Corporation, Pictorial Products Division, 140 West 51st St., New York, New York 10020 / Rear projection screens, viewers.

Gruber Products Co. / Viewers with stands. *See also* Screens and Pointers—Rear Projection Screens.

Heindl Masks 'n' Mounts / Viewers. *See also* Mounts/Binding Materials.

Karl Heitz, Inc. / *See* Mounts/Binding Materials.

Josten's Library Services, 1301 Cliff Road, Burnsville, Minnesota 55337 / Viewers.

Kalt Corporation / Pocket slide viewer. *See also* Mounts/Binding Materials.

Keystone Ferrule and Nut Company / Slide sorters. *See also* Carrying Cases.

Kinderman / Viewer. *See also* Mounts/Binding Materials.

Leedal, Inc. / *See* Matrix Systems Ltd.

Logan Electric Specialty Manufacturing Co. / Slide sorters. *See also* Carrying Cases.

Macbeth, Division of Kollmorgen, P.O. Box 950, Little Britain Road, Newburgh, New York 12550 / Previewer.

Matrix Systems Ltd., Division Leedal Ind., 2929 South Halsted, Chicago, Illinois 60608 / Slide and transparency viewers.

Multiplex Display Fixture Co. / Viewers. *See also* Filing and Storage Cabinets.

Seebamil Sales Corporation / *See* GAF Corporation.

Smith-Victor Corporation / Slide sorters. *See also* Carrying Cases.

Texwood A/V Systems / *See* Engstrom Enterprises.

Tru-Vue Company / *See* GAF Corporation.

MISCELLANEOUS

Edmund Scientific, 100 Edscorp Building, Barrington, New Jersey 08007 / Photo and optical items (color wheels for slide projectors).

IDenticard Systems Inc., 630 East Oregon Road, Box 5349, Lancaster, Pennsylvania 17601 / AV laminators, color lifts equipment and supplies.

DIRECTORY OF SLIDE SOURCES

"See also" references refer to the source listing under which the complete address of a distributor and/or slide producer is provided.

GENERAL SOURCES

American Library Color Slide Company, Inc., Box 5810 Grand Central Station, New York, New York 10017 / Art, earth science, history, science.

American Museum of Natural History, Photography Division, Central Park West at 79th St., New York, New York 10024 / Animals, anthropology, archaeology, art, geography, science.

The Center for Humanities, Inc., Two Holland Ave., White Plains, New York 10603 / Arts, communications, earth sciences, home economics, social sciences (sound-slide sets).

Creative Arts Studio, Inc., 1611 Connecticut Ave., Washington, D.C. 20009 / Produces slides from script to screen, any area; e.g., art, and care and treatment of diabetes.

Robert Davis Productions, P.O. Box 12, Cary, Illinois 60013 / Art (American, Asian, and European architecture, painting and sculpture), geography/travel, history, music, science.

Demco Educational Corporation, 2120 Fordem Ave., Madison, Wisconsin 53704 / Agriculture, arts, geography/travel, history, home economics, history, science, etc.

Denoyer-Geppert Audiovisuals, 355 Lexington Ave., New York, New York 60640 / Art, earth science, geography/travel, science.

Educational Dimensions Group, Division of Educational Dimensions Corp., Box 126, Stamford, Connecticut 06904 / Arts, education, humanities, language arts, social sciences.

Encyclopaedia Britannica Educational Corporation, 425 North Michigan Ave., Chicago, Illinois 60611.

Environmental Communications, 62 Windward Ave., Venice, California 90291 / Man's relationship to his environment; e.g., Paolo Soleri, urban crowd behavior, art, architecture videotapes; groups, social groups and environment; pollution, cities, communes, television.

European Art Color Slides, Peter Adelberg, Inc., 120 West 70th St., New York, New York 10023 / Art (American painting, European architecture, painting, sculpture, Egyptian, Central American, Mexico and Guatemala), geography/travel, history, science.

The Field Museum of Natural History, The Education Dept., Roosevelt Road at Lake Shore Drive, Chicago, Illinois 60605.

John Fraser Associates, P.O. Box 157, Alamo, California 94507 / Education, performing arts, sports, travel, training for library aides ("library page training").

GAF Corporation, Pictorial Products Division, 140 West 51st St., New York, New York 10020 / Apollo moon landing, art, geography/travel.

Goldsmith's Music Shop, Inc., Language Dept., 301 East Shore Road, Great Neck, Long Island 11023 / Art, geography/travel, history, science; agent for Veronesi Slide Company of Paris.

Guidance Associates. / *See* Harcourt Brace Jovanovich, Inc.

Harcourt Brace Jovanovich, Inc., 757 Third Ave., New York, New York 10017 / Biology, history, mathematics, science.

Johnson's Farm, 1729 Laurel St., Madison, Wisconsin 53705 / Slides, films and filmstrips for education, slides that document present status of Chicago architecture and ancient to modern architecture.

McIntyre Visual Publications, Inc., 716 Center Street, Lewistown, New York 14092 / Arts, earth sciences, travel/geography, humanities, etc.

C.V. Mosby Company, Subsidiary of Times Mirror Company, 11830 Westline Industrial Drive, St. Louis, Missouri 63141 / Earth sciences, education, medicine, science, social sciences, sports.

National Audiovisual Center, National Archives and Records Service, General Services Administration, Reference Section GA, Washington, D.C. 20409 / General.

National Film Board of Canada, 1251 Avenue of the Americas, New York, New York 10020 / Arts and crafts, health, science, social studies (Canadian).

Playette Corporation, 301 East Shore Rd., Great Neck, New York 11023 / Art, geography/travel, history, science.

Roloc Color Slides, P.O. Box 1715, Washington, D.C. 20013 / Art, geography/ travel, history, science (Apollo 14 slides).

SECAS International Company, 400 Notre Dame St. East, Montreal, 127 Quebec, Canada / Art, geography/travel, history, science.

Smithsonian Institution, Photographic Services, Washington, D.C. 20560 / Anthropology, art, geography/travel, history, science, and exhibitions at the Smithsonian Institution.

Smithsonian Institution, The Conservation Information Program, Office of Museum Programs, Smithsonian Institution, Washington, D.C. 20560 / Slide series on the Conservation Information Program, includes a script, cassette or single-side audio tape and one-two carousel trays. Samples of titles: Removing Tape from Paper Objects; The Cleaning of Prints, Drawings, and Manuscripts on Paper.

Society for Visual Education, Inc. (SVE), Division of The Singer Company, 1345 Diversey Parkway, Chicago, Illinois 60614 / Art, geography/travel, history, science.

State University of New York at Buffalo, Instructional Communication Center, Media Library, 22 Foster Annex, Buffalo, New York 14214 / Art, geography/travel, history, technology.

Unipub, Box 433, Murray Hill Station, New York, New York 10016 / U.S. source for publications (books, slides, records) of United Nations agencies and other international publishers.

Universal Color Slides Company, 136 West 32nd St., New York, New York 10001 / Art, geography/travel, history.

G. W. Van Leer and Associates, 1850 North Fremont Ave., Chicago, Illinois 60614 / Custom design and production in all visual communication media internationally.

World Color Slides, 21 Schoen Place, Pittsford, New York 14534 / Arts, life and culture of 72 countries.

AGRICULTURE

Covalda Date Company, P.O. Box 908, Coachella, California 92236 / Date growing, desert culture, desert scenes.

The Fertilizer Institute, 1015 18th St. N.W., Washington, D.C. 20036 / Agriculture, agronomy, safety and maintenance.

Media Services, New York State College of Agriculture and Life Sciences, Cornell University, Department of Communication Arts, 412 Roberts Hall, Ithaca, New York 14850 / Agriculture, human ecology.

NASCO, 901 Janesville Ave., Fort Atkinson, Wisconsin 53538 / Home economics, science, vocational agriculture.

Pan American Development Foundation / *See* Housing.

U.S. Department of Agriculture, Office of Information, Photography Division, Washington, D.C. 20250 / Activities of the U.S. Department of Agriculture.

Vocational Education Productions, California State Polytechnic College, San Luis Obispo, California 93401.

ART (INCLUDES ARCHAEOLOGY AND ARCHITECTURE)

Ancora, Consejo de Ciento, 160, (Edificio Creta), Barcelona 15, Spain / Ancient, Asian, Egyptian, and modern art, and Spanish architecture, painting, sculpture, and decorative arts.

Archaeological Institute of America, 260 West Broadway, New York, New York 10013 / Archaeology, European and South American architecture, painting, and sculpture.

Art Color Slides, Inc. / *See* Francis G. Mayer.

Art Council Aids, P.O. Box 641, Beverly Hills, California 90213 / African, American Indian, American painting, pre-Columbian and primitive art.

ART IN AMERICA, 850 Third Avenue, New York, New York, 10022 / Selected visual content of ART IN AMERICA magazine on high-quality slides.

Art Now, University Galleries, Inc., 144 North 14th St., Kenilworth, New Jersey 07033 / Emphasis on contemporary art.

Arts in Society, University of Wisconsin Extension, Room 728 Lowell Hall, 610 Langdon St., Madison, Wisconsin 53706 / Offers instructional research packages: The Arts and Crafts in Kenyan Society; Art and Environment; Art and Social Revolution; Art and Technology; The Street As a Creative Vision.

Austrian Institute, 11 East 52nd St., New York, New York 10022 / European art, geography/travel, history, science. Will loan to universities and colleges.

Avid Corporation / *See* Budek Films and Slides, Inc.

Blackhawk Films, Eastin-Phelan Corporation / *See* Geography/Travel.

Blauel Art Slides, Postfach 1121, Gauting, Germany.

Budek Films & Slides, Inc., Box 4309, 1023 Waterman Ave., East Providence, Rhode Island 02914 / Architecture and related arts. *See also* Visual Education, Inc.

Barney Burstein, Photographer, Original Color Slides, 29 Commonwealth Ave., Boston, Massachusetts 02116 / Minor arts, painting, and sculpture. Emphasis on art in American museums and galleries.

Carman Educational Associates, Inc. / Modern typography. *See also* Geography/Travel.

Le Centre de Documentation Yvan Bouler , Box 292, Postal Station "E," Montreal, Quebec H2T 3A7, Canada / Promotion of Canadian visual arts by publishing and distributing slide series: architecture, painting, photography, printmaking, and sculpture.

Color Slide Enterprises, Box 150, Oxford, Ohio 45056 / Ancient Greek and Roman sculpture and works in the Louvre.

Creative Concepts of California, P.O. Box 649, Carlsbad, California 92008 / American and European art and architecture, North and West Africa, Byzantine art, Mexico, Egypt, and "color slides of nature" (e.g., lines, forms, colors).

The Dunlap Society, Visual Documentation Program, Essex, New York 12936 / Visual archive of American Art, includes microfiche and slides, *The Architecture of Washington, D.C.*, Volume I.

The Eastin-Phelan Distributing Corporation / *See* Blackhawk Films Eastin-Phelan Corporation.

Les Editions Yvan Boulerice / *See* Le Centre de Documentation Yvan Boulerice.

Educational Art Transparencies / *See* Geography/Travel.

Educational Audio Visual, Inc. (EAV), Pleasantville, New York 10570 / African, American, Asian, and European architecture, painting, and sculpture.

Educational Lantern Slide Project, College Art Association, 16 East 52nd St., New York, New York 10022.

Embassy of the Polish People's Republic, Press Office, Information Officer, 2640 Sixteenth St. N.W., Washington, D.C. 20009 / Polish architecture, painting and sculpture.

FACSEA, Society for French-American Cultural Services and Educational Aid, 972 Fifth Ave., New York, New York 10021 / European architecture, painting and sculpture, geography/travel.

Four Continent Book Corporation, 156 Fifth Ave., New York, New York 10010 / U.S.S.R.: architecture, art, geography/travel (cities, gardens, resorts).

Graphic Arts Technical Foundation, Inc., 4615 Forbes Ave., Pittsburgh, Pennsylvania 15213 / Graphic arts.

Harper and Row Publishers, Inc. / Women artists. *See also* Science.

Heaton-Sessions, 313 West Fourth Street, New York, New York 10014 / Slides for standard art history/appreciation texts.

Hispanic Society of America / *See* Geography/Travel.

Imago Color Slides, P.O. Box 811, Chapel Hill, North Carolina 27514 / Emphasis on ancient architecture, minor arts, and medieval sculpture.

Instruction Resources Corporation, 12121 Dove Circle, Laurel, Maryland 20811 / Achievements of American women, development of U.S. cities, events in transportation history, etc., taken from photos and drawings in the files of the Library of Congress, the National Archives, the Smithsonian Institution, and other public and private sources.

International Museum of Photography, Office of Extension Activities, 900 East Ave., Rochester, New York 14607 / The history of photography.

Kahana Film Productions / Central American architecture, painting, and sculpture. *See also* Geography/Travel.

McGraw-Hill Book Company, 330 West 42nd St., New York, New York 10036 / "Color Slide Program of Art Enjoyment."

Francis G. Mayer, Art Color Slides, Inc., 235 East 50th St., New York, New York 10022 / American, Asian, European architecture, painting, and sculpture, and South American painting.

Miniature Gallery, 60 Rushett Close, Long Ditton, Surrey, England / African, American and Asian painting and sculpture, European and South American architecture, painting, sculpture, and decorative arts.

Museum of Fine Arts, Slide Library, Boston, Massachusetts 02115 / "Slide Sets 1978-79."

The Museum of Modern Art, Museum Bookstore, 11 West 53rd St., New York, New York 10019 / American and European painting and sculpture, other slides from MOMA collection are available from Sandak, Inc.

National Gallery of Art, Extension Service, Washington, D.C. 20565 / Slides of National Gallery's collection.

William Rockhill Nelson Gallery of Art and Mary Atkins Museum of Fine Arts, 4525 Oak St., Kansas City, Missouri 64111 / American architecture, painting, and sculpture; Asian and European painting and sculpture.

Pan American Development Foundation / Pre-Columbian pottery and sculpture; South American architecture, painting and sculpture. *See also* Housing.

Philadelphia Museum of Art, Slide Library, Parkway at 26th St., Philadelphia, Pennsylvania 19130 / African, American, Asian, European, South American architecture, painting, and sculpture.

William Protheroe, P.O. Box 898, Chula Vista, California 92102 / Graphic art, sculpture, twentieth century painting.

Prothmann Associates, Inc., 650 Thomas Ave., Baldwin, New York 11510 / African, American, Asian, European architecture, painting, and sculpture. Exclusive distributor for following slide producers: Bijutsu Shuppan-Sha, Tokyo; Editions Rencontre, Switzerland; Educational Productions, England; Hannibal, Athens; Kunsthistorisches Museum, Vienna; Polygoon, Amsterdam; Publications of Art and Art History, Paris; Sans Vega, Madrid; Slide Center, England; Dr. Franz Stoedtner, Berlin; Valdagno, Italy.

Rosenthal Art Slides, 5456 South Ridgewood Court, Chicago, Illinois 60615 / Emphasis on contemporary American and European architecture, painting, and sculpture; advertising art; Australian Aboriginal art; Mexican and Mohammedan architecture.

Sandak, Inc., 180 Harvard Ave., Stamford, Connecticut 06902 / Emphasis on eighteenth century to present American and European art. African, American, Asian and European architecture, painting and sculpture, graphic arts.

Saskia Cultural Documentation, Renate Wiedenhoeft, 6931 South Yukon Way, Littleton, Colorado 80123 / American and European painting, sculpture, and architecture.

Scala Fine Arts Publishers, Inc., 28 West 44th St., New York, New York 10036 / European architecture, painting and sculpture.

Spitz Laboratories, Inc. / *See* McGraw-Hill Book Company.

Taurgo Slides, 154 East 82nd St., New York, New York 10028 / African, American, Asian, European architecture, painting, and sculpture; South American architecture and sculpture.

The United Presbyterian Church, Mission Program Information, Commission on Ecumenical Mission and Relations. Room 1268, 475 Riverside Dr., New York, New York 10027 / African, Asian, and South American painting and sculpture.

University of Washington Press / African sculpture. *See also* Science.

The University Prints, 21 East St., Winchester, Massachusetts 01890 / African, American, Asian, and European architecture, painting, and sculpture.

Visual Education, Inc., Box 6039, Santa Barbara, California 93111 / Architecture and related arts. *See also* Budek Films & Slides, Inc.

Visual Resources, Inc. (Eva Wisbar), 152 West 42nd St., No. 1219, New York, New York 10036 / Emphasis on twentieth century contemporary arts.

The Walters Art Gallery, 600 North Charles St., Baltimore, Maryland 21201 / American and European painting and sculpture.

Architecture and Architectural Sculpture

American Institute of Architects, 1735 New York Avenue, N.W., Washington, D.C. 20006 / Produces slides sets, arts, social sciences.

Wayne Andrews, 521 Neff Road. Gross Pointe, Michigan 48230 / American and European architecture.

Architectural Color Slides, 187 Grant St., Lexington, Massachusetts 02173 / American, Australian, Canadian, European, Mexican, and New Zealand architecture.

Architectural Delineations, 20 Waterside Plaza, New York, New York 10016 / American, Asian, European, and South American architecture and sculpture, art nouveau, European history.

Educational Art Transparencies, Richard N. Campen Architectural Color Slide Collection, 27 West Summit St., Chagrin Falls, Ohio 44022 / American, Canadian, European and Mexican architecture, geography/travel.

FACSEA / French architecture. *See also* Art.

Kai Dib Films International / *See* Geography/Travel.

Robert F. McConnell, Producer of Travelslide Classics, 4447 Que St., N.W., Washington, D.C. 20007 / American, Asian, Central American, European, Mexican, and South American architecture, geography/travel, history.

Joseph P. Messana, Photographer, 5574 Lakewood, Detroit, Michigan 48213 / American, European, South American architecture and sculpture.

National Cathedral Association, Slides and Film Section, Washington Cathedral, Mount St. Alban, Washington, D.C. 20016 / Washington Cathedral.

Soleri Slide Series, Cosanti Foundation, 6433 Doubletree Road, Scottsdale, Arizona 85253.

State Historical Society of Wisconsin / Wisconsin architecture. *See also* Costume.

U.S. Department of Housing and Urban Development / American and European architecture. *See also* Housing.

Black Art

Educational Dimensions Corporation / Black studies. *See also* Art.

The Ethnic American Art Slide Library, College of Arts and Sciences, University of South Alabama, Mobile, Alabama 36608 / Published catalog of art slides of works by Afro-Americans, Mexican-Americans, and Native Americans.

Harmon Foundation, Inc., 598 Madison Ave., New York, New York 10801.

Prothmann Associates, Inc. / *See* Art.

Sandak, Inc. / *See* Art.

SEMA (Sanders Educational Media Association), 5271 West Pico Boulevard, Los Angeles, California 90019 / Black art and art of West Africa.

Crafts and Folk Arts

American Crafts Council, 44 West 53rd St., New York, New York 10019 / Slides for rent and purchase. Slide kits on clay, fiber, glass, metal, multimedia (e.g., American Indian jewelry, ceramics and wood sculpture, cultural artifacts, et.), wood. Sets on women artists.

Cooper Hewitt (Smithsonian Institution), 9 East 90th St., New York, New York 10028 / Kit of 35 color slides of embroideries in its collection.

Craft and Folk Art Museum, 5814 Wilshire Boulevard, Los Angeles, California 90036 / Slide registry of current works by professional crafts artists. Includes the work of about 400 artists.

Indian Arts and Crafts Board, Tipi Shop, Inc., Box 1270, Rapid City, South Dakota 57701 / Organized by the United States Department of the Interior (Indian Arts and Crafts Board). Contemporary Indian and Eskimo crafts of the United States, "Contemporary Sioux Painting," and slide lecture kits.

The Museum of the American Indian, Heye Foundation, Broadway at 155th St., New York, New York 10032 / Kits of 100 objects each from its collections, North, Middle, and South American Indian art.

Silvermine Publishers, Inc., Comstock Hill, Norwalk, Connecticut 06850.

CONSUMER EDUCATION

Architectural Aluminum Manufacturers Association / Home safety. *See also* Industry and Industrial Management.

Eastman Kodak Company, Audio-Visual Library Distribution, 343 State St., Rochester, New York 14650 / Safety (consumer protection).

The Superior Electric Company, Media Manager, 383 Middle St., Bristol, Connecticut 06010.

Underwriters' Laboratories, Inc., 207 East Ohio St., Chicago, Illinois 60611 / Consumer education: how the company tests products for the safety of the public against hazards to life, limb, and property.

U.S. Consumer Product Safety Commission, Modern Talking Picture Service, 2323 New Hyde Park Road, New Hyde Park, New York 11040 / Slides on hazardous substances, accidents in the home.

COSTUME/FASHION

Fairchild Visuals, Division of Fairchild Publications, Inc., 7 East 12th St., New York, New York 10003 / Display, fashion history, fashion and merchandising careers, retail trends, textiles.

Milady Publishing Corporation, 3839 White Plains Rd., Bronx, New York 10467 / Cosmetology, fashion history, vocational education, etc.

State Historical Society of Wisconsin, 816 State St., Madison, Wisconsin 53706 / Costume (major emphasis), history (blacks in Wisconsin history), Wisconsin architecture.

GEOGRAPHY/TRAVEL

Austrian Institute / Austria. *See also* Art.

BEE Cross Media, Inc., 36 Dogwood Glen, Rochester, New York 14625 / Emphasis on the Philippines.

Blackhawk Films Eastin-Phelan Corporation, 1235 West Fifth St., Davenport, Iowa 52808 / Landmarks and areas of interest in Europe.

British Information Services, 845 Third Ave., New York, New York 10022.

Broadman Films, 127 Ninth Ave., North, Nashville, Tennessee 37203.

Carman Educational Associates, Inc., Box 205, Youngstown, New York 14174 / China, U.S.A., U.S.S.R. (comparative study slide sets).

The Eastin-Phelan Distributing Corporation / *See* Blackhawk Films Eastin- Phelan Corporation.

Educational Art Transparencies / Europe, Mexico, U.S.A. *See also* Art, Architecture and Architectural Sculpture.

FACSEA / France. *See also* Art.

Four Continent Book Corporation / U.S.S.R.: cities, gardens, resorts. *See also* Art.

Ginn and Company, A Xerox Company, 2550 Hanover St., Palo Alto, California 94303.

Martha Guthrie Slides, Distributed through BEE Cross Media Inc., 36 Dogwood Glen, Rochester, New York 14625 / Japan and Korea.

Hispanic Society of America, Publications Dept., 613 West 155 St., New York, New York 10032.

Hubbard Scientific Company / *See* Science.

Imperial Film Company, Inc. / Slide sets on Hawaii; Japan; Moscow and other Soviet cities; Washington, D.C. *See also* Science.

Kahana Film Productions, 1909 North Curson Place, Los Angeles, California 90046 / Central American architecture, painting, and sculpture; geography/ travel with emphasis on Central America, East Africa, Europe, Israel, and Japan.

KaiDib Films International, P.O. Box 261, Glendale, California 91209.

Robert F. McConnell / Asia, Bermuda, Canada, Europe, Latin America, U.S.A. *See also* Art—Architecture and Architectural Sculpture.

Francis G. Mayer / *See* Art.

National Park Service, Audio-Visual Arts Division, Harper's Ferry, West Virginia 25425.Rhode

Rhode Island Department of Economic Development / *See* Industry and Industrial Management.

Scala Fine Arts Publishers, Inc. / Europe. *See also* Art.
Scientificom / *See* Science.
South Dakota Department of Highways, Film Librarian, Communications Division, Pierre, South Dakota 57501 / Geography/travel, history. For tourism promotion only.
Swedish National Tourist Office, 75 Rockefeller Plaza, New York, New York 10017 / Sweden.
John Wiley and Sons, Inc., 605 Third Ave., New York, New York 10016 / Physical geography (the Earth, atmosphere and oceans, climate, soils, and vegetation, landforms of the Earth's crust).
World in Color Productions, Box 392, Elmira, New York 14902.

HEALTH SCIENCES

American Dental Association, 211 East Chicago Ave., Chicago, Illinois 60611 / Dentistry and dental health education.
American Dietetic Association, 620 North Michigan Ave., Chicago, Illinois 60611 / Food service in nursing homes.
The American Journal of Nursing Company, Educational Services Division, 10 Columbus Circle, New York, New York 10019 / Topics to aid nursing and allied health personnel.
American Optometric Association, 7000 Chippewa St., St. Louis, Missouri 63119 / Health care: vision.
American Podiatry Association, Audio-Visual Section, 20 Chevy Chase Circle, N.W., Washington, D.C. 20015 / Medical, foot disorders.
American Society for Microbiology, 1913 I St., N.W., Washington, D.C. 20006 / Microbiology.
Cleveland Health Museum and Education Center, 8911 Euclid Ave., Cleveland, Ohio 44106 / Health education.
Harwyn Medical Photographers, Green Hill Lower Merion, 1001 City Ave., Suite 918B, Philadelphia, Pennsylvania 19151 / Photo-micrographic slides of medical subjects.
Hubbard Scientific Company / Human reproduction. *See also* Science.
Otologic Medical Group, Inc., 2122 West Third St., Los Angeles, California 90057 / Otological surgery slides.
W. B. Saunders Company, West Washington Square, Philadelphia, Pennsylvania 19105 / Medical and nursing for education of students and continuing education of physicians and nurses. Science.
Sister Kenny Institute of the American Rehabilitation Foundation, A/V Publications Office, 1800 Chicago Ave., Minneapolis, Minnesota 55404 / Teaching care of patients.
University of Washington Press / *See* Science.
John Wiley and Sons, Inc. / Nursing instruction. *See also* Geography/Travel.

HISTORY

Architectural Delineations / European history. *See also* Art—Architecture and Architectural Sculpture.
Austrian Institute / Austrian history. *See also* Art.

Colonial Williamsburg Foundation, AV Distribution Section, Box C, Williamsburg, Virginia 23185 / General history.

Cultural History Research, Inc. / General French history. *See also* Art.

FACSEA / French civilization. *See also* Art.

Imperial Film Company, Inc. / American history. *See also* Geography/Travel.

Library of Congress, Photoduplication Service, Department C, Washington, D.C. 20540 / Set of six color slides from exhibit, "To Set a Country Free" (Revolutionary scenes).

Robert F. McConnell / American history. *See also* Art—Architecture and Architectural Sculpture.

Francis G. Mayer / *See* Art.

National Institute of Anthropology and History, Cordoba 45, Mexico 7, D.F.

Pan American Development Foundation / Latin American civilizations. *See also* Housing.

Olcott Forward, Inc. / Social studies. *See also* Consumer Education.

South Dakota Department of Highways / For tourism promotion only. *See also* Geography/Travel.

State Historical Society of Wisconsin / Blacks in Wisconsin history. *See also* Costume.

HOUSING

National Association of Home Builders, National Housing Center, 140 South Dearborn St., Chicago, Illinois 60603.

Pan American Development Foundation, 17th and Constitution Ave., N.W., Washington, D.C. 20006 / Latin America: agriculture, ancient civilizations, art, housing, scenery. Pre-Columbian pottery and sculpture.

U.S. Department of Housing and Urban Development, 451 7th St., S.W., Washington, D.C. 20410 / American and European architecture. Publication: *U.S. Department of Housing and Urban Development, A Selected Bibliography of Films, Filmstrips, Slides and Audiotapes*, Washington, D.C., June 1969.

INDUSTRY AND INDUSTRIAL MANAGEMENT

American Institute of Timber Construction, 333 West Hampden Ave., Englewood, Colorado 80110 / Timber industry.

Architectural Aluminum Manufacturers Association, 35 East Wacker Dr., Chicago, Illinois 60611 / The glass revolution for home safety.

Chamber of Commerce of the U.S., 1615 H St., N.W., Washington, D.C. 20006 / Explaining the American business system.

Education and Training Consultants Company, Box 49899, 12121 Wilshire Boulevard, Los Angeles, California 90049.

Hobart School of Welding Technology, Trade Square East, Troy, Ohio 45373 / Sets of slides about welding training.

Instruction Resources Corporation / *See* Art.

Milady Publishing Corporation / *See* Costume/Fashion.

Petroleum Extension Service, University of Texas, Box S, University Station, Austin, Texas 78712 / Petroleum industry: technical training, drilling and production.

Rhode Island Department of Economic Development, 1 Wybasset Hill, Providence, Rhode Island 02903 / Business, communications, travel.

NUMISMATICS

American Numismatic Society, Broadway at 155th St., New York, New York 10032 / Numismatics.

Interbook, Inc., 545 Eighth Ave., New York, New York 10018 / Oriental (including Asia House exhibits), French, and Spanish numismatics.

ORNITHOLOGY

Interbook, Inc. / *See* Numismatics.

Cornell University, Film Center, Box 41, Roberts Hall, Ithaca, New York 14853 / Bird sets.

National Audubon Society, Photos and Film Department, 950 Third Ave., New York, New York 10022 / J. J. Audubon's birds and mammals, natural history.

SCIENCE

American Meteorite Laboratory, P.O. Box 2098, Denver, Colorado 80201 / Meteorites.

Austrian Institute / Austrian inventors. *See also* Art.

Carolina Biological Supply Company, Burlington, North Carolina 27215.

Harcourt Brace Jovanovich, Inc., 757 Third Ave., New York, New York 10017 / Algebra and geometry, earth and life sciences, world history; designed for grades K-12.

Harper and Row, Publishers, Inc., College Department, 49 East 33rd St., New York, New York 10016.

Hubbard Scientific Company, 1946 Raymond Dr., Northbrook, Illinois 60062 / Astronomy, biology, geography, geology, human reproduction, meteorology, science, space exploration.

Imperial Film Company, Inc., 4404 South Florida Ave., Lakeland, Florida 33803 / Animal tissue, bacteria, complex life forms, plant sciences, reproduction, simple life forms. Apollo XI. Geography, history (small selection).

Macalaster Scientific Company / *See* Raytheon Company.

Moody Institute of Science, Educational Films Division, 12000 East Washington Blvd., Los Angeles, California 90021.

NASCO / *See* Agriculture.

National Teaching Aids, Inc., 120 Fulton Ave., Garden City Park, New York 11040.

Prentice-Hall Media, Inc., 150 White Plains Road, Tarrytown, New York 10591 / Science slides.

Raytheon Company, 141 Spring Street, Lexington, Massachusetts 02173 / General physics.

W. B. Saunders Company / *See* Medicine.

School Specialty Supply Company, Box 1327, Salina, Kansas 67401 / Earth sciences, life sciences, space exploration, weather.

Science Slides Company, Division of Communications International, 22 East 42nd St., New York, New York 10017.

Scientificom, Division of Mervin W. LaRue Films, Inc., 708 North Dearborn Ave., Chicago, Illinois 60610 / Geography/travel, science.

Scott Education Division / *See* Prentice Hall Media.

University of Washington Press, Film Division, 1416 N.E. 41st St., Seattle, Washington 98105 / Art, medicine, science.

Ward's Natural Science Establishment, Inc., P.O. Box 1712, Rochester, New York 14603 / Biology, earth sciences.

MISCELLANEOUS

New York Zoetrope, 31 East Twelfth St., New York, New York 10003 / Exclusive U.S. distributor of l'Avant-Scène Slide Collections. Each collection includes a 30-48 page annotated filmography, a biographical outline, bibliography and guide to the slides. Especially on film directors' careers, general, etc., on cinema.

Vedo Films, 85 Longview Rd., Port Washington, New York 11050 / Anthroplogy, sociology.

DIRECTORY OF SLIDE LIBRARIES

Only those 83 slide libraries in the United States that have been cited in the text are listed here. See the *Directory of Art Libraries and Visual Resource Collections in North America* (compiled by the Art Libraries Society/North America) for a comprehensive inventory of slide collections in the United States and Canada (1978). As noted in Chapter 3, the majority of slide libraries do not have detailed descriptions of their cataloging and classification systems available. For those collections known by the author to have a guide to their cataloging and/or classification procedures, the abbreviation (c) is placed at the end of the entry.

The following outline of entry format and abbreviations is that used in the Directory:

STATE

City

INSTITUTIONAL TITLE, library, department, school and/or college, address, zip code.
Title of individual in charge of slide library. Collection title. Date of establishment (Estab.). Number of slides. Number of full-time staff (FT), and part-time staff (PT).

(c) Cataloging and/or classification guide prepared for the collection.

unk. Information requested unknown.

CALIFORNIA

(Berkeley) University of California, Berkeley, Art History Department, 94720. Curator. Slide Collection. c.225,000.

—University of California, Berkeley, Department of Architecture, 94720. Assistant Librarian. Visual Aids Collection. 115,000. 1 FT, 3 PT.

(La Jolla) University of California, San Diego, Medical School, 92093. Librarian. Learning Resources Center. c.10,000. 1 FT.

(Los Angeles) University of California, Los Angeles, Art Department, 405 Hilgard Ave., 90024. Slide Curator. Slide Library. Estab. 1957. 200,000. 3 FT, 3-5 PT. (c)

(Northridge) California State University, Northridge, Art History Department, 18111 Nordhoff St., 91330. Slide Curator. Art Slide Library. Estab. 1958. 80,000. 1 FT, 1+ PT.

(Riverside) University of California, Riverside, Department of the History of Art, 92521. Slide & Photo Curator (University job title: Museum Scientist). Slide & Photo Collection. unk. 68,000. 1 FT, 1-6 PT.

(San Jose) San Jose State College, Department of Art, 93106. Slide Curator. Estab. c.1938. 95,000. 1 FT, 3 PT.

(Santa Cruz) University of California, Santa Cruz, University Library, 95060. Slide Librarian. Slide Library. Estab. 1966. 120,000. 2 FT, 0 PT. (c)

(Stanford) Stanford University, Department of Art, 94305. Slide Curator. Slide Collection. Estab. 1950s. 140,000. 2 FT, 12 PT.

(Valencia) California Institute of the Arts, School of Art, 24700 McBean Parkway, 91355. Art/Slide Librarian. Library. Estab. 1960. 20,000. 1 FT, 1 PT.

CONNECTICUT

(New Haven) Yale University, Art and Architecture Library, Box 1605 A Yale Station, 06520. Librarian. Slide and Photograph Collection. Estab. c.1924. 218,000. 4 FT, 5 PT.

DELAWARE

(Winterthur) The Henry Francis du Pont Winterthur Museum, 19735. Librarian in Charge of Photography and Slide Collection. Slide Collection. Estab. 1954. 90,000. 5 FT, 1 PT.

FLORIDA

(Gainesville) University of Florida. College of Fine Arts, 32611. Audio-Visual Librarian. Audio-Visual Library. Estab. C.1952. c.100,000. 1 FT, 2 PT.

(Sarasota) Ringling School of Art, Library, 1191 27th St., 33580. Slide Curator. RSA Collection. Estab. 1975. 30,000. 1 FT, 1 PT. (c)

GEORGIA

(Atlanta) Emory University, Art History Department, Annex "B," 30322. Slide
Curator. Slide Library. Estab. 1965. 100,000. 1 FT, 2 PT.
—Georgia Institute of Technology, School of Architecture, 30332. Librarian.
34,000. 1 FT, 1 PT.

ILLINOIS

(Chicago) The Art Institute of Chicago, Ryerson & Burnham Libraries, Michigan
Avenue at Adams Street, 60603. Slide Librarian. Slide Library. Estab. c.1904.
233,800. 5 FT, 5-8 PT. (c)
—University of Chicago, Department of Art, History of Art, 401 Goodspeed Hall,
60637. Curator of Slides. Estab. 1938. 130,000. 1 FT, 1 PT.
—University of Illinois at Chicago Circle, College of Architecture and Art, Box
4348, 60680. Audio-Visual Curator. Slide and Photograph Library. Estab.
1947. 106,000. 2 FT, 20 PT.

(De Kalb) Northern Illinois University, Art Department, 60115. Slide Librarian.
Slide Library. Estab. 1961. 135,000. 2 FT, 3 PT.

(Elmhurst) Elmhurst College, A. C. Buehler Library, 60126. Special Collections
Librarian. Estab. 1967. c.6,000 slides. 1 FT, 2 PT.

(Urbana-Champaign) University of Illinois, Urbana-Champaign, Architecture
Building, 61820. Slide Curator. Slide Library. Estab. 1880s. 150,000.
1 FT, 4-6 PT.

INDIANA

(Bloomington) Indiana University, African Studies Program, Slide Archives, Wood-
burn Hall, 47405. Estab. 1967. 5,000. 0 FT, 1 PT.
—Indiana University, Fine Arts Department, 47405. Slide Librarian. Slide Library.
Estab. c.1935. 220,000. 2 FT, 10 PT.

(Muncie) Ball State University, Department of Library Service, 47306. Architecture Slide Collection Assistant. Architecture Library—Slide Collection.
Estab. 1965. 1 FT, 0 PT.

IOWA

(Davenport) Marycrest College, 52804. Cone Library, Educational Materials Center.
Estab. 1952. c.15,000. 1 FT, 1 PT. (c)

(Iowa City) University of Iowa, School of Art, 52240. Curator of Visual Materials.
Estab. 1935. 185,000. 1.5 FT, 10-12 PT.

KENTUCKY

(Louisville) University of Louisville, Fine Arts Department, Belknap Campus,
40208. Curator of Slides. Slide Collection. Estab. c.1950. c.180,000. 1 FT,
1 PT.

MARYLAND

(Baltimore) Enoch Pratt Free Library, Audiovisual Department, 400 Cathedral St., 21201. Administrative Assistant. Estab. c.1922. 36,075. 1 FT (varies), 0 PT.

—Johns Hopkins University, Department of the History of Art, Charles & 34th St., 21218. Curator. Slide and Photograph Collection. Estab. 1948. c.90,000. 3 FT, 0 PT.

MASSACHUSETTS

(Boston) Boston Museum of Fine Arts, 465 Huntington Ave., 02115. Slide Librarian. The Slide Library. Estab. 1905. 90,000. 2 FT, 0 PT.

(Cambridge) Harvard University, Fogg Art Museum, Fine Arts Library, Quincy Station, 02138. Curator of Visual Collections. Visual Collections. Estab. c.1927. 250,000. 5 FT, 12-15 PT. (c)

—Massachusetts Institute of Technology, Rotch Library, 02139. Visual Collections Librarian. Visual Collections. Estab. 1900. 165,000. 2 FT, 6 PT.

(Northampton) Smith College, Art Department, Hillyer Art Gallery, 01063. Curator of Slides. Hillyer Slide Room. Estab. 1920s. 134,000. 3 FT, 3 PT.

(Wellesley) Wellesley College, Department of Art, Jewett Arts Center, 02181. Slide Librarian. Library. Estab. 1892. 48,000. 2 FT, 2 PT.

(Williamstown) Sterling and Francine Clark Art Institute, Library, South St., 01267. Slide Cataloguer. Photograph and Slide Collections. Estab. 1967. 65,000. 4 FT, 2 PT.

MICHIGAN

(Ann Arbor) University of Michigan, Department of the History of Art, Tappan Hall, 48104. Curator of Slides and Photographs. Slide and Photograph Collection. Estab. 1911. 203,000. 6 FT, 26 PT. (c)

MINNESOTA

(Minneapolis) Minneapolis Public Library & Information Center, 300 Nicollet Mall, 55401. Films Specialist in Charge of Slide Collection. Art/Music/Films Department. Estab. 1913. 45,000. 1 FT.

—University of Minnesota, Department of Art History, 109 Jones Hall, 55455. Slide Librarian. Slide Room. Estab. 1947. 100,000. 1 FT, 3 PT.

—Walker Art Center, Library, Vineland Place, 55403. Slide Librarian. Walker Art Center Slide Collection. Estab. 1971. 55,000. 0 FT, 1 PT.

MISSOURI

(Kansas City) University of Missouri—Kansas City, Department of Art and Art History, 64110. Curator of Slides and Photographs. Slide and Photograph Collection. Estab. 1948. 65,000. 1 FT, 7 PT.

(St. Louis) St. Louis Art Museum, Richardson Memorial Library, 63110. Librarian. Estab. c.1925. 19,000. 1 FT, 0 PT.

NEW JERSEY

(Newark) The Public Library of Newark New Jersey, Art and Music Department, 5 Washington St., 07101. Art Slide Collection. Estab. 1964. 15,000. None specifically for the Slide Collection. (9 FT for the department; 5 PT for the department).

(Princeton) Princeton University, Department of Art and Archaeology, McCormick Hall, 08540. Director of the Section of Slides and Photographs. Section of Slides and Photographs. Estab. 1882. 193,000. 6 FT, 2 PT.

NEW MEXICO

(Albuquerque) University of New Mexico, Fine Arts Slide Library, Room 2010, Fine Arts Center, 87131. Slide Librarian. Estab. c.1948. 220,000. 3 FT, 8 PT.

NEW YORK

(Binghamton) State University of New York at Binghamton and Harpur College, Department of Art and Art History, 13901. Curator of Visual Resources. Estab. 1951. 70,000. 1 FT, 7 PT.

(Brooklyn) Pratt Institute, Library, 215 Ryerson St., 11205. Librarian. Estab. 1959. 40,000. 1 FT, 4 PT.

(Buffalo) State University of New York at Buffalo, Art History, 345 L Richmond Quadrangle, Ellicott Complex, 14261. Slide and Photograph Curator. 127,000. 1 FT, 5-8 PT.

(Corning) Corning Community College, The Arthur A. Houghton, Jr. Library, 14830. Curator of Slides. Estab. 1959. 16,000. 1 FT, 0 PT.

(Ithaca) Cornell University, College of Architecture, Art and Planning, Sibley Hall, 14850. Curator. Slide Library. Estab. c.1880. 200,000. 1 FT, 1 PT.
—Cornell University, Department of the History of Art, 35 Goldwin Smith Hall, 14850. Curator of Slides and Photographs. Slide Library. Estab. c.1935. 100,000. 1 FT, 9 PT.

(New York) Columbia University in the City of New York, Department of Art History and Archaeology, Schermerhorn Hall, 10027. Slide Collection. Estab. 1934. 300,000. 1 FT, 15-20 PT.
—Metropolitan Museum of Art, Fifth Avenue & 82nd Street, 10028. Chief Librarian. Photograph and Slide Library. Estab. 1907. 347,000. 9 FT, 4-8 PT.
—The School of Visual Arts, Library, 209 East 23rd St., 10010. Slide Curator. Estab. 1967. c.15,000. 2 FT, 0 PT.

(Poughkeepsie) Vassar College, Art Department, 12601. Curator of Slides and Photographs. Slide Collection. Estab. 1915. 98,000. 1 FT, 1-6 PT.

(Rochester) University of Rochester, Fine Arts Department, River Campus Station, 14627. Slide and Photograph Curator. Estab. 1900s. 82,000. 1 FT, 4 PT.

(Saratoga Springs) Skidmore College, Library, Art Reading Room, 12866. Curator of Slides. Estab. 1933. 14,000. 1 FT.

(Syracuse) Syracuse University, Ernest Stevenson Bird Library, 205A, 13210. Slide Curator. Slide Library. Estab. 1917. 144,000. 3 FT, 10 PT. (c)

(West Point) United States Military Academy, Library, Department of the Army, 10996. Fine Arts Librarian. 12,000. 0 FT, 1 PT.

NORTH CAROLINA

(Chapel Hill) University of North Carolina, Department of Art, The William Hayes Ackland Memorial Art Center, 27514. Curator of Slides and Photographs. Estab. c.1940. 70,000. 2 FT, 5 PT.

OHIO

(Cincinnati) Cincinnati Art Museum, Library, Eden Park, 45202. Curator of Slides and Photographs. Slides and Photographs. Estab. 1977. 3,600. 1 FT, 0 PT.
—The Public Library of Cincinnati and Hamilton County, Films and Recordings Center, 800 Vine St., 45202. Head, Films and Recordings Center. Estab. 1947. c.25,000. 12 FT, 0 PT (staff of Films and Recording Center).

(Cleveland) Cleveland Museum of Art, 11150 East Boulevard, 44106. Slide Librarian. Slide Library. Estab. 1916. 230,000. 5 FT, 10 PT. (c)

(Columbus) Ohio State University, Department of the History of Art, 126 North Oval Dr., 43210. Curator of Slides and Prints Collection. Slides and Prints Collection. Estab. 1920s. c.160,000. 2 FT, 2-4 PT.

(Oberlin) Oberlin College, Department of Art, Library, 44704. Slide Curator. Slide Room. Estab. 1917. 225,000. 1 FT, 3 PT.

(Oxford) Miami University, Department of Art, School of Fine Arts, 203 Hiestand Hall, 45056. Slide Librarian. Department of Art Slide Collection. Estab. 1952. c.32,500. 0 FT, 5 PT.

(Toledo) Toledo Museum of Art, Box 1013, Monroe Street at Scotwood Avenue, 43601. Slide Curator. Art Library. Estab. c.1930. 36,500. 1 FT, 4 PT.

OREGON

(Eugene) University of Oregon, Architecture and Allied Arts Library, School of Architecture and Allied Arts, 279 Lawrence Hall, 97403. Slide Curator. Slide Library. Estab. 1949. c.140,000. 2 FT, 2 PT.

PENNSYLVANIA

(Philadelphia) Philadelphia College of Art. Broad & Pine Streets, 19102. Supervisor. Slide Library. Estab. 1958. 140,000. 1 FT, 6 PT.
—Philadelphia Museum of Art, Slide Library, Parkway at 26th St., 19101. Curator of Slides. Slide Library. Estab. 1939. 175,000. 1 FT, 0 PT.
—University of Pennsylvania, Graduate School of Fine Arts, 34th and Walnut St., 19174. Head of Slides. Fine Arts Library, University of Pennsylvania Slide Collection. Estab. c.1900. c.180,000. 3 FT, 8-10 PT.

(University Park) Pennsylvania State University, Department of Art History, College of Arts and Architecture, 229 Arts II, 16802. Slide and Photograph Archivist. Estab. 1930s. 90,000. 1 FT, 4-6 PT.

(Valley Forge) C-E Refractories, Research and Development Library, 19482. Research Librarian. Estab. 1977. 6,000. 1 FT.

RHODE ISLAND

(Providence) Rhode Island School of Design, Library, Box B, 2 College St., 02903. Slide Librarian. Estab. 1915. 46,000. 0 FT, 1 PT.

TEXAS .

(Austin) University of Texas at Austin, Department of Art, FAB 2.210, 78712. Visual Arts Curator. Slide & Photograph Collections. Estab. 1938. 225,000. 3 FT, 15 PT.

(Houston) University of Houston, College of Architecture, Cullen Boulevard, 77004. Slide Librarian. Slide Library. Estab. 1970. 35,000. 1 FT, 2 PT.

WASHINGTON

(Olympia) Evergreen State College, Generic Library, 98501. Slide Curator. Library 2300. 21,000. 1 FT, 1 PT.

(Seattle) University of Washington, School of Art, DM-10, 98105. Slide Curator. Slide Library. unk. 165,000. 2 FT, 1 PT.

WISCONSIN

(Madison) University of Wisconsin, Department of Art History, Elvehjem Art Center 314, 53706. Curator of Slides & Photographs. Art History Slide & Photograph Collection. Estab. 1923. 190,000. 1 FT, 4 PT. (c)

WASHINGTON, D.C.

—Howard University, Architecture and Planning Library, 20059. Architecture and Planning Librarian. Estab. 1974. 28,000. 3 FT, 6 PT. (c)

—National Collection of Fine Arts, Smithsonian Institution, Eighth and G. Streets, N.W., 20560. Chief, Office of Slides and Photographs. Librarian, Slide and Photograph Archive. 41,100. 4 FT, PT varies. (c)

—National Gallery of Art, Smithsonian Institution, Sixth and Constitution, N.W., 20565. Curator in Charge of Educational Work. Slide Librarian. Slide Library. Estab. 1941. 81,000. 2 FT, 0 PT. (c)

—The World Bank, Information & Public Affairs Department, Photo Library, 1818 H St., N.W., 20433. Photo Librarian, Information and Public Affairs. 31,300. 1 FT, 0 PT. (c)

INDEX

Page numbers in bold refer to pages having photographs. Specific names of distributors and manufacturers of equipment, slides and supplies are cited as they appear in the text. *All* bibliographic references in the text have been indexed. Direct references to the directories is necessary for complete addresses and information on types of material handled by each source.